INTELLIGENCE
IN THE
NATIONAL
SECURITY
ENTERPRISE

INTELLIGENCE
IN THE
NATIONAL
SECURITY
ENTERPRISE

AN INTRODUCTION

ROGER Z. GEORGE

GEORGETOWN UNIVERSITY PRESS / WASHINGTON, DC

Library of Congress Cataloging-in-Publication Data

Names: George, Roger Z., 1949- author.
Title: Intelligence in the National Security Enterprise : An Introduction / Roger Z. George.
Description: Washington, DC : Georgetown University Press, 2020. | Includes bibliographical references and index.
Identifiers: LCCN 2019009528 (print) | LCCN 2019016763 (ebook) | ISBN 9781626167445 (ebook) | ISBN 9781626167421 (hardcover : qalk. paper) | ISBN 9781626167438 (pbk.: qalk. paper)
Subjects: LCSH: Intelligence service—United States. | Military intelligence—United States. | National security—United States.
Classification: LCC JK468.I6 (ebook) | LCC JK468.I6 G47 2020 (print) | DDC 327.1273—dc23
LC record available at https://lccn.loc.gov/2019009528

♾ This book is printed on acid-free paper meeting the requirements of the American National Standard for Permanence in Paper for Printed Library Materials.

21 20   9 8 7 6 5 4 3 2 First printing

Printed in the United States of America.

Cover design by Jeff Miller, Faceout Studio.

*To Cindy—my life partner and best friend—for her patience,
understanding, and love*

Contents

Illustrations

BOXES

FIGURES

TABLES

Acknowledgments

This book is the product of many years of learning from my mentors, supervisors, and peers about intelligence practices and principles. In this regard I want to thank a long list of former colleagues who read chapters or parts of chapters to ensure I got my facts right. In particular, I want to express special appreciation to Thomas Fingar at Stanford University, Gregory Treverton at the University of Southern California, and Peter Clement at Columbia University for reviewing various chapters from their vantage point of being former intelligence practitioners and now teachers themselves. Also I need to acknowledge the indispensable advice I received from former policy and intelligence officials at the National Security Council, such as Gregory Schulte, Steven Simon, Stephen Flanagan, and Steven Slick. Along the way, I also consulted with a wide range of former colleagues regarding particular events, processes, or facts: Brad Knopp, James Carson, Tim Kilbourn, Craig Chellis, John Lauder, Mathew Burrows, Aris Pappas, Daniel Wagner, and Cindy Storer. Of course, if I have committed any errors of fact or reached ill-conceived conclusions, those rest solely on my shoulders.

Special thanks is also reserved for three individuals who have shaped my academic and professional career and offered assistance in this book project. First, my earliest and longest mentor, Larry Caldwell, is responsible for encouraging me to pursue a career in international affairs but also for providing a model for someone who had one foot in academia and another in the intelligence world. Second, my closest intelligence colleague, James Bruce, and I have collaborated on several writing projects over the past decade. He encouraged me in this textbook project as part of a career-long conversation. Last, Harvey Rishikof has been a close writing partner during and after a decade teaching with him at the National War College. Like Larry and James, Harvey has been both friend and colleague and one who brings both insight and integrity to the study and teaching of national security decision-making. He has deepened my own understanding of the labyrinth within which the national security and intelligence enterprises operate.

Last, I wish to thank Georgetown University Press for encouraging me to write this book. For the past decade, we have collaborated on several edited volumes examining the national security decision-making process as well as intelligence analysis. In particular, I want to express my gratitude to Donald Jacobs, who has been a wise and gentle editor and overseer of several book projects before this one. Don has been a trusted partner on my intelligence publications as well as those of many other practitioners and scholars, which has made Georgetown University Press one of the foremost publishers of intelligence scholarship.

Abbreviations

ABM	antiballistic missile
ACH	analysis of competing hypotheses
ACIS	Arms Control Intelligence Staff
BNE	Board of National Estimates
BTF	Balkan Task Force
BW	biological weapons
C^3	command, control, and communications
C^4	command, control, communications, and computer
CBJB	congressional budget justification book
CFE	conventional forces in Europe
CI	counterintelligence
CIA	Central Intelligence Agency
CIB	*Current Intelligence Bulletin*
CIG	Central Intelligence Group
CJCS	chairman of the Joint Chiefs of Staff
COI	coordinator of information
COMINT	communications intelligence
COMIREX	Committee on Imagery Requirements and Exploitation
CTC	Counterterrorism Center
CW	chemical weapons
CYBERCOM	United States Cyber Command
D&D	deception and denial
DA	Directorate of Analysis
DC	Deputies Committee
DCI	director of central intelligence
DEA	Drug Enforcement Administration
DHS	Department of Homeland Security
DI	Directorate of Intelligence
DIA	Defense Intelligence Agency
DINSUM	*Defense Intelligence Summary*
DIRNSA	director of the NSA
DMA	Defense Mapping Agency
DNI	director of national intelligence

DO	Directorate of Operations
DOD	Department of Defense
DOJ	Department of Justice
E-O	electro-optical
EPIC	El Paso Intelligence Center
FBI	Federal Bureau of Investigation
FEMA	Federal Emergency Management Agency
FISA	Foreign Intelligence Surveillance Act
FISC	Foreign Intelligence Surveillance Court
FISINT	foreign instrumentation intelligence
FOIA	Freedom of Information Act
G-2	Army intelligence
GEOINT	geospatial intelligence
HPSCI	House Permanent Select Committee on Intelligence
HSC	Homeland Security Council
HUMINT	human intelligence
IAEA	International Atomic Energy Agency
I&A	Office of Intelligence and Analysis
I&W	indications and warning
IC	intelligence community
ICBM	intercontinental ballistic missile
ICD	Intelligence Community Directive
IG	inspector general
IMINT	imagery intelligence
INF	intermediate nuclear forces
INFOSEC	information security
INR	Bureau of Intelligence and Research
INT	intelligence-collection discipline
IOB	Intelligence Oversight Board
IPC	interagency policy committee
IRTPA	Intelligence Reform and Terrorism Prevention Act of 2004
ISG	Iraq Survey Group
ISIS	Islamic State of Iraq and Syria
J-2	JCS intelligence section
JCS	Joint Chiefs of Staff
JSOC	Joint Special Operations Command
JTTF	joint terrorism task force
LEGAT	legal attaché
LG	NSC Lawyers Group

MASINT	measurement and signature intelligence
MIB	Military Intelligence Board
MID	*Military Intelligence Digest*
MIP	Military Intelligence Program
NATO	North Atlantic Treaty Organization
NCPC	National Counterproliferation Center
NCSC	National Counterintelligence and Security Center
NCTC	National Counterterrorism Center
NEC	National Economic Council
NGA	National Geospatial-Intelligence Agency
NIB	National Intelligence Board
NIC	National Intelligence Council
NID	*National Intelligence Daily*
NIE	National Intelligence Estimate
NIM	national intelligence manager
NIMA	National Imagery and Mapping Agency
NIO	national intelligence officer
NIO/W	national intelligence officer for warning
NIP	National Intelligence Program
NIPF	National Intelligence Priorities Framework
NPIC	National Photographic Interpretation Center
NPT	Non-Proliferation Treaty
NRO	National Reconnaissance Office
NSA	National Security Agency
NSB	National Security Branch
NSC	National Security Council
NSE	national security enterprise
NSPD	national security presidential decision
NTM	national technical means
OCI	Office of Current Intelligence
ODNI	Office of the Director of National Intelligence
OFAC	Office of Foreign Assets Control
OTFI	Office for Terrorism and Financial Intelligence
OIA	Office of Intelligence and Analysis
ONE	Office of National Estimates
ONI	Office of Naval Intelligence
OOB	order of battle
OPC	Office of Policy Coordination
OSD	Office of the Secretary of Defense

OSINT	open-source intelligence
OSR	Office of Strategic Research
OSS	Office of Strategic Services
PC	Principals Committee
PCLOB	Privacy and Civil Liberties Oversight Board
PDB	*President's Daily Brief*
PIAB	President's Intelligence Advisory Board
POTUS	president of the United States
PSP	President's Surveillance Program
R&A	Research and Analysis branch (OSS)
RFE	Radio Free Europe
RL	Radio Liberty
SALT	Strategic Arms Limitation Talks
SAS	Senior Analytical Service
SEIB	*Senior Executive Intelligence Brief*
SIGINT	signals intelligence
SME	subject-matter expert
SSCI	Senate Select Committee on Intelligence
TECHINT	technical intelligence
UAV	unmanned aerial vehicle
UN	United Nations
UNVIE	UN Mission to International Organizations in Vienna
USAF/IN	Air Force Intelligence
USCG	US Coast Guard
USDI	undersecretary of defense for intelligence
USMC/IN	Marine Corps Intelligence
USTR	US special trade representative
VTC	video teleconference
WINPAC	Weapons Intelligence, Nonproliferation, and Arms Control Center
WIRe	*Worldwide Intelligence Report*
WMD	weapon of mass destruction

1

HOW TO USE THIS BOOK

Keep giving me things that make me think.
—Henry Kissinger to CIA director Richard Helms

Intelligence is often an invisible player in presidential formulation and execution of national security policy. New occupants of the Oval Office often are perplexed as well as amazed about how intelligence works and contributes to their policy processes. It is no less challenging to explain the business of intelligence to students just learning about American foreign policymaking. When I joined the **intelligence community (IC)** in the late 1970s after studying international relations as an undergraduate and in graduate school, I knew virtually nothing myself. For many students of my era, intelligence was simply too secret and arcane to be understood. But with the benefit of working in the IC and interacting with many policy agencies and officials, I believe that the relationship between intelligence and policy can and should be more transparent. Having taught courses on intelligence at both the graduate and undergraduate levels, however, I realize that intelligence is still scarcely and often simplistically presented in most books and courses about the conduct of American foreign and security policy. There are plenty of critiques, memoirs, and studies on specific aspects of intelligence but far fewer that survey the multifaceted role intelligence plays in US statecraft in a more systemic way.

Accordingly, this textbook is intended to inform students about the ways in which intelligence supports the national security decision-making process. It quite consciously does not survey all the wide range of internal intelligence processes that are common in other intelligence textbooks. Many intelligence books and studies concentrate much more attention on the operational side of intelligence collection. For example, they describe how technical collection systems such as satellites and listening stations vacuum up massive amounts of data, or they recount how former spies conducted their espionage against key adversaries. These are, indeed, important topics for understanding the internal organizational cultures, methods, and challenges of the intelligence business. However, such a focus on the inside of the IC can detract from a student's understanding of what the actual output and value of such collection is and how the finished analysis produced from such exotic, expensive, and risky efforts actually is used in national-level decision-making.

This book captures my understanding of how the IC and the policy community attempt to work together. It is a symbiotic relationship. When it is working well, policy decisions are usually more systematic and better informed; when it is not, policies are often poorly shaped, either because the intelligence was incorrect or simply ignored. Granted, even with a good relationship, there is no guarantee that policies will succeed, but in the author's view the odds are surely better.

The book takes the approach of illustrating with practical examples how intelligence has played a significant part in national security policymaking. The author's own experiences as a political-military analyst at the Central Intelligence Agency (CIA), including serving in policy rotations at the State Department and Defense Department in the late 1980s and early 1990s, have shaped the way this book addresses the intersection of policy and intelligence. Most intelligence practitioners have had some good experiences when intelligence was useful as well as bad ones when intelligence was flawed, dismissed, or misused. Indeed, my own opinions are on display in this book, which I might summarize as being convinced that intelligence is a necessary, if never perfect, part of the national security enterprise.

USE AND ORGANIZATION OF THE BOOK

This book deepens a student's understanding of how American national security policy is conducted with a more detailed description of how intelligence contributes to the development of such policies. Most textbooks about American foreign policy or national security provide scant attention to the intelligence contribution, but that is a gap that should be filled. This book thus can complement textbooks on American foreign policy by providing concrete examples of how intelligence informs and influences national security deliberations.

For students taking general courses in intelligence, this book can provide two important additions to what is often left out of other intelligence textbooks. First, this volume provides a clear explanation of the expanding US national security enterprise (NSE), in which intelligence operates.[1] The term itself suggests a set of agencies and operations that conduct US national security policies. As the definition of national security has broadened well beyond traditional military and diplomatic concerns to include more transnational and socioeconomic issues, the enterprise and the agencies it comprises has continued to expand. It is often assumed that the student is already familiar with the NSE and its interagency process. In this author's experience, students taking an introductory intelligence course often are not aware of the details of that decision-making process, so it is hard for them to put the intelligence contribution into proper context.

A second feature of this book is its focus on distinguishing among a range of intelligence functions that contribute to the NSE. Other intelligence textbooks will typically address intelligence support to policy in a single chapter, perhaps accompanied by a chapter on analysis. Instead, this volume examines the varied forms of intelligence support to policymakers, ranging from strategic intelligence and warning analysis to more actionable daily intelligence support and covert action.

Accordingly, this book's chapters are organized around the kinds of decisions that policymakers often confront. At times their intelligence questions revolve more around mysteries than secrets—to use Joseph Nye's characterization of the different sets of problems facing a senior policymaker or commander.[2] Will China's economic model collapse? This is a mystery about which the IC can speculate and develop alternative scenarios to help national decision-makers prepare strategies and options for dealing with different circumstances. However, other questions might be how potent China's military modernization effort is likely to become and how it might impact the South China Sea maritime rivalry. Here there are specific facts and trends that the IC can bring into the discussion in order for policymakers to assess the risks the United States and its allies face in challenging Chinese territorial claims. Sometimes policymakers are simply asking how to "think about" a problem—whether it is the geopolitics of climate change or how Vladimir Putin views the world—while others might be seeking specific facts about the size and location of Syria's chemical weapons stocks or the nature of Russia's new "hybrid warfare."

The wide range of questions posed to the IC lends itself to characterizing a range of functions that are being performed constantly. The book's chapters are organized around those key functions. Chapter 2 first defines what intelligence is and its various dimensions in general terms. Students will learn about intelligence-collection methods, including technical, human, and open sources, and the contributions they make to analysis. This foundation will then enable students to focus more on intelligence "outputs" than "inputs" in order to highlight the value of intelligence to the policymaking process.

Chapter 3 will outline the current structure and decision-making processes of the NSE. It highlights the policy agencies and interagency mechanisms that are used to develop and implement national security strategies. Students can then appreciate the complexity of the decision-making process and the role that particular senior policymakers play in running the process or shaping its outcomes. Importantly, the chapter also will illustrate how intelligence fits into the formal interagency process for national security decision-making.

Chapter 4 will outline the current structure of the IC and identify some of the key agencies that participate regularly in the NSE. Attention will be focused principally on the national and departmental intelligence provided to National Security Council (NSC) members as well as senior departmental decision-makers, who are principal customers for the IC. This chapter will also introduce students to some of the continuing challenges leaders face in managing this huge intelligence enterprise.

Chapter 5 lays out a framework for how to think about the distinct and diverse roles that intelligence plays in the national security process. It describes the "intelligence cycle" concept and moves to the practical discussion of more-specific missions that support the decision-making process. Thereafter, chapters 6 through 10 will examine each of those missions in more detail, providing examples of how intelligence has contributed to major policy decisions.

To start, chapter 6 will describe "strategic intelligence" and its use for developing long-term strategies and policies. Students will gain an understanding of what kinds of strategic intelligence, as opposed to tactical intelligence, are available to policymakers. This discussion will explore the role of National Intelligence Estimates (NIEs) and how they are produced. It will identify the actors and processes that produce NIEs, using recent examples such as the deeply flawed 2002 NIE on Iraqi weapons of mass destruction (WMDs) as well as the rising importance of the Global Trends documents aimed at each incoming president.

Chapter 7 will describe the IC's enduring responsibility to provide warning of threats to the United States and its interests abroad. Students will be introduced to the concept of warning, including how it is conducted and organized. A brief examination of some of the famous warning events—beginning with Pearl Harbor and including the 9/11 attacks—will help students to identify lessons to be learned from past warning cases. The chapter will conclude with an examination of how the warning function has been organized in the past and how recent practices are shifting the burden of warning from specialized warning staffs to every analyst.

Chapter 8 will shine a light on the usually invisible mission of direct policy support provided to virtually every major national security agency in the US government. Students as well as scholars sometimes misunderstand the term to imply that the IC openly supports an administration's policy agenda. That is not the meaning or intent of this term. Rather, the chapter will illustrate how intelligence supports policymakers with information and analysis relevant to their decisions, without intending to favor or oppose them. Students will gain an understanding of the ***President's Daily Brief*** (*PDB*) and the process behind it. It also describes other unique forms of intelligence support to policymakers engaged in ongoing international negotiations, crisis management, and counterterrorism efforts.

Chapter 9 focuses on the special and controversial intelligence mission of "covert action." Students will gain an appreciation for how covert actions are authorized and monitored by both the executive and legislative branches. It will review some successes and failures of covert action, using historical as well as more recent (acknowledged) operations to illustrate the benefits, costs, and risks of such activities. Students will be able to appreciate how national security policy and intelligence are even more intertwined and less distinct than usual, which raises additional ethical and analytical challenges.

Chapter 10 is designed to bring the discussion back to the critical and often fractious relationship between intelligence and the policymaking process. Students will learn how the IC is sometimes placed in a position of evaluating the effectiveness of US policies. If the intelligence judgments are largely pessimistic, an administration's opponents—in Congress or in other political arenas—can attack those policies. Hence, this chapter will expose students to the risks of "politicization" of intelligence. Classic cases can be found in analysis conducted during the Vietnam War as well as during the run-up to the invasion of Iraq during the presidency of George W. Bush, even though the forms of politicization in these two cases were very different. Students can then analyze various forms of politicization and also consider how it can be minimized if not entirely eliminated.

Chapter 11 concludes with an examination of how intelligence can best operate within American democracy while safeguarding both civil liberties and national security. It highlights the ethical and legal challenges to conducting secret intelligence gathering and covert action while remaining within the bounds of the US Constitution and accountable to senior policymakers, Congress, and ultimately the American public. Students will become familiar with the mix of executive branch and congressional oversight mechanisms that are in place to guarantee accountability. It raises the question of whether those oversight mechanisms have been sufficient to deal with the kinds of complex and intrusive intelligence operations conducted in a post-9/11 environment. The chapter concludes with a recommendation that American intelligence become as transparent as possible so that it is not only more easily understood by students and scholars but also finds more public support for its essential role in the policymaking process.

As students work their way through this introduction to intelligence, they will be confronted with a variety of terms involving intelligence processes, organizations, and concepts. This arcane vocabulary is often difficult to comprehend. Therefore, to provide a study aid, the author has set in boldface these terms that have a special meaning or significance. Short definitions of these highlighted items are located in the extensive glossary found at the back of the book. For instructors and students interested in going further into any of the topics covered in each chapter, there is also a short list of key readings at the end of each chapter, which the author considers excellent sources on a wide range of intelligence and national security topics. Last, at the end of the chapters where relevant there are sections variously titled Useful Documents, Useful Websites, and Further Reading with links to additional intelligence studies, declassified intelligence products, and related materials. With these additional aids, the author hopes to make a student's introduction to intelligence more accessible and comprehensive.

NOTES

Epigraph: As cited in Charles Lathrop, *The Literary Spy: The Ultimate Source of Quotations on Espionage and Intelligence* (New Haven, CT: Yale University Press, 2004), 10.

1. See Roger George and Harvey Rishikof, eds., *The National Security Enterprise: Navigating the Labyrinth*, 2nd ed. (Washington: Georgetown University Press, 2017). This book outlines the many government agencies involved in national security decision-making along with descriptions of other key actors, such as Congress, the courts, think tanks, and the media. It provides students with an overview of the interagency processes and challenges that the NSE faces and is likely to face for the foreseeable future.

2. Joseph Nye, "Peering into the Future," *Foreign Affairs*, July/August 1994, 82–93.

2

WHAT IS INTELLIGENCE?

It is not enough, of course, to simply collect information. Thoughtful analysis is vital to sound decision-making.
   —President Ronald Reagan, 1981

Our country's safety and prosperity depend on the quality of the intelligence we collect and the analysis we produce, our ability to evaluate and share this information in a timely manner and our ability to counter intelligence threats.
   —2010 US National Security Strategy

The Intelligence Community exists to provide political and military leaders with the greatest possible decision advantage. We understand, now more than ever, that the best possible way to accomplish our goal is through integration of all national intelligence capabilities.
   —James Clapper, director of national intelligence, 2014

US national security decision-making relies on intelligence. Although the relationship between policy action and information seems so obvious, the actual uses of intelligence for making decisions on war and peace are seldom well understood by scholars and students of international affairs. This chapter will explore what intelligence is and introduce students to some of the basic terminology surrounding intelligence **collection** and **analysis**.

   The organization and operation of American intelligence agencies is itself a complicated subject that is hard for students to grasp. Intelligence involves the use of specialized methods and processes for *collecting* information and then *processing* it (if it must be converted into more usable forms or translated). That information is then *analyzed* by regional or technical experts to determine what significance it holds for US national security interests. Once the information is *analyzed* and fully evaluated for its credibility and accuracy, it is compiled into finished analysis (i.e., fully evaluated information) reports and *disseminated* to government officials for their use in shaping national security policies. Policymakers then may provide *feedback* and levy new intelligence **requirements** for additional information and analysis on those topics. This sequence of steps has become known as the **intelligence cycle.** All of these phases are important, but they reveal little about how intelligence informs policy or how policymakers use intelligence. Moreover, the alphabet soup of more than a dozen intelligence agencies is bewildering. They are not all equally important to national-level decision-making. Knowing where, when, and how intelligence has been critical to a national security decision is far more critical to understanding how US national security policies are formulated and implemented.

The intelligence-policy relationship is fundamentally one of a support function involving a wide range of intelligence agencies, activities, and assessments. Identifying the roles and responsibilities of both sides of this relationship is critical to understanding why sometimes it can become a very contentious one. Policymakers expect and depend on intelligence to provide more clarity if not total comprehension of complex international issues; however, they consider intelligence only one input and not always the decisive one. Intelligence officers do not wish to make policy, but they must often provide information and analysis that complicates or raises questions about an administration's decisions or actions. This symbiotic relationship, as we shall see in subsequent chapters, is not always evident or easy to manage. The intelligence-policy relationship often suffers from distrust on both sides, partly owing to poor understanding of the different cultures that drive them.

INTELLIGENCE: AN ENABLER OF STRATEGY

When the Cold War broke out, the United States began developing a national security strategy as well as a national security system (see chapter 3 for more discussion). US containment strategy was soon in place along with seminal legislation titled the **National Security Act of 1947**, which set up the now well-known **National Security Council** and its various components. At that time, there was no set idea of how intelligence would support a growing US international role. However, an early participant in US wartime intelligence, Professor Sherman Kent, wrote perhaps the most influential book on intelligence. In it, he argued that intelligence should "raise the level of discussion" around the policymaking table.[1] At the same time, intelligence should not advocate any specific policy option but rather should provide information that is tailored to those policies being considered by decision-makers. Kent was aware of the dangers of being too close or too far from the policy process. Being too close ran the risk of intelligence becoming skewed to suit policymakers' preferences; being too far

---

Box 2.1   Sherman Kent on Intelligence

"I suppose if we in intelligence were one day given three wishes, they would be to know everything, to be believed when we spoke, and in such a way to exercise an influence to the good in the matter of policy."

—Sherman Kent, former director, Board of National Estimates

---

removed from policy discussions risked being irrelevant to or uninformed about the policies being debated and the options being considered (see box. 2.1).

An important by-product of the 1947 National Security Act was the institutionalization of intelligence support to senior policymakers. According to the legislation, the NSC would be expanded beyond just the president's diplomatic and military advisers to include the **director of central intelligence (DCI)** as its key intelligence adviser. This usually placed intelligence at or near the policy table when presidents and secretaries of state and defense were making momentous decisions. That intelligence advisory role took the form of providing the president with his own daily intelligence reports, which later came to be known as the *President's Daily Brief*, as well as preparation of more comprehensive intelligence reports such as **National Intelligence Estimates** on which major policies were often based. In addition, the Cold War and the threat of nuclear war obliged the United States to find methods short of a "hot" conflict for combating Soviet subversion around the world. In short order, President Harry Truman and virtually every president thereafter authorized the CIA to conduct other "special activities"—later known as **covert action**. This became an important secret tool of presidents and also placed the CIA in a unique position to both formulate policy initiatives and implement them. In the post-9/11 era, this covert action tool has become even more important and ironically more visible than the original shapers of the US national security system could have imagined.

Today the United States maintains the largest and most elaborate and capable set of intelligence agencies in the world. This intelligence system employs more than one hundred thousand people and spends over $70 billion annually on its activities. It supports the national security enterprise by providing tailored intelligence to virtually every national security body, from the White House to the Department of State and Department of Defense to the economic and law enforcement agencies. Important intelligence subjects go far beyond the politico-military realm, and the concept of national security now encompasses such broad topics as infectious disease, climate change, and the cyberspace domain. Since 9/11, national security has also required significant domestic intelligence functions. Simply stated, intelligence is a significant player in forming and conducting all aspects of US foreign policy but also aspects of domestic public safety.

WHAT IS INTELLIGENCE?

The term *intelligence* has a variety of meanings and uses. The most common usage is to encompass just information (both classified and unclassified) provided to policy officials, in order to distinguish it from a broader body of information available to those inside and outside the US government. So the term is often applied to the collection of raw (i.e., unevaluated) information that the intelligence agencies collect and distribute to a select group of civilian and military decision-makers. A second usage is when intelligence refers to the analysis that is produced when regional and technical experts evaluate the raw information and then prepare "finished" intelligence reports of various kinds. The word *finished* denotes that all the information included in those reports has been reviewed and evaluated for its accuracy and significance.

Intelligence Is Collection

Intelligence is most often but not always focused on the collection of secret information. That is to say, intelligence organizations are especially interested in gathering information that a foreign actor wishes to conceal from the US government. In this sense, clandestinely acquired intelligence is doubly secret—it concerns the secrets of foreign actors that US intelligence can gather secretly. The acquisition of the information is done so that the collection operation as well as the source and identity of the **collector** are concealed. This allows the US IC the ability to know things that a foreign government or actor does not want to be shared, but it also keeps that target in the dark regarding what the US government has learned about its plans and capabilities. This is the essence of secret intelligence—giving the United States a decision-advantage in dealing with a foreign threat.

The two most well-known categories of intelligence are **technical intelligence (TECHINT)** and **human intelligence (HUMINT)**. First, intelligence can be gathered by technical (i.e., TECHINT) systems involving ground-based electronic systems and aerial platforms or satellites in earth orbit that gather electronic signals or images using different technologies. These systems produce the bulk of the raw intelligence used by the IC. Alternatively, raw information can be collected through **clandestine** (i.e., conducted in order to assure the secrecy of the activity) or overt means involving people (i.e., HUMINT). Here, the goal is to understand the activities but also the intentions of foreign government officials or other nonstate actors. A third but entirely unclassified form of intelligence collection has been the widespread use of

---

Box 2.2   Intelligence Disciplines: Their Uses

Human intelligence (HUMINT) is gained overtly by diplomats and military attachés or secretly from foreign agents who have access to the plans, intentions, and capabilities of foreign adversaries. Examples:
- Diplomatic reporting on foreign government policies and actions
- Attaché reporting on the readiness and capabilities of foreign militaries
- Clandestine reports on internal foreign government plans and intentions

Signals intelligence (SIGINT) is the technical interception and exploitation of an adversary's communication and other electronic systems. Examples:
- Communications between a hostile government's ministries or offices
- Electronic test results from an adversary's missile firing
- Air-defense radar capabilities of a hostile power's defense installations

Imagery intelligence (IMINT) is collected from ground, aerial, and space-based imaging systems (often satellites) using visual photography, electro-optics, radar, or infrared sensors. Examples:
- Images of battlefield preparations and combat operations
- Measurement and assessment of an adversary's air-defense systems
- Location and assessment of airfields for emergency evacuations of US nationals

Geospatial intelligence (GEOINT) is derived from imagery and other geospatial information that describe the physical features and geographically referenced activities on Earth. Examples:
- Geolocation of hidden defense installations
- Targeting data for unmanned airborne vehicles
- Physical geographic and environmental changes following natural disasters

Measurement and signature intelligence (MASINT) is information derived from a diverse set of technical sensors that collect acoustic, radiological, chemical, biological, and other signatures from fixed or moving targets. Examples:
- Presence of chemical or biological toxins in soil samples near factories
- Air samples containing radioactive isotopes from nuclear tests
- Electromagnetic analysis that can distinguish foliage from camouflage

Open-source intelligence (OSINT) is unclassified, publicly available information on key foreign developments found in foreign broadcasts, news media, or Internet sites. Examples:
- Public speeches by foreign officials on national security policies
- Online terrorist propaganda and recruitment efforts
- Technology reports of foreign scientific and technical research institutes

---

open-source intelligence (OSINT) (see box 2.2). Collectively, these intelligence-collection disciplines (often referred to as "**INTs**") make up the body of classified and unclassified information from which analysts will try to identify significant international developments. Each of these approaches is worth exploring in greater detail because they provide the foundation for later exploration of the role intelligence plays in informing the policymaking process.

Within the TECHINT category, **signals intelligence (SIGINT)** collects the wide array of electronic signals and communications produced by foreign actors. It is collected via ground stations as well as aircraft and satellites that suck up all the signals emanating from multiple sources and locations. SIGINT is further broken down into other more distinct categories of collection techniques and targets. For example, **communications intelligence (COMINT)** comprises all the signals produced by telecommunication systems such as telephones, fax machines, radios, and Internet data streams. COMINT is particularly useful in providing insights into the conversations among foreign actors and any activities that might be revealed in the collected phone, fax, or Internet activity. In addition, there is **electronic intelligence (ELINT)**, which is produced by the signals emanating from foreign radars and other electronic military systems; it is especially useful for observing and assessing military capabilities and operations. Finally, the SIGINT family is rounded out by **foreign instrumentation signals intelligence (FISINT)**, the electronic signals produced by a foreign government's military, commercial, and scientific testing. When a foreign government sends performance data from a rocket test, for example, these signals can sometimes be intercepted by US collectors.

Also within the TECHINT category is **imagery intelligence (IMINT)**. The United States led the way in developing overhead imagery systems such as the U-2 and SR-71 aircraft, which carried cameras (as well as SIGINT sensors) to observe foreign military activities. These have been dramatically augmented by large satellite systems, which today are mostly electro-optical (E-O) systems capable of returning vast numbers of images of selected targets in near-real time.[2] These satellites have the advantage of being well above enemy air defenses and can loiter in long-duration earth orbits to give them ability to reaccess important target locations on a regular basis. Technology has advanced to the point that these systems can pick up targets that are far less than a square meter in size.[3] Other technical sensors on such satellites can also capture infrared images of ground and even underground targets that E-O systems would not detect. Managed from the ground, satellites can be programmed to take images at precise times and places based on the priorities established by the imagery analysts.

Satellites are typically operated for many years and are expensive to replace. While they can produce many images, they are in great demand, so they are used only on high-priority targets. The advent of commercial imagery satellites now permits the US IC to purchase images of lower-priority targets, which otherwise might not be covered. Most recently, imagery has been supplemented as well by the appearance of unmanned aerial vehicles (UAVs), which can also provide real-time imagery on specific locations, installations, or operations being conducted by foreign governments or nonstate actors.

As technology has advanced in the development of sensors as well as computer software applications, the technical collection of raw information has led to the development of a new category of intelligence. **Geospatial intelligence (GEOINT)** is the use of these advanced technologies along with imagery that has even more applications than simply producing high-resolution pictures. To give a simple example, IMINT might produce pictures of a terrorist camp or refugee center somewhere in Africa; however, GEOINT would overlay those images with other social media and signals intelligence geolocated there to describe who might be in those structures and what their plans or activities are.

A final element of the TECHINT discipline is **measurement and signature intelligence (MASINT)**. This discipline is an even more arcane set of sensors and collection methods on the technical side of intelligence. MASINT aims to detect, identify, and describe significant features of the earth or other fixed or dynamic targets. Often mentioned are radar **signatures** that can capture activities hidden from normal imagery, seismic detectors of nuclear and natural events, or air-sampling sensors that can identify the presence of nuclear, chemical, or biological materials.[4] In many cases, some combination of these technical collection systems is used to give the most complete picture of an important target.[5]

HUMINT, or human-source collection, is the oldest and most common method of collecting secret (as well as overt) information. Called "spying" or "espionage," clandestine HUMINT involves the use of trained intelligence officers (called "case officers") who recruit agents (termed "sources" and sometimes "assets"). These agents are foreign nationals who for a variety of reasons—such as greed, ego, disgruntlement or trouble with their superiors or governments, or ideology—are prepared to commit treason. That is, they will pass a foreign government's or other organization's secrets to the IC at the risk of incarceration and possibly execution. Compared to TECHINT, HUMINT is relatively cheap in terms of resources. However, it requires substantial training in espionage methods (termed **"tradecraft"**) that enables the case officer to evade detection, evaluate and run the source, and protect those **sources and methods**. These HUMINT operations can lead to a case officer's arrest, expulsion, lengthy imprisonment, or death; often it is far worse for a source that is uncovered. Hence, human-source collection is reserved for some of the most important intelligence missions and justifies keeping the information about such sources limited to only those who **"need to know."**[6] That principle aims to keep detailed knowledge of a source's identity, activities, and location to an absolute minimum and to compartmentalize these details so as to reduce the risk of exposure. Few if any intelligence analysts need that kind of information, and policymakers almost never see it.

A key advantage of HUMINT is that it can reveal the plans and intentions of foreign officials and other human targets who have shared their information with others, including an intelligence source. This kind of direct knowledge of a foreign government's thinking and plans is hard to develop. It can take years for a HUMINT asset to be identified, recruited, developed, and managed as a reliable source of a foreign government's or terrorist organization's innermost secrets. American HUMINT programs are run overseas by placing officers "under cover" (i.e., provide a false identity) in order for them to work clandestinely. This status allows them to operate clandestinely without a foreign government's or nonstate actor's knowledge. Such operations are termed "unilateral" since the host government is unwitting of their existence.

HUMINT need not be clandestinely collected. Many HUMINT reports come from the normal diplomatic interactions between US diplomats and their foreign counterparts. Military attachés serving in US embassies also meet with foreign military officials or observe military exercises, which result in HUMINT reports. US intelligence officers may also use formal liaison relationships with foreign intelligence agencies to share information on targets they both view as a threat. In these cases, American case officers may work jointly (termed a "joint or bilateral operation") with a host government's intelligence service to gather intelligence on that target. These forms of HUMINT are declared to a foreign government and are considered acceptable, so they do not carry the risk that clandestinely acquired HUMINT normally involves. Nonetheless, since these reports reflect confidential information or views that a foreign government has shared with US diplomats, military officers, or case officers, they are also classified.

There has been a long-standing debate over whether the United States relies too much on TECHINT and has failed to develop sufficient HUMINT capability. US technological sophistication gives it a natural advantage in building technical collection systems capable of gathering huge volumes of electronic data, images, and other information. However, it is costly to process and sift through that mountain of data to find the nuggets of unique and compelling information. This raw information can be degraded or misleading as well as denied to the United States through a variety of concealment, deception, and operational security measures. Interpreting images requires special understanding of the telltale signatures of complex targets, which can be hidden if the foreign intelligence target understands how US technical systems operate.

HUMINT—if it provides unique access to a government's or another target's plans and intentions—can be indispensable to alerting intelligence analysts and policymakers to an emerging threat. Yet HUMINT also has disadvantages and weaknesses. First, as mentioned earlier, it takes time and good tradecraft skills to recruit and protect reliable sources with real access. Reviewing and validating a human source's information also takes time, and it is not always easy to develop high confidence about a source. Second, those sources can often be fabricators, who tell a case officer what they believe the US government expects to hear. Third, a human source might actually be part of a foreign **counterintelligence (CI)** operation. In this case, the source is a foreign intelligence officer working to penetrate US intelligence. Such CI operations are designed to provide misinformation, collect against US intelligence agencies, and disrupt American intelligence programs.

Having surveyed the main sources of largely secret intelligence collection, it is important not to minimize the value of open-source intelligence. OSINT includes the vast array of publicly available news reporting, government documents, academic and scientific scholarship, and social media that are carried in publications, on television or radio, or over the Internet. In fact, open-source materials had been used throughout the Cold War, when translations of Soviet newspapers and television and radio broadcasts provided insight into internal Kremlin politics, domestic economic conditions, and foreign policy positions. In the post–Cold War period, with the decline in so-called denied areas (i.e., authoritarian states where information is closely guarded) and the growth of the Internet and social media, the volume of open-source material has grown exponentially. While these sources are easily accessible, they still require systems and processes to retrieve, store, and evaluate their significance to American national security. Translation services, data mining, and other technical processes are often used to put those information sources into a form that is useful for analysts and ultimately for policymakers.

Open sources are in many ways ubiquitous, and they provide a useful starting point for understanding a foreign government's or nonstate actor's behavior. Intelligence analysts often use open sources to assist them in pointing TECHINT and HUMINT collectors to targets where their unique access might provide more insight and details about an emerging problem. In some cases, where a target is considered a low priority for expensive TECHINT or risky HUMINT operations, OSINT might be the most likely source of information.

Intelligence comprises all these sources, which are collected to produce the best understanding of complex issues. A good example of the combination of intelligence disciplines was the successful targeting of Osama bin Laden. Human intelligence derived from agents and interrogation of terrorist detainees was used to ascertain the possible location of the al-Qaeda leader in the Pakistani town of Abbottabad. Imagery provided details of the compound in which he was living, while communication intercepts were used to determine who was in touch with Bin Laden and how alert Pakistani officials were to the activities inside that compound. No single intelligence source was sufficient to locate and identify Bin Laden. Even so, as participants said after the fact, they were never 100 percent sure Bin Laden was there. But the combination of all the sources helped to raise confidence that this was the location. Typically, good intelligence relies on a combination of clandestine, technical, and even open-source intelligence to give analysts and policymakers a more complete picture of an important topic or target.

Intelligence Is Analysis

Intelligence, as President Reagan's comment at the beginning of this chapter notes, is more than the collection of raw information. That information must be assembled into a consolidated picture of what international developments might affect US national security interests. Many of the book's later chapters will delve deeply into the nature of intelligence analysis, but understanding the contribution that analysis makes to collection of raw information is important to understand. The old adage that "the facts speak for themselves" is almost never true. In an intelligence context, arraying all the facts is not enough, for many reasons. First, all the facts may not address the question policymakers are asking. Experts need to determine which facts are relevant. Second, not all the information may be accurate or reliable. The data must be examined and compared with other information known to be accurate to see if this new information can be validated. Third, the relevant and validated information must be developed into a narrative or story that explains why this development is significant for US policy. Last, when policymakers react to these finished reports and pose further questions, analysts must determine what new information needs to be collected to fill gaps in their understanding and to continue monitoring those intelligence issues. In sum, analysts must guide the collection for new information so that they can address policymakers' critical intelligence needs.

Analysis can take a number of forms, depending on where it occurs in the intelligence cycle. Within each **INT**, there are **single-source** analysts who examine and evaluate the collected raw information. They assemble a picture of the intelligence target or topic based on their understanding of the imagery, signals, or human sources that their collection system produces. Although single-source analysts have access to information from other INTs and their work is often informed by other collection disciplines (usually termed "collateral information"), they are not authorized to produce "**all-source analysis**," or "finished" intelligence. Instead, sole-source reports go to other all-source analysts, where they will collate all relevant information that sole-source analysis has on a specific topic.

For example, take the case of Saddam Hussein's efforts to develop **weapons of mass destruction** in the late 1990s and early 2000. Single-source imagery analysts would evaluate many photos taken of suspected WMD research or production sites to determine if there might be proof of renewed activities. SIGINT analysts would cull through many intercepted phone conversations of senior Iraqi officials to determine if they were talking about the development or transfer of "special weapons" (e.g., what analysts believed was the euphemism for WMDs) among suspect sites. HUMINT reports officers (now called "collection management officers") would evaluate the accuracy and reliability of human assets (a combination of agents or defectors or foreign liaison reporting) and disseminate any credible reports on the supposed plans of senior Iraqi officials regarding their WMD programs or on reactions to US policies to restrict Baghdad's weapons research. These single-source reports across all INTs would be available to all-source analysts in other agencies. All-source analysts would then be responsible for assessing whether Saddam had plans to restart WMD programs and whether he could develop a nuclear, chemical, or biological weapons capability over the next several years. Their "finished" intelligence assessments were then provided to the president and his senior civilian and military advisers. In this particular case, George W. Bush administration officials were convinced that Saddam had restarted his programs. Their feedback tended to criticize analysts for not providing more conclusive evidence of Saddam's WMD programs. Later chapters will examine how this kind of policymaker bias and feedback can distort analysis and sometimes misdirect collection priorities toward confirming a policy bias rather than searching as well for disconfirming information.

Intelligence Is Risky Business

Whether intelligence is looked at as a collection effort or as an analytical one, it carries risks of imperfection, if seldom complete failure. First, it is impossible to collect perfect information or to have total confidence in what intelligence reporting means for US national security. Each intelligence-collection discipline has its limits and flaws. Hostile foreign actors have worked hard to hide their plans and capabilities; many of America's foremost rivals, such as Russia, China, and Iran, have formidable intelligence services that are conducting espionage and disinformation campaigns against the United States. Also, as a former mentor of many intelligence analysts put it, analysis is not "fortune telling."[7] Such assessments can, as another practitioner has phrased it, "reduce uncertainty," but they cannot entirely remove it.[8] Necessarily, some intelligence will prove to be wrong or off base. Making "predictions" in the sense of forecasting precise outcomes is a fool's errand. Few policymakers seriously expect the IC to have crystal balls, and the IC attempts not to give that impression. However, policymakers do expect intelligence to bound that uncertainty, so they have a clear sense of the "knowns" and "unknowns" in the decisions they make.

A second risk is that the intelligence sources and methods often carry political, financial, and personal costs if they are exposed or lost. US intelligence officers overseas run the risk of exposure, expulsion, and possible imprisonment if they are discovered by foreign governments. Many intelligence operations are fragile, so they must be protected through good operational security practices. This, too, is intelligence.

Box 2.3   Counterintelligence Explained

As defined in the Executive Order 12333, which governs US intelligence activities, counterintelligence is "information gathered and activities conducted to identify, deceive, exploit, disrupt or protect against espionage, other intelligence activities, sabotage, or assassinations conducted for or on behalf of foreign power, organizations or persons, or their agents, or international terrorist organizations or activities."

US intelligence agencies conduct counterintelligence analysis and operations to ensure that they understand which specific threats hostile foreign intelligence agencies may present to the United States. US CI activities also include careful screening of US government employees, requiring a security clearance to ensure they are not under the control of a foreign intelligence service. Travel restrictions as well as reporting of any contact with foreign nationals are required of all employees; moreover, periodic reinvestigation and often polygraph exams are used to verify their adherence to strict rules about the handling and sharing of classified information.

Formal responsibility for counterintelligence is shared by several US intelligence agencies. The CIA is principally responsible for monitoring and combating foreign counterintelligence overseas, while the FBI is responsible for investigating foreign counterintelligence activities within the United States.

Protecting US sources and methods (via counterintelligence) often involves having to penetrate foreign intelligence services (**counterespionage**) in order to know if US intelligence operations have been compromised (see box 2.3). Recent exposure of large amounts of **classified intelligence** by Edward Snowden, including sensitive collection operations, has compromised or ended some of the most productive sources of counterterrorism information. Many are probably irreplaceable and have now been exploited by other hostile actors. Moreover, it has damaged the United States' reputation with allies and in some cases made their intelligence services less willing to cooperate with Washington. Conducting counterintelligence and counterespionage can also carry risks. When US efforts to recruit foreign intelligence officers are revealed, it inevitably has negative effects on those intelligence relationships. An alleged CIA effort to recruit a German intelligence officer in 2014, according to various news sources, led to official German complaints and demands that the senior US intelligence official in Germany leave the country.[9]

Third, intelligence operations can raise serious ethical concerns about their acceptability in democratic societies. "Spying" and secrecy more generally are seen by some as antithetical to the openness of democratic societies, yet the protection of American democracy may require compromises in how far the United States is prepared to let its intelligence agencies operate. Excessive domestic surveillance at the expense of Americans' civil liberties—as occurred during the Vietnam War—cost the IC credibility with Congress and the public. Similar operations against foreign targets tend to be less controversial. Covert actions to influence foreign governments or to weaken hostile nonstate actors often rely on activities that would be reprehensible within our own society and constitutional system. Since the early 1980s, those operations have required **presidential findings** and **congressional notifications** (discussed in later chapters). Today measures to collect intelligence, whether they are enhanced interrogation techniques or technical surveillance of private citizens, raise serious human rights and civil liberties questions that our legislative and judicial institutions must protect. Providing as much transparency and accountability as possible will remain important if intelligence agencies are to be able to operate with the support of the American public. These challenges will be examined in more detail in chapter 11.

WHY INTELLIGENCE MATTERS

Good strategy is dependent on understanding the nature of the international system, key actors in that system, and major challenges facing US national interests. Inherently, then, a national security strategy must be based on good intelligence. Historically, leaders have depended on good intelligence. Moses sent spies into Canaan, Napoleon's diplomats were operating as spies in the royal courts of Europe, and Paul Revere provided the first intelligence warning of the British advance on the colonists. Indeed, Gen. George Washington became America's first spymaster, directing the Committee of Correspondence and dispensing funds to agents working against the Redcoats. In both world wars, American intelligence operations were established to support the military campaigns, only to be eliminated in peacetime.

After 1947, however, intelligence became a permanent feature of America's national security system. However, it was little discussed or understood outside of the government. As mentioned above, the 1947 National Security Act set up a new decision-making process, with the president at the center. Most important for our purposes, that legislation established the need for a peacetime intelligence function, making it a central player in the national security decision-making process. The NSC not only would contain the president's closest foreign policy advisers from the Department of State and Department of Defense but also the DCI as its key intelligence adviser—a body most recently revised to reflect the creation of the **director of national intelligence (DNI)**. This was a realization that classified and specialized information would be useful in determining what kinds of threats and opportunities the United States faced and which tools—diplomatic, economic, and military as well as intelligence— might be brought to bear.

The 1947 act says very little about the internal organization and operation of US intelligence. That would evolve over the next sixty or more years into an elaborate set of agencies. Proof of the connection between intelligence and national security can be seen in the simultaneous expansion of American global influence and military presence abroad and the comparable growth of American intelligence. As America became a superpower, so too the US IC went "global," covering virtually any topic that might be discussed in the Oval Office, by the NSC, or by military officials in the Pentagon.

This growth also reflected more sophistication in intelligence techniques—both for collection of information as well as its analysis. As the US national security policy structure grew into a major enterprise, it created an ever-larger and more diverse set of civilian and military users of intelligence. Important legislation and presidential **executive orders**—sometimes secret—authorized the creation of new intelligence agencies. The position of DCI was established in 1947. After some debate over whether analysis and espionage should be run separately by the State Department and the CIA, respectively, the CIA began its slow evolution into the multimission organization that it is today.[10] President Truman secretly authorized the establishment of the National Security Agency (NSA) in 1952, unifying previously separate signals intelligence agencies of the military services. In the early 1960s, Presidents Dwight Eisenhower and John F. Kennedy pushed for the National Reconnaissance Office (NRO) to monitor Soviet military activities and the Defense Intelligence Agency (DIA) to strengthen military analysis. Other elements of the IC came into being as each major department became a player in international diplomatic, economic, or legal affairs and needed tailored intelligence in order to conduct its business.

Another expansion occurred in the wake of the 9/11 terrorist attacks. President George W. Bush introduced the most far-reaching intelligence reforms to defend the homeland against terrorist attacks and to better coordinate the vast IC. He established the Office of Director of National Intelligence (ODNI) to oversee the sixteen individual intelligence agencies, gave the CIA new authorities to conduct covert action against global terrorist organizations, and created a **National Counterterrorism Center (NCTC)** to better orchestrate the development of counterterrorism policies. Separately, he created the new Department of Homeland Security (DHS), which has intelligence functions as well as domestic policy authorities. All of these measures highlight just how interrelated intelligence and policy are.

Today intelligence is central to defeating terrorism, preventing proliferation of WMDs, and deterring the actions of resurgent or rising powers such as Russia and China. Indeed, the 2019 National Intelligence Strategy lists countering cyber threats, terrorism, and WMD proliferation as key missions as well as conducting broad strategic intelligence analysis of enduring security issues and anticipating emerging threats.[11]

Each president has recognized the crucial role of intelligence in formulating national security decision-making. Most presidents have been dissatisfied with the

IC's performance at various points in their tenures, while praising the community at other times. Failures receive the lion's share of attention in the form of presidential criticisms, congressional inquiries, and media attention. Most successes must remain secret or are of such little interest that they seldom garner attention. Many are simply getting good information in a timely way to senior policymakers that helps to shape policies; some are early warnings that lead to decisions that avert or at least reduce the risks or impact of damaging trends. Still others are invisible covert actions that reinforce diplomacy or military operations. However, dramatic failures are often seen as particularly damning and cause for major investigations and additional reforms. There can be double standards. For example, the successful tracking and elimination of Bin Laden has been generally applauded, but the "targeted killings" by **drone** operations and enhanced interrogation techniques have been strongly questioned by the media. Consider how few people will recall or appreciate the IC's successful discovery of secret Syrian or North Korean nuclear weapons facilities during George W. Bush's presidency, whereas everyone is aware of the **intelligence failures** leading to 9/11 and the Iraq War.

Intelligence has also become a much more visible feature of America's national security policy debates. Intelligence agencies during the early Cold War years largely operated under the cloak of secrecy, having less oversight and arguably less influence over the direction of foreign policy. Today intelligence judgments or operations are now widely reported in major news media. Whereas one seldom heard from or saw the CIA director in public during the 1950s and 1960s, today the DNI or CIA director regularly presents major public addresses or open congressional testimonies. For example, the DNI's annual Worldwide Threat Assessment to congressional oversight committees is now a standard presentation of the IC's assessment of major threats. Of course, intelligence reports are periodically and unofficially "leaked" to the media. Sometimes they are part of the government's efforts to highlight important issues to the public or to warn adversaries that Washington is aware of their activities. Other times leaks are the result of internal policy debates over controversial methods or actions, in which disgruntled government employees or others with access to classified information want to disclose secrets to start a public discussion. Official declassification of significant intelligence assessments has also become the subject of congressional and public debates over not only those intelligence judgments but also the national security policies they support. Again, we see that the two are intertwined more and more.

Intelligence is also a force multiplier for the United States in terms of providing critical information or methods that can reduce the costs of conducting effective US national security policies. To cite just one historical example, a former Soviet spy for the United States provided critical information regarding Soviet radar developments that the US Air Force credited with saving at least $1 billion in research-and-development funds.[12] Assessments of major adversaries' weapon systems today are equally important in ensuring that US armaments are well designed and effective. The use of drones is another example of a cost-effective way to disrupt and destroy terrorist targets without placing US forces on the ground. The counterterrorism policies of the Barack Obama administration often were favored over more expensive and risky counterinsurgency policies because they could rely more heavily on intelligence operations.

Finally, as mentioned above, intelligence remains a controversial ethical issue in American foreign policy. Democratic governments are wary of creating strong organizations that operate in secret and by definition are breaking the laws of other governments. US intelligence agencies have been involved in many scandals since their creation and will continue to operate by "playing to the edge" of what is permissible, as one former CIA director put it.[13] Some critics often dismiss the utility of intelligence when it fails in some of its operations or analysis. Others question the ethics of intelligence operations conducted around the world or even domestically. The revelations of NSA collection operations, the secret detention of alleged terrorists, and the use of enhanced interrogation techniques are only the latest examples of what will demand a tricky balance between safeguarding national security and preserving Americans' civil liberties. Many security specialists believe that intelligence is more important than ever given the threats the United States faces in the twenty-first century. In turn, this era has ushered in more complexity as the world has become more connected, nonstate actors have risen in importance, great power rivalry has returned, and the concept of national security has further blurred the line between foreign and domestic policies. For all these reasons, understanding how intelligence contributes to national security decision-making is now even more essential for the study of American foreign policy.

USEFUL DOCUMENTS

ODNI, *A Consumer's Guide to National Intelligence, 2009*, https://www.dni.gov/files/documents/IC_Consumers_Guide_2009.pdf

ODNI, *US National Intelligence: An Overview*, 2013, https://www.dni.gov/files/documents/USNI%202013%20Overview_web.pdf

ODNI, *National Intelligence Strategy of the United States*, January 2019, https://www.dni.gov/index.php/newsroom/reports-publications/item/1943-2019-national-intelligence-strategy

FURTHER READING

Richard Betts, *Enemies of Intelligence: Knowledge and Power in American National Security* (New York: Columbia University Press, 2007).

Offers a recapitulation of the author's many excellent articles on intelligence that takes a balanced view between many critics and the few apologists for US intelligence.

Thomas Fingar, *Reducing Uncertainty: Intelligence and National Security* (Stanford, CA: Stanford University Press, 2011).
    Gives an insider's view of the challenges of post-9/11 intelligence, with special attention to the intelligence-policy relationship and how intelligence weathered the controversies surrounding the 2002 Iraq WMD NIE.
Robert Jervis, *Why Intelligence Fails: Lessons from the Iranian Revolution and the Iraq War* (Ithaca, NY: Cornell University Press, 2010).
    An excellent postmortem by a recognized intelligence scholar on the sources of cognitive and bureaucratic bias in intelligence analysis.
Mark Lowenthal, *Intelligence: From Secrets to Policy*, 6th ed. (Washington, DC: CQ Press, 2015).
    The best-known treatment of the intelligence process and cycle.
Mark Lowenthal and Robert Clark, *The Five Disciplines of Intelligence Collection* (Washington, DC: CQ Press, 2015).
    An excellent survey of the technical, human, and open-source collection systems, written by individual scholars and practitioners.
Paul Pillar, *Intelligence and US Foreign Policy: Iraq, 9/11, and Misguided Reform* (New York: Columbia University Press, 2011).
    Provides a practitioner's view of the 9/11 and Iraq War intelligence controversies and criticizes both the politicization of intelligence as well as recent intelligence reforms.
Amy Zegart, *Flawed by Design: The Evolution of the CIA, JCS, and NSC* (Stanford, CA: Stanford University Press, 1999).
    Provides a controversial description of how the national security and intelligence enterprises came about largely because of bureaucratic and legislative rivalries.

NOTES

First epigraph: White House, *National Security Strategy*, May 2010, 15.

Second epigraph: Office of the Director of National Intelligence, *The National Intelligence Strategy of the United States*, 2014, 21.

1. Sherman Kent, *Strategic Intelligence for an American World Policy* (Princeton, NJ: Princeton University Press, 1966).

2. "Near-real time" refers to the speed with which electro-optical images can be transmitted from overhead satellites to ground stations and then processed so that they can be viewed by imagery analysts within a very short period of time.

3. Imaging resolution of small targets far less than a square meter in size are now possible by classified satellite systems, but commercial satellites are prohibited from exploiting the full capability, for national security reasons.

4. A "signature" is commonly understood as a unique characteristic of a target that is observable or measurable. In imagery it might be the design of a particular kind of weapons facility; in ELINT it might be a particular radio frequency or radar band used by a foreign military's radar or air-defense systems; in MASINT a signature might be a chemical compound

or nuclear isotope that is characteristic of a WMD or an acoustic signal typical of a nuclear-powered submarine.

5. For an excellent survey of technical intelligence, see Robert M. Clark, *Technical Collection of Intelligence* (Washington, DC: CQ Press, 2014); and Mark Lowenthal and Robert M. Clark, *The Five Disciplines of Intelligence Collection* (Washington, DC: CQ Press, 2015).

6. Two excellent memoirs of how case officers are trained and how they operate are to be found in Robert Baer, *See No Evil: The True Story of a Ground Soldier in the CIA's War on Terrorism* (New York: Random House, 2002); and Henry A. Crumpton, *The Art of Intelligence: Lessons from a Life in the CIA's Clandestine Service* (New York: Penguin, 2012).

7. See Jack Davis, "Facts, Findings, Forecasts, and Fortune-Telling," *Studies in Intelligence* 39, no. 3 (1995): 25–30.

8. Thomas Fingar, *Reducing Uncertainty: Intelligence Analysis and National Security* (Stanford, CA: Stanford University Press, 2011).

9. Alison Smale, Mark Mazzetti, and David E. Sanger, "Germany Demands Top U.S. Intelligence Official Be Expelled," *New York Times*, July 10, 2014, http://www.nytimes.com/2014/07/11/world/europe/germany-expels-top-us-intelligence-officer.html?_r=0.

10. Secretary of State George C. Marshall wanted his own intelligence bureau, which meant that the functions of the Research and Analysis Branch of the Office of Strategic Services that were assigned to the State Department became the beginnings of a much smaller Bureau of Intelligence and Research, while the CIA's analytical side grew much larger throughout the 1950s and 1960s.

11. DNI, *National Intelligence Strategy of the United States*, September 2014, www.http://www.dni.gov/files/documents/2014_NIS_Publication.pdf.

12. David E. Hoffman, *The Billion Dollar Spy: A True Story of Cold War Espionage and Betrayal* (New York: Penguin Random House, 2015).

13. Michael V. Hayden, *American Intelligence in the Age of Terror: Playing to the Edge* (New York: Penguin, 2016).

3

WHAT IS THE NATIONAL
SECURITY ENTERPRISE?

The buck stops here.
  —President Harry Truman

A particular virtue of the National Security Act is its flexibility.
  —McGeorge Bundy, John F. Kennedy's national security adviser

The US national security system has evolved over the past half century into an elaborate set of organizations and processes. As vast as this national security enterprise
has become, it still rests on some fundamental concepts that make it responsive to
American leaders and the US Constitution. Key to understanding what American
national security officials do is the role of the president as commander in chief and
his reliance on key advisers and institutions to support his decisions. This chapter
will describe the way national security policy is made and how intelligence fits into
that decision-making process. It will also highlight some of the ongoing issues facing
a president's organization of his national security team.

Article 2 of the Constitution bestows on the president the authority as commander
in chief of US military forces and as chief diplomat over US foreign relations. The
president's authority to appoint ambassadors, negotiate treaties, and implement all
laws and policies through his direction of the huge executive branch agencies gives
him unparalleled control over national security decisions. To be sure, Article 1 of the
Constitution gives Congress the power of the purse to set budgets for military, diplomatic, and intelligence activities and to confirm his appointments of cabinet officers, diplomats, and military leaders. The president must often act in concert with
Congress, but in many circumstances he or she can take the initiative and announce
a policy or commence a military operation, knowing that Congress is hesitant to challenge presidential authority abroad. Given the far-flung US national interests around

the globe, presidents have relied on an increasingly complex set of national security agencies and processes to conduct American statecraft. That decision-making system has been orchestrated through the National Security Council and its so-called **interagency process**. The intelligence community plays a key role in both, as this chapter will make clear.

WHAT IS THE NATIONAL SECURITY SYSTEM?

The US national security system has grown larger and more complicated since it was established in 1947. At that time, the intent was both to reorganize the postwar military establishment and to centralize the national-level decision-making process. It created a secretary of defense as well as the **Joint Chiefs of Staff (JCS)**, a body that would organize and direct the previously more independent military services. The intent was to give the president the ability to seek the advice of his closest political and military advisers on how to use all instruments of national power—political, military, economic, and informational—to protect and advance US national interests. In fact, President Truman tended not to rely on it heavily until confronted with the Korean War, when he was obliged to fashion a more robust "containment strategy" to halt the spread of communism.

Even so, it was a bare-bones operation. The newly established Office of the Secretary of Defense had only a few assistants and was easily overpowered by the well-established secretaries of the army and navy. The State Department was the true center of foreign policy authority. President Truman, like President Franklin D. Roosevelt, relied heavily on the wisdom of his secretaries of state, George C. Marshall and Dean Acheson. He made most foreign policy decisions on his own, based on their advice and counsel, but generally shied away from allowing the NSC to become a decision-making body. That began to change as America's world involvement deepened into a bipolar conflict. Indeed, one of the major contributions of the early NSC system was the now famous NSC 68 policy document, which laid out a containment strategy that continued for more than forty years.

Subsequent presidents have altered what began as occasional meetings of key advisers into a complicated set of national security–related committees and staffs that meet virtually nonstop to consider a myriad of international crises and decisions. By the 1960s, the national security adviser—not specifically mentioned in the 1947 act—had become a key advisory position, comparable to the secretary of state in influence if not formal status. Dr. Henry Kissinger, who assumed this job for President Richard Nixon in 1968, single-handedly created the NSC staff as we know it today, although it comprised a mere dozen or so experts. As will be discussed later, the NSC staff has become its own powerful organization, with several hundred professional staff members. For many observers, this trend has made the NSC the most power-ful "agency" of the US government, which was not the original intent of the 1947 National Security Act.[1] "Staffing the president" has come to mean ensuring that the president is fully informed on every aspect of US national security policy. As we will see, the NSC staff has become one of the key consumers of intelligence, especially as it has grown in size over the past seventy years.

An important by-product of the 1947 National Security Act was the further institu-tionalization of intelligence support to senior policymakers. According to the legisla-tion, the NSC would be expanded beyond just the president's diplomatic and military advisers to include the director of central intelligence as its key intelligence adviser. This usually placed intelligence at or near the policy table when presidents and sec-retaries of state and defense were making momentous decisions. That intelligence advisory role took the form of providing the president with his own daily intelligence reports, which later came to be known as the *President's Daily Brief,* as well as prepa-ration of more comprehensive intelligence reports such as National Intelligence Esti-mates, on which major policies were often based.

In addition, the Cold War and the threat of nuclear war obliged the United States to find methods short of a "hot" conflict for combating Soviet subversion around the world. In short order, President Truman and virtually every president thereafter autho-rized the CIA to conduct other "special activities"—later known as covert action. This became an important secret tool of presidents and also placed the CIA in a unique position to influence policy as well as implement it. In the post-9/11 era, this covert action tool has become even more important and ironically more visible than the original shapers of the US national security system could have imagined.

Most importantly, the 1947 legislation also established the NSC as part of the Exec-utive Office of the President in order to provide him or her with advice on foreign and security issues. By statute, the president, the vice president, and the secretar-ies of state and defense are members; in addition, the chairman of the Joint Chiefs and the director of central (now national) intelligence are advisers from the military and intelligence communities (see box 3.1).[2] Since that act first established the NSC, presidents have felt free to modify the structure as well as add other agency heads to the list of attendees of NSC-sponsored meetings. For example, when nuclear matters are discussed, it has been routine for the secretary of energy to be included in NSC meetings, as this department oversees the operations of America's nuclear weapons laboratories.

Another example of a major structural change occurred when President Bill Clin-ton entered office wanting to highlight the importance of economics. In this case, he created the National Economic Council (NEC), somewhat modeled after the NSC but attended by key economic departments, agencies, and advisers.[3] Accordingly, when

---

Box 3.1   The National Security Act of 1947
(Excerpts from Original and Amended Act)

Sec. 101 (original):

(a) There is hereby established a council to be known as the National Security Council (here-inafter in this section referred to as the "Council").

The President of the United States shall preside over meetings of the Council.

The function of the Council shall be to advise the President with respect to the integration of domestic, foreign, and military policies relating to the national security so as to enable the military services and the other departments and agencies of the Government to cooperate more effectively in matters involving the national security.

Sec. 102 (original):

(a) There is hereby established under the National Security Council a Central Intelligence Agency with a Director of Central Intelligence, who shall be the head thereof. The Director shall be appointed by the President, by and with the advice and consent of the Senate, from among the commissioned officers of the armed services or from among individuals in civilian life.

Section 102 (amended in 2004*):

1.a. There is a Director of National Intelligence who shall be appointed by the President and with the consent of the Senate. . . .

1.b. The DNI shall:

    (1) Serve as head of the Intelligence Community.

    (2) Act as the principal adviser to the President, the National Security Council, and the Homeland Security Council for matters related to national security.

* Section 102 was amended with the passage of the Intelligence Reform and Terrorism Prevention Act (Public Law 108-458) on December 17, 2004.

---

the NSC meets to discuss international economic issues, it has been usual to include the NEC adviser as well as the secretaries of the treasury and commerce. A more recent addition has been the creation of the Homeland Security Council (HSC), which President George W. Bush established after the 9/11 attacks. The HSC includes key foreign policy advisers as well as law enforcement and counterterrorism officials for examining issues such as terrorism, WMDs, and natural disasters.[4] During the Bush administration, the HSC operated somewhat separately from the NSC; however, the Barack Obama administration later integrated the two staffs under the NSC, resulting in a dramatic enlargement of the size of the professional staff.

Two factors serve to restrict the role of the NSC. First, the NSC serves only to "advise" the president and is not a decision-making body. Secretary Marshall worried that the new National Security Act would undermine the constitutional authority of the president as well as the prerogatives of the secretary of state.[5] However, in practice, the president, as George W. Bush famously said, has remained the "decider." Second, each president can alter the composition of the NSC to suit his or her preferences. Early in the Donald Trump presidency, there was controversy surrounding the appointment of Stephen Bannon, Trump's onetime strategic adviser, to the NSC's **Principals Committee (PC)** while neglecting to retain the chairman of the Joint Chiefs of Staff (CJCS) and the DNI.[6] While it is not unheard of for presidents to include personal advisers in NSC meetings, it was unusual to include them in all aspects of NSC official business. This decision was shortly reversed. Like his predecessors, President Trump altered the composition to suit his own desires and like them ultimately decided to include both the DNI and the CJCS in NSC deliberations.

Expanding Role of the NSC and Its Staff

Historically, different presidents have used the NSC differently. Harry Truman initially ignored it—fearing it would become more of a decision-making than advisory body—until the outbreak of the Korean War in June 1950 demanded that there be better integration of America's diplomatic and military efforts to bring the war to an end.[7] Dwight Eisenhower institutionalized an "NSC system" of policy reviews and committees, much as he had used his military staffs during World War II. Eisenhower preferred to have plans developed at lower government levels and then be reviewed by more senior officials before they were presented to him for a decision. A young John F. Kennedy chose to operate more informally and dismantled the extensive military staff system he inherited from Eisenhower. However, he created the role of a "national security adviser," who acts as the president's eyes and ears in monitoring the NSC system. He selected his former Harvard professor McGeorge Bundy to keep him informed regarding international events and ensure that other agencies responded to presidential directives and requests for information.[8]

President Nixon, through his selection of Henry Kissinger as his national security adviser, had the most profound impact on the NSC's role. First, Kissinger established the position as de facto equal with those of the secretaries of state and defense and was able to put himself in the position of setting the national security agenda. Second, he built up the first real NSC staff of regional and functional experts, who could provide himself and the president more independent views on issues, which previously had been largely the domain of the State and Defense Department officials. Those senior experts carried the title of "senior director" for their respective region or issue and were also named "special assistants to the president"—titles that tended to carry real clout. These two actions dramatically centralized power over foreign affairs in the hands of the president and his national security adviser, weakening the influence of the other presidential advisers.

Subsequent presidents from the 1960s to the present day have largely continued to use the NSC staff as a way to keep decision-making within the Oval Office. The size of the NSC staff has grown tenfold since Kissinger first built the staff, from roughly a dozen professionals to several hundred. Moreover, its control over the foreign policy agenda—if the president so chooses—is unparalleled. Each president has shaped the NSC system by issuing presidential directives that describe its structure, participants, and review process in order to prioritize the issues that matter most to him and direct how the interagency process will operate for that particular administration.

The Interagency Process: How It Works

As noted in box 3.1, a key function of the NSC and of the NSC staff is to ensure the smooth integration of all national elements of power—that is, diplomatic, military, economic, and intelligence. Hence, the NSC and subsidiary committees established by each president are key to providing presidential guidance and the development of comprehensive policy reviews, directives, and decisions. Given the growth in the size of the NSE, the national security adviser and his or her staff must work hard to orchestrate the operations of hundreds of diplomats, military officers, law enforcement officials, and intelligence officers so that they are working smoothly together. Fashioning national-level policies that are also supported and implemented by those same agencies requires substantial coordination.

To do this, the NSC cannot simply have the secretaries of state and defense meet with the national security adviser. Such high-level interactions do occur, both formally and informally. However, much more elaborate sets of meetings must be held at lower levels of the bureaucracy to ensure that all agencies have contributed to the development of sound foreign and security policies and to achieve some consensus on how policies should be formulated as well as executed. Hence, each president has constructed subcommittees of the NSC that focus on specific regions, countries, or issues, on which all the relevant agencies are represented.

Since the early 1990s, the NSC committee structure has been set up to have four operational levels. At the highest level is the NSC itself. In this forum, the president presides, and the cabinet-level officers (e.g., the secretaries of state and defense, the national security adviser, the CJCS, and the DNI) attend. These meetings are fairly rare and largely used to announce major presidential decisions. Much more frequent are the PC meetings, which the national security adviser chairs and cabinet-level officers attend to finalize policy reviews in which options will be presented to the president. These PC meetings are usually preceded by **Deputies Committee (DC)** meetings, where subcabinet officials (deputy- or undersecretary-level officials or their

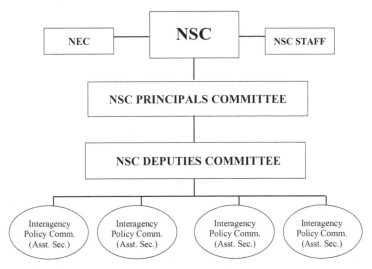

Figure 3.1. The NSC Committee Structure

equivalent) will discuss, debate, and complete policy reviews and recommendations that would then go to the PC. The DC is also used extensively for "crisis management," meaning the deputies will monitor those situations and implement any emergency measures. Below the DC, there will typically be a long list of country, regional, or issue-specific **interagency policy committees (IPCs)**, which the appropriate assistant secretaries from departments (or their equivalent) will attend (see fig. 3.1).

To give one hypothetical example of the interagency process, imagine if the president were interested in promulgating a new policy on China. In this case, his national security adviser might issue an NSC directive to all departments and agencies calling for an IPC meeting to review possible policy options. The senior director of the NSC for East Asia would chair this meeting; in attendance would be representatives from the national security agencies (see fig. 3.2). The assistant secretary of state for East Asia would attend and might cochair the meeting, along with counterparts from the Defense Department—the assistant secretary for international security affairs and the chairman's senior representative from the Joint Staff, who represents the views of the chairman of the Joint Chiefs. Economic and law enforcement agencies also would send their equivalent representatives on the presumption that policy options might touch on commercial or financial relations as well as counterterrorism or copyright laws.

Senior analysts from both the DNI and the CIA would also participate in this IPC. Most likely, the national intelligence officer for East Asia would represent the IC, while the CIA might send a senior substantive analyst on China. Together these intelligence officials might provide a briefing as well as an intelligence assessment

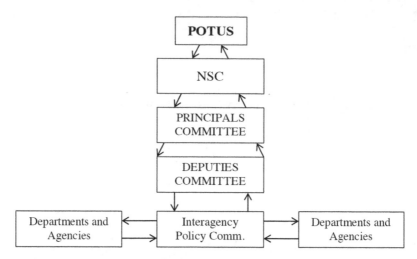

Figure 3.2. The Interagency Process for Decision-Making

on any key questions raised by the national security adviser's directive calling for a policy review. The briefing and intelligence assessment may have been coordinated across major intelligence agencies if there was a White House desire to have a more authoritative IC assessment of the issues. If military intelligence issues are to be discussed—such as China's defense programs or the "militarization" of the South China Sea—the DIA might also send a representative to this IPC in order to support Department of Defense (DOD) policy counterparts.

Once the IPC has reviewed the intelligence and the key issues to be addressed, the NSC senior director would assign an agency, most likely the Department of State, to prepare a policy options paper. This paper would later be circulated and reviewed by the agencies attending the IPC, and additional IPC meetings might be necessary to finalize the policy options. That policy review document would then go to the DC for review, where the deputies would either approve it or remand it for changes if there are disagreements about the policy options. Once approved by the DC, the PC would meet to discuss the options and agree on recommendations to be made to the president. At each of these PC and DC meetings, the DNI and CIA representatives might provide an updated intelligence brief as a foundation for the discussion of the policy options.

At the PC, chaired by the national security adviser, there would be a full and candid discussion of the intelligence surrounding the various policy options. The DNI and the CIA director might be asked to assess the Chinese military threats to US interests in the region; alternatively, if the policy review was focusing more on the US-Chinese trade issues or on a possible American diplomatic initiative, the intelligence brief might concentrate on the state of the Chinese economy or on the current Chinese leadership's views of the United States. At the end, the national security adviser would transmit the final policy review with the PC's recommendations to the president for his approval or disapproval. All through this process, intelligence will have been a key input to understanding the pros and cons of various policy options as well as key uncertainties regarding Chinese intentions, plans, operations, or responses to US decisions. The interagency participants would also be responsible for monitoring agencies' progress in implementing presidential decisions.

Because this interagency review process can extend over several weeks or even months, constant intelligence updates might be required as new events occur in the Far East. In some crisis situations, of course, the process can be extremely compressed, with a series of nonstop meetings of the PC and DC over a period of hours or a few days. In place of face-to-face meetings, some interagency sessions would be held via secure video-teleconference (VTC) facilities. This is especially useful for quickly emerging issues or crisis management. The White House Situation Room is connected to all major national security agencies' operations centers via such VTC systems, so classified discussions can be conducted without leaving one's office.[9] This has greatly increased the US government's ability to operate in crisis mode, with the capability of including military commands and overseas embassies in the VTC discussions.

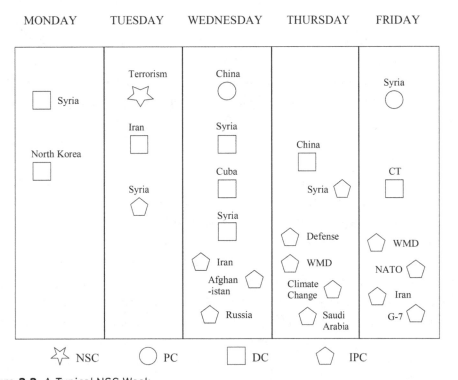

Figure 3.3. A Typical NSC Week

Typically, the IPC convenes most frequently, with the DC overseeing its work and the PC meeting only to validate the work of lower-level committees or to iron out disagreements. One hypothetical but fairly typical week in the life of the interagency process is provided in figure 3.3. As is represented there, not only is China on the agenda but there are also a number of other pressing international issues that compete for senior officials' time and attention. There might be an ongoing crisis—such as has occurred in Syria or Venezuela—that demands frequent meetings at various committee levels; in general, however, issues are placed on the NSC agenda as events demand. Likewise, senior substantive experts from the IC participate and support multiple interagency meetings at any given time.

THE EXPANDING NATIONAL SECURITY ENTERPRISE

The set of institutional players within the NSE has vastly grown since the 1947 National Security Act. That original system was largely focused on the president, his secretaries of state and defense, and his military and intelligence advisers. But now "national security" issues are spread virtually across every department. When the NSC meets to discuss critical international issues, it will often have to include not only foreign and security policy agencies but also economic and law enforcement agencies. To capture this complex web of agencies and processes, the term *national security enterprise* has often been used. Embedded in the word *enterprise* is the realization that a set of agencies and institutions must work together in a "whole-of-government" fashion to achieve a common vision or purpose. In a sense, the NSE suggests a whole that is greater than the sum of its parts as it strives to create better synergies among the various departments' and agencies' activities and capabilities.[10]

State Department

As the oldest federal department with the longest tradition of conducting foreign relations for the United States, this department carries the largest share of the diplomatic mission. The State Department maintains over 190 diplomatic missions overseas and employs slightly more than eight thousand Foreign Service officers (diplomats) and eleven thousand civil servants. In FY 2017, it had a budget of $50.1 billion, far less than the DOD budget of nearly $600 billion and smaller even than the IC's budget.[11] As the US global role has grown, so too has the size of US embassy operations. Today a US embassy has become a platform for the programs of many other departments of government, to the point that often the State Department's complement of Foreign Service officers amounts to far less than half of the American officials present in their diplomatic mission.

By tradition and statute, America's ambassadors are the personal representatives of the president, making them the senior-most US official in any foreign capital. Accordingly, senior officials from other agencies, such as the DOD and the IC, must report to the ambassador and serve there at the ambassador's pleasure. The CIA station chief is also seen as the senior IC representative who has responsibility to interact with the host government's intelligence services and keep the ambassador informed of the IC activities in that country.[12]

When the National Security Act of 1947 was promulgated, the State Department was by far the most influential agency in shaping US foreign policy. Secretaries of state were typically seen as the president's senior-most foreign policy adviser. Early on, a much less complex interagency process was often driven by the State Department because the secretary was often in charge of major policy reviews or diplomatic initiatives. The appropriate assistant secretary of state—for East Asia, for example, if the review or initiative was on China or for international security affairs if it was on security assistance or arms control—would chair an interagency policy review meeting. However, over time, as the stature of the national security adviser grew and as the NSC staff expanded to oversee more of the nation's security policies, the influence of the secretary of state and his subordinates has generally declined.

There have been obvious exceptions, such as James Baker, who was a close personal friend and confidant of George H. W. Bush. However, in today's NSE, the secretary of state must compete with powerful defense secretaries who control far more resources and people and with a national security adviser who spends far more time with the president and has an able and energetic NSC staff monitoring, as well as often initiating, policy decisions. In the interagency process, it is often observed that that the State Department has an organizational culture that encourages cautious and incremental moves. First, it has trouble developing new policy initiatives because it is made up of a large number of competing regional and functional bureaus. Headed by strong-minded assistant secretaries, bureaus often propose competing ideas or initiatives, leading to internal compromises. Second, Foreign Service officers seek continuity in American relations with key foreign partners, so they are often wary of White House initiatives that might be seen as rocking the boat. The State Department is, thus, eager to minimize American policy shifts and soften harsh presidential rhetoric toward partners and even adversaries.

Department of Defense

Created by the promulgation of the 1947 National Security Act and subsequent legislation in 1949, the DOD has become what some call the "eight-hundred-pound gorilla" in the interagency process. By virtue of commanding so many resources—roughly 1.1 million men and women under arms, with a budget of over $600 billion annually—the secretary of defense has enormous power to exert. The secretary also now has a considerable professional staff in the Office of the Secretary of Defense (OSD), and his undersecretary for policy has become a key player in the interagency process. This undersecretary and his subordinate assistant secretary for international security affairs are active participants in the NSE. If they are team players, then much can be accomplished. However, if they choose to oppose actions by the NSC or the State Department, the DOD can be a major hurdle to effective policy formation or implementation.[13]

This clout is not simply due to the personality of the secretary of defense or his closeness to the president, although that can be a factor. Rather, the resources that the DOD commands—to support military, peacekeeping, or humanitarian relief operations or to provide military hardware, training, or technical advice to foreign governments—gives the department huge advantages over the relatively tiny NSC staff or the resource-poor State Department. By virtue of its military mission, the DOD's organizational culture is dominated by long-term planning (e.g., in developing and fielding weapons, positioning forces around the world, and designing elaborate war plans) that is not found in any other national security department. The DOD resists the ad hoc approaches sometimes proposed by the State Department if they do not fit into a more cohesive, long-term strategy.

The DOD is also unique in that it is both a producer and user of the largest portion of US intelligence. Given its mandate to fight and win the nation's wars, it needs vast amounts of highly sensitive intelligence information on foreign military adversaries. Since its creation, the department has established a number of designated **combat-support agencies**, which make up the bulk of the US intelligence community. Although they are discussed in more detail in the next chapter, it is worth mentioning that these combat-support agencies—including the DIA, the NSA, the NRO, and the National Geospatial-Intelligence Agency (NGA)—account for roughly 70 percent of the budgets of the **National Intelligence Program (NIP)**. Hence, the secretary of defense controls most of the US intelligence program, and it is important that the DNI be able to work closely with him and his undersecretary of defense for intelligence (USDI).[14] As will be discussed later, cooperation among the sixteen national intelligence agencies is not always easy, especially when the DOD controls so much of the IC's budget, technology, and personnel.

The Pentagon also is unique in that it will have two representatives on the NSC and its subcommittees. That is because the CJCS is the senior military adviser to the president and the NSC. As such, he represents the chiefs of the individual military services (army, navy, air force, and Marine Corps). While it is desirable to have the secretary of defense and the chairman take the same position on a military policy issue, the chairman has the responsibility to give his best military advice, even if he disagrees with the defense secretary.

In the 1986 Goldwater-Nichols Act, the CJCS was given more independence and an enhanced policy role. Moreover, his Joint Staff has grown to more than fifteen hundred military officers from all the services, which are among the best and brightest in the Pentagon. Arranged into sections ranging from intelligence (J-2) to operations (J-3) to strategy, plans, and policy (J-5), these professional military officers will attend key NSC meetings relevant to their responsibilities. Often the director of J-5 will represent the chairman at the IPC level and be the plus one at PC and DC meetings. The director of J-2 works closely with the director of the DIA in order to maximize the combined resources of the Joint Staff's intelligence section as well as the entire DIA in support of the intelligence requirements of the secretary of defense, the chairman, the overseas military commands, and the vast array of military intelligence consumers.

NEWER NATIONAL SECURITY AGENCIES

The customary membership of the NSE includes the NSC, the State Department, the Defense Department, the Joint Staff, and the IC. However, the definition of "national security" and the NSE itself has now broadened to include a much larger array of agencies and departments that have responsibilities for protecting the nation from foreign and domestic threats. National security now not only includes traditional military and economic threats but also covers more unconventional but increasingly dangerous ones from terrorism, proliferation, cyber operations, and even climate change.

Accordingly, this expanded notion of national security has drawn agencies normally seen as more domestically oriented into discussion of international security. Leading the list of those agencies and departments are the Federal Bureau of Investigation (FBI) and DHS for domestic law enforcement and counterterrorism purposes, but also included are the Treasury Department and the Commerce Department for dealing with illicit financial and commercial crimes that touch on the sale of prohibited weapons-related technologies as well as funding of terrorist organizations. Moreover, US actions to impose economic, trade, and financial sanctions make economic departments central national security players in using hard economic power to deter potential proliferators and their state sponsors or to disrupt financial operations that would support terrorist plots.

Federal Bureau of Investigation

Historically, the FBI—commonly referred to as "the bureau"—has been involved in national security cases primarily through its responsibilities for countering foreign espionage and organized criminal activities conducted in the United States. However, since the 9/11 attacks, the bureau has assumed major new responsibilities for uncovering, preventing, and prosecuting international terrorist plots aimed at the American homeland. The FBI has developed an elaborate set of offices both domestically and overseas to coordinate the federal, state, and municipal law enforcement assets to assess, identify, and prevent possible terrorist plots. Currently the FBI has fifty-six field offices around the country, which consider one of their major missions the investigation of terrorist plots and prosecution of terrorists. In this regard, it also operates over one hundred joint terrorism task forces (JTTFs) in major cities, which are made up of over four thousand representatives from fifty federal agencies as well as hundreds of state and municipal law enforcement organizations.

As many such plots originate overseas, the FBI also maintains over sixty legal attaché (LEGAT) offices in major US embassies in major foreign capitals. The LEGAT works closely with other counterterrorism officials—including the CIA's chief of station and the defense attaché—in order to share information as well as coordinate their interactions with the local host security services. Since 9/11, the FBI has also reorganized its headquarters operations to make counterterrorism and counterproliferation high priorities. Its national security branch now encompasses units covering terrorism and WMDs as well as counterintelligence. To support these priority missions, the FBI also has developed its own major intelligence analysis operation, employing over three thousand analysts.[15]

Department of Homeland Security

The Department of Homeland Security is the newest member of the NSE. Created by the 2004 intelligence and counterterrorism reform efforts, it was given the important mission of preventing terrorist attacks at home. However, much of that responsibility was also shared with the CIA and FBI. As a result, DHS has largely become the agency responsible for managing the domestic preventive measures at borders, airports, and ports as well as for assessing vulnerabilities of critical infrastructure to terrorism and cyber threats. An important additional responsibility of DHS is to develop information-sharing relationships with state and municipal law enforcement agencies who are the "first responders" to many domestic terrorist operations.

DHS is one of the largest federal departments, having an annual budget of nearly $70 billion (FY 2018) and employing more than 240,000 people.[16] Its size reflects the fact that it combines the previous missions and operations of twenty-two separate agencies, including the Secret Service, the Coast Guard, the Federal Emergency Management Agency (FEMA), and Immigration and Customs Enforcement—just to name some of the largest. DHS's major challenge has been to balance its important counterterrorism responsibilities against its other public safety missions, which range from protecting US presidents and other VIPs to responding to natural disasters to rescuing American sailors at sea or interdicting maritime narcotics transfers to apprehending undocumented foreign nationals and smugglers attempting to enter the United States illegally. With such a broad set of responsibilities, it has not yet been able to develop the same level of expertise, competence, and organizational cohesion that the more established agencies such as the CIA and FBI have built up over many decades.[17]

Economic Agencies

While America's diplomatic and military instruments of power are concentrated in the Department of State and the Department of Defense, its economic instruments are spread across a number of departments and special offices. This reflects the fact that the American economy has a range of sectors—financial, commercial, agricultural, and technological, to name only the most obvious—over which the federal government has only partial control. Depending on the actions a president might desire, one or another department will be the key executor of policy. So, if the president wishes to begin trade negotiations, he will instruct the US special trade representative (USTR) to lead those talks. However, if he wants to impose financial or commercial sanctions, he will have to instruct the secretary of treasury and/or commerce to work with Congress to legislate new restrictions on international financial or commercial transactions vis-à-vis specific countries or individuals. Other economic tools include foreign sales of weapons, food, and technology, which again can involve a number of different agencies as well as the State Department and Defense Department, which together are responsible for much of the foreign economic and military assistance programs.[18]

Without going into detail about each economic office or agency, it is useful to examine the expanding role of the Department of the Treasury. Since 9/11, it has become an increasingly active participant in national security policymaking regarding counterterrorism and other illicit international activities. As a former deputy secretary noted, there is now a strong argument for including the Treasury Department as a statutory member of the NSC because its financial tools for punishing state sponsors of proliferation and terrorism and for squeezing off the financial support for such operations have become so powerful.[19] Its Office for Foreign Assets Control (OFAC) has the authority to name and shame individuals who are breaking US laws, making major international banks and other financial institutions wary of doing business with them. Likewise, Treasury's Office of Intelligence and Analysis (OIA) and Office for Terrorism and Financial Intelligence (OTFI) have become powerful tools for monitoring rogue foreign governments, criminals, and terrorists. Its ability to design effective sanctions has worked tremendously in bringing pressure on Iran to negotiate a nuclear arrangement with the United States and the other permanent members of the UN Security Council.[20]

Other Players in the NSE

The interagency process, of course, only describes how the president and the executive branch shape national security policies. These are by no means simply implemented without further deliberations. In fact, the decision-making process is complicated by congressional involvement via the budget process, hearings and investigations, and other legislative authorities. No president can ignore Congress when proposing new funding for national security programs, announcing new strategies for dealing with international problems, or negotiating new international agreements. Congress can complicate a president's policies by refusing to fund them, by interrogating his advisers in public hearings, by publishing critical investigative reports, and by failing to give its consent to a president's appointments or negotiated treaties. Numerous examples can be cited from virtually every administration. Congressional disapproval of President Obama's negotiation of an Iranian nuclear deal and two separate investigations into the Russian meddling in the 2016 presidential election of President Trump illustrate how active Congress can become in foreign policy. As the Russian "hacking" scandal illustrates, congressional investigations conducted by both the House and Senate intelligence committees can play a major role in surfacing intelligence issues and in shaping intelligence policies (as discussed in more detail in later chapters).

At the same time, one must not dismiss the power of the media to throw a spotlight on a president's conduct of foreign policy. Often a president and his advisers want to highlight a policy initiative by giving influential journalists or media outlets an "exclusive" as news breaks, or an administration will announce its latest decisions as part of a broader public diplomacy and communication strategy. There might be an entire "roll-out" plan for announcing presidential actions and subsequent stories provided by the State Department and Defense Department on what progress the administration is making. Within the Obama NSC, for example, there was a deputy national security adviser for "strategic communications and speechwriting," who had a very influential role with the president as well as the media. This more formal or systematic media plan has now been altered by President Trump's preference to make policy by Twitter messages. In at least one case, DNI Dan Coats had to acknowledge that he first learned about a presidential summit after the president tweeted about it and the media reported it.

In addition, there are frequently unauthorized leaks from inside the executive or legislative branches that can lead to major controversies surrounding presidential initiatives or actions. When there is an internal executive branch struggle over a policy, or when there is a disagreement between the White House and Congress over a major policy, participants in the dispute are tempted to leak information favorable to their positions. The first indications that the George W. Bush administration had set up secret "black sites" for enhanced interrogations reportedly came from a former NSC official who disagreed with those actions.[21] Leaks have been a nemesis to every president, and few leakers are ever prosecuted successfully. Yet there are also times when a White House may itself produce leaks to mislead or confuse congressional opponents or keep the media off the scent of another story. The leak weapon is one that is available to a variety of executive and legislative branch officials for lots of different reasons.

What is most significant about the media's role for understanding the role of intelligence, however, is its skill in bringing information to light that otherwise would have remained secret. The media is very much in the forefront of revealing controversial intelligence programs that become topics of debate in Congress and the executive branch. For instance, stories in the *Washington Post* and *New York Times* revealed the CIA's **rendition** programs that placed Afghan detainees in secret prisons outside the United States, where enhanced interrogation methods (considered torture by many) were conducted. Later the then chairman of the Senate Select Committee on Intelligence, Sen. Dianne Feinstein, released a sanitized summary (more than six hundred pages long) of an extensive staff report on torture; she did this prior to losing her chairmanship, after which it was likely that the new Republican chairman would block its release. In many cases, leaked intelligence judgments or findings can become part of the public policy debate because they have appeared in the *New York Times* or the *Washington Post*. In a few cases, such as the recent Russian hacking into the computers of the Democratic National Committee and efforts to penetrate American electoral systems, the IC might even produce a declassified assessment to publicize the seriousness of the issue and gain public and congressional support for more forceful presidential actions.[22]

KEY ISSUES FOR THE NSE

Every president must make some major decisions on how to organize the national security decision-making process. Sometimes presidents have wished to radically alter the system used by their predecessors, while at other times they retained much of the system they inherited. But inevitably there are issues that have to be addressed or that will confront presidents in one way or another. Among the most enduring are the role presidents see for their national security adviser, the extent to which they wish to see national security decisions made in the White House, and the degree to which they are comfortable relying on formal structures and the career bureaucrats.

Role of the National Security Adviser: Advocate versus Honest Broker

Looking back on the many national security advisers who have held that title, there have been a variety of roles played, sometimes well and sometimes poorly. As many experts have noted, presidents have to feel comfortable with their national security adviser, who will spend more time with them than their secretaries of state or defense. The national security adviser has traditionally maintained a small office close to the Oval Office, allowing the adviser to brief the president on fast-moving events, participate in morning briefings and international phone calls to heads of state, and generally control the flow of foreign affairs information reaching the president. Nonetheless, presidents have to decide if they want to be more personally engaged in foreign policy or devolve that to their national security adviser and cabinet officers. Some scholars have described Bill Clinton as "indecisive" because he held lengthy NSC meetings without decisions emerging, while George W. Bush relished being "the decider" and wanted "actionable" intelligence so he could make swift decisions. Barack Obama, as a constitutional lawyer, was more deliberative, and some criticized him as "procrastinating" in how long he took to make important policy decisions.[23] How a president answers those questions will dictate the type of national security adviser with whom he is likely to feel most comfortable.

A useful way of thinking about the national security adviser's role is to outline what the position entails. First, the national security adviser must advise the president, meaning provide him or her with information in the form of staff memoranda or briefings on specific topics. Second, the adviser is responsible for running what has become a large NSC staff of several hundred foreign policy experts. Third, but not unimportant, the adviser must manage the interagency process by setting the agendas for NSC, PC, DC, and IPC meetings. Embedded in these duties is also the responsibility to present to the president the views of other cabinet officers and their agencies so that the president has the widest possible set of perspectives and options.

Different national security advisers have prioritized those duties differently. In the early days, those serving as quasi–national security advisers were primarily interested in administering and scheduling the meetings of NSC principals with the president and distributing policy papers for review. These were essentially "administrators" of the national security process.[24] Later, national security advisers became more personal "counselors" to the president in terms of giving the president advice and information privately to assist presidential decision-making. Other advisers have defined their role as more the "honest broker" who would ensure that the interagency process fairly aired all agencies' views and options, which should be shared with the president. And finally, there have been strong-minded national security advisers who have exercised their own closeness to the president and strongly advocated their own positions as opposed to simply presenting the views of the secretaries of state and defense.

Most scholars have concluded that the honest-broker role is the proper one, most likely to succeed in generating the best decisions. President George H. W. Bush's national security adviser, Brent Scowcroft, is often held up as the classic honest broker who was able to maintain an even playing field for all cabinet officers and agencies to get their views on the table and before the president, without any fear that he would bias the president. Partly, this model works when there is a good teamwork spirit among the NSC principals. President Bush is reputed to have insisted on this early in his administration.

Other models have also been prevalent with other presidents. Henry Kissinger, under President Nixon, and Zbigniew Brzezinski, under President Jimmy Carter, are often described as advocates who held strong views and worked to have theirs accepted by the president. President George W. Bush's national security adviser, Condoleezza Rice, often described her first responsibility as being a counselor to the president rather than a manager of the interagency process; many have criticized her weak control over a strong-minded defense secretary, Donald Rumsfeld, and Vice President Dick Cheney for a dysfunctional NSC process. During the Obama era, the NSC principals were sometimes described as a "team of rivals" as there were strong personalities in the cabinet, such as Hillary Clinton as secretary of state and Robert Gates as secretary of defense.

National security advisers also serve as key customers of intelligence and often are the gatekeepers for intelligence reaching the president. As the adviser who shapes the president's daily agenda of foreign policy discussions, the national security adviser can walk intelligence reporting into the Oval Office if it is deemed critically important or can simply dismiss it. Photos of Soviet missiles in Cuba were first shown to McGeorge Bundy, who then escorted the briefers into the Oval Office to brief President Kennedy. Both Henry Kissinger and Zbigniew Brzezinski had the *PDB* delivered directly to them, choosing which items to then discuss with their presidents that morning. Other national security advisers have organized separate *PDB* sessions for themselves prior to the president's in order to be better prepared to address the policy implications of the intelligence issues contained in the *PDB*. In today's environment, it would appear that President Trump's national security adviser, John Bolton, is the most likely reader of daily intelligence because the president himself appears not to value intelligence highly and has repeatedly shown indifference if not disdain for its contributions. (To be examined further in later chapters.)

Centralize Foreign Policy or Not?

Part of the presidential decision on the type of national security adviser rests on how much the occupant of the Oval Office wishes to be involved in foreign affairs. Some presidents come with considerable foreign affairs experience or none at all. For example, George H. W. Bush had been CIA director, ambassador to the UN, envoy to China, and vice president. In contrast, George W. Bush and Bill Clinton were former governors, with far less exposure to foreign affairs. If presidents wish to be involved, then there is a natural tendency to pick strong national security advisers who will try to control national security decisions from the White House. Such national security advisers will build a strong NSC staff, take charge of meetings, and insist on the NSC adviser being as much of a policymaker as any cabinet officer. That model prevailed under President Nixon, where Kissinger was virtually single-handedly in charge of American foreign policy.

Other presidents have preferred to have less to do with foreign affairs and have devolved onto the secretaries of state and defense much of the responsibility for formulating and implementing presidential decisions. President Ronald Reagan began his eight years in office with such a view, selecting a national security adviser who had little responsibility other than scheduling meetings, while relying on strong secretaries of state, retired general Al Haig and later George Shultz, for big foreign policy ideas. This departmentally driven foreign policy might have worked, except that a weak national security adviser was unable to moderate the bitter rivalry between Shultz and Defense Secretary Caspar Weinberger. Reagan's model of weak presidential interest in the NSC also permitted the Iran-Contra scandal to occur and threaten his presidency.

A more recent model of less centralized foreign policy occurred during George W. Bush's tenure, when he empowered Defense Secretary Rumsfeld to run the war in Iraq, leaving the NSC and State Department relatively uninvolved or at least uninfluential in shaping the president's policies in his first term. Finally, the Obama presidency tried to learn from the mistakes of the Bush years and again centralized foreign policy in the hands of the NSC staff in the White House. This was perhaps an overcorrection. Several cabinet officials would later criticize President Obama for allowing relatively inexperienced NSC staffers to shape policy and allow political considerations to creep into national security discussions.[25]

Structured or Informal?

The preceding discussion described a range of approaches presidents have taken in selecting and organizing their national security teams. Often, however, the description of the formal process cannot capture the complexity and variety of decision-making styles that presidents adopt. Truman shunned the NSC meetings and relied heavily on his secretaries of states. Eisenhower participated in a huge number of NSC meetings over which he presided, to the point his advisers thought they might exhaust him. Kennedy preferred informal gatherings and violated bureaucratic hierarchy regularly—often calling junior desk officers himself. Nixon liked to make his decisions on long walks or privately with his equally secretive national security adviser. So, presidents are prone to make decisions outside the normal processes.

This informality is partly driven by a president's confidence in a few close advisers and a wish to keep big decisions within those circles of trust. Sometimes over regularly scheduled lunch meetings, NSC principals will compare notes or reach consensus on issues prior to formal meetings with the president.[26] Presidents also use informal mechanisms to surface more radical ideas that the bureaucratic process might not support. Nixon and Kissinger famously concocted the opening to China in 1972 outside of any NSC process, expecting agencies to oppose it or leak to the press. George H. W. Bush also used an NSC "ungroup" to meet regarding sensitive US-Soviet issues that were considered as the USSR was collapsing; the topics were seen as so sensitive that no meetings were ever listed on the formal calendars of those included. More recently, President Obama, after hearing all the arguments by his NSC advisers for taking a forceful line against Syrian use of chemical weapons, changed his mind after a walk in the Rose Garden with his chief of staff.

INTELLIGENCE AND THE NSC

As described above, the NSC system is a complex set of policy discussion and options-generating processes that ultimately allow the president to make national security decisions. Intelligence contributes in a number of ways to this process. First, it informs the president and by extension his national security team with both current and **estimative intelligence**. The daily intelligence publications, including the *PDB*, contain valuable information and analysis that is purposely aimed at addressing issues that are of presidential interest (see box 3.2). One former CIA director recalls the "rain of requests" for information from the national security adviser following such briefings.[27] Other publications are also designed to inform the president's national security staff as well as the staffs supporting other NSC members across the government.

Second, intelligence provides direct input to the interagency discussions—at the PC, DC, and IPC levels—in the form of oral briefings by IC representatives as well as written assessments requested as part of the policy reviews. Longer-term assessments in the form of NIEs often are tasked to support significant NSC deliberations. Intelligence support to the almost continuous set of PC, DC, and IPC meetings has become a major part of the DNI's and the CIA's responsibilities. Both CIA offices and the ODNI's national intelligence council spend much of their time preparing memos and briefings for their respective directors who attend the PC meetings.

Third, the IC often has to put forth options for covert action, which is an additional policy tool at the disposal of the president and his closest advisers. The CIA director (as will be discussed in chapter 9) is responsible for developing covert means to support broader national security policies where the US role must be hidden. In this way,

---

Box 3.2   Typical *PDB* for George H. W. Bush

George H. W. Bush:
"One important fixture was the 8:00 am national security meeting in the Oval Office, at which the CIA briefed me on the latest developments around the world. It had two parts. The first portion was the intelligence briefing, at which I was joined by Brent [NSC adviser Scowcroft], Bob Gates [deputy NSC adviser], usually John Sununu [chief of staff], and, once or twice a week, Bill Webster [CIA director]. A CIA officer would bring in the President's Daily Brief (PDB), which was a written rundown of important intelligence reports and analysis put together during the night and small hours of the morning. I made it a point from day one to read the PDB in the presence of a CIA briefer and either Brent or his deputy. This way I could task the briefers to bring in more information on a certain matter or, when the reading would bring to mind policy matters, ask Brent to follow up on an item of interest. The CIA officers would write down my questions; in a day or so, I would get an answer or an elaboration.

Knowing of my interest in the oft-berated but essential clandestine service, Webster would occasionally ask to bring along some individual who had risked his or her life to gather critically important intelligence. I found those sessions fascinating, and I was always impressed with the courage, the patriotism, and the professionalism of those who served in the Directorate of Operations."

Brent Scowcroft:
"After the CIA briefing, the second part of the national security meeting would begin. The Vice President, already briefed separately by a different CIA team, would arrive and I would go over pertinent events of the day, items where the President's guidance was needed, and anything else requiring discussion."

Source: George H. W. Bush and Brent Scowcroft, *A World Transformed* (New York: Knopf, 1998), 30.

---

the IC is put in more of a policymaking role than an intelligence-support one. This has become especially important in the fight against terrorism and efforts to disrupt the dangerous spread of WMD technologies.

Finally, the IC is often called on to evaluate the feasibility of the policy options under consideration or assess their actual impact. In this role, it is often seen as an unhelpful player if intelligence does not favor a policy agency's preferred option or judges a presidential initiative to have failed to achieve its objectives (discussed further in chapter 10). As mentioned above, intelligence assessments can become ammunition in the internal administration debates or in executive-legislative disputes over appropriate foreign policies. As the IC is responsible for providing intelligence to both branches of government, it can become especially tricky to provide objective yet significant intelligence evaluations to a White House when those same findings might become available to critics on Capitol Hill.

THE FUTURE OF THE NATIONAL SECURITY ENTERPRISE

This brief description of the national security decision-making process and the role that intelligence plays cannot capture the full complexity of the huge NSE. One thing is very clear. What began as a fairly simple structure has grown over seventy years into an unwieldy and often unresponsive tangle of agencies, organizational cultures, and competing authorities. Government practitioners as well as scholars have lamented this development but have seemed unable to convince presidents and Congress to make the needed improvements. Former secretary of defense Donald Rumsfeld bemoaned the reality of "incredible amounts of time that just kind of suck the life out of you at the end of the day spending 4, 5, 6 hours in interagency meetings and the reason is, because the organization of the government fit the last century instead of this century."[28] The bureaucracies within the NSE have also been reluctant to modify the well-trodden paths and processes with which they have become comfortable. At the heart of the problem are the distinct organizational cultures resident in the different national security agencies. Efforts to produce "jointness"—coordination of military, diplomatic, law enforcement, and intelligence activities—remain elusive. Congress adds to the problem by its refusal to reform its own committee structure, which tends to separate rather than integrate the military, diplomatic, economic, law enforcement, and intelligence tools. Congressional leaders' personal status and clout over their committees' jurisdiction have often inclined them to resist organizational reforms that might somehow reduce their own importance.[29] The NSE today continues to suffer from a lack of sufficient coordination and development of capabilities that are needed for the twenty-first century.

Major reforms to the national security decision-making process usually result only from a major crisis that can generate a temporary consensus on next steps. The 1947 National Security Act bubbled up from the many lessons learned in World War II, particularly those regarding the need for better coordination of America's military, diplomatic, and intelligence activities. The post-9/11 reforms that created the ODNI and DHS were also driven by a major shock to the nation. Most likely, the next set of reforms will be similarly driven by a surprise or shock, perhaps one associated with the new cyber domain or growing environmental threats posed by climate change. Whatever those changes to the NSE amount to, intelligence is likely to be one of the major areas where change will be needed.

USEFUL WEBSITES

Center for a New American Security, https://www.cnas.org/
   A forum for former civilian and military officials, the center advocates for strong and pragmatic national security policies.

Council on Foreign Relations, https://www.cfr.org
    The oldest American think tank, the council publishes the leading international affairs jour-
    nal, *Foreign Affairs*, where additional materials for educators and students are also available
    online.
Federation for American Scientists, https://www.fas.org
    An association of American scientists concerned about the control of nuclear weapons that main-
    tains a website that hosts a variety of documents related to national security and intelligence.
Project on National Security Reform, https://www.thepresidency.org/programs/project-on
-national-security-reform
    A nonpartisan, nonprofit organization mandated by Congress in 2009 to recommend major
    improvements in the US national security system.

FURTHER READING

Cody M. Brown, *The National Security Council: A Legal History of the President's Most Power-
    ful Advisers* (Washington, DC: Center for the Study of the Presidency, 2008).
        A concise legislative history of the evolution of the NSC across numerous presidencies.
Ivo Daadler and I. M. Destler, *In the Shadow of the Oval Office: Profiles of the National Security
    Advisers and the Presidents They Served—from JFK to George W. Bush* (New York: Simon &
    Schuster, 2009).
        An excellent study of the personalities who held the position of national security adviser
        and how they dealt with their presidents.
Roger Z. George and Harvey Rishikof, *The National Security Enterprise: Navigating the Laby-
    rinth*, 2nd ed. (Washington, DC: Georgetown University Press, 2017).
        A compendium of practitioners' assessments of the principal national security agencies,
        Congress, the courts, think tanks, and the media.
Peter W. Rodman, *Presidential Command: Power, Leadership, and the Making of American For-
    eign Policy from Richard Nixon to George W. Bush* (New York: Knopf, 2009).
        A leading political scientist's assessment of presidential style in directing US foreign
        policy.
David Rothkopf, *Running the World: Inside the National Security Council and the Architects of
    American Power* (New York: PublicAffairs, 2005).
        A recognized think tank expert's analysis of the NSC's evolution and his critique of US
        foreign policy.
Charles A. Stevenson, *America's Foreign Policy Toolkit: Key Institutions and Processes* (Los
    Angeles: SAGE, 2013).
        A concise description of the major tools and agencies that direct US military, diplomatic,
        economic, and intelligence missions.

NOTES

Second epigraph: Quote from McGeorge Bundy, "Letter to Jackson Subcommittee," in *Fateful
Decisions: Inside the National Security Council*, ed. Karl E. Inderfurth and Loch K. Johnson
(New York: Oxford University Press, 2004), 44.

1. For a good discussion of the expansion of the NSC, see David Rothkopf, *National Insecurity: American Leadership in an Age of Fear* (New York: PublicAffairs, 2014), 206–8.

2. Typically the secretary of energy is also considered a statutory member, as the Department of Energy oversees the operation of the national laboratories that research, develop, and build America's nuclear weapons.

3. Typical attendees include the assistant to the president for national economic policy, who directs the NEC, and the secretaries of commerce, treasury, agriculture, energy, and transportation.

4. Spenser Hsu, "Obama Combines Security Councils," *Washington Post*, May 27, 2009, http://www.washingtonpost.com/wp-dyn/content/article/2009/05/26/AR2009052603148.html.

5. See Cody M. Brown, *The National Security Council: A Legal History of the President's Most Important Advisers* (Washington, DC: Center for the Study of the Presidency, 2008), 3.

6. "Principals" refers to secretary-level or equivalent positions of the departments and agencies attending NSC meetings. A principal often is allowed to bring a "backbencher" to expanded meetings, who is termed "plus one."

7. Truman attended very few NSC meetings prior to the Korean War, and the council's reviews and policy papers had far less impact than its workload would have suggested. See Stanley Falk, "The NSC under Truman and Eisenhower," in *Fateful Decisions: Inside the National Security Council*, ed. Karl Inderfurth and Loch Johnson (London: Oxford University Press, 2004), 38.

8. See Ivo Daalder and I. M. Destler, *In the Shadow of the Oval Office: Profiles of the National Security Advisers and the Presidents They Served—from JFK to George W. Bush* (New York: Simon & Schuster, 2009), for a comprehensive review of the changes that early presidents made to the NSC system.

9. Operations centers are continuously manned to receive and send messages or conduct secure telephone- and/or video-conferencing among key agencies and foreign military and diplomatic posts. The operations staffs at the White House Situation Room and at other departments are responsible for alerting the president and key advisers to any rapidly emerging crisis or event requiring presidential or departmental attention.

10. In a similar fashion, the Department of Homeland Security has highlighted its "Homeland Security Enterprise," which strives to knit together the twenty-two DHS agencies and their disparate missions into a single integrated approach to homeland security. Also, the ODNI often discussed the "National Intelligence Enterprise" that aims to integrate the activities of the sixteen national intelligence organizations under a set of common missions.

11. For fuller treatment of the Department of State's role, mission, and culture, see Marc Grossman, "The State Department: Culture as Interagency Destiny," in *The National Security Enterprise: Navigating the Labyrinth*, 2nd ed., ed. Roger Z. George and Harvey Rishikof (Washington, DC: Georgetown University Press, 2017), 81–96.

12. "Chief of station" refers to the senior CIA official in a country who directs the intelligence activities there. He or she is responsible for managing relationships with that country's security services and in this way has unique access to a foreign government's thinking and operations.

13. For discussion of how the secretaries of defense have treated the interagency process, see Joseph McMillan and Frank C. Miller, "The Office of the Secretary of Defense," in George and Rishikof, *National Security Enterprise*, 120–41.

14. The USDI is the senior-most intelligence official who reports to the secretary of defense. In turn, the directors of the NSA, DIA, NRO, and NGA report to this official.

15. For a fuller discussion of the FBI's evolving national security role, see Harvey Rishikof and Brittany Albaugh, "The Evolving FBI: Becoming a New National Security Enterprise Asset," in George and Rishikof, *National Security Enterprise*, 223–45.

16. This budget figure includes more than $7 billion in disaster-relief funds used by FEMA.

17. For an analysis of DHS's organizational challenges and missions, see Susan Ginsburg, "The Department of Homeland Security: Civil Protection and Resilience," in George and Rishikof, *National Security Enterprise*, 247–78.

18. An excellent overview of the many economic instruments and agencies can be found in Charles A. Stevenson, *America's Foreign Policy Toolkit: Key Institutions and Processes* (Los Angeles: SAGE, 2013), 170–299.

19. Robert Kimmitt, "Give Treasury Its Proper Role on the National Security Council," *New York Times*, July 23, 2012, http://www.nytimes.com/2012/07/24/opinion/give-treasury-its-proper-role-on-the-national-security-council.html?mcubz=1.

20. See Dina Temple-Raston and Harvey Rishikof, "The Department of Treasury: Brogues on the Ground," in George and Rishikof, *National Security Enterprise*, 162–82.

21. Dafna Linzer, "CIA Officer Fired for Leaking Classified Data," *Washington Post*, April 25, 2006, http://www.washingtonpost.com/wp-dyn/content/discussion/2006/04/24/DI2006042401026.html.

22. Adam Entous, "Secret CIA Assessment Says Russia Was Trying to Help Trump Win the White House," *Washington Post*, December 9, 2016, https://www.washingtonpost.com/world/national-security/obama-orders-review-of-russian-hacking-during-presidential-campaign/2016/12/09/31d6b300-be2a-11e6-94ac-3d324840106c_story.html?utm_term=.6bcd00fcdcfe.

23. Illustrative of Obama's deliberative style, he took more than sixty days to review his Afghan strategy before announcing a major increase in troops sent there in 2008.

24. See Alexander L. George, "The Case for Multiple Advocacy in Making Foreign Policy," *American Political Science Review* 66, no. 3 (September 1972): 751–85.

25. Former CIA director Leon Panetta and Defense Secretary Robert Gates both criticized President Obama for allowing relatively junior NSC staff to drive policy and marginalize more senior cabinet officials. See "Hagel's Predecessors Decry White House Micromanaging," NBC News, November 24, 2014, https://www.nbcnews.com/politics/first-read/hagels-predecessors-decried-white-house-micromanaging-n255231; and Robert M. Gates, *Duty: Memoir of a Secretary at War* (New York: Alfred A. Knopf, 2014), 587.

26. Lyndon Johnson held his Tuesday lunches with his secretaries of state and defense, while during the Clinton administration, Defense Secretary William Perry, Secretary of State Warren Christopher, and National Security Adviser Anthony Lake would have their "PCL" ("pickle") meetings. Likewise, Secretary of State Madeleine Albright, National Security Adviser Sandy Berger, and Defense Secretary William Cohen ("ABC") would continue this habit. See David Auerswald, "The Evolution of the NSC Process," in George and Rishikof, *National Security Enterprise*, 36.

27. Recalled by former DCIA Frank Carlucci in Inderfurth and Johnson, *Fateful Decisions*, 175.

28. Quoted in Christopher J. Lamb and Joseph C. Bond, "National Security Reform and the 2016 Election," *Strategic Forum*, no. 293 (March 2016): 2.

29. For a more complete discussion of these challenges, see Harvey Rishikof and Roger Z. George, "Navigating the Labyrinth of the National Security Enterprise," in George and Rishikof, *National Security Enterprise*, 382–94.

4

WHAT IS THE INTELLIGENCE COMMUNITY?

Before Pearl Harbor the United States did not have an intelligence service comparable to that of Great Britain or France or Russia or Germany or Japan. We did not have one because the American people would not accept it. It was felt that there was something un-American about espionage and intelligence in general.
—Lt. Gen. Hoyt Vandenberg, second DCI, 1947

The National Intelligence Program straddles six cabinet departments, an independent agency [the CIA], and an independent staff [ODNI]. . . . It's a challenge to manage—a challenge but not an impossibility.
—DNI James Clapper, 2015

The US intelligence community exists to provide the best available information to the nation's senior civilian and military decision-makers. As the previous chapter makes clear, that set of customers or users continued to grow throughout the Cold War period and up to the present. The IC currently encompasses sixteen separate national intelligence agencies, which employ—conservatively measured—at least one hundred thousand people and spend more than $70 billion annually on the combined national and military intelligence programs (see box 4.1).[1] These funds are spread across the agencies somewhat unevenly. Specific details regarding individual agency budgets remain classified, and much of the National Intelligence Program remains "hidden" in the DOD appropriations (see later discussion regarding budgets).

This is a significant amount of money and is often a source of criticism when an intelligence failure occurs and policymakers ask whether they are getting their money's worth. This chapter will survey the changes and expansion of the IC to keep

---

Box 4.1   National Intelligence Program: Members and Missions

Office of Director of National Intelligence: integration, cooperation, and budgetary management

Department of Defense Intelligence Community Members
1. Defense Intelligence Agency: all-source analysis, defense HUMINT, MASINT
2. National Geospatial Intelligence Agency: geospatial intelligence
3. National Security Agency: SIGINT, information security
4. National Reconnaissance Office: IMINT and SIGINT satellite development and operation
5. Army Intelligence (G-2): land warfare intelligence
6. Office of Naval Intelligence (ONI): maritime intelligence
7. Marine Corps Intelligence (USMC/IN): tactical intelligence
8. Air Force Intelligence (USAF/IN): air and space intelligence

Non-DOD Intelligence Community Members
9. Central Intelligence Agency: all-source analysis, HUMINT collection, covert action, foreign counterintelligence
10. Department of State's Bureau of Intelligence and Research: all-source analysis
11. Department of Energy's Office of Intelligence and Counterintelligence: nuclear and energy intelligence
12. Department of Treasury's Office of Intelligence and Analysis: financial intelligence
13. Department of Homeland Security's Office of Intelligence and Analysis: homeland security intelligence
14. Department of Homeland Security's US Coast Guard Intelligence: maritime intelligence
15. Department of Justice's FBI National Security Branch: homeland security, counterterrorism, and domestic counterintelligence
16. Department of Justice's Drug Enforcement Agency's Office of National Security Intelligence: narcotics intelligence

---

pace with the expanding set of users and their diverse intelligence requirements. It will examine these agencies' basic functions and their involvement in both collecting and producing intelligence. It will also identify some continuing challenges that such a large and diverse set of agencies face in coordinating their operations for supporting the policy community.

BRIEF HISTORY OF GROWTH

In 1947, America's new national security system also brought into existence its first peacetime civilian intelligence community. Prior to the outbreak of World War II, having a permanent peacetime intelligence agency was deemed both unnecessary and essentially undemocratic. After World War I, civilian involvement in the modest US military intelligence effort was terminated. Much later, Secretary of State Henry Stimson said, "Gentlemen do not read each others' mail." In spite of this, the American military retained modest intelligence functions: the army's G-2 and the navy's Office of Naval Intelligence (ONI) focused on assessing foreign armies and navies in the event of future conflicts. And the relatively young FBI did maintain some foreign intelligence capabilities—including operations in Latin America—to monitor possible foreign espionage and criminal activities. But the notion of having a large-scale foreign intelligence function in peacetime was entirely new for the United States.

As Europe went to war in 1939, President Roosevelt began to see the need for information on Europe as he worried that the United States might be dragged into the fighting. He first instructed a close confidant, William J. "Wild Bill" Donovan, to make a fact-finding trip to Europe in order to assess whether Britain would be willing and able to resist the Third Reich's military onslaught. Donovan came back reporting that the British would resist. Also, he was impressed with Britain's intelligence services, which openly expressed a willingness to help Washington build up its own. Roosevelt thereafter assigned Donovan the role of "coordinator of information" (COI) to carry out "supplementary activities" for information not available to the US government.[2]

Following the Pearl Harbor attack in 1941, President Roosevelt soon established the **Office of Strategic Services (OSS)**, and he put Donovan in charge. However, this was to be largely a military-focused intelligence effort, with the OSS operating under the authority of the military chiefs. In addition to running agents behind enemy lines for conducting sabotage and collecting information on the Axis powers, the OSS also established the first research-and-analysis function (its R&A branch), which would later serve as a model for the CIA's own analytical directorate.

At the end of World War II, President Truman disbanded the OSS. Donovan argued, unsuccessfully, that the growing problems with the Soviet Union justified maintaining and expanding the OSS; however, he faced bureaucratic resistance from the military intelligence services, the State Department, and the FBI.[3] But as the Cold War deepened, the need for a peacetime intelligence community became overwhelming. Truman gradually agreed to a modest national intelligence effort, led by a newly named first director of central intelligence—Sidney Souers, who already had been a presidential adviser. In 1947, Truman signed the National Security Act, which gave the DCI a more formal role in advising the president and his NSC; in short order, this led to the creation of the CIA. Nonetheless, Truman continued to have serious reservations that it would create rivalries among the already existing intelligence agencies and might create an American "Gestapo."[4]

The CIA's Central Role

The CIA's origins emerged from the surprise attack on Pearl Harbor as well as the wartime OSS experience. In 1941, the early morning attack on the US Navy's Pacific

Fleet highlighted the inadequacy and disorganization of American intelligence. As discussed in later chapters, this failure to warn was the result of poor information gathering, failure to disseminate and share intelligence quickly, and a faulty mindset of what to expect from the Japanese military. Combined with the utility seen in having an organization such as the OSS supporting the war effort, Truman accepted the need for a single organization that could pull together all relevant information collected and held by different government agencies. As Roosevelt's initial 1942 mandate to Donovan made clear, there needed to be a way for a president to get all the information he or she needed to make national security decisions. Thus was born the idea of a "central" agency that reported to the president rather than the military services or the secretary of state.

Creating a CIA did not guarantee its successful operation. In the early years, there was considerable friction between the new CIA and the already existing military intelligence organizations and the FBI. The 1947 National Security Act was purposely vague on exactly what the scope and missions of this new organization would be. First, the act was primarily designed to unify the military services under a newly created DOD; accordingly, the drafters of the legislation did not want to complicate passage with controversial language regarding a new secret intelligence organization. Second, the White House also did not wish to lay out the details of this new organization, because it would reveal that the CIA would not only be correlating and disseminating existing information found in the government but also collecting it clandestinely as well as conducting "special activities" at the request of the president (later known as covert action).

Given the vague mandate found in the 1947 act, the CIA's success would depend on the efforts and energy of its first directors to define and expand its missions and capabilities. Prior to the 1947 creation of the CIA, its small predecessor operated as the Central Intelligence Group (CIG), which was led by DCI Souers. He viewed his appointment as temporary and thus was largely content to have the CIG correlate and evaluate intelligence on national security. It had limited people and resources, which were drawn from other agencies. Moreover, the CIG also faced competition from the military services as well as the State Department, which continued to believe it had the responsibility for providing the president with intelligence. With Lt. Gen. Hoyt Vandenberg's appointment as its new director in 1946, however, the organization grew from fewer than a hundred staff members to more than eighteen hundred, with emphasis on the collection of foreign intelligence in addition to evaluation.[5] With increased resources and a more ambitious leadership, the establishment of the CIA in 1947 promised to create an even more powerful institution. Very quickly the CIA was able to grab control over the FBI's Latin American human intelligence operations, as it became the premier civilian HUMINT collection agency.[6]

There also ensued an interagency debate and eventually decisions to distinguish what CIA produced in the way of reports—**"strategic analysis"** and "interdepartmental intelligence assessments"—from State Department reporting that was essentially **"departmental intelligence."** Most importantly, Vandenberg won the right to have his organization's reporting transcend departmental assessments and be the linchpin of the national security decision-making process.[7]

The CIA's reputation, resources, and clout grew quickly in the 1950s and 1960s as successive presidents came to rely on its responsiveness. The 9/11 Commission's report makes clear that the CIA remains unique among the sixteen intelligence agencies: "The sole element of the IC independent from a cabinet agency is the CIA. As an independent agency it collects, analyzes and disseminates intelligence from all sources. The CIA's number one customer is the president of the United States who also has the authority to direct covert operations."[8]

This quotation neatly captures three of the CIA's four major missions:

1. It is the principal HUMINT collector run by the **Directorate of Operations (DO)**.
2. Its **Directorate of Analysis (DA)** also is the largest producer of all-source intelligence.
3. The DO's Special Activities Division conducts covert action at the direction of the president.
4. The CIA also conducts foreign CI against foreign intelligence threats to the United States that are located overseas.

These functions make it a truly central player in the national security decision-making process. First, as the major collector of HUMINT, it recruits spies to provide information on some of the most sensitive and important national security issues. DO case officers (those who recruit agents) are asked to operate in highly risky foreign environments, focused on stealing secrets that can be gotten no other way. Secrets gained through daring operations naturally draw special attention from the White House. Many presidents often wish to understand "how we know" certain secrets that foreign adversaries hope to conceal from Washington.

Second, the CIA manages the largest number of all-source intelligence analysts, who produce assessments on a global set of issues, including most of the material finding its way into the important *President's Daily Brief*. The DA not only has analysts focused on regional issues such as Russia, China, and Iran, but it also covers special topics such as CI, counterterrorism, and counterproliferation and supports a variety of national intelligence centers (operated by the DNI and discussed later).

Third, the DO and its Special Activities Division plan and conduct covert action at the direction of the president. In this case, the CIA is actually implementing policy, not just supporting other policy agencies with information (discussed in more detail in chapter 9). The CIA's unique direct reporting role to the president makes it the obvious choice to be the agency that conducts covert operations because only the president can authorize those activities.

Fourth, the CIA runs CI and **counterespionage** operations as well as produces CI analysis to identify, monitor, exploit, and disrupt foreign intelligence services' efforts to penetrate US intelligence and national security agencies. Along with the FBI, which is responsible for CI activities domestically, the CIA has uncovered numerous instances of Russian, Chinese, and other hostile intelligence services' efforts to recruit agents; steal classified military, scientific, and economic information; and penetrate critical American civilian and government information systems.

For much of its history, the CIA was considered the agency with the most clout, given these critical missions. On top of that, the director of the CIA was also simultaneously the DCI, making him the president's senior intelligence adviser as well as giving him responsibility for overseeing other IC agencies. This clout, however, was diminished with the passage of the **Intelligence Reform and Terrorism Prevention Act of 2004 (IRTPA).** The act established the director of national intelligence, who not only became the senior intelligence adviser to the NSC and the president but also took over the role of managing the IC. In so doing, the CIA director now reports to the DNI, which has caused the CIA to lose some status within the IC as well as the White House. Some CIA careerists viewed this action as punitive, to reflect dissatisfaction with the CIA's failure to prevent the 9/11 attacks and its flawed Iraq WMD analysis. However, other commentaries stress that previous CIA directors were never able to juggle the day-to-day management of the CIA with effective oversight of the huge IC. That said, the relationship between the CIA director and the DNI continues to be an evolving one.

Today the CIA remains the most visible IC member, whose analysis is often considered the unofficial record of intelligence performance, and thus often it is the one agency that attracts the most criticism if those assessments prove to be off the mark.[9] It remains the agency most responsive to the president's intelligence requirements and is said to generate upward of 80 percent of the *PDB* articles for the president. Moreover, in this era of terrorism, insurgencies, and WMD proliferation, its covert action programs have become all the more critical to presidential efforts to prevent future attacks or other threats to the nation. Most recently, the CIA's management of covert detention and interrogation programs has also drawn attention and criticism, even though these have been authorized by two presidents from both major political parties.

EXPANSION OF DEFENSE INTELLIGENCE

Military intelligence is perhaps the oldest part of the intelligence discipline. As one military analyst has argued, "Military intelligence is the basis of operations."[10] Military strategists (such as Sun Tzu and Carl von Clausewitz) as well as better-known American generals (from George Washington to Dwight Eisenhower to David Petraeus) have relied on spies, deception, and sabotage to gain military advantages over their opponents. Not surprisingly, America's IC has long been dominated by the military. The earliest American intelligence organizations were the ONI, established in 1882, and the army's military intelligence directorate, established in 1885. They gathered information on the great European and Asian militaries prior to, during, and between the two world wars through a system of military attachés assigned to American embassies.

World War II and the onset of the Cold War later demanded a large, diverse, and permanent military intelligence community in its own right. The military intelligence failure at Pearl Harbor led both the army and navy to reorganize and expand their own use of HUMINT and SIGINT collection in an effort to give Allied forces the intelligence needed to defeat the Axis powers. And as the Soviet Union loomed larger as a military and nuclear threat in the 1950s, the newly created Defense Department demanded more intelligence to conduct **military analysis** focused on key threats facing the US homeland and overseas commitments.

Defense intelligence today commands roughly two-thirds to three-quarters of the NIP's budgets and includes some of the largest intelligence agencies in terms of collection operations and personnel. In addition to the service intelligence organizations tied to the army, navy, air force, and Marine Corps, there are the large combat-support agencies that include the DIA, the NSA, the NRO, and the NGA. These big four are responsible for collecting, exploiting, and analyzing all national-level military intelligence required by the president and the NSC but especially by the secretary of defense, the JCS, and the senior generals and admirals spread across the globe in nearly a dozen unified and specified commands. Among the many intelligence requirements these agencies must satisfy are:

- **Order-of-battle (OOB)** data (location, size, readiness, and capability of enemy forces)
- Scientific/technical assessments of foreign military weapon systems
- Strategic and theater-level targets for US forces
- Military and civilian infrastructure and lines of communication
- Defense economics and spending levels of foreign adversaries
- Environmental/cultural characteristics of foreign militaries
- Military CI threats

- Basic geographical, topographical, and weather conditions in foreign theaters
- Command, control, communications, and computer (C^4) systems
- Assessments of foreign military strategies, plans, and intentions
- Foreign military leadership assessments[11]

Fulfilling such a wide array of intelligence requirements for such a long list of military and civilian customers helps to explain the huge size and cost of defense intelligence. With so many separate service and combat-support intelligence agencies within a single department, the secretary of defense decided in 2003 to create an undersecretary of defense for intelligence (USDI) to whom all defense intelligence agencies would report. This change has put him in charge of a high percentage of the NIP that comes through DOD appropriations. In terms of lines of authority, the directors of the DIA, the NSA, the NRO, and the NGA must now report both to the USDI as defense "combat-support agencies" but also to the DNI as members of the national intelligence community.

Defense Intelligence Agency

The DIA was established in 1961 following an extensive study of problems in coordinating the separate military service intelligence agencies during the Korean War (1950–53) and thereafter. As the DIA's own official history describes the problem, "Although the need for timely military intelligence was widely recognized, the Army, Navy, and newly founded Air Force still separately collected, produced, and disseminated information. The system proved duplicative, costly, and ineffective, as services provided separate, and at times, conflicting estimates."[12]

Secretary of Defense Robert McNamara, who in the 1960s was intent on making the department more efficient as well as introducing civilian evaluation of defense programs, was particularly eager to challenge service intelligence estimates of the Soviet threat. He feared that parochial service interests in larger military budgets might be driving up intelligence estimates of the Soviet military capabilities. Therefore, he strongly endorsed a more independent DIA that reported to him through the Joint Staff. Once fully staffed, he hoped that the DIA would provide him with a more independent source of intelligence assessment. That said, the DIA's creation did not eliminate all service biases, but it probably did help to economize on some defense intelligence resources. For example, the DIA was able to take over central management of the military attaché program from the services. Still, the services retained their own intelligence divisions and continue to this day to produce their own separate assessments that are not always in line with the DIA's estimates.

Over the years, the DIA has grown to take on major intelligence-collection and analysis functions. Four critical missions include (1) producing all-source intelligence on defense-related and military issues; (2) managing defense HUMINT collection (both overt through defense attachés and clandestine through espionage); (3) managing technical collection programs, including MASINT; and (4) conducting military-related CI analysis.

Regarding analysis, the DIA maintains one of the largest cadres of both civilian and military analysts in the US government. The majority of those analysts work in Washington, but increasingly analysts are deployed to military theaters to provide direct support to combatant commanders. Running the defense attaché program for all the military services involves placing army, navy, Marine Corps, and air force officers in US embassies so they can represent the Defense Department to foreign military officials. In addition, with close cooperation and joint training with the CIA, the DIA operates a DOD HUMINT service that collects military information clandestinely. Regarding technical collection, the DIA serves as the national manager of MASINT, which involves operating a variety of technical sensors to collect environmental data (e.g., acoustic, seismic, and radiological) that can reveal important military technologies. Finally, along with the CIA, the DIA collects and analyzes CI information related to foreign intelligence service efforts to penetrate US military departments and to recruit spies.

Like many combat-support elements, the DIA is headed by a serving three-star general officer who is selected by the secretary of defense, approved by the DNI, and confirmed by the Senate. Importantly, the director of the DIA chairs the Military Intelligence Board (MIB), which the heads of the separate military intelligence services as well as the directors of the NSA, the NGA, and the NRO use to reach decisions and often consensus on defense intelligence-collection priorities, budgets, and programs. In this capacity, the DIA director will often represent the combined military intelligence views of all those combat agencies.

National Security Agency

The NSA is perhaps second only to the CIA in terms of the fascination that journalists and scholars have regarding its activities. Much like the CIA, it operates in the dark, given the highly classified nature of its SIGINT operations. Like the DIA, the NSA was created to help centralize the separate and poorly coordinated SIGINT activities of the military services. In 1949, the JCS were charged with creating an armed forces security agency to better coordinate the separate army, navy, and air force programs. Those steps proved inadequate, and after further study the NSC proposed, and President Truman signed, a secret executive order establishing the NSA in 1952.[13] Its creation remained officially a secret until the mid-1970s, when the House and Senate conducted investigations into the illegal activities of the NSA regarding domestic surveillance of American anti–Vietnam War protesters. To this day, the NSA's powerful SIGINT-collection capabilities provoke Americans' civil liberties concerns. Most recently, the Edward Snowden leaks of the NSA's worldwide collection of communications—including some reportedly directed at America's allies—have caused Congress and the public to question whether the NSA's activities go well beyond what the law permits.

Today the NSA is the principal US cryptologic organization, with a dual mission. First and foremost, it must protect US national security information by creating secure, encrypted communication equipment and systems. The NSA produces what is commonly referred to as information security (INFOSEC) or information assurance—encrypted codes and encryption gear (e.g., secure phones and other communication devices) used throughout the US government. Second, it must collect, exploit, and analyze foreign SIGINT, including missile telemetry systems; military command, control, and communications (C^3) systems; commercial telephone and Internet networks; and foreign information networks. In layperson's terms, the NSA attempts to collect, process, and then analyze virtually any significant form of foreign electronic signals. For example, when a foreign military tests a new weapon system, the NSA will collect FISINT; when foreign diplomats or military commanders talk to each other, the NSA will collect COMINT; and when a foreign military is operating a variety of electronic devices such as radars, the NSA will collect ELINT. To do all this, the NSA manages a large workforce of both civilian and military professionals with skills in cryptoanalysis, cryptography, mathematics, computer science, and foreign languages. It is sometimes suggested that the NSA is the largest employer of mathematicians and computer "geeks" in the United States.

Like the DIA, the director of the NSA (often abbreviated DIRNSA) is a serving three-star officer who reports to the USDI. The DIRNSA not only directs the activities of the NSA but also oversees the individual military service SIGINT activities, which ensures their smooth cooperation with the NSA. At the time of this writing, the DIRNSA also has the job of being the commander of the United States Cyber Command (CYBERCOM). This is a unified military command established in 2010 with the mission to protect US defense information networks from foreign cyberattacks and to conduct a full spectrum of cyber operations in support of US military operations. There continue to be discussions of whether the DIRNSA should be separated from CYBERCOM in order to give this command its own dedicated senior military commander.[14]

National Reconnaissance Office

As the saying goes, a "picture is worth a thousand words," but only if it can be interpreted and understood correctly for what it signifies. The National Reconnaissance Office is the agency charged with building and operating overhead satellites that collect IMINT as well as SIGINT. The NRO came into existence as the Space Age began in the 1950s. Cold War intelligence requirements for Soviet nuclear and missile tests posed great risks to pilots of "spyplanes" trying to overfly Soviet airspace. In 1958, President Eisenhower directed his science and military advisers to begin a crash program for developing space-based satellite systems that could photograph Soviet test ranges and missile sites. By 1960, the first such system, designated Corona, produced the reconnaissance photos that helped to dispel the myth of a "missile gap."[15]

Early development of reconnaissance satellites was spurred on by the fact that the US Air Force, the US Navy, and the CIA all wished to develop overhead collection capabilities for their own organizational reasons. The air force was interested in targeting information for bombing attacks, the CIA needed information on Soviet missile tests, and the navy wanted to monitor Soviet maritime operations. This resulted in a hybrid organization, made up of military service personnel, CIA employees, and civilian staff and contractors.

These three separate programs were brought under central management when, in 1961, Secretary McNamara placed them all under the newly created NRO. As an assistant secretary of the air force, the director of the NRO would report to both the secretary of defense and the DCI (after 2005, the DNI). The organization's existence and even its name were secret and remained so until 1992, when Secretary of Defense Dick Cheney declassified the name.

The NRO's first decade was focused on revealing the military capabilities and intentions of the Soviet Union and the People's Republic of China. Although considered a temporary fix to satisfy American intelligence needs, the Corona program continued to operate through the early 1970s. However, the demand for higher volume and higher-resolution imagery pressed the United States to introduce the KH-7 and KH-9 satellite systems, which were able to produce thousands of linear feet of film during their more than one hundred missions. These film-return systems were replaced in 1976 by the first electro-optical KH-11 system, which transmitted electronically much higher-resolution images in near real time to ground stations and then on to Washington for rapid processing and interpretation.[16] Avoiding military surprises such as the 1968 Soviet invasion of Czechoslovakia and the 1973 Arab attack on Israel were strong drivers to develop such capabilities to give policymakers adequate warning time to take appropriate action.

In the 1990s, as defense and intelligence budgets suffered through cuts (à la the "peace dividend"), the NRO reorganized and integrated the three separate air force, navy, and CIA programs and their personnel. The expense of large satellites also put a premium on integrating the diverse IMINT- and SIGINT-collection capabilities onto single satellite platforms to get the most "bang per launch."

During the Cold War, the NRO systems were largely focused on collecting against Soviet and Chinese strategic and tactical military targets, as those were seen as the most direct military threats to the United States. However, even more diverse and capable satellite programs are used for a variety of national security challenges:

- monitoring the proliferation of WMDs
- tracking international terrorists, drug traffickers, and criminal organizations
- developing highly accurate military targeting data and bomb-damage assessment
- supporting international peacekeeping and humanitarian relief operations
- assessing the impact of natural disasters, such as earthquakes, tsunamis, floods, and fires

As there are many applications for imagery, the NRO has found itself working closely with the NGA, which combines satellite imagery and SIGINT with other data to produce unique GEOINT. In addition, there are domestic agencies interested in exploiting the NRO's considerable resources for disaster relief and environmental monitoring, so there is now a Civil Applications Committee within the Department of the Interior, where representatives from other domestic agencies such as DHS and the Department of Health and Human Services can make their requests for imagery.[17]

The NRO, like other combat-support agencies, has to operate with split loyalties to both the secretary of defense and the DNI. The original charter for the NRO had it reporting directly to the secretary of defense but allowed the then DCI to assign its intelligence requirements. President Carter first established the NRO as a member of the national foreign intelligence program, giving the then DCI authority over its budget. For many years, a special Committee on Imagery Requirements and Exploitation (COMIREX) functioned to ensure that all IC agencies—not just military ones—relying on IMINT could jointly determine imagery priorities, including their urgency, frequency, and resolution.[18] A 2010 memorandum of agreement between the DNI and the secretary of defense has stipulated that the NRO director is the senior adviser on overhead systems to both; in practice, this means that both the DNI and the secretary of defense must validate future intelligence requirements for satellite systems. As one historian phrased it, "A certain amount of conflict between the Defense Department and the Intelligence Community is an inherent part of the NRO's history, and remains a challenge for running the organization today."[19]

National Geospatial-Intelligence Agency

The NGA is unique in its own way, as it relies on close relationships with other collection agencies, such as the NSA (for SIGINT), the NRO (for IMINT), and the CIA (for HUMINT) to produce a wide variety of geospatial intelligence (GEOINT). Before briefly tracing its history, a working definition of GEOINT is required. The IC considers GEOINT to be the exploitation and analysis of imagery and other geospatial information that "describe, exploit and visually depict physical features and geographically referenced activities on the earth."[20] In layperson's terms, GEOINT has to take advantage of not just images but also combines them with data and information from all the other INTs as well. Imagery information has been and remains the foundation on which much geospatial information and analysis is based. But it must be enhanced with other information—often referred to as "collateral collection"—to give meaning or value to the imagery itself.

Two examples might help explain how GEOINT is more than just imagery. First, when a tsunami hit the Philippines in 2004 and reshaped the landscape, the NGA used digital mapping imagery to revise maritime maps used by rescue ships. It exploited social media being used by the victims to update existing maps to highlight new physical hazards, closed roads, and displaced populations.[21] Second, the NGA was a key contributor to locating Osama bin Laden and many other so-called high-value targets. During the planning of Operation Neptune Spear, the NGA helped to produce an exact replica of Bin Laden's Abbottabad residence, using various forms of imagery of the compound to measure it. This information reportedly helped show US Navy SEALs where to land their helicopters and detailed the number, gender, and even heights of the compound's occupants.[22]

This new discipline is really not that new. Ancient and modern armies and navies have always relied on topographical and maritime mapping to describe difficult terrain features of the battlefield as well as favorable and dangerous maritime routes. In 1803, for example, President Thomas Jefferson sent the US Army's Lewis and Clark Expedition off to map significant features of the huge Louisiana Territory purchased from the French. The US Navy also has been conducting defense-related mapping as far back as the 1830s, so as not to rely on the British navy's charts.[23] Likewise, there has long been the practice of aerial reconnaissance to assist in targeting an enemy as well as assessing the damage done by strategic bombing campaigns. The world wars saw the steady expansion and greater sophistication of such aerial reconnaissance for mapping battlefields, landings, and enemy targets. All of this was done by the individual services that were primarily interested in their unique domains—land, naval, and air battle spaces.

The CIA produced further early advancements in the use of the U-2 and the SR-71/AR-12 spyplanes and eventually space-based imagery satellites. Increasing imagery collection also required a dedicated set of analysts to interpret this growing volume of data. Thus began the gradual reorganization and centralization of GEOINT. In 1961, President Eisenhower created the National Photographic Interpretation Center (NPIC) by combining the imagery analysis found in the CIA with similar activities in the army, navy, and air force. The NPIC made an early contribution in its identification of the Soviet missiles secretly placed in Cuba in 1962. During the Vietnam War in the 1960s and 1970s, the need for better coordination of mapping services led to a comparable consolidation of the separate military services' mapping function into a single Defense Mapping Agency (DMA). But it was not until the mid-1990s that Secretary of Defense William Perry and DCI John Deutch agreed to combine all imaging and mapping services into a single National Imagery and Mapping Agency (NIMA).

Shortly after 9/11, James Clapper became the director of NIMA, and he quickly determined that the agency was now producing more sophisticated products for more and more customers. Increasingly, NIMA was producing geospatial information well beyond military maps or finished imagery analysis. In fact, it was combining imagery with a host of other data to support humanitarian relief efforts, support international negotiations, and plot the locations and movement of terrorists, criminals, and pirates. With such a wide array of applications and government users, General Clapper pushed to rename NIMA as the NGA to highlight this shift in focus.

The NGA is also unlike the NSA and the DIA, as it now has a senior civilian rather than a general military officer as its director. This is understandable given that the NGA has to work with a variety of nonmilitary departments and agencies that also have geospatial missions and requirements. Any number of domestic agencies produce geospatial data that the NGA might need to access to develop actionable intelligence for national security purposes. While the director of the NGA is the senior manager of all GEOINT produced by the DOD, it must work with many of those agencies outside the DOD. Some of those nontraditional and nonmilitary applications include environmental problems such as desertification and climate change, geological and environmental challenges caused by natural disasters, human rights and war crimes data, population movements, energy production and disruption, and food security problems caused by weather and other natural causes.

STATE DEPARTMENT'S BUREAU OF INTELLIGENCE AND RESEARCH

The Bureau of Intelligence and Research (INR) provides all-source intelligence support to the secretary of state and other State Department policymakers, including ambassadors, special negotiators, and other Foreign Service professionals throughout the department. The assistant secretary for INR requires Senate confirmation, reports directly to the secretary of state, and is his or her senior intelligence adviser. In this capacity, INR is therefore responsible for producing its own departmental intelligence analysis, crafting an intelligence policy for the department, and coordinating national intelligence activities in support of American diplomacy.

INR has claimed the distinction of being the direct descendent of the OSS. In fact, its R&A branch was transferred to the State Department at the end of the war and was huge at the time (sixteen hundred employees) compared to its size today (slightly more than three hundred).[24] It was the foundation for later all-source analysis. At the same time, however, the OSS's collection and special operations functions were transferred to the CIA and the US military, respectively. Unlike the CIA, DIA, or NSA, INR has no formal collection activities. That said, it has considerable insight into the quality of the extensive diplomatic reporting that comes to the US government from American embassies and consulates. Its analytical workforce comprises civilian regional and functional experts, who tend to remain on their accounts far longer than analysts at other agencies. Historically, roughly 30 percent have been Foreign Service officers who have served overseas, know their regions and countries well, and have excellent connections with those embassies and their diplomatic reporting. INR's organization not surprisingly aligns well with the various regional and functional bureaus, as these are key consumers of INR assessments.

Importantly, INR is close to the policymaking process at the department. Its analysts are routinely included in each of the regional or functional bureaus' daily and weekly staff meetings. This puts INR in a unique position of being able to tailor its assessments to current and longer-term issues on the agendas of assistant secretaries and higher-level officials in the department. Until 2002, INR also produced its own daily intelligence bulletin, called the *Secretary's Morning Summary*, which was also sent to the White House and other *PDB* consumers; it often received kudos for being better written than the *PDB*, if not as highly classified. This daily and broadly circulated current intelligence publication was eventually ended when INR and key consumers determined the bureau could have more impact if State Department customers received specially tailored memoranda with detailed analyses on issues of direct interest to them.

INR has a well-deserved reputation for being able to assert its independence from policy, even as it reports to senior political appointees such as the secretary of state. During the Vietnam War, INR famously dissented from Secretary McNamara's rosy assessments that the United States was "winning the hearts and minds."[25] During the early 1960s, it routinely dissented from National Intelligence Estimates on South Vietnam it considered too optimistic, and later it also disputed the Pentagon's numbers of North Vietnamese fighters. This reputation for independence was more recently demonstrated in the well-publicized dissent INR took to the 2002 Iraq WMD estimate (discussed in chapter 10) regarding the status of Saddam Hussein's nuclear program. INR has also stood by its analysts whenever political appointees have pressed them to hew to a political line.[26]

INR also has the responsibility to advise the secretary of state on intelligence matters that could impact the conduct of US diplomacy and US foreign relations more broadly. INR is responsible for managing the department's relationship with the CIA. In this capacity, INR acts on behalf of the department to ensure that CIA activities are consistent with American diplomacy vis-à-vis foreign governments. Overall, INR will represent Department of State interests to other intelligence agencies as well, especially when intelligence sharing is involved. For example, if the secretary of state wishes to share sensitive intelligence with a foreign official, INR would need to gain approval from the intelligence agency producing that report, whether it is based on NSA SIGINT or CIA HUMINT. Also, a senior INR official is responsible for coordinating any proposed covert action or other special intelligence activities and assessing whether they might have diplomatic repercussions or require that such plans be shared with a foreign government.

THE FBI'S GROWING INTELLIGENCE ROLE

The FBI has been involved in intelligence-related activities almost from the beginning of its existence in the early twentieth century. Prior to September 11, 2001, however, it principal focus was on CI—on threats coming from hostile intelligence services. Historically, terrorism was not treated as a core mission; instead, such cases were handled individually out of single field offices without much interaction with or input from the FBI's Washington headquarters. The subsequent investigation of the 9/11 plotters highlighted major flaws in the FBI's handling of counterterrorism cases, including the way FBI procedures "stove-piped" investigative information, prevented effective FBI headquarters oversight, and assigned inconsistent priorities to terrorism cases.[27] Since 9/11 and the 2004 intelligence reforms, the FBI has become America's principal "domestic intelligence" organization.[28] In this new era, the bureau has had to modify its mission statements, which previously focused on "law enforcement," to something closer to "national security." The fusing of these two has required a new set of missions and forced a change in the law enforcement culture at the FBI.

In recognition of the new era and its new missions, the FBI created its National Security Branch (NSB), which is led by a senior FBI deputy director. This branch has special agents and analysts who investigate crimes and threats to the United States involving counterterrorism, CI, and WMDs. After 9/11, an Intelligence Directorate was added to ensure careful management of intelligence resources across the bureau and to establish its intelligence strategy and programs. As of 2014, the FBI went a step further and created an entirely separate Intelligence Branch, whose mission continues to be the integration of FBI intelligence activities but also ensuring that analysis and information are shared across the government and with international partners.

Beyond the Washington Beltway, the FBI's joint terrorism task forces, located in major metropolitan areas, increased from a couple dozen prior to 9/11 to over a hundred since then. These bring together FBI law enforcement and intelligence experts from across the federal government as well as state and municipal law enforcement organizations. Overseas, the FBI operates over sixty legal attaché offices that are part of the law enforcement and IC presence in foreign countries. These LEGATs work with other US intelligence agencies operating overseas as well as foreign law enforcement and security services. It is the LEGAT who, in most cases, is responsible for pursuing extradition and most renditions of suspected terrorists and WMD proliferators whom the United States wishes to bring to justice.

The FBI organizational culture of being simply America's "top cop" has also changed. In addition to being populated and run by FBI "special agents" (who carry badges and guns and have arrest authorities), the FBI has developed a large cadre (nearly three thousand) of intelligence analysts. These analysts work in the NSB located at FBI headquarters in downtown Washington as well as in the fifty-six field offices across the United States, which still take the lead on individual investigations. Increasingly, especially since the Russian interference with the 2016 US elections, the FBI has played a leading role in presenting intelligence findings and warnings to US policymakers, Congress, and the American public.

Other Intelligence Agencies

The remainder of the sixteen intelligence agencies all reside in their own departments and probably make up far less than 10 percent of the IC's budget and manpower. Nonetheless, they each play key roles in providing critical intelligence to their departments and in some cases to the president and his senior advisers. Not much has been written about the intelligence-related activities conducted by the small intelligence units of the Treasury Department and Energy Department that are focused on international financial crimes, illicit WMD technology transfers, and nuclear-related proliferation problems. The Treasury Department's OIA has received more notoriety recently because of its ability to monitor and disrupt financial transactions of terrorist cells, narcotic traffickers, and weapon proliferators as well as enforce effective sanctions against Russia, Iran, and North Korea.

The Drug Enforcement Administration (DEA) also is now considered an intelligence agency as well as law enforcement agency focused on collecting and acting on intelligence related to narcotic trafficking. As part of the Department of Justice (DOJ), it has a significant presence overseas as DEA special agents deployed to American embassies are collecting drug-related intelligence and cooperating with and conducting counterdrug operations with the host governments' services. The

DEA also runs the El Paso Intelligence Center (EPIC), a multiagency center that is focused on illicit drug trafficking and smuggling on the southwestern US border.[29]

And, finally, DHS contains two separate intelligence functions. The first is its Office of Intelligence and Analysis (I&A). When the department was first being created, there was some support for giving DHS a more expansive counterterrorism intelligence role, but this was quickly batted down by proponents of leaving the FBI and CIA largely responsible for collecting and analyzing domestic and foreign CT intelligence, respectively. Instead, the I&A was restricted to taking the intelligence collected by other intelligence agencies and using it to inform other DHS leaders of major threats to the homeland. In addition, the office is responsible for communicating threat information to state, municipal, tribal, and private sector partners. That said, DHS does play a major role in cyber issues. As recently reported, DHS joined the FBI in producing the first public reports on Russian government sponsorship of cyberattacks on US election systems and the Hillary Clinton campaign.[30] This was partly designed to alert local officials of cyber threats and to encourage closer cooperation among all levels of government to enhance their cyber security.

The second DHS intelligence agency is the US Coast Guard (USCG). The USCG is a hybrid organization as well, operating as a military service in its own right but with substantial law enforcement and intelligence functions. It always had a military intelligence mission but joined the IC only when it was transferred to DHS in 2005. The USCG's most visible intelligence mission focuses on drug interdiction through maritime routes.[31] But it has many additional roles, perhaps most importantly assessing and combating maritime and port security threats to the homeland.[32]

THE GROWING ROLE OF THE DNI

The preceding description of the many agencies and missions within the IC underlines the challenge of organizing and directing their activities in a way that can support the president and the national security enterprise. For more than half a century, the CIA director carried the burden of overseeing the IC as his "second hat" as director of central intelligence. Numerous studies over that period had argued for reforms that would strengthen the DCI's budgetary and programmatic authority versus the powerful secretaries of defense, who controlled most of the resources. The most radical call for strengthening central management came from former national security adviser Brent Scowcroft, who in 2001 reportedly recommended to President George W. Bush that the three largest defense intelligence organizations—the NSA, the NRO, and NIMA (precursor to NGA)—be placed under the budgetary authority of the DCI, leaving the secretary of defense with day-to-day management of only the military service intelligence programs.[33] That plan, never made public officially, was strongly resisted by Defense Secretary Rumsfeld at the time. And like previous efforts, any notion of creating a "national intelligence czar" was met with strong congressional reluctance to give up control over large parts of the defense budget to the intelligence oversight committees.[34]

All of that changed with the 9/11 attacks on the World Trade Center and the Pentagon. Analysis of this surprise attack pointed to weaknesses in information sharing across the IC, divided management responsibilities, and the DCI's inability to direct other agencies to take the Bin Laden threat more seriously. The flawed 2002 NIE on Iraq's WMD program only added fuel for congressional pressure to pass new legislation that would reorganize the IC to improve both collection and analysis.[35]

Accordingly, the 2004 Intelligence Reform and Terrorism Prevention Act created the position of DNI, who became the new head of the IC and now shoulders all the responsibility once held by the DCI for developing the IC's budgets, setting intelligence priorities, protecting classified information, and overseeing the production of NIEs. Most importantly, the DNI replaces the DCI as the senior intelligence adviser to the president and the NSC. In particular, the DNI now represents the IC at NSC meetings and at Principals Committee meetings; members of his staff also represent the DNI at the Deputies Committee and IPC-level meetings. The DNI's responsibilities are laid out in Executive Order 12333, which has been modified since the IRTPA was promulgated (see box 4.2).

As similar as it sounds to that of the former DCI, the DNI's job is very different, for a number of reasons. First, unlike the former DCIs, the new DNI does not simultaneously run the CIA or any other intelligence agency. Rather, his sole job is to represent the broader IC, advise the president and the NSC, and oversee and implement the NIP. This has mixed effects. On the one hand, the DNI can concentrate on his responsibilities to advise the president, oversee the broader IC, and prepare a consolidated intelligence program and budget. In this way, he is a far better adjudicator of budget disputes because he does not have any personal control or investment in the CIA's budget or programs as former DCIs did. On the other hand, the DNI lacks the backing of a large organization like the CIA to support his efforts. Congress directed that the Office of the Director of National Intelligence *not* become another agency and not become too large or bureaucratic and create another layer of management. In fact, the ODNI currently has roughly eighteen hundred employees, many of whom are on rotational assignments from other intelligence agencies or are contractors.

Second, the pre-9/11 walls between domestic and foreign intelligence as well as between law enforcement and intelligence have been broken down. Now the DNI has

Box 4.2 Excerpts from Executive Order 12333
(1981, as Amended in 2003)

1.2 **The National Security Council.**

(a) **Purpose.** The National Security Council (NSC) shall act as the highest ranking executive branch entity that provides support to the President for review of, guidance for, and direction to the conduct of all foreign intelligence, counterintelligence, and covert action, and attendant policies and programs. . . .

1.3 **Director of National Intelligence.** Subject to the authority, direction, and control of the President, the Director of National Intelligence (Director) shall serve as the head of the Intelligence Community, act as the principal adviser to the President, to the NSC, and to the Homeland Security Council for intelligence matters related to national security, and shall oversee and direct the implementation of the National Intelligence Program and execution of the National Intelligence Program budget. The Director will lead a unified, coordinated, and effective intelligence effort. In addition, the Director shall, in carrying out the duties and responsibilities under this section, take into account the views of the heads of departments containing an element of the Intelligence Community and of the Director of the Central Intelligence Agency. . . .

(b) In addition to fulfilling the obligations and responsibilities prescribed by the Act, the Director:

(1) Shall establish objectives, priorities, and guidance for the Intelligence Community to ensure timely and effective collection, processing, analysis, and dissemination of intelligence, of whatever nature and from whatever source derived. . . .

(7) Shall ensure that appropriate departments and agencies have access to intelligence and receive the support needed to perform independent analysis;

(8) Shall protect, and ensure that programs are developed to protect, intelligence sources, methods, and activities from unauthorized disclosure. . . .

(14) Shall have ultimate responsibility for production and dissemination of intelligence produced by the Intelligence Community and authority to levy analytic tasks on intelligence production organizations within the Intelligence Community, in consultation with the heads of the Intelligence Community elements concerned. . . .

(17) Shall determine requirements and priorities for, and manage and direct the tasking, collection, analysis, production, and dissemination of, national intelligence by elements of the Intelligence Community, including approving requirements for collection and analysis and resolving conflicts in collection requirements and in the tasking of national collection assets of Intelligence Community elements (except when otherwise directed by the President or when the Secretary of Defense exercises collection tasking authority under plans and arrangements approved by the Secretary of Defense and the Director).

Source: Executive Order 12333, United States Intelligence Activities. As amended by Executive Orders 13284 (2003), 13355 (2004), and 13470 (2008), https://fas.org/irp/offdocs/eo/eo-12333-2008.pdf.

not only foreign intelligence duties but also duties overseeing intelligence aspects of domestic and homeland security. It is important to remember he or she is the senior intelligence adviser to the Homeland Security Council as well as the NSC. Thus, the DNI has to coordinate not just the large defense intelligence agencies, the powerful CIA, and the smaller departmental intelligence units, but now he or she must also oversee the intelligence-related activities of a growing FBI's national security responsibilities and DHS's intelligence and analysis functions.

Third, the legislation modestly strengthened the DNI's authorities compared to the former DCIs regarding the control over financial resources and people. But it fell far short of a new "Department of Intelligence" or of bringing all DOD intelligence-related activities under the DNI. The secretary of defense and the powerful armed services committees were aligned against such a move, and they insisted on legislative language that essentially prohibited the DNI from undermining the "statutory responsibilities of the heads of the departments."[36] For example, the DNI can reprogram (move funds from one part of the intelligence budget to another) a few million dollars and transfer a few dozen personnel from one program to another; however, in both cases these numbers are small, and anything larger has to be done with the concurrence of the department in which the action was to be taken.

Fourth, the DNI has the responsibility for overseeing a number of national intelligence centers, which are designed to centralize management of critical functions and improve information sharing across the community. These centers help account for the considerable size of the ODNI and wield considerable influence:

- The **National Intelligence Council (NIC)** predated the IRTPA and has the responsibility for preparing long-term, strategic intelligence analysis that represents the collective judgments of the IC. The NIC prepares NIEs that are approved by the DNI. The council is composed of a dozen **national intelligence officers (NIOs)** with regional and functional responsibilities, who oversee the production of NIEs and other community-based assessments for senior policymakers. NIOs are usually the senior IC representatives to the interagency policy committees and often support the DNI at NSC and PC meetings as a backbencher (termed the "plus one") participant.
- The National Counterterrorism Center has primary responsibility for conducting CT analysis as well as counterterrorism strategic planning. It uniquely bridges the foreign and domestic intelligence agencies responsible for counterterrorism, as it oversees all activities for accessing, integrating, and analyzing all intelligence related to terrorism. Likewise, it is responsible for ensuring that other agencies with CT missions have access to this information. Perhaps its most unique role is that it must conduct strategic operational planning for the

entire US government and ensure the effective use of all military, diplomatic, law enforcement, and intelligence disciplines. Therefore, the director of NCTC reports both to the DNI and to the president in his capacity as senior adviser on counterterrorism operations.

- The **National Counterproliferation Center (NCPC)** facilitates the counterproliferation activities of IC agencies and conducts strategic planning designed to prevent the spread of WMD technologies and systems. Unlike the NCTC, the NCPC does not produce WMD-related intelligence analysis but rather identifies intelligence gaps, promotes new techniques and technologies, and fosters cooperation among intelligence agencies, other federal agencies, and American industry and academia. In this manner, its smaller workforce is a management function rather than an intelligence-production element.
- The **National Counterintelligence and Security Center (NCSC)** serves as the focus of the national CI effort, which aims at integrating the CI activities of the CIA, FBI, and other agencies as well as coordinating their budgets and evaluating their effectiveness. Importantly, NCSC is responsible for investigating CI cases to assess their damage and also for establishing common security practices across the US government.

Finally, the DNI has taken over responsibility—as the president's senior intelligence adviser—for the preparation of the *PDB*. Under the prior DCIs, the *PDB* was almost exclusively a CIA publication, written and briefed by CIA analysts. Under the DNI, the *PDB* has become an IC document that includes assessments prepared by CIA but also DIA and INR analysts. This ensures that a range of analytical views are available to the president and senior advisers; it also allows the DNI to give feedback to agencies beyond the CIA as to the president's agenda and intelligence priorities. New procedures introduced by the DNI include *PDB* editorial and briefing teams that include non-CIA analysts (primarily from the DIA and INR). CIA offices still produce the vast majority of *PDB* articles, but many also contain input from other contributing agencies. But the principle of DNI control of the most sensitive information reaching the Oval Office has given the DNI greater influence, even if he does not control a large bureaucracy like the CIA.

In sum, the DNI has become a key participant in the national security decision-making process. The DNI or his deputy has usually chosen to join the *PDB* briefings in the Oval Office, and they are regular participants at the many NSC, PC, and DC meetings. The DNI has to approve the content of the *PDB* and NIEs reaching senior officials. Moreover, the DNI prepares and defends the IC programs and budgets on Capitol Hill and often has to take the heat for intelligence activities gone wrong or judged to be controversial. Last, he gives an annual Worldwide Threat Assessment to the armed services and intelligence oversight committees in early spring that often generates great media attention and reveals the latest IC assessments regarding cyber and terrorism threats as well as Russian, Iranian, or North Korean military challenges. The 2019 presentation by DNI Dan Coats produced its own media attention as it was widely reported that the IC's views on Russia, North Korea, and Iran were judged widely at odds with President Trump's own assessments.[37]

KEY ISSUES FOR THE INTELLIGENCE COMMUNITY

The intelligence reforms contained in the 2004 IRTPA have now been in existence for more than a decade along with the DNI and other new intelligence organizations and processes. The question remains as to whether these reforms have been sufficient to improve the IC's performance. Perennial issues still remain on how best to manage, resources coordinate, and oversee the IC.

Managing the IC's Budgets

The size and growth of the IC's budgets have reflected the expanding set of intelligence challenges as well as the growing list of intelligence users. In talking about intelligence activities, senior IC leaders have also adopted the language of an "intelligence enterprise" that reflects the reality of a diverse set of agencies and functions that must increasingly coordinate and integrate their operations to maximize its effectiveness. Understanding this enterprise is difficult because of the classified nature of the IC's business and budgets. As these programs and budgets remain largely classified, it is difficult to shed light on how money is spent and which intelligence priorities have been chosen. Historically, however, the IC's budgets have been driven by large and multiyear investments in expensive technical-collection infrastructure and equipment—such as ground sites, computer-processing systems, and satellites—for SIGINT and IMINT.

These take years to design, build, and deploy. For example, during the 1970s and 1980s, when the United States was building much of its space-based satellite reconnaissance systems, more than half of the NIP was most likely devoted to the NRO and NSA satellite programs. Such systems were instrumental in permitting the United States to negotiate nuclear arms control agreements with the Soviet Union. Without them, monitoring Soviet compliance with the terms of the strategic arms reduction and other major agreements would have been impossible. These so-called legacy systems continue to provide useful intelligence, but more agile and multisensor satellites have become available to deal with post-Soviet intelligence threats.

Some in Congress have argued that satellites are less useful in tracking down and monitoring terrorists than plain old spies. The question is often posed whether too much attention and spending on technical systems comes at the expense of HUMINT collection. After 9/11, for example, President Bush authorized a 50 percent increase in CIA operations officers in order to strengthen human-source reporting. Those increases cannot immediately guarantee results because human-source recruitment can take years to come to fruition. It is generally believed that budget increases are aimed at greatly expanded efforts directed against terrorism, proliferation, and insurgencies in the Middle East but may also reflect growing concern about cyber issues and the need for an active information-operation capability. In 2013, James Clapper noted that even though today's environment is so fluid, the IC is spending far less than 1 percent of the gross national product on intelligence: "The United States has made a considerable investment in the Intelligence Community since the terror attacks of 9/11, a time which includes wars in Iraq and Afghanistan, the Arab Spring, the proliferation of weapons of mass destruction technology, and asymmetric threats in such areas as cyber-warfare."[38]

As in the past, more than half of the NIP was consumed by the big defense intelligence agencies—the NSA, the NRO, and the NGA. As reported in 2010, these three agencies were consuming a large portion of the $60 billion intelligence budget. It was pointed out earlier in this chapter that the intelligence reforms did not go so far as to give the newly created DNI sole control over the NIP's budgets. While the DNI can set priorities, most of the money is found in the defense appropriations bills. In addition, the military services control their own tactical military intelligence programs—termed the **Military Intelligence Program (MIP)**—which are separate from the NIP. This MIP totals roughly $20 billion annually and is submitted to the USDI first and is approved by the secretary of defense. Thus, in reality, the secretary of defense has huge influence over both the NIP and the MIP. Specifically, he must concur in any DNI changes to defense-related budgets of any magnitude. Moreover, the Senate and House intelligence and armed services committees all get a chance to review, critique, and approve the intelligence agencies' programs and budgets that come under their jurisdiction, so, the DNI's budgetary authority is far from supreme.

Integration versus Centralization

Ever since the 1947 National Security Act was signed, there has been a debate regarding the extent to which intelligence should be coordinated rather than centralized. The many intelligence agencies, most of which report to separate department secretaries, value their autonomy and ability to be responsive to their immediate bosses. However, the president and Congress are also eager to streamline, economize, and rationalize the expensive IC. Hence, there is the common complaint that too much of what it does is duplicative or redundant. Critics argue there is no reason why multiple agencies should be producing finished intelligence on the same topics. For example, the CIA produces analyses on Russia, China, Iran, WMDs, and other national security issues, just as the DIA and INR do for their departmental customers. Policy agencies, however, have particular and often different types of questions regarding foreign policies, military capabilities, or economic and financial practices of China, Iran, and so forth, and thus their departmental intelligence units produce uniquely tailored assessments on the same countries or topics. In addition, proponents of rigorous **analytical tradecraft** argue that multiple perspectives are needed to guard against **groupthink**. As a former DNI put it, "**Competitive analysis** avoids single points of failure and unchallenged analytic judgments."[39]

The creation of the DNI has once again raised the question of how much integration is enough without losing the autonomy that the IC agencies clearly desire. While praising the value of orchestrating the operations of a large intelligence enterprise for efficiency and effectiveness, few senior intelligence leaders support centralization if that means the DNI can direct individual agencies' daily activities and order them to stop producing intelligence for their departmental policymakers. During the debate of the DNI's role, many in the CIA believed the authorities of the then DCI could have been modestly strengthened without creating an entirely new organization and more bureaucracy. Congress, in particular, has been adamant that the ODNI not grow into a new agency of its own or presume to take on the roles of other agencies. Hence, it has placed limits on the number of personnel the ODNI can hire.

At the same time, nearly every senior intelligence official recognizes the need for better coordination of the collection-exploitation-analysis process in order to ensure that all available information is examined and evaluated properly. Close cooperation between the NSA and the NGA has enabled the US military to target key terrorists operating in Iraq and Afghanistan. Former NGA director Robert B. Murrett described this as "horizontal integration" that could have a multiplier effect on military operations.[40] Moreover, when covert joint operations are planned, it requires close coordination between the CIA and the DOD's Joint Special Operations Command (JSOC) for managing paramilitary activities in Iraq and Afghanistan. As one participant described it, the Abbottabad operation amounted to "a complete integration of special forces into a CIA operation."[41]

NSC Oversight of the Intelligence Community

There has been almost constant if not always sufficient oversight of the CIA and the IC by the president and the NSC. Even as early as 1946, when the tiny CIG amounted to fewer than one hundred people, representatives from secretaries of state, war (i.e., army), and navy, along with a presidential representative, oversaw its activities.[42] As the IC grew through the 1950s and 1960s, oversight continued to be conducted by a special subcommittee of the NSC. As Henry Kissinger noted in his memoirs,

President Gerald Ford was the first president to acknowledge "the existence of a committee of the NSC—then known as the 40 Committee—which had for over two decades reviewed covert programs before they were submitted to the President for approval."[43]

The NSC interagency groups overseeing intelligence activities have been given a variety of names over the years, reflecting each president's preferences for how to handle sensitive intelligence matters. But as the 1981 Executive Order 12333 makes clear, the NSC should play a central role in intelligence:

> 1.2 *The National Security Council.*
>
> (a) *Purpose.* The National Security Council (NSC) shall act as the highest ranking executive branch entity that provides support to the President for review of, guidance for, and direction to the conduct of all foreign intelligence, counterintelligence, and covert action, and attendant policies and programs.
>
> (b) *Covert Action and Other Sensitive Intelligence Operations.* The NSC shall consider and submit to the President a policy recommendation, including all dissents, on each proposed covert action and conduct a periodic review of ongoing covert action activities, including an evaluation of the effectiveness and consistency with current national policy of such activities and consistency with applicable legal requirements. The NSC shall perform such other functions related to covert action as the President may direct, but shall not undertake the conduct of covert actions. The NSC shall also review proposals for other sensitive intelligence operations.[44]

This authority, combined with the 1947 National Security Act, placed special responsibility on the NSC and indirectly the national security adviser to supervise and evaluate intelligence activities. Within the NSC staff, there is a senior director for intelligence programs, who is customarily charged with supporting the president, the national security adviser, and the NSC and Homeland Security Council on intelligence matters. Thus, this directorate participates with the ODNI and OMB in determining the IC's budget, helps set up the administration's priorities on collection and analysis (see below), and oversees ongoing covert actions as well as proposed sensitive collection operations. The senior director for intelligence programs also chairs an interagency committee that reviews intelligence policy questions—including sensitive operations—and makes recommendations to the Deputies Committee and the Principals Committee.

As with other senior appointments, the senior director's influence depends on his relationships to the president, the national security adviser, and senior intelligence officials, especially the DNI and DCIA. In some cases, this officer has been largely invisible to the policy process and little known. In others, he can become a key player. For example, George Tenet was the senior director for intelligence policy for Bill Clinton and from that position rose to become deputy director of CIA and finally director. Likewise, President Barack Obama selected former CIA careerist John Brennan, who oversaw the NSC's Directorate of Intelligence, to become deputy national security adviser for terrorism and homeland security. Brennan later became CIA director when Leon Panetta left that position to become secretary of defense.

Since 2003, there has been a greater emphasis placed on having the NSC "drive" the intelligence process. This has meant having senior interdepartmental officials review current and longer-term intelligence-collection and analysis priorities, which are used to allocate IC funds to various programs. This review takes the form of a **National Intelligence Priorities Framework (NIPF)**, which arrays key intelligence targets and topics on separate axes in a matrix format. This then allows senior officials to rank the target and topic cells by a 1-to-5 numbering system. For example, hypothetically North Korea (country target) and "nuclear program" (intelligence topic) might receive the highest ranking of a "1," while Argentina (country target) and "political unrest" (intelligence topic) might only rank a "4." The ranking method allows intelligence agencies then to prioritize—as well as justify—their collection and analysis efforts.

In reality, most NSC principals have little time or patience to review the elaborate NIPF priorities. The list of intelligence issues is almost endless, and the matrix of topics and targets has grown to have over nine thousand individual entries.[45] Thus, the NSC is likely to review the NIPF no more than twice annually. However, the IC leadership led by the DNI will examine it regularly to ensure it is consistent with presidential and other official actions and directives. Naturally, policymakers are inclined to attach high importance to many intelligence problems without realistically weighing the opportunity costs that the IC must incur with its finite resources. Many practitioners have lamented that too many topics are assigned higher priorities than can possibly be serviced. Moreover, any set priorities list can be upset by a quickly breaking crisis that will shoot an issue or a country to the top priority. Most likely, political conditions in Tunisia prior to the outbreak of the Arab Spring had a low ranking, but undoubtedly this was given much more attention as the crisis spread across North Africa and eventually to Syria.

Presidents and their advisers are seldom proponents for major intelligence reforms because they often are focused more on their own policy challenges and less on the effectiveness and efficiency of the IC. Sadly, major reforms are usually the result of major intelligence failures, which generate pressure for reforms. Even more than a decade since the tragedy of 9/11, there continue to be questions regarding the necessity and wisdom of the DNI's creation and its associated moves to integrate the huge IC. As of 2019, however, the necessity for having a senior official responsible for the overall operation of such a massive intelligence enterprise remains unquestionable, even if the job is nearly impossible to perform without periodic clashes within the IC or with senior policy consumers.

USEFUL WEBSITES

Central Intelligence Agency, www.cia.gov
 Offers a huge library of declassified intelligence documents as well as many speeches, testimonies, and reports of CIA officials on major intelligence issues.
Defense Intelligence Agency, www.dia/mil
 Offers the DIA's Latest News reports, which include various unclassified military assessments on Russia and other military adversaries.
Office of the Director of National Intelligence, www.odni.gov
 Hosts the ODNI's Worldwide Threat Assessment testimonies to Congress, special reports issued by the ODNI, a large number of declassified NIEs, and the series of NIC Global Trends reports.

FURTHER READING

James Clapper, *Facts and Fears: Hard Truths from a Life in Intelligence* (New York: Penguin Press, 2018).
 The first memoir by a DNI and relates the challenges of orchestrating such a diverse set of agencies.
Michael E. DeVine, *Intelligence Community Spending: Trends and Issues* (Washington, DC: Congressional Research Service, 2018), https://fas.org/sgp/crs/intel/R44381.pdf.
 Gives an excellent overview of IC budgets, including both the NIP and the MIP.
Richard Immerman, *The Hidden Hand: A Brief History of the CIA* (West Sussex: Wiley & Sons, 2014).
 A brief history with special emphasis on controversies involving covert action and CI.
Rhodri Jeffreys-Jones, *The CIA and American Democracy*, 3rd ed. (New Haven, CT: Yale University Press, 2003).
 An excellent, if critical, history of CIA activities.
Mark M. Lowenthal and Robert M. Clark, *The Five Disciplines of Intelligence Collection* (Washington, DC: CQ Press, 2016).
 Provides a clear and concise explanation and history of the technical, human-source, and open-source collectors.
Jeffrey Richelson, *The US Intelligence Community*, 7th ed. (New York: Routledge, 2015).
 Provides a comprehensive description of the organizations, methods, and operations of the entire US intelligence community.
Michael Warner, *The Rise and Fall of Intelligence: An International Security History* (Washington, DC: Georgetown University Press, 2014).

Covers intelligence history from ancient to modern times, with special attention paid to the IC.

Amy Zegart, *Flawed by Design: The Evolution of CIA, JCS, and the NSC* (Stanford, CA: Stanford University Press, 1999).

Describes the creation of the NSC, FBI, and CIA as a bureaucratic battle that impeded effective intelligence management.

NOTES

First epigraph: Lt. Gen. Hoyt Vandenberg, "Testimony before the Senate Armed Service Committee," April 29, 1947, found in Office of Legal Counsel, *Legislative History of the CIA and National Security Act of 1947*, July 25, 1967, declassified, https://www.cia.gov/library/reading room/docs/DOC_0000511045.pdf.

Second epigraph: James Clapper, in Loch K. Johnson, "A Conversation with James R. Clapper, The Director of National Intelligence in the United States," *Intelligence and National Security*, vol. 30, issue 1 (2015): 6.

1. These figures were cited by former DNI Michael McConnell in 2008. In 2016, the ODNI released the 2016 figure for the National Intelligence Program as $53.0 billion. See ODNI, News Release NR-20-16, October 28, 2016, https://fas.org/irp/news/2016/10/nip-2016.pdf. Simultaneously, the DOD released the official FY 2016 requests for the Military Intelligence Program controlled by the individual service intelligence agencies. See DOD News Release NR-286-16, October 28, 2016, https://fas.org/irp/news/2016/10/mip-2016.html.

2. Rhodri Jeffreys-Jones, *The CIA and American Democracy*, 3rd ed. (New Haven, CT: Yale University Press, 2003), 16.

3. For discussion of the bureaucratic resistance to establishing a new Central Intelligence Agency, see Richard Immerman, "Birth of an Enigma 1945–49," *The Hidden Hand: A Brief History of the CIA* (West Sussex, UK: Wiley Blackwell, 2014), 11–12.

4. Harry Truman, *Memoirs by Harry S. Truman: Years of Trial and Hope* (New York: Doubleday, 1955, Vol. 2), 51–60. Legend has it that when Truman conferred the title of first director of central intelligence on Sidney Souers, one of his close staff aides, he gave him a black hat, a black coat, and a wooden dagger and called him the first "director of centralized snooping." See Jeffreys-Jones, *CIA and American Democracy*, 34.

5. Vandenberg began expanding current intelligence operations by gaining the authority to hire staff rather than borrow from other agencies. See Immerman, "Birth of an Enigma," 17.

6. See Michael Warner, *The Rise and Fall of Intelligence: An International Security History* (Washington, DC: Georgetown University Press, 2014), 140.

7. Warner, 17.

8. 9/11 Commission, *The Final Report on the National Commission on Terrorist Attacks upon the United States* (New York: Norton, 2003), 86.

9. An example of this is the infamous 2003 Iraq WMD estimate's key judgments, which all other agencies largely concurred in, but only the CIA was singled out publicly for having produced flawed analysis.

10. David Thomas, "US Military Intelligence Analysis: Old and New Challenges," in *Analyzing Intelligence: Origins, Obstacles, and Innovations*, ed. Roger Z. George and James Bruce (Washington, DC: Georgetown University Press, 2008), 143.

11. Thomas, 143–45.

12. Office of the DIA Historical Research, *A History of the Defense Intelligence Agency*, 2007, https://fas.org/irp/dia/dia_history_2007.pdf.

13. President Truman signed an NSC intelligence directive on October 24, 1952, creating the NSA within the new DOD. See Records of the National Security Agency / Central Security Service, National Archives, https://www.archives.gov/research/guide-fed-records/groups/457.html.

14. Morgan Chalfant, "Pentagon Mulling Whether Split of NSA-Cybercom Command," *The Hill*, February 23, 2017, http://thehill.com/policy/cybersecurity/320736-pentagon-mulling-split-of-nsa-cyber-command.

15. See Bruce Berkowitz, *The National Reconnaissance Office at 50 Years: A Brief History* (Chantilly, VA: Center for the Study of National Reconnaissance, 2011), 1, 11.

16. Darryl Murdock and Robert M. Clark, "Geospatial Intelligence," in *The Five Disciplines of Intelligence Collection*, ed. Mark M. Lowenthal and Robert M. Clark (Washington, DC: CQ Press, 2016), 124. See also Bruce Berkowitz with Michael Suk, *The National Reconnaissance Office at 50 Years: A Brief History* (Chantilly, VA: Center for the Study of National Reconnaissance, 2018), https://www.nro.gov/Portals/65/documents/about/50thanniv/The%20NRO%20at%2050%20Years%20-%20A%20Brief%20History%20-%20Second%20Edition.pdf?ver=2019-03-06-141009-113×tamp=1551900924364.

17. Murdock and Clark, 124.

18. COMIREX was reorganized as the Central Imagery Office in 1992 and placed within the DOD.

19. Berkowitz, *National Reconnaissance Office*, 15.

20. See Murdock and Clark, "Geospatial Intelligence," 111–54, for a much more in-depth explanation of GEOINT's characteristics, processes, and applications.

21. Murdock and Clark, 131.

22. David Brown, "10 Things You Might Not Know about the National Geo-spatial Intelligence Agency," News and Career Advice, ClearanceJobs.com, March 22, 2013, https://news.clearancejobs.com/2013/03/22/10-things-you-might-not-know-about-the-national-geospatial-intelligence-agency/.

23. See Office of the Historian, United States Military Academy, NGA History, http://www.usma.edu/cegs/siteassets/sitepages/research%20ipad/nga_history.pdf.

24. Mark Stout, "Bureau of Intelligence and Research at 50," *INR*, December 1997.

25. John Prados, "The Mouse That Roared: State Department Intelligence in the Vietnam War," National Security Archive, http://nsarchive.gwu.edu/NSAEBB/NSAEBB121/prados.htm.

26. In 2002, former undersecretary John Bolton is alleged to have threatened to fire INR analysts for publishing findings at odds with his views on a number of issues, which was well publicized during his ambassadorial nomination hearings in 2005. See Jonathan S. Landay, "Ex-State Official Describes Bolton as Abusive, Questions Suitability," McClatchy DC Bureau, April 12, 2005, http://www.mcclatchydc.com/latest-news/article24445810.html.

27. See Harvey Rishikof and Brittany Albaugh, "The Evolving FBI: Becoming a New National Security Enterprise Asset," in Roger Z. George and Harvey Rishikof, *The National Security Enterprise: Navigation the Labyrinth* (Washington, DC: Georgetown Press, 2016), 229.

28. Former FBI intelligence officials will argue there is no official definition of "domestic intelligence" but rather a redefinition of "national intelligence" that includes any information collected anywhere that relates to security within US borders. See Maureen Baginski, "Domestic Intelligence," in *Analyzing Intelligence: Origins, Obstacles, and Innovations*, 2nd ed., ed. Roger Z. George and James Bruce (Washington, DC: Georgetown University Press, 2014), 267.

29. See DEA, Drug Enforcement Center, El Paso Intelligence Center: Intelligence, https://www.dea.gov/ops/intel.shtml#epic.

30. Katie Williams, "FBI, DHS Release Report on Russian Hacking," *The Hill*, December 29, 2016, http://thehill.com/policy/national-security/312132-fbi-dhs-release-report-on-russia-hacking.

31. See Ron Nixon, "Coast Guard Faces Challenges at Sea and at the Budget Office," *New York Times*, July 4, 2017, https://www.nytimes.com/2017/07/04/us/politics/coast-guard-faces-challenges-at-sea-and-at-the-budget-office.html?smprod=nytcore-ipad&smid=nytcore-ipad-share&_r=0.

32. USCG, Publication 2–0, *Intelligence*, May 2010, https://www.uscg.mil/doctrine/CGPub/CG_2_0.pdf.

33. Walter Pincus, "Sweeping Revamp of Intelligence System Drafted," *Washington Post*, November 8, 2001, http://www.chicagotribune.com/chi-0111080259nov08-story.html.

34. For an overview of many intelligence reforms, see Michael Warner and J. Kenneth McDonald, *US Intelligence Reform Studies since 1947* (Washington, DC: Center for the Study of Intelligence, 2005), www.cia.gov/library/center-for-the-study-of-intelligence/csi-publications/books-and-monographs/US%20Intelligence%20Community%20Reform%20Studies%20Since%201947.pdf.

35. For an eyewitness account of IRTPA's legislative history, see Michael Allen, *Blinking Red: Crisis and Compromise in American Intelligence after 9/11* (Washington: Potomac Books, 2013).

36. Cited in Richard Best, *Intelligence Reform after Five Years: The Role of the Director of National Intelligence*, Congressional Research Service, June 22, 2010, 4, https://www.fas.org/sgp/crs/intel/R41295.pdf.

37. Daniel R. Coats, *Worldwide Threat Assessment of the US Intelligence Community: Statement for the Record*, to the Senate Select Committee on Intelligence, January 29, 2019, https://www.dni.gov/files/ODNI/documents/2019-ATA-SFR—-SSCI.pdf.

38. "DNI James Clapper's Statement to the *Post*," *Washington Post*, August 29, 2013, https://www.washingtonpost.com/world/national-security/dni-james-clappers-statement-to-the-post/2013/08/29/52d52090-10e1-11e3-85b6-d27422650fd5_story.html?utm_term=.5fd6ce866caf.

39. Questions and Answers, ODNI, 2010.

40. Robert Murrett, "Issues Confronting Military Intelligence," Incidental Paper, Center for Policy Research, Harvard University, December 2006, http://www.pirp.harvard.edu/pubs_pdf/murrett/murrett-i06–1.pdf.

41. Nicholas Schmidle, "Getting Bin Laden," *New Yorker*, August 8, 2011, http://www.newyorker.com/magazine/2011/08/08/getting-bin-laden.

42. Jeffreys-Jones, *CIA and American Democracy*, 35.

43. Henry Kissinger, *Years of Renewal: The Concluding Volume of His Memoirs* (New York: Simon & Schuster, 1999), 316. He notes this committee was first established in 1948, was in continuous existence under a variety of designations, and reviewed every covert operation undertaken by the US government.

44. Excerpt from Executive Order 12333, ODNI, United States Intelligence Activities, December 4, 1981, https://www.dni.gov/index.php/ic-legal-reference-book/executive-order-12333.

45. Former assistant DNI for analysis Thomas Fingar notes that the NIPF matrix arrayed more than 280 "actors against thirty-two intelligence topics." See Thomas Fingar, *Reducing Uncertainty: Intelligence Analysis and National Security* (Stanford, CA: Stanford University Press, 2011), 51.

5

FROM INTELLIGENCE CYCLE
TO POLICY SUPPORT

America's ability to identify and respond to geostrategic and regional shifts and their political, economic, military, and security implications requires that the U.S. Intelligence Community (IC) gather, analyze, discern, and operationalize information. In this information-dominant era, the IC must continuously pursue strategic intelligence to anticipate geostrategic shifts, as well as shorter-term intelligence so that the United States can respond to the actions and provocations of rivals.

—National Security Strategy, 2017

The traditional intelligence cycle may adequately describe the structure and function of an intelligence community, but it does not describe the intelligence process.

—Robert M. Clark, *Intelligence Analysis*

The preceding chapters have outlined the national security decision-making process and described the large national intelligence enterprise. This chapter will address how intelligence works in both theory and practice by examining the concept of the "intelligence cycle," then dissecting its key components and in the process describing its challenges and limitations. It will then explore a more practical way of distinguishing the separate missions that intelligence performs for the national security enterprise.

As cited above, national security strategies rest on good information. They depend on careful analysis of the international environment in which the United States operates and development of courses of action that can be implemented. Expanding a bit on this "simple" process, there are always difficulties involved. American foreign policies require good information for assessing the international environment, which is not always available. Defining American interests is also a somewhat ambiguous process, as those can change depending on the international and domestic conditions at the time. Even if those interests are clearly defined, identifying the major threats and opportunities to those interests rests as well on good information. And, of course, once those threats and opportunities are laid out, there is the challenge of formulating and weighing the advantages and disadvantages of different policy options. Without accurate information, decision-makers are prone to fail in assessing the international environment as well as the costs and risks associated with their policy decisions. The challenge for intelligence then is in providing the most relevant, accurate, and timely information and analysis in order to give policymakers a realistic picture of the world they face.

THE INTELLIGENCE CYCLE

How does a national security decision-maker get intelligence? Over the past half-century, the American intelligence bureaucracies have developed processes designed to collect, analyze, and disseminate critical information that senior officials can use in making decisions. As mentioned in an earlier chapter, this system is often called the "intelligence cycle." As the US intelligence apparatus has grown, practitioners and scholars have developed elaborate ways to describe this cycle. Graphically, it can be displayed as in figure 5.1.

As the graphic shows, the intelligence cycle suggests a linear process that begins with policymakers ranging from the president of the United States (POTUS) on down laying out intelligence requirements for tasking (step 1) of the intelligence community. These information needs, as discussed in previous chapters, can be expressed in the NIPF rankings as well as many ad hoc requirements from the White House or other senior officials. They can be conveyed during in-person briefings, written directives to senior intelligence officials, or at interagency meetings focused on high-priority policy issues. **Collection** (step 2) will then seek to fulfill those intelligence requirements via the various intelligence disciplines. This "raw intelligence," or unevaluated information, is not yet ready for analysis but often requires further *processing* (step 3). For example, collected communications intelligence usually needs to be translated, and other types of electronic signals intelligence may need to be decrypted and put into a format that is usable by analysts. Raw CIA clandestine reports also have to be reviewed for relevance and validity; this often involves expunging much information regarding the source and determining whether the new information is not only valid and credible but also provides what analysts are seeking to confirm or disconfirm in any previous reporting.

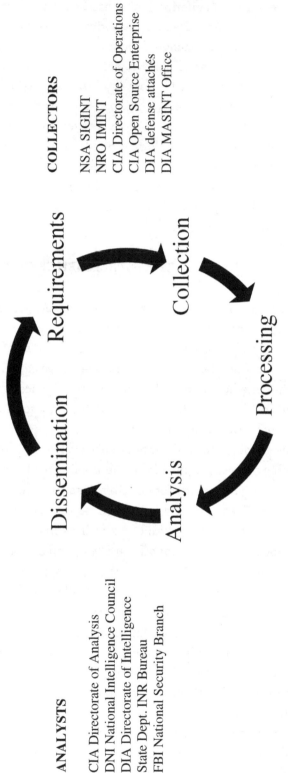

POLICYMAKERS
POTUS
NSC Principals
Departments
Military

COLLECTORS
NSA SIGINT
NRO IMINT
CIA Directorate of Operations
CIA Open Source Enterprise
DIA defense attachés
DIA MASINT Office

ANALYSTS
CIA Directorate of Analysis
DNI National Intelligence Council
DIA Directorate of Intelligence
State Dept. INR Bureau
FBI National Security Branch

Requirements

Collection

Processing

Analysis

Dissemination

Figure 5.1. The Intelligence Cycle

Likewise, open-source intelligence—in addition to requiring language translation—needs to be filtered to root out disinformation or irrelevant reporting. All of this collection is typically **"single-source"** as it comes from one SIGINT, HUMINT, IMINT, MASINT, or open source. All-source analysis (step 4) involves analysts taking all information available on a topic and assessing whether there are important trends, patterns, or relationships among the data points that have significance for US national security. The analytical process may require significant collaboration with collectors for understanding the strength and validity of the reporting. Once analyzed, the findings are *disseminated* (step 5) to policymakers via oral briefings or written assessments in a variety of hard-copy or electronic formats.

Policymakers

Figure 5.1 also highlights the three principal groups of actors in the intelligence cycle. First, of course, are the policymakers who work in the White House, the foreign and homeland security–related departments, the military, and many other parts of the executive and legislative branches. They are mostly involved in the *tasking* of the IC in the form of intelligence needs or requirements. They also will provide *feedback* to the analysis provided them, either by asking for more information, critiquing the analysis, or sometimes challenging intelligence judgments that require further explanation or review by the analysts. The other factor to keep in mind is that many policymakers have sources of information other than the IC. They are in close contact with foreign officials who may represent their governments and policies in ways that do not reflect the IC's assessments. Naturally, policymakers may form opinions at variance with IC analyses, and their own sources may contradict or at least diverge from intelligence assessments. In a few cases, policymakers will consider themselves to be "super analysts" and ask to receive as much raw intelligence as they can absorb without having intelligence analysts put this reporting into proper context. This has a way of undermining the purpose of the intelligence cycle—namely, to carefully collect, evaluate, and integrate all available information into an all-source finished intelligence analysis.

As suggested above, policymakers use a certain strategic logic in making their national security decisions. First, they must assess the international environment to determine what major trends and factors are critical to understand. In many cases, policymakers bring to their jobs strongly held views, partly shaped by their own political ideologies and partly by their own backgrounds and experiences. Each administration will formulate a set of national security objectives based on traditional "national interests" such as protection of the homeland, promotion of economic prosperity, maintenance of a stable international order, and preservation of American values and institutions. In an effort to articulate these objectives, recent administrations have issued a long list of "national security strategies" focused on terrorism, proliferation, homeland security, and even intelligence.[1] Once those goals and objectives are established, then they must assess what threats there are to those interests and objectives as well as what opportunities for advancing those goals exist. Based on these assessments, policymakers will review the types of policy actions (options) that they can use to protect or advance US interests. Typically policymakers will consider a range of instruments—military, economic, political, and so forth—and construct and assess a range of options to achieve them. Depending on how much they cost or the risk policymakers are prepared to run, they will select an option and execute it. Most often, policies take time to have any impact, and some reassessment is likely, depending on whether the policy is having the desired effects. Intelligence plays a critical role in all these steps, in informing broad policy discussions, identifying threats and opportunities, supporting policy options, and evaluating those executive actions.

In their deliberations, policymakers face many challenges in using intelligence. First and foremost, decision-makers crave certainty, but intelligence officers live in a world of ambiguity and uncertainty. Hence, policymakers are perennially dissatisfied with intelligence. As one former senior intelligence manager noted, they can start out highly skeptical of intelligence and then are pleasantly surprised, or they begin with high expectations that are almost immediately dashed.[2] Either way, policymakers want intelligence that serves their agenda. They are generally highly skilled in their own professions and confident of their own analytical judgments. Thus, they are prone to ignore intelligence that conflicts with their views or are at least tempted to skew intelligence judgments to make them fit their own preconceptions.

Second, policymakers have little time for complex issues and want their intelligence boiled down to the one-page summary and "bottom lines." Will China attack Taiwan or not? What's the likelihood of Iran building a nuclear weapon secretly? What will be the next threat to the homeland? Most likely, analysts cannot satisfy these black-and-white questions. Answers like "it depends on x, y, z" or "we cannot confirm" or "there are a range of possibilities" only frustrate policymakers who want **actionable intelligence**. If all intelligence can provide is low-confidence guesses about the future, decision-makers are left to decide how much risk they are prepared to take when there is no certainty that the intelligence is correct.

Third, and related to the previous point, policymakers must usually act before the intelligence is sufficiently detailed or certain to guarantee successful action. As will be explained in later chapters, strategic assessments and warnings must be issued well in advance of a potential event, otherwise policymakers will have little opportunity to prepare for those exigencies. President Obama approved the operation against Osama bin Laden knowing there was a fair amount of uncertainty regarding his location. Only after they were on the ground in Abbottabad could US commandos confirm they had found bin Laden.

Collectors

The second group of actors includes collection agencies such as the NSA and CIA that take policymaker tasking or requirements and translate them into collection priorities and directives for their SIGINT and HUMINT operations. Often decisions have to be made regarding the most relevant, reliable, and rapid methods for answering policymakers' questions. Keep in mind that open-source intelligence is the most readily available, least costly, and least risky in answering many questions. But when "secret" information is required, then senior intelligence officials must determine whether a technical or human operation is needed. In the case of technical intelligence collection, the challenge may be whether a SIGINT or IMINT satellite can access the needed information better than a risky HUMINT operation that puts a CIA case officer and a clandestine source at risk of detection by a foreign government. Collection priorities may also play a role. For a hypothetical example, tasking an imaging satellite to monitor Chinese maritime activities in the South China Sea might reduce the availability of that same satellite system to image North Korean nuclear test sites or perhaps some other activity in South Asia. Collection managers will have to juggle competing collection requirements to best satisfy the most customers. Adjusting a satellite's orbit, collection priorities, or frequency of accessing a particular target is almost always an "opportunity-cost" decision. In the past decade, however, the availability of less costly commercial satellite imagery has allowed the United States to satisfy lower-priority collection needs without compromising coverage of higher-priority topics.

Collection faces its own challenges in providing the best information available to analysts and decision-makers. First, some information simply might not be accessible—that is, there is a **collection gap**. Information on a foreign adversary's intentions is usually hard to come by. If it exists, it is usually carefully guarded by a small number of people. Imagine how few people knew about the 9/11 attack plans being formulated. Sometimes foreign plans or decisions are not fully known even by the adversary. One good example is that until shortly before the Soviet invasion of Afghanistan in 1979, the IC had no indication of such plans; however, it later became known that there was a serious division within the Soviet leadership regarding the invasion that only resolved itself just before the decision was taken. Second, collection is often impeded by an adversary's **deception** and **denial** (D&D) plans. Many US adversaries use camouflage over their military equipment or hide nuclear activities in underground facilities; they also can put out false or misleading information on their plans or activities. Saddam Hussein was able to deceive US intelligence prior to the 1990–91 Gulf War, allowing him to develop a potent WMD capability includ-ing nuclear programs. Adversaries can deny US access to their information by using encrypted communications or couriers instead of telephones or observing other prin-ciples of "operational security" to keep their plans hidden. Overcoming these D&D efforts by adversaries such as Russia, China, and Iran can be nearly impossible. Third, failure to share information among collection agencies can impede their ability to develop a composite picture of an adversary's plans and capabilities. Information not shared might in some cases reveal the deeper significance of additional information held by other agencies. Collectors all have so-called **need-to-know** rules that com-partmentalize their sensitive intelligence to protect sources and methods. In many cases, this need-to-know principle is well placed; however, too much compartmental-ization can withhold valuable data to other agencies. After the 9/11 attacks, a **need-to-share** principle took precedence since it became clear that information held by the CIA and FBI had not been adequately shared. In the wake of the WikiLeaks and Edward Snowden revelations of intelligence-collection programs, the pendulum may be shifting away from a need to share back toward a need to know. All of these factors can contribute to a less than complete or accessible set of raw intelligence reporting.

Analysts

The third set of actors is the analytical community. As described in chapter 4, there are several agencies that have such all-source analysts, who are able to access vir-tually everything the IC collects. The CIA's Directorate of Analysis has the largest cadre of analysts, who regard themselves as covering virtually the entire world. The DIA's Directorate of Intelligence (DI) also contains thousands of specialists in for-eign military intelligence topics. Much smaller in size, the State Department's Bureau of Intelligence and Research is nonetheless regarded as highly skilled and often hav-ing analysts who have worked on their accounts for decades, compared to CIA and DIA analysts, who tend to move from account to account as they advance up through their much larger bureaucracies. Last, the FBI has a large contingent of analysts who work in investigations regarding domestic counterintelligence, counterterrorism, and counterproliferation threats. The IC's analytical tasks are many, but some basic kinds of analysis include the following:

- Trend analysis: Data can be analyzed over time to establish increasing or decreasing trends in a foreign actor's military programs, economic develop-ment, or political stability. Examples include monitoring military buildups or arms races in the Middle East, tracking China's economic growth rates, and assessing the levels of terrorism, corruption, or instability in Afghani-stan and Iraq.

- Pattern recognition: Data can also reveal interesting patterns in military deployments and other activities over time or space. Examples include modeling of terrorism incidents to uncover patterns to their occurrences by their time, locations, or methods. Cyberattack data can be analyzed by type of attack, Internet provider address, and volume to determine an attacker's affiliation or identity.
- Relationship identification: Data can be used to establish whether relationships exist among foreign actors. Examples include link analysis, which uses Internet and phone-call metadata to connect suspected terrorist plotters to other foreign actors. Such relationship analysis can also dissect foreign governments or terrorist organizations to determine key players, their organizational structure, and decision-making processes.[3]

Becoming an intelligence analyst involves developing a range of skills not entirely found in academic institutions. Naturally, a good analyst requires expertise on the politics, economics, and military programs found in key foreign countries and regions, not to mention a host of topics such as WMD proliferation and terrorism. Analysts must also be well versed in US policies in order to understand what policymakers' agendas and intelligence questions might be. More uniquely, the analyst must become an expert in tasking the exotic intelligence-collection systems; this cannot be learned outside the IC but typically is the result of years of collaborating with collectors and even working on an assignment inside those organizations to better understand collection methods and procedures. Perhaps most important, analysts must develop a good sense of their own analytical biases and a set of analytical practices—commonly called "tradecraft"—that can prevent those biases from skewing their assessments. Last, analysts must be good team players, in the sense of working collaboratively on intelligence targets that are multidimensional and require expertise from a range of experts.

Analysts are the critical links between the collectors and the policymakers. In many respects they are the ones who must direct collection efforts to ensure they get the best information possible to answer questions posed by policymakers. And, indeed, the analysts are often in the best position to understand the customer's needs because they are in the most direct contact with the White House, the State Department, and the Defense Department. This puts a premium on analysts' ability to work with the collectors to develop strategies for getting the information needed in the most efficient and reliable way. Analysts must also be sensitive to the strengths and weaknesses of different collection methods (see table 5.1). No single source is likely to be sufficient to answer complicated questions regarding a foreign adversary's plans and capabilities. Analysts must, accordingly, weigh the value that signals, imagery,

Table 5.1. Collection Disciplines: Their Contributions and Constraints

INTELLIGENCE DISCIPLINES	CONTRIBUTIONS	CONSTRAINTS
HUMINT: human reports collected by case officers who run agents in denied foreign areas; also diplomats' and defense attachés' reports	Provides information on a foreign government, foreign officials, or nonstate actor's plans and intentions.	Time required to develop and vet sources. Hard to get access to decision-making circles. Risky to agents and case officers for fear of counterintelligence.
IMINT/GEOINT: imagery and geospatial reports collected remotely from overhead systems; UAVs transmitting live action on battlefields or other sensitive sites	Provides quick graphic display of foreign defense, industrial facilities, and test sites as well as geographically significant physical targets.	Imagery captures only one point in time and is subject to weather/malfunction. Requires proper interpretation that can be difficult if D&D is used.
SIGINT: communications and electronic signals collected remotely by ground sites, aerial, or space-based platforms	Provides voluminous information on foreign government, foreign officials, or nonstate actors' plans and intentions.	Massive volume of material must be decrypted, translated, and identified as involving significant actions/actors.
MASINT: measurements and reporting of changes in environmental conditions via variety of seismic, radiological, and materials sensors	Provides unique insight into environmental conditions (e.g., temperature changes, composition, chemical) surrounding a target.	Hard to evaluate and explain to policymakers. Usually requires unique access to a target and special processing.
OSINT: open sources from foreign print, broadcast, and social media	Provides a baseline understanding of a target that can be corroborated by other sources.	Voluminous material that requires translation and time to identify false or misleading information.

human reporting, and open-source media bring to answering such questions. In a real sense, analysts are performing synthesis of many data points and trying to make sense of that information. Some critics have charged that the 9/11 attacks were the result of analysts not "connecting the dots," a rather simplistic notion that presumes all the dots were available and easily numbered like on a child's coloring book. A better metaphor is that of a thousand-piece jigsaw puzzle for which there is no box-cover illustration; moreover, analysts have to select from thousands of related and unrelated puzzle pieces to begin to make out a pattern or shape.

THE ANALYTICAL PROCESS: A DESCRIPTION

To understand how finished intelligence is produced, a description of the analytical process is helpful. First, the analyst needs to consider which key questions policymakers have.[4] Part of the challenge is determining what senior officials are trying to decide and what they already know about the subject. Close interaction with the policymakers and their senior staff can help determine whether policymakers' background knowledge is accurate or complete; likewise, analysts might need to be prepared for the possibility that decision-makers have preconceptions or biases regarding the answers they hope to receive. A second task is to determine how much information and analysis decision-makers want, what kind of time horizon they might be considering, and also where the policymaker is in the decision-making process. In the latter case, it will matter whether an interagency discussion is only just beginning or whether the broad outlines of a strategy have been set and policymakers are more interested in intelligence focused on an adversary's likely response to US actions.

To take one hypothetical example, consider the kinds of strategic intelligence questions that a new administration might have regarding Iran's nuclear program. The IC might produce a National Intelligence Estimate on the development of Iran's nuclear program, with a time-horizon of no more than four years—as this is the furthest out a newly formed NSC team might be prepared to look. On the other hand, if two years later the NSC team has developed a set of policies for dealing with Iran's nuclear program, it would be looking for more focused intelligence assessments regarding how Iran is responding to those policies, the steps Iran might take to undermine US goals, and the likely consequences of Iran's countermeasures. Thus, strategic intelligence has to be very much tailored to the needs and time frames of decision-makers.

A third step in developing strategic intelligence is to gather, organize, and evaluate the available intelligence reporting on the topic. Having defined the specific set of intelligence questions to be answered, analysts must gather all relevant intelligence information, whether classified or open-source, that bears on the subject. At this point, analysts may well need to generate new requests—officially described as "requirements"—for additional information from collectors. Most **strategic intelligence** topics have an enduring quality so that analysts can expect to be asked to update or amend their assessments over time. Soviet military developments dominated strategic intelligence throughout the Cold War, while counterterrorism, counterproliferation, and now cyber threats are most prominent today. Hence, analysts need to remind collectors of their interest in new information on these and other targets such as Russia, China, Iran, and North Korea.

Continuing with the Iran nuclear example, analysts would task HUMINT, IMINT, and SIGINT systems to collect any information on the state of Iran's nuclear program. Whatever assessment the analyst might produce today, it is likely to be amended in a few months as new information becomes available. As analysts organize and evaluate available information, they also need to be wary of taking each report at face value. Just because reports are classified does not make the information true. Indeed, HUMINT sources are hard to recruit, difficult to manage, and can turn out to be self-promoters, fabricators, or double agents. SIGINT intelligence can require tremendous resources to collect and process but can provide important insights into the motivations and plans of an adversary, depending on the quality and reliability of the interception, decryption, and translation processes. Much of what we know about al-Qaeda and ISIS has been the result of intercepting terrorist cells' communications or capturing computer data, which can contain terabytes of information. Imagery, too, can detect planned military operations or nuclear test preparations of countries such as North Korea, but it also needs to be carefully interpreted; that imagery can be of poor quality or misleading as the result of weather, geography, or an adversary's use of camouflage and deception.

In many cases, well over half of an analyst's information may come from open sources, which also need to be evaluated for their accuracy and validity. Analysts must be alert to the danger that OSINT may be promoting what a foreign government wants the United States to believe. On the other hand, good journalists can sometimes ferret out important facts regarding a government's policies or personalities that analysts can use. In general, analysts need to keep five factors in mind when weighing evidence provided by human sources:

- Accuracy: Is an intelligence report consistent with other data that has been validated as accurate?
- Expertise: Do sources have the knowledge or background to report accurately on an intelligence target?
- Access: Has a report come directly from a source having observed the event, or is it secondhand information?
- Reliability: Has a source been accurately reporting over time, or is it a new source who requires further vetting?
- Objectivity: Is a source motivated by a hidden agenda or personal gain that distorts reality?

After analysts have evaluated the reliability and validity of available reporting, they also have to consider whether the information gathered is both relevant and plausible. Some reporting may appear relevant to policymakers' concerns but be highly implausible. In the case of Iraq's WMD program in 2002, there were rumors but scant reliable reporting that Saddam Hussein was prepared to share WMDs with al-Qaeda; to analysts, it was implausible for the Iraqi leader, who despised and feared Islamic fundamentalism, to give al-Qaeda access to weapons it might use against him. At other times, data may be too incomplete or insufficient to be of much value. In the 1962 Cuban Missile Crisis, for example, among the hundreds of anecdotal reports of Soviet activities, there were fewer than a half dozen credible HUMINT reports that the USSR had placed missiles on the island. Also, the reliability of most of these sources was judged to be very poor as they were uneducated émigrés who knew next to nothing about Soviet weaponry.[5]

A fourth step in the analysis process is to generate key hypotheses that explain the validated intelligence reporting. In intelligence, the facts do not speak for themselves. Rather, they must be organized, evaluated, and put into a framework of some understanding. As analysts sift through the data, they will begin to formulate plausible explanations for what they are observing. For seasoned analysts, they will have accumulated a body of knowledge about the target and can imagine how data may fit into how the target has behaved in the past. Often analysts are looking for patterns, relationships, and trends in the data. They may detect some similarities as well as differences in how the new information describes a target's actions.

There usually is more than one possible explanation that is worth pursuing. Analysts must be alert to keeping an open mind regarding alternative hypotheses, as additional data may confirm or disconfirm their current interpretation. It is wise for them to ask themselves what future developments they would expect to see if a particular hypothesis is accepted. Alternatively, what information might disconfirm the current hypothesis in favor of an alternative one? In 2007, for example, the controversial NIE on Iran postulated a halt in parts of Iran's nuclear weapons program beginning in 2003, which was a major shift from the 2005 NIE. That earlier estimate had concluded Iran was continuing its nuclear activities and was intent on building a bomb.[6] Clearly these earlier hypotheses had to be altered in favor of a more nuanced one—namely, that Iran had curtailed for several years key aspects of its weaponization research program.

A fifth step in the analysis process is making an argument. Having weighed the evidence and developed alternative hypotheses or explanations for a target's behavior or actions, analysts must present findings or conclusions. Those findings—sometimes termed an assessment or in an NIE captured in summary form as the "key findings" or "key judgments"—have to rest on a clear logic and rigorous use of evidence. In most cases, analysts will begin with a strong key message, followed by a succession of facts and reliable intelligence reporting. Analysts must be objective in reporting the **level of confidence** they have in the sources used so that policymakers can independently judge whether they find the argument compelling. Typically analysts will not have *high confidence* in their findings unless they are corroborated by multiple high-quality sources from a variety of collection disciplines.[7] *Low confidence* levels result when there is scant information or the sources are not considered to be fully vetted and reliable. *Medium confidence* often reflects a mixed set of reporting, some of which might be contradictory. Even if analysts have high confidence in a judgment, it is wise to consider including alternative explanations in order to highlight how much uncertainty might still exist in these findings and also to convince policymakers that the analysts considered a range of scenarios that might yet occur if circumstances change.

Analytical challenges are equally as important as those facing the collection agencies. First, analysts must accept the fact that the available information is going to be incomplete, contradictory, and sometimes false. To prepare first-rate all-source assessments, the analyst must be able to deal with a high degree of ambiguity. Seldom will analysts have all the information they want in order to answer a policymaker's questions; at times they will be overwhelmed by too much information, which in itself can make finding what is truly significant even more difficult. At other times there will be huge intelligence gaps because of collection limitations or an adversary's D&D efforts. Compensating or accounting for the so-called missing information in an intelligence assessment is a very difficult exercise.[8] As the saying goes, there are known unknowns but also unknown unknowns that can change an intelligence problem dramatically. To cite only one example, American intelligence analysts incorrectly assessed that the shah of Iran was not in danger of being toppled in 1979 because they believed he would have acted more decisively if he felt threatened. Unknown to analysts at the time was the fact that the shah was deathly ill with cancer (he would die a few months later in exile), causing him perhaps to be much less decisive than he had been previously.

A second challenge is the reliance on **analytical assumptions** and **mind-sets** in formulating intelligence judgments. Analysts often operate on what others might call "conventional wisdom." These are the bedrock assumptions that analysts use to build their intelligence assessments. These assumptions can prove to be either out of date or flatly wrong. But analysts must often rely on assumptions when there is no hard evidence. A classic example of a bedrock assumption that later proved wrong was that Saddam Hussein was deceiving the UN inspectors about his renewed chemical, biological, and nuclear programs. This assumption formed after the Gulf War revealed he had been hiding massive amounts of WMD stockpiles and was dangerously close to having a nuclear bomb. Thereafter, analysts assumed Saddam would be effective in deceiving UN inspectors. So, in 2002, the IC assessment was that he was again hiding WMDs when American collection efforts did not produce much new and corroborated information regarding Iraq's programs (see chapter 6). The point is that analysts must be attuned to their reliance on such assumptions and challenge them periodically to revalidate them.

Closely related to the assumptions problem is the mind-set challenge. Every analyst has in his or her mind an image of how the world operates and in particular how a particular target behaves. These mind-sets or mental maps help to filter information coming to the analysts, who are prone to accepting a report as "confirming" their mind-set or to dismissing it as inconsistent with the ways the target had previously behaved. Analysts need these mental maps to organize their thinking, but they must be careful not to allow them to become out of date.[9]

The IC can be faulted for not appreciating in the late 1980s that Mikhail Gorbachev was a new style of Soviet leader. The USSR had gone through a rapid series of leadership changes as one aging Politburo chairman after another struggled to maintain the Soviet Union's hardline stances vis-à-vis the West. Inside the CIA, there was a debate among military and political analysts about the authenticity of Gorbachev's reforms and whether they indicated a fundamental shift in Soviet thinking. For many analysts, the dominant mental map was of a conservative communist leadership unprepared for radical reforms that might threaten the socialist system itself. Gorbachev's behavior challenged that mental map, and many analysts were slow to appreciate it.[10] Hence, their analysis underestimated Gorbachev's willingness to jettison Soviet practices and positions vis-à-vis the West. Gorbachev subsequently surprised analysts by agreeing to far-reaching arms control agreements as well as to German unification in 1990 and the ultimate withdrawal of Soviet power from Eastern Europe.

Underlying both the assumptions and mind-set problems is the broader challenge of **"cognitive bias."** Scientists as well as intelligence scholars have written about the way the human brain perceives, filters, and integrates information. The cognitive process involves distilling huge volumes of information in an efficient way. Humans develop thinking styles for perceiving the world that enable them to make inferences or draw conclusions rapidly. In a major study, two psychologists termed this habitual cognitive process as "thinking fast"—that is, using mental shortcuts that allow new information to be quickly absorbed and integrated to an existing cognitive map.[11] Such mental processes can cause analysts to make incorrect inferences or to dismiss new information that "doesn't fit." Among the many analytical biases that can interfere with more objective weighing of information, the following are often at the center of flawed analysis:

- **Confirmation bias:** A human tendency to interpret information in a way that confirms existing preconceptions. Analysts will seek out or give more weight to information that confirms an accepted hypothesis or belief, while dismissing or devaluing disconfirming information.
- **Anchoring bias:** Previous analysis prevents analysts from reassessing their judgments and allows for only incremental change in their forecasts. Analysts are thereby "anchored" to those earlier assessments and unable to move away from them.
- **Mirror-imaging:** Analysts presume that a foreign actor would behave much as they would in the same situation. Thus, analysts look at a foreign actor and

see themselves (i.e., in a mirror), disregarding the possibility that in other cultures or political systems decision-makers might behave differently.

- **Groupthink:** Although not a cognitive bias, this group behavior can afflict analysts who work together and strive for consensus rather than seek alternative hypotheses or explanations for information. In large agencies such as the CIA and DIA, there develops an "agency line," which can be hard to shift. The phenomenon is even more prevalent among decision-makers working under great time pressure and stress.

There are a few ways that analysts can work to overcome cognitive and other analytical biases. Most importantly, most CIA and DIA analysts receive some training in the perils of cognitive biases and measures that can be taken to uncover them. They are expected to employ **structured analytical techniques (SATs)**, which can challenge these unconscious biases. While there are dozens of such techniques today, the most often employed and powerful SATs are the following:

- Structured brainstorming: A structured discussion of a topic among a diverse set of experts in which new ideas are actively encouraged and recorded (never dismissed out of hand) in an effort to stimulate new analytical insights or alternative hypotheses. This guards against a single consensus view or groupthink errors.
- Key assumptions check: Early identification of key assumptions underlying an assessment, which are then reviewed to see how much confidence analysts have in the logic and evidence for them. They should also examine what evidence might disprove them. This can uncover hidden biases that are preventing more rigorous weighting of evidence.
- Analysis of competing hypotheses (ACH): Analysts create a matrix of individual data points and information alongside multiple hypotheses for explaining a problem. Then they evaluate each data point to see if it confirms or disconfirms the hypothesis. Information that confirms every alternative is judged less useful than information that can disconfirm all but one explanation. This prevents single-hypothesis analysis and forces more rigorous examination of what reporting is truly significant.
- Scenario analysis: A group-designed technique for building multiple long-term scenarios for complex and highly uncertain intelligence problems (e.g., the future of China), it relies heavily on bringing together a large group of experts with diverse backgrounds and typically developing at least three or four alternative futures based on critical uncertainties. This forces analysts outside their conventional mind-sets and identifies plausible major discontinuities that might occur.[12]

A second remedy to analytical bias is the IC's maintenance of a healthy degree of competitive analysis. This permits different agencies to simultaneously look at information and draw their own independent conclusions. In this way, competing analyses can challenge each agency's use of information and logic. Throughout the Cold War, the CIA and DIA were constantly producing competing analyses of Soviet military programs and budgets, which helped maintain analytical rigor and expose any biases. Similar competitive analysis exists today on Russian, Chinese, and other major military programs. Such multiple advocacy has long been identified as a good check on groupthink or stove-piped thinking found within individual agencies.

A more recent mechanism has been the creation of a number of **"Red Cell"** analytical units within CIA and DIA, where analysts are allowed to develop contrarian analysis (sometimes termed **"alternative analysis"**).[13] The CIA set up such a unit after the 9/11 attacks, and it continues to this day, along with smaller groups operating as Red Cells within individual analytical offices. The notion of Red Cell work involves "thinking like the enemy" (an adversary's Red Team versus the US Blue Team) and using that enemy's perspective in assessing how best to defeat US strategies and actions. These groups are empowered to challenge prevailing lines of analysis, where mistakes might have catastrophic consequences for the United States. More generally, they are instructed to "think outside the box" regarding unlikely but still plausible outcomes that most analysts had discounted. Red Cells have now produced hundreds of such contrarian analysis, using a variety of SATs.

A third corrective is more use of "analytical outreach" that allows nongovernment experts to discuss and challenge intelligence judgments. To some degree, this has always been a practice, when intelligence analysts wished to meet with outside scholars on the Soviet Union regarding its military programs and budgets or regarding the CIA's analysis of worldwide energy production. Selectively, a few cleared outside experts were allowed to review NIEs in draft and provide their critiques. Perhaps one of the best-known and respected outside consultants has been Professor Robert Jervis of Columbia University. In his own writing, he describes his involvement in a number of reviews he conducted of CIA analysis regarding the 1979 Iranian Revolution and the 2002 estimate of Iraqi WMDs.[14]

The 2004 9/11 Commission's report encouraged the IC to engage even more in this type of outreach to guard against its "lack of imagination" regarding terrorist plots. Immediately after the report was issued, there was a surge in outreach efforts and a loosened set of rules for analytical exchanges. Many analysts welcomed this opportunity to interact with academics and other outside experts to sharpen their own skills, develop networks of expertise, and prevent too much insular thinking on their part. Such analytical outreach is limited, naturally, by the IC's "security culture" of classifying and compartmentalizing information. This inherent reluctance to share its views—even in unclassified ways—with academics or other private-sector experts without security clearances still hampers effective challenging of long-held agency views.[15] Rules governing contacts with nongovernment experts can sometimes seem so burdensome as to discourage the less enterprising analysts from attempting to develop such relationships.

BEYOND THE INTELLIGENCE CYCLE:
AN ANALYST-CENTRIC PROCESS

The steps highlighted in figure 5.1 give the impression that there is a logical progression from requirement to collection and processing and ultimately to analysis and dissemination of reporting. That, however, is highly theoretical and seldom reflects the real process by which information in gathered, analyzed, and provided to senior policymakers. In reality, there are any number of complexities that impede the notion that policymakers are the initiators of intelligence collection and analysis. First, policymakers seldom want to invest the time in prioritizing their intelligence needs, although they will routinely ask for additional information in more of an ad hoc fashion. In reality, senior intelligence managers must often identify key requirements based on impressions—if not direct instructions—of presidential and cabinet officials' intelligence needs. Agencies cannot wait for explicit instructions to collect what they believe are essential intelligence data. Analysts are also important in directing collectors to access the information they need to answer key intelligence questions they have about their targets. They do not need the NSC or a senior official to tell them that information on China's military buildup in the South China Sea is important to access, nor do they need to ask policymakers whether they would be interested in knowing more about the cyber capabilities of America's key adversaries.

Second, the notion of a linear or sequential "intelligence cycle" is also very simplistic. Analysts and collectors are working most often in parallel or simultaneously to answer policymakers' questions. Analysts prepare analyses even as collectors are continuing to search for new information on any given topic. A written assessment is only a snapshot in time of what is known about a subject, but as new information is collected, analysts will update, amend, or correct their earlier assessments to fit the newly collected and evaluated information. A good example of this is to be found in the 2007 NIE on Iran's nuclear program.[16] Based on new information, the IC abandoned previous judgments and assessed that Iran had halted a critical part of the program in response to international pressure.

Third, the intelligence cycle also is less a linear process and more an interactive one. That is to say that there is often communication back and forth between analysts and policymakers as well as between analysts and collectors regarding intelligence topics. Analysts often refine their assessments based on conversations with senior

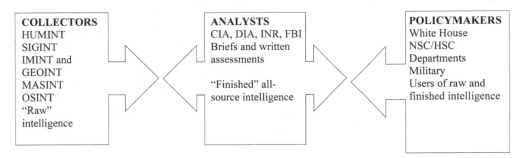

Figure 5.2. Analyst-centric Intelligence Process

policymakers, in order to address their policy agenda more directly; similarly, collectors may alter their collection strategies to fit analysts' views of the kinds of information they need to answer policymakers' questions. Ironically, then, these interactions run the intelligence cycle somewhat in reverse. Indeed, analysts are typically at the center of the process of fielding intelligence requirements from policymakers and working with them and collectors to satisfy their questions. A more realistic, if still overly simplified, depiction of the analyst-centric intelligence process might be what is shown in figure 5.2.

This analyst-centric process highlights how critical it is to define more precisely the kinds of analytical tasks that must be undertaken to satisfy the long list of intelligence concerns by American decision-makers across the government and now including even state and local officials responsible for homeland security. Analysts must be subject-matter experts on countries such as China, Russia, and Iran as well as on transnational threats such as international terrorism, narcotic trafficking, and WMD proliferation. They must also be knowledgeable about US national security policies designed to deal with these issues. In other words, they are expected to know as much about US foreign policy as they are to understand a foreign government's policies. If not, they will not be able to accurately gauge what constitutes a significant development for presidents and their key advisers.

Analyst as Enabler

Today the analyst has the benefit—and the challenge—of understanding a long list of explicit US strategies on security, homeland defense, counterterrorism, and intelligence that have been drafted in the wake of the terrorist attacks of September 11, 2001. The 2010 National Security Strategy goes further than earlier ones in mentioning the critical role of intelligence in shaping American strategies: "Our country's safety and prosperity depend on the quality of the intelligence we collect and the analysis we produce, our ability to evaluate and share this information

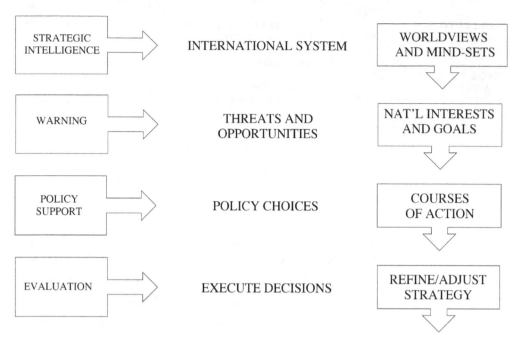

Figure 5.3. Intelligence as "Enabler of National Security Strategy"

in a timely manner and our ability to counter intelligence threats. This is true for the strategic intelligence that informs executive decisions as it is for intelligence support to homeland security, state and tribal governments, our troops and critical national missions."[17]

Likewise, the 2019 National Intelligence Strategy lays out the various missions of the IC, including strategic intelligence, anticipatory (i.e., warning) intelligence, and current operations as critical support to the decision-maker.[18] Figure 5.3 graphically displays how the analyst makes contributions throughout the decision-making process. An analyst who has studied the strategic thinking of key policymakers is in a better position to enable those individuals to improve their performance at each step of the decision-making and policy-execution processes. Seen in this context, virtually all intelligence analysis is strategic, for it seeks to enable policymakers to achieve their goals with the required means. That is, whether the analyst is describing the general strategic environment, providing warning of some attack, merely describing the details of an adversary's military potential or infrastructure, or providing very tactical targeting information, the endeavor itself is in support of an overall strategy to achieve certain specific ends. As shown in figure 5.3, the analytical mission will change as policymakers move from developing an understanding of the problem to defining the major goals for US national security and then designing policy options and implementing them:

- The decision-maker brings to the process a worldview or perceptions about the international environment to the strategy-making process. The analyst brings expertise and analytical assessments to improve the policymaker's understanding of that environment.
- As the president and his advisers define the national interests and the principal threats and opportunities posed by the international environment, the key function of the analyst is then to identify—that is, "warn" of—events or trends that might constitute such threats or opportunities.
- As an administration formulates policy objectives and courses of actions, the analysts support these deliberations by describing the opposing actor's strengths and weaknesses, possible foreign responses to any US course of action, and perhaps unforeseen consequences of potential policy actions— that is, information that relates to the real and potential costs and risks of such policy actions.
- Finally, the NSC principals must assess the effectiveness of their policies and refine or restructure the overall strategy. At this juncture, the analyst's role is to provide an assessment of how adversaries and allies have reacted to US policies, what intended and unintended consequences those policies might have had, and what future actions foreign state and nonstate actors might contemplate to comply with or oppose US actions.

The next few chapters will examine in greater depth these four unique ways in which intelligence analysis can enable effective strategy. The remainder of this chapter will briefly outline their differences to illustrate that intelligence analysis is not a one-size-fits-all proposition. Indeed, the IC must be sensitive to the stage at which American policies are being formulated or implemented. Analysis that focuses too much on broad trends when the strategist is already poised to select courses of action or implement specific policy decisions is likely to be disregarded. Likewise, if a decision-maker does not share the analytical community's general views of a problem early in the strategy-formulation process, then trying to provide policy support can be doubly difficult for the IC.

Strategic Intelligence

The most fundamental goal of both the policymaker and analyst must be to comprehend the strategic environment in which the United States and other friendly and adversarial actors are operating. However, the vantage point of the decision-maker and analyst are very different. Whereas a policymaker such as a president usually comes to the problem with a well-formed set of values, preconceptions, and policy goals, the analyst must attempt to examine the strategic context from a less explicitly American perspective.

In the Cold War, US strategists were both contemptuous toward and alarmed by the communist system. They could see the faults of the system but may have ascribed more ideology to the factors driving Soviet policy than was actually the case. It was the analysts' responsibility to view the Soviet Union in its totality. Hence, the analyst was obliged to assess the limits of the Soviet Union's national economic, political, and military power, the importance of Russian self-interest (vis-à-vis other competing communist power centers such as China), and understand how interest groups inside the Soviet Union (e.g., the party, the military, the government ministries) might be competing or working at cross purposes.

Today, as during the Cold War, analysts must consider the world as it exists, not as one wishes it to be. Moreover, analysts must remain consciously more self-critical than most policymakers; sometimes analysts can become too complacent or overconfident about their knowledge and too resistant to alternative explanations and thus miss important changes in the international environment or in the attitudes of US adversaries. Hence, the analyst must constantly challenge his or her views on an intelligence subject and use different analytical techniques to check whether key assumptions are flawed; information is incomplete, misleading, or flatly wrong; or the known facts about an issue could legitimately produce multiple thoughts rather than a single conclusion.[19]

Informing the policymaker about the changing strategic environment is the most all-encompassing role that the analyst performs. Adding knowledge to the policy discussion is what Sherman Kent described as the intelligence analyst's goal of elevating the level of the policy debate. Many policymakers do not always acknowledge this quiet yet pervasive function of intelligence. But it is one that intelligence analysts perform almost unconsciously in their everyday interactions with policymakers via finished analysis, oral briefings, or telephone and face-to-face conversations. Sometimes providing a different perspective to a policymaker can be the most important contribution to a strategy debate if it can put the decision-maker in the adversary's position or demonstrates that the American perspective on an issue is not the only possible interpretation of the current problem.

The Warning Function

In most cases, intelligence analysts are ultimately—if not always fairly—judged on whether they provided adequate strategic and tactical **warning analysis** of an impending change in the world. For the policymakers, however, the challenge is far more difficult. The policy community must first define what are the enduring American interests, which must be protected—for example, a secure homeland, a democratic way of life, a prosperous economy, access to energy supplies, effective alliances and defenses, and the like—and how American hard and soft power will be used to achieve these goals.

Defining what are critical national interests at a given moment is not easy, nor is it simple to prioritize, choose among, or balance those interests that might at times be in conflict.[20] If, in fact, US decision-makers have difficulty defining what are the most critical US interests worth defending or advancing, then it stands to reason that intelligence analysts will have an equally difficult time determining which issues need to be watched to provide effective warning or—more positively—notification that an opportunity exists to advance an important US interest. A case in point is the recent intelligence findings that indicated the highest levels of the Russian government authorized hacking into the US electoral system. It must be puzzling to intelligence managers that President Trump has dismissed the issue as a "hoax," which might suggest the IC should not prioritize collecting and analyzing information on this. On the other hand, other policy agencies, including the FBI and DHS, as well as Congress seem adamant about getting to the bottom of the issue. There appears to be a division of opinion on whether Russian hacking poses a serious threat to American democracy, putting US intelligence in the middle of this controversy.

In the post-9/11 world, it is now axiomatic that a central mission of the IC is warning of any terrorist attack. A huge national effort has been launched to create large analytical centers to identify and prevent such threats from materializing. Not only is there a National Counterterrorism Center to which many national intelligence agencies contribute, but there also are separate, departmental counterterrorism activities throughout the government, most especially at the CIA, the FBI, the Treasury Department, DHS, the DIA, and the State Department's INR. In this sense, the analysts' mission is clear. However, there is still a long list of other US national interests that must also be protected and advanced, most of which have not been as clearly enunciated as counterterrorism or counterproliferation. How many analysts also should be following and reporting regularly on international human and drug trafficking, illegal border crossings, and organized crime activity that can threaten and potentially kill US citizens? Moreover, are senior officials, to whom analysts might report their concerns, paying attention to these issues?

Policy Support: Analysts' Tactical Role

Compared to the warning mission of analysts, the job of providing intelligence that can support policy actions is far more frequent but far less noticed or appreciated by those outside the decision-making process. The reality is that decision-makers spend far more time on the selection and implementation of courses of actions—that is, choosing policy instruments and determining how to apply them—than they do on their initial assessment of the strategic context and identification of principal threats.

Once policymakers believe they understand the international environment and the principal challenges facing the nation, they are concerned primarily about using the military, diplomatic, economic, and other instruments of power at their disposal.

The role of the analyst, then, becomes one of providing information and analysis that can enable the best tactical application of those courses of action—for example, the imposition of sanctions, the offer or cancellation of foreign military assistance, the threat of military intervention, or the use of public diplomacy. Few writers outside the IC, however, recognize the wide range of analytical contributions to this phase in the policy process, which do not fall into the category of a major intelligence warning or prescient reassessment of an important international development. There are literally thousands of transactions between analyst and policymaker that fall into the category of policy support. These involve the analyst providing bits and pieces of information and insight on a specific policy issue—for example, where a diplomat is trying to determine how best to use an instrument such as a foreign aid package or to construct convincing arguments in a planned conversation with a foreign counterpart or to contemplate possible countermeasures an adversary might take if the United States were to initiate certain actions designed to increase US influence. As Professor Jennifer Sims has argued, this kind of intelligence support is often judged by whether it can give "decision advantage" to US policymakers.[21] What is meant is that timely intelligence can enable American decision-makers to react more quickly and more effectively than an adversary can. Few of these activities are ever transparent to the outside observer. Analysts are being instrumental in providing information, which "supports" current policy objectives, regardless of whether analysts think the policy is correct or likely to succeed.

Policy Evaluation

It would be naive to assume that a president's policies, once set, run their course "automatically" until they achieve their stated goals. As military commanders often say, "No plan survives first contact with the enemy." Likewise, when developing strategic plans, there is the danger that the decision-makers will fall into the trap sometimes known as the "fallacy of the first move"—presuming that the adversary will accept the inevitability of an American action and comply in the ways imagined by its creators. Sadly, the world is far more complex and less predictable than this. Numerous times overconfident presidents or commanders have proclaimed that a stated policy action will be successful and then were shocked by the persistence of an enemy's resistance or an actor's clever response to some US policy action. One thinks immediately of Bush administration officials' claims that only a few Iraqi "bitter-enders" remained, just prior to the onset of the violent Iraqi insurgency in 2005. The analysts' role in the postimplementation phase of strategy formulation is to report back to policymakers on the effectiveness of their actions taken. This role is more feedback rather than forecasting; in this case, analysts are required to draw up "after-action" reporting that can assist policymakers in reassessing or redirecting their policies. Not surprisingly, this is a contribution that is needed but not always welcomed, particularly when it amounts to a failing grade or a less-than-overwhelming success for an American administration. As former deputy national security adviser Leon Fuerth used to muse, "There are no policy failures, only intelligence failures."

Hence, the analyst must tread carefully in providing feedback to the strategist if he or she is to maintain the trust of a president or other senior official. As another former deputy national security adviser, James Steinberg, has noted, a smart policy-maker would be foolish to dismiss analytical evaluations of policy simply because they do not conform to his expectations.[22] However, there are examples of where the policymaker's expectations and the analyst's assessment of a policy action were widely disputed. The long record of IC evaluations of US military policies in Vietnam and American policymakers dismissing them is recorded by numerous intelligence practitioners and policymakers and recounted in later chapters in this volume.

In sum, policy evaluation of all the specific intelligence tasks is most likely to breed distrust between the intelligence and policy communities. As the next chapters lay out, strategic intelligence lays the groundwork for a dialogue about the international environment between those two groups, while warning and policy support are directed especially at assisting decision-makers in formulating and executing effective policies. But where the IC is most likely to encounter problems is when its analysis suggests policies are not working or intelligence is perceived to be undermining a president's agenda. That is where the intelligence-policy relationship becomes most challenging.

USEFUL DOCUMENTS

CIA Analytical Tradecraft Primer, https://www.cia.gov/library/center-for-the-study-of
-intelligence/csi-publications/books-and-monographs/Tradecraft%20Primer-apr09.pdf
    A good summary of more recent analytical methods used to guard against mind-sets and
    cognitive bias.
The Intelligence Cycle, https://fas.org/irp/cia/product/facttell/intcycle.htm
    Gives a description of the intelligence process as a linear process.

FURTHER READING

Robert M. Clark, *Intelligence Analysis: A Target-Centric Approach* (Washington, DC: CQ Press,
    2004).

A good examination of the analytical process and analysts' role in the policy-collection-analysis process.

Donald C. Daniel, "Denial and Deception," in *Transforming US Intelligence*, ed. Jennifer Sims and Burton Gerber (Washington, DC: Georgetown University Press, 2005).

A concise description of the role that D&D plays in complicating US intelligence assessments.

Richards Heuer, *The Psychology of Intelligence Analysis* (Washington, DC: Center for the Study of Intelligence, 1999).

A ground-breaking examination of how analysts are prone to cognitive biases and mind-sets and what measures can be taken to guard against them.

Mark Lowenthal and Robert M. Clark, *The Five Disciplines of Intelligence Collection* (Washington, DC: CQ Press, 2011).

An excellent collection of articles written by practitioners who examine each intelligence discipline.

Douglas MacEachin, *The Tradecraft of Analysis: Challenge and Change in the CIA* (Washington, DC: Consortium for the Study of Intelligence, 1994).

A foundational examination of how analysts must guard against analytical biases.

Stephen Marrin, *Improving Intelligence Analysis: Bridging the Gap between Scholarship and Practice* (New York: Routledge, 2012).

An intelligence scholar's critique of intelligence analysis as practiced in the IC and how social science scholarship might assist in improving the IC's performance.

Mark Phythian, ed., *Understanding the Intelligence Cycle* (New York: Routledge, 2013).

An outstanding collection of articles on the origins, development, and limitations of the concept, which may have outlived its usefulness.

NOTES

First epigraph: White House, *National Security Strategy of the United States*, December 2017, 32.

Second epigraph: Robert M. Clark, *Intelligence Analysis: A Target-Centric Approach* (Washington, DC: CQ Press, 2004), 12.

1. A "national security strategy" refers to the development of plans for preventing a range of threats to the United States, utilizing all elements of national power, including diplomatic, military, economic, and information power. Typically they require coordination among all the national security agencies, such as the State and Defense Departments and the Department of Homeland Security, as well as the intelligence and law enforcement communities.

2. To paraphrase an anonymous senior intelligence official quoted in the CIA monograph *Intelligence and Policy: An Evolving Relationship* (Washington, DC: Center for the Study of Intelligence, 2003), 3, https://www.cia.gov/library/center-for-the-study-of-intelligence/csi-publications/books-and-monographs/IntelandPolicyRelationship_Internet.pdf.

3. For detailed discussion of analysts' model building, see Robert M. Clark, *Intelligence Analysis: A Target-centric Approach* (Washington, DC: CQ Press, 2004), 39–62.

4. The author wants to acknowledge that much of this discussion of the analytical process is drawn from a former colleague's unclassified paper produced for the CIA's Global Futures

Partnership in 2008. See Timothy Walton, "An Intelligence Analysis Primer: Six Steps to Better Intelligence Analysis," Global Futures Forum's Community of Interest on the Practice and Organization of Intelligence, Vancouver, Canada, March 2008.

5. See Sherman Kent, "A Crucial Estimate Relived," *Studies in Intelligence* (Spring 1964): 185–87.

6. Thomas Fingar, chairman of the NIC at the time, described this new estimate in detail in his chapter "Tale of Two Estimates," in *Reducing Uncertainty: Intelligence Analysis and National Security*, ed. Thomas Fingar (Stanford, CA: Stanford University Press, 2013), 89–125.

7. NIEs now contain a scope note laying out what the terms *high, medium,* and *low confidence* imply about analysts' views of the information on which their judgments are based. In the 2007 NIE on Iran's nuclear program, the following statement was included in the Scope Note and repeated in all subsequent NIEs:

  • *High confidence* generally indicates that our judgments are based on high-quality information, and/or that the nature of the issue makes it possible to render a solid judgment. A "high confidence" judgment is not a fact or a certainty, however, and such judgments still carry a risk of being wrong.
  • *Moderate confidence* generally means that the information is credibly sourced and plausible but not of sufficient quality or corroborated sufficiently to warrant a higher level of confidence.
  • *Low confidence* generally means that the information's credibility and/or plausibility is questionable, or that the information is too fragmented or poorly corroborated to make solid analytic inferences, or that we have significant concerns or problems with the sources.

8. On the impact of missing information, see James Bruce, "The Missing Link: The Analyst-Collector Relationship," in *Analyzing Intelligence: National Security Practitioners' Perspectives*, 2nd ed., ed. Roger George and James Bruce (Washington, DC: Georgetown University Press, 2014), 157–77.

9. The best source on the assumptions and mind-set problems is the book by Richards Heuer Jr., *The Psychology of Intelligence Analysis* (Washington, DC: Center for the Study of Intelligence, 1999), https://www.cia.gov/library/center-for-the-study-of-intelligence/csi-publications/books-and-monographs/psychology-of-intelligence-analysis/PsychofIntelNew.pdf.

10. One senior analyst involved in those debates has recounted to the author that the internal CIA debate was won by those whose assessment was largely based on the continued high defense spending by the USSR, which they believed was a reflection of a continuation of prevailing Soviet foreign and security policy objectives. Separately, in the Aspen Security Forum in the mid-1980s, a senior CIA official reflected this military perspective when he told an audience that that nuclear deterrence of the Soviet Union as we know it would be with us for as long as one could imagine. See a description of scenario planning in Peter Schwartz, *The Art of the Long View: Paths to Strategic Insight for Yourself and Your Company* (New York: Currency Press, 1991).

11. Daniel Kahneman and Amos Tversky wrote about common analytical errors made by people in reaching decisions. See Daniel Kahneman and Amos Tversky, *Thinking Fast Thinking Slow* (New York: Farrar, Straus and Giroux, 2011). Richards Heuer Jr. also produced a

groundbreaking book on the role of cognitive bias found in intelligence analysis. See Heuer, *Psychology of Intelligence Analysis*.

12. For a fuller explanation of SATs and their purpose and process, see Randolph Pherson and Richards Heuer Jr., "Structured Analytical Techniques: A New Approach to Analysis," in George and Bruce, *Analyzing Intelligence*, 231–48.

13. Micah Zlenko, "Inside the Red Cell," *Foreign Policy*, October 30, 2015, http://foreign policy.com/2015/10/30/inside-the-cia-red-cell-micah-zenko-red-team-intelligence/.

14. See Robert Jervis, *Why Intelligence Fails: Lessons from the Iranian Revolution and the Iraq War* (Ithaca, NY: Cornell University Press, 2010). Jervis describes his long-standing relationship as an outside consultant and how it enabled him to identify a number of analytical and collection pathologies that are endemic in intelligence failures.

15. For a comprehensive overview of recent academic outreach, see Susan H. Nelson, "Academic Outreach: Pathway to Expertise Building and Professionalization," in George and Bruce, *Analyzing Intelligence*, 319–38.

16. See the discussion of the 2007 Iran NIE in Thomas Fingar, *Reducing Uncertainty*, xxx.

17. White House, *National Security Strategy of the United States*, May 2010, 15, http://nssarchive.us/NSSR/2010.pdf.

18. ODNI, *The National Intelligence Strategy of the United States of America: 2014*, 6, https://www.dni.gov/files/documents/2014_NIS_Publication.pdf.

19. See Roger George, "Fixing the Problem of Analytic Mindsets: Alternative Analysis," in *Intelligence and the National Security Strategist: Enduring Issues and Challenges*, ed. Roger A. George and Robert D. Kline (Lanham, MD: Rowman & Littlefield, 2005), 311–26.

20. Today the homeland security debate often focuses on balancing American citizens' right to privacy against their right to feel secure at home. Equally challenging is proper prioritization of domestic well-being in the form of spending on education, health care, or airport security against defense spending or foreign assistance programs designed to avert failing states that can become havens for future terrorists.

21. See Jennifer E. Sims, "Decision Advantage and the Nature of Intelligence Analysis," *Oxford Handbook on National Security Intelligence*, ed. Loch Johnson (Oxford: Oxford University Press, 2010).

22. James Steinberg, "The Policymaker's Perspective: Transparency and Partnership," in George and Bruce, *Analyzing Intelligence*, 95.

6

STRATEGIC INTELLIGENCE

No matter what we tell the policymaker, and no matter how right we are and how convincing, he will upon occasion disregard the thrust of our findings for reasons beyond our ken. If influence cannot be our goal what should it be? Two things. It should be relevant within our competence, and above all it should be credible.

—Sherman Kent, former director, Board of National Estimates, 1968

The primary purpose of most intelligence estimates is, or should be, to enhance decision maker understanding of complex and potentially consequential issues shrouded in mysteries, secrets and enigmas. The goal is to help them anticipate, abet, alter, avoid, or ameliorate developments that they find desirable, dangerous, or disruptive.

—Thomas Fingar, former chairman, National Intelligence Council, 2011

This chapter will examine the topic of strategic intelligence and how it supports the national security enterprise. It will describe how strategic intelligence is conducted and lays the foundation for other intelligence missions. The key role of the National Intelligence Council and the National Intelligence Estimates process will be used to illustrate the practice of preparing strategic intelligence, although other intelligence agencies also produce strategic analysis. Last, the chapter will examine some of the enduring challenges of such analysis to have impact as well as to ensure its accuracy and quality.

WHAT IS STRATEGIC INTELLIGENCE?

For both the intelligence analyst and the policymaker, the principal concern is the strategic international environment in which the United States and other friendly and

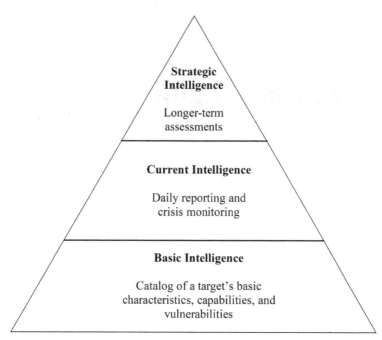

Figure 6.1. Types of Intelligence

adversarial actors are operating. Intelligence analysts' first task is to comprehend the major trends and factors that are shaping the world in which the American government is operating. **Strategic intelligence,** then, is defined as information and analysis that informs policymakers about those critical trends and factors that will impinge on broad and enduring US national security interests. As illustrated in figure 6.1, strategic intelligence goes beyond simply reporting of known facts (**basic intelligence**) and daily events (**current intelligence**). Basic intelligence is best understood as catalogs of known information such as economic statistics, demographic data, and infrastructure and logistics information (location of ports, airports, military installations, power plants, etc.). Current intelligence is the daily production of short assessments that distill the vast flow of diplomatic, military, clandestine, and open-source reporting that comes into the US intelligence community. Because of their time urgency and brevity, current intelligence permits very little analysis of those reports. Yet good current intelligence rests on solid strategic analysis.

In turn, strategic intelligence does rest on the analysts' understanding of both basic intelligence information and an awareness of current intelligence reporting. To be able to produce solid strategic intelligence, analysts must have a good grasp of the basic geographic, historical, political, and economic conditions of their country targets or functional topics. On top of that, analysts must integrate the latest information on their target with past reporting; however, strategic analysis must avoid being driven solely by the current development. Instead, strategic intelligence must integrate that new information with a much larger body of past reporting to form a comprehensive picture of a country's or target's actions and likely behavior. Thus, analysts working on a country or functional subject will build up extensive knowledge about a country—its history, economy, leadership, and politics.

In the precomputer age, a new analyst was sometimes directed toward a large four-drawer file cabinet full of past intelligence reporting on his new intelligence account (e.g., Iran, China, Russia, or ballistic missiles, chemical weapons, etc.). His supervisor would point and say, "Read everything in that file drawer, and then we'll see if you are ready to write intelligence analysis." While this is only a slight exaggeration, the process of becoming a subject-matter expert (SME) on targets such as Iran or North Korea or WMDs could take considerable time. Figure 6.2 lays out the layers of knowledge that a senior intelligence analyst might be expected to achieve in order to prepare strategic intelligence analysis. The analyst must understand a target country's political history, regional setting, and resource potential, which in turn feeds into a broader international environment in which the analyst must understand the existing division and dynamics of power. Factoring in a particular state's political culture, government structure, and leadership styles will then permit the analyst to assess how a particular national leadership will define its vital national interests, develop policy objectives, and utilize the diplomatic, military, and economic power at its disposal in dealing with the United States and US partners.

The first challenge for analysts is to determine what strategic intelligence trends are of most importance to senior policymakers and to gather the best intelligence available to help inform policymakers' discussions and decisions regarding these strategic issues. In wartime, strategic intelligence is obviously focused principally on the opponent's military capabilities, plans, and intentions; even in peacetime, however, strategic intelligence also can often be focused on military issues. Indeed, during the Cold War, strategic intelligence focused extensively on the Soviet military challenge. However, it was never limited to the military domain alone. The CIA and other IC agencies also had to examine nonmilitary factors such as an adversary's economic performance (which can support its military potential) and its political system and leadership characteristics, as those can inform US policymakers on how a foreign adversary might behave or react to American policies.

Like intelligence analysts, policymakers undertake to both understand the international environment and attempt to shape it to the advantage of the United States. Neither is necessarily easy. At times the international environment is difficult to comprehend. Particularly at times of great change, as the United States finds itself today, policymakers are often confronted with difficult questions about how the international system is changing, how power is distributed, and which states are likely to

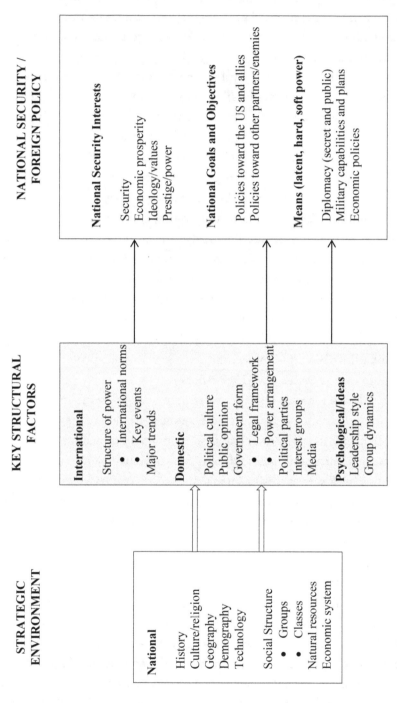

Figure 6.2. Determinants of Foreign Actors National Security Policy

pose the greatest challenges to US interests. At the end of the Cold War, for instance, the IC was focusing as much as 80 percent of its collection and analysis resources on the so-called Soviet target, and it took considerable time to both reduce this preoccupation and expand its global coverage of other issues.

Unlike during the Cold War, policymakers today do not have the luxury or clarity to focus on a single actor or adversary. There are broader, more diffuse trends or factors that may alter the international conditions in which the United States must operate. For example, global climate change is likely to create new environmental as well as geopolitical conditions in which US diplomacy must operate; if scientists are correct, climate change may produce more failing states, humanitarian crises, and interstate conflicts, for which the US will have to develop policies.[1] Unlike intelligence analysts, however, policymakers must go beyond identifying these factors to fashioning strategies and enunciating policies designed to exploit opportunities and prevent or at least reduce the threats that might emerge from changing international conditions.

Informing the policymaker about the changing strategic environment is the most challenging role that the analyst performs, and it can come in many forms. Providing knowledge is what Sherman Kent described in 1949 as the intelligence analyst's goal of elevating the level of the policy debate. Many policymakers do not always acknowledge this quiet yet pervasive function of intelligence. But it is one that intelligence analysts must perform in their everyday interactions with policymakers via finished analysis, oral briefings, or telephone and classified email communications and face-to-face conversations. Sometimes providing a different perspective to a policymaker can be the most important contribution to a strategic decision if it can put the decision-maker in the adversary's position or demonstrates that the policymaker's perspective on an issue is not the only possible interpretation of the current problem.

STRATEGIC ISSUES YESTERDAY AND TODAY

As mentioned above, strategic intelligence is designed to give the policymaker a broad sense of how the international environment operates and which actors and factors are critical to understanding how it is operating. Intelligence gathering and analysis for such a strategic perspective requires a more comprehensive look at the dynamics in the international environment. For example, when the IC was created in the 1940s, the Cold War demanded strategic intelligence focused on the military, economic, and political actions and capabilities of the Soviet Union, its Warsaw Pact allies, and Communist China. Contrast that today with the far greater focus on the global terrorism threat, the economic rise of China, and the proliferation of dangerous WMD technologies and cyber threats. The annual DNI Worldwide

Threat Assessment outlines the top-tier strategic intelligence challenges, and these days that list begins with the transnational issues such as cyber domain, counter-intelligence, Internet manipulation terrorism, proliferation, and more traditional adversarial relations with China, North Korea, Iran, and Russia, just to name the most obvious.[2] Clearly, the international environment has shifted with the end of the bipolar US-Soviet global competition. Nonetheless, Russia remains a strategic challenge, even though it is nowhere near the top of the list of major threats facing the United States today.

So, what is seen as having strategic importance will change, and necessarily US intelligence has adapted its collection and analysis priorities to make sure it can provide strategic intelligence on a whole range of subjects that were unknown or unimportant before the 1989 fall of the Berlin Wall. One way of understanding what has become strategic is to look at the long list of national "strategies" that several presidents have promulgated since 2000. These documents have been issued by the White House or by individual agencies but often include in their titles the word *National* to indicate they reflect a strategic priority that demands high-level attention across the entire national security enterprise. It is hoped that also will carry a high priority for intelligence. Even a short and incomplete list (and accompanying issue dates) would include the following:

National Security Strategy (2017, 2015, 2010, 2008, 2002, etc.)
National Strategy for Counterterrorism (2018, 2011, 2006, 2003)
National Strategy to Combat Weapons of Mass Destruction (2003, 2002)
National Strategy for Combating Biological Threats (2009)
National Strategy for Bio-surveillance (2012)
Strategy for Cyberspace (2011, 2002)
National Strategy to Combat Transnational Crime (2011)
National Security Space Strategy (2011, 2006)
National Strategy for the Arctic Region (2013)[3]

As this only partial list demonstrates, there is a wide range of international issues for which there needs to be broad strategies that can orchestrate the activities of numerous federal (and, in many cases, state and municipal) agencies. These enunciated strategies are the results of NSC deliberations outlined in chapter 3. Many more topics remain in classified channels, so they cannot be discussed as examples here. Nonetheless, these classified interagency studies and decision memoranda are prepared and coordinated by the interagency process. Presidents then approve strategies for dealing with those problems. Many of those documents contain intelligence assessments either as part of the national security decision memoranda or as separate appendices or accompanying intelligence assessments that support the deliberations of the NSC principals.

To provide one example, following the 9/11 terrorist attacks, President George W. Bush's national security team developed a classified strategy for combating WMDs. This National Security Presidential Decision 17 (NSPD 17) directed federal agencies to develop a three-pronged approach to preventing the spread, use, and consequences of WMDs. It also laid out the controversial policy of "preventive" attacks against adversaries who might intend to develop or use WMDs against the United States or its allies. In September 2002, President Bush issued a six-page unclassified version of NSPD 17, which declared that the United States "will not permit the world's most dangerous regimes and terrorists to threaten us with the world's most destructive weapons." This first National Strategy to Combat Weapons of Mass Destruction highlighted the need to orchestrate the use of diplomacy and deterrence, to develop better counterproliferation defenses, and to expand the use of economic sanctions and export controls on sensitive technology. However, equally important, it also emphasized the need for better strategic intelligence: "A more accurate and complete understanding of the full range of WMD threats is, and will remain, among the highest U.S. intelligence priorities, to enable us to prevent proliferation, and to deter or defend against those who would use those capabilities against us. Improving our ability to obtain timely and accurate knowledge of adversaries' offensive and defensive capabilities, plans, and intentions is key to developing effective counter- and nonproliferation capabilities."[4] This is about as clear a statement of the interconnection between strategy development and intelligence support as one can find. Policymakers focused on combating WMD proliferation and potential use—like many other issues—rely on timely, accurate assessments of the evolving strategic environment.

FORECASTING: WHAT DISTINGUISHES STRATEGIC INTELLIGENCE

Strategic intelligence—unlike basic or current intelligence—must be forward-looking and longer-term, so analysts are expected to reach reasoned judgments about the future conditions that policymakers could face. This requires that they **forecast** how the target and/or its behavior might change over time and give some sense of the probability of those changes occurring. This is perhaps the most challenging part of the analyst's job. Sherman Kent once said, "Estimating is what you do, when you do not know."[5] Intelligence is *not* about prediction, but it is often judged on whether it correctly predicts the actions of a foreign adversary. That said, analysts must reduce the levels of uncertainty facing policymakers to the extent possible. Hence, they are usually expected to assign some probability to their judgments—for example, highly or more likely, less likely, or improbable. Whatever the adjectives used by analysts, they are impressions and judgments, not facts. As a rule of thumb, analysts will attach qualifiers—often termed "**caveats**"—to their judgments to imply that an improbable or unlikely event carries a probability of less than 50 percent, while likely or almost certain events carry a probability of much more than 50 percent.

More precision is both impossible and reckless when so many known and unknown factors can influence a foreign actor's behavior. To manage this probability challenge, analysts will also resort to developing alternative scenarios that permit them to rank them in terms of their relative probability depending on which key factors become more prominent in a foreign actor's behavior. In many cases, analysts will distinguish the most likely from the least likely cases based on their understanding of which key factors and forces are most powerful in determining how a target might behave. Among the scenarios, analysts might also highlight those likely to have the most positive or negative consequences for US interests.

To take one example, if analysts were asked to assess the probability of China attacking Taiwan, they might construct several scenarios based on factors such as the nature of the Chinese leadership and the foreign policies of the current Taiwanese government. Analysts would determine which factors might be most likely to generate pressure for one or another scenario, and from those factors there would be a set of **indicators** most likely to accompany increasing chances of one or another scenario. So, for example, one scenario might judge an attack as unlikely, if the Beijing leadership was stable and confident and the Taiwanese government had eschewed any notion of independence from China. However, a second scenario might be judged much more likely if the Beijing was undergoing a leadership struggle between hardliners and moderates, and a new Taiwanese government was toying with the idea of declaring independence. Under the latter scenario, the risk of a preemptive Chinese invasion might be significantly higher, and intelligence analysts would be looking for new evidence (e.g., indicators) in Beijing and Taipei for radical departures from past policies of coexistence.

One of the most critical yet challenging tasks for analysts is also laying out key assumptions used in a strategic assessment. When forecasting the future, there is seldom strong evidence for actions not yet taken by an adversary, so in place of facts analysts must rely on past behavior and patterns. These assumptions, often unappreciated and usually unstated, may disguise potential analytical errors. In 1941, American military intelligence dismissed a Japanese attack on Pearl Harbor in part because of well-formed biases that the Japanese were culturally inferior and did not have the military capabilities or skills to attack the US Pacific Fleet. In 1962, Sherman Kent's CIA analysts largely dismissed Soviet placement of offensive missiles on Cuba because of the assumptions that the Soviets had never before deployed their missiles outside of the USSR and that the Soviets would surely understand that the United States would never tolerate such weapons ninety miles from American shores. Such assumptions should be made as transparent as possible so that other analysts can challenge them and policymakers can decide if they are well founded. In some cases, it is useful to allow a diverse set of outside experts to review intelligence assessments because they will often bring a different perspective and set of assumptions regarding a topic and thus are then able to quickly identify and challenge the intelligence analysts' assumptions.

WHO DOES STRATEGIC INTELLIGENCE?

Strategic intelligence comes in a variety of forms from a diverse set of producers. Customarily, strategic intelligence products have been focused largely on future or longer-term problems as opposed to current intelligence, which is principally reporting on what is happening today. This distinction has blurred a bit as many decisions taken by the president and the national security team regarding a current problem will have strategic and longer-term implications. That said, the traditional format for strategic intelligence is the National Intelligence Estimate and other products that reflect the views of the sixteen intelligence agencies. In the 1950s, the director of central intelligence created an Office of National Estimates (ONE), which comprised senior analysts from the CIA who wrote these assessments on behalf of the entire IC.

The most influential director of the ONE was Professor Sherman Kent, a Yale academic who had been recruited into the OSS during World War II and later joined the newly formed CIA in 1950 to lead the new estimates process. Under his leadership, the ONE became the most authoritative intelligence group within the US government. It recruited some of the leading academics from Ivy League universities along with professional military, diplomatic, and intelligence officials.[6] Kent largely conflated "strategic" intelligence with "national" intelligence, by which he meant it had to go beyond the usual departmental intelligence produced by one agency for its own narrow list of consumers. This gave the large ONE staff and its smaller Board of National Estimates (BNE) experts an elevated status beyond the analytical staffs found in the military services or even in other parts of the CIA.[7] The ONE, with its BNE, continued to operate until the early 1970s, but it had become too "academic" and out of touch with real policy issues in the eyes of many. CIA director William Colby replaced that organization with the NIC and its group of national intelligence officers in an effort to tie strategic intelligence closer to policy.

Even though the ONE was the principal body for providing strategic intelligence to the president and the NSC in the early days of the IC, naturally the CIA, the DIA, and even INR were also producing their own strategic intelligence products. Early in the Cold War, the CIA organized its analysts into groups with different functions; one large group was the Office of Strategic Research (OSR), and the other was the Office of Current Intelligence. The former focused on broad questions of Soviet military and scientific developments. This is where much of the analysis of the USSR's military programs was conducted, including ballistic missile developments, nuclear programs, and their strategic doctrines that guided their use of military force. These analysts were producing a wide range of CIA assessments used by the Department of Defense but also valuable to senior civilian leaders trying to understand how the Soviet military planned to use nuclear weapons, how the Kremlin thought about war, and what strategic plans the Soviets had for expanding their sphere of political and military influence in Europe and Asia. Complementing this work on strategic military questions, the CIA's then Office of Economic Research developed the best models of the Soviet economy's performance, its growth rates, and, importantly, the extent of the defense burden on the Soviet economy. These CIA analysts were also regularly participating in the preparation of NIEs and might be the principal estimate drafters if they were among the IC's recognized experts.

At the same time, the DIA maintained its own cadre of senior military analysts who focused on Soviet military power and its capabilities vis-à-vis the United States. Within the DIA, there was a Directorate of Estimates, where longer-term estimates of missiles, tanks, planes, and ships were developed. Those military estimates became part of the broader IC's development of NIEs. Over the years, disagreements between DIA and CIA analysts over the size and growth rates of Soviet military programs and budgets were quite controversial and heated. In a somewhat simplistic sense, defense intelligence analysts tended to see the Soviets as "ten feet tall," while civilian intelligence analysts at the CIA and elsewhere tended to see a smaller and more backward Soviet military threat.[8] Disputes over the Soviet strategic capabilities and intentions persisted throughout the 1970s and 1980s, when very elaborate studies of Soviet weapon systems and military doctrine were deemed critical to whether the United States could deter and survive a Soviet nuclear attack. Those assessments also played a key part of the debate of the 1970s strategic arms control agreements negotiated by President Richard Nixon and National Security Adviser Henry Kissinger (discussed in more detail in a later chapter).

The State Department's INR bureau never had the staff to support a large-scale intelligence-estimate effort. Nonetheless, it would periodically prepare its own longer-term assessments that could be considered of strategic and national interest. INR analysts were also drafters of NIEs on occasion, when the bureau had an outstanding expert on the estimate's topic. INR's own all-source analysts were just as able to use intelligence reporting from all national collectors as CIA and DIA analysts could, and sometimes they could produce alternative views on major issues regarding Soviet strategic intentions or prospects for success in Vietnam; in the latter case, INR's pessimistic forecasts proved to be much more accurate than many of those produced by other intelligence agencies.

THE NATIONAL INTELLIGENCE COUNCIL

Today strategic intelligence continues to be produced both within individual agencies as well as in the NIC. Because of its historical roots in the ONE, the NIC retains its status as the IC's premier strategic intelligence producer. As laid out in the 2004 IRTPA, the NIC "shall be composed of senior analysts within the intelligence community and substantive experts from the public and private sector . . . [and] the members of the National Intelligence Council shall constitute the senior intelligence advisers for the purposes of representing the views of the intelligence community within the United States Government."[9]

The NIC is currently made up of roughly one hundred experts and support staff spread across the global set of strategic intelligence priorities of the US government. The NIC chairman oversees the work of roughly a dozen or more national intelligence officers, who cover major regional areas as well as critical functional topics. The chairman is either a very senior intelligence official or often a highly regarded academic or former policymaker. Some recent chairmen have included Professor Joseph Nye of Harvard University, Dr. Gregory Treverton from the RAND Corporation, and Christopher Kojm, who served as former staff director of the 9/11 Commission; all had served previously in senior policy positions and were thus uniquely placed to work closely with counterparts in the NSC, the State Department, and the Defense Department. The council itself comprises the NIOs, their deputy NIOs, and a Long-Range Assessments Group, which prepares a range of NIC products. A snapshot of the NIC's organization would include NIOs for the following regional and functional areas:

- Regional: Africa, Asia, Europe, Western Hemisphere, Near East, Russia/Eurasia, and South Asia
- Functional: WMDs, cyber threats, transnational threats (e.g., terrorism), global economics, technology

The NIC has distinguished itself by containing a diversity of experts with varied military, diplomatic, academic, or private-sector backgrounds. As one former NIC chairman pointed out, the NIC attracted senior CIA and DIA officers but also experts from other IC agencies, the Federal Reserve, the West Point faculty, and prestigious think tanks.[10] As he put it, the NIC "wanted officers who were widely recognized inside and outside government, and respected for their expertise."[11] The NIO's job was not only to be a substantive expert but also a leader of the community of analysts and a bridge to the policy world. An NIO was responsible for representing the IC's collective views on international topics, not primarily their personal judgments. As such, NIOs usually attended the interagency policy committee meeting on their respective areas and were often the plus one supporting the DNI's participation at the Principals Committee meetings. NIOs meet regularly with senior NSC, State Department, and Defense Department officials to brief them on community intelligence assessments and to develop an intelligence research agenda that suits their needs.

In most cases, NIOs would propose topics for NIEs and other NIC products based on their understanding of policymakers' needs. Alternatively, senior policymakers or even congressional committees can request a national estimate. It is then the NIC's and NIOs' responsibility to prepare those along the lines and timetable of the requestors. The NIOs are responsible for developing outlines (called a "terms of reference") for each project, assign and manage the drafting of the assessments, lead interagency "coordination" sessions of analysts that reviewed and revised the drafts, and then edit and finalize those products. At the end of the process, the NIO would present the estimate for review by the National Intelligence Board (NIB), comprising the heads of all IC agencies and chaired by the DNI. This would be the final step when any amendments or dissents to the NIE would be considered.

As of 2005, the NIC became part of the Office of the Director of National Intelligence and now reports directly to the DNI. In his capacity as head of the IC, the DNI would approve all NIEs produced by the NIC. While policymakers recognize the NIE as the most authoritative product by the IC, it is by no means the most widely read or popular NIC publication. Typically NIEs involve the most exhaustive drafting and review process, often taking weeks if not months. Historically, the NIEs tended to be lengthy, detailed studies that could run into tens if not hundreds of pages or even several volumes, depending on the complexity of some technical topics such as weapon technologies. In some cases, policymakers were not prepared to read such documents, so the NIOs have often resorted to quicker memos—called "sense of the community memoranda"—that are more focused on current priority issues and did not require the lengthy review by the DNI and other IC chiefs. One recent example of such an interagency memo was the January 2017 Intelligence Community Assessment titled "Assessing Russian Activities and Intentions Regarding Recent US Elections."[12] These products, combined with individual NIO memos prepared for specific policy consumers, have totaled more than seven hundred publications annually.[13] Moreover, recent NIC chairmen have dictated that NIEs should be no longer than twenty pages in length, with a three-page "Key Judgments" (major conclusions) preface. This is all designed to make the NIEs themselves more useful and increase the likelihood that busy policymakers will actually read the products.

NIES: PROCESS AND PRODUCTS

Producing authoritative strategic intelligence depends on having a deep bench of senior analysts within the IC who can provide insight into significant long-term problems. It also requires a rigorous process of shifting through past assessments on those topics, assessing the new trends and developments, and developing a forecast of what the problem might look like anywhere from six months to several years into the future. That process includes weighing past reporting against new reporting and ensuring that all the perspectives of IC agencies are represented. The results come in a variety of forms, from the NIE, to more focused interagency products and NIO memoranda, to the elaborate and multiyear projects now known as the Global Trends series.

Process

The NIE is considered the most authoritative form of strategic intelligence because it has the most time-consuming and senior-level review of all IC products. The typical NIE is often the result of senior policymaker interest in a subject on which decisions must be made or an NIO having determined that such an NIE may be needed either to review past judgments made on a priority subject or to anticipate decisions that might be made by the policy community. Often the focus of an NIE is derived from interactions between the NIO and his counterparts at the NSC, the State Department, and the Defense Department. Once the topic is agreed on, the NIO will chair an IC-wide meeting of experts to develop an outline focused on the key questions that the NIE is designed to address. NIOs will assign drafting responsibility to one or more analysts from the CIA, the DIA, INR, and so forth, and he or his deputy NIO will oversee the drafting process and act as a first-level reviewer and editor. Once a draft is prepared, the NIO will circulate the NIE draft among the IC agencies for comment, using that feedback to revise it. Most NIEs require several face-to-face meetings—part of the **coordination process**—at which analysts representing their agencies will review the draft line by line; this can be an exhausting day- or weeklong process, depending on the complexity and scope of the NIE. Despite the term *coordination*, the experience can be both frustrating and not entirely collegial.

At the end of the day, the NIO will determine if there is consensus on the subject or whether further review and some "dissents" are needed to capture the difference of opinion among the agencies. In the past, NIEs were often written as consensus documents, with minor footnotes inserted when an agency disagreed on particular points; they would appear at the bottom of the page and identify those agencies dissenting and a brief discussion of their reasons. In the post-Iraq-WMD era, however, such disagreements are highlighted in the text, allowing individual agencies to lay out in more detail why their judgments differ and whether they believe the evidence is available to support the majority's line of argumentation.

Today senior NIC officials are averse to minimizing differences in the interest of consensus; rather, the emphasis is on "clarity" in each agency's views. Importantly, each agency gets a vote, and directors of those agencies will have to ultimately confirm their approval at the final NIB meeting on the paper. This process, instituted since the flawed 2002 Iraq WMD estimate, is designed to force agencies to review in a zero-based fashion their previous judgments on a subject and stand by those views before it can be approved and disseminated by the DNI. At that final NIB meeting, not only do agency heads need to confirm their agreement to the judgments but collection agencies must also review the use of their source material and confirm that they are confident in that information's validity and use in the NIE. All of this is designed to connote as much authority and responsibility for an NIE's accuracy as can be expected.

Estimative Products

NIEs come in all shapes and sizes. In the Cold War era, it was not unusual for estimates on Soviet strategic nuclear forces to run into several volumes of several hundred pages each. They truly were strategic research of the most basic kind. Those estimates on Soviet strategic forces were given the series designation of "NIE 11-3/8" (see excerpt in box 6.1) and were an annual exercise that was used by the Defense Department to size US strategic forces and develop strategic plans to deter any plausible Soviet nuclear strike. Based on those estimates, US policymakers developed a nuclear triad of American land-based, sea-based, and airborne delivery systems to complicate any Soviet temptation for "first strike." Those estimates also became controversial in the 1970s, when President Nixon and National Security Adviser Kissinger were promoting détente and signed the first major Strategic Arms Limitation Talks (SALT) agreement with the USSR. Disagreements between the CIA and DIA on future Soviet force projections led to later charges that the CIA had politicized its lower force projections to fit Kissinger's détente policies; outside critics attacked those estimates, claiming CIA analysts were prone to "best-casing" Soviet programs by assuming Moscow was content on parity rather than superiority in strategic forces.[14]

Those days of lengthy NIEs and long, drawn-out disagreements over Soviet strategic doctrine and forces are long past. Estimates run the gamut from very short and focused on a narrow question of a foreign government's survivability to longer-term prospects of threats to the US homeland. There has been a steady stream of shorter

---

**Box 6.1   *Soviet Forces for Intercontinental Attack*
(Key Findings)**

The intercontinental attack forces considered in this paper include intercontinental ballistic missiles (ICBMs), submarine-launched ballistic missiles (SLBMs) and heavy bombers. In the course of the past 10 years, the Soviets have engaged in a vigorous and costly buildup of these elements of their military establishment. While all defense spending increased during the period, the estimated share allocated to these forces doubled, going from about 5 percent in 1960 to more than 10 percent in the later years of the decade. The 1969 level—an estimated 2.3 billion rubles (the equivalent of $5.6 billion)—was more than three times as high as the 1960 level. For the decade as a whole, spending on intercontinental attack forces accumulated to about 16 billion rubles (about $36 billion) with ICBMs accounting for 80 percent of this amount. . . .

As a result of this effort, the Soviets had on 1 October 1970 an estimated 1,291 operational ICBM launchers at operational ICBM complexes, and they will have an estimated 1,445 launchers operational by mid-1972. . . . Of the 1,445 ICBM launchers estimated to be at operational complexes by mid-1972, 306 probably will be of the large SS-9 type and 850 the smaller SS-11. . . .

In the early 1960s, the Soviet leaders, politically and ideologically hostile to the US, and thinking and behaving as rulers of a great power, perceived that in this particular respect their military forces were conspicuously inferior to those of their most dangerous rival, the US. Consequently, they set themselves to rectify the imbalance—to achieve at a minimum a relation of rough parity. Parity in this sense cannot be objectively measured; it is essentially a state of mind. Such evidence as we have, much of it from the strategic arms limitation talks, indicates that Soviet leaders think that they have now achieved this position, or are about to achieve it, at least in respect to weapons of intercontinental range.

Source: Declassified excerpts from NIE 11-8-70 found in CIA, *Intentions and Capabilities: Estimates on Soviet Strategic Forces, 1950–1983* (Washington, DC: Center for the Study of Intelligence, 1996), 263–67.

NIEs estimating the prospects for stability in such hot spots as Afghanistan and Iraq that become part of the NSC interagency discussions on US strategies toward those conflicts. One example of this is the January 2007 NIE on the prospects for Iraq (see box 6.2), which was one major contribution to the decision about how to "surge" American forces to defeat the Sunni insurgency.

Seeing a deteriorating security situation, well documented in the NIE, President George W. Bush simultaneously announced a new strategy that increased US forces in Iraq by twenty thousand troops and embedded them in the Iraqi Security Forces, which the NIE had also identified as a major weak point. This estimate was quickly followed by several others, which updated the IC's judgments on how well the surge was working and whether progress was being made. In August 2007, for example, the NIC disseminated an updated NIE titled *Prospects for Iraq's Stability:*

Box 6.2 Excerpts from January 2007 NIE *Prospects for Iraq's Stability: A Challenging Road Ahead*

Key Judgments

Iraqi society's growing polarization, the persistent weakness of the security forces and the state in general, and all sides' ready recourse to violence is collectively driving an increase in communal and insurgent violence and political extremism. Unless efforts to reverse these conditions show measurable progress during the term of this estimate, the coming 12 to 18 months, we assess that the overall security situation will continue to deteriorate at rates comparable to the latter part of 2006. If strengthened Iraqi Security Forces (ISF), more loyal to the government and supported by Coalition forces, are able to reduce levels of violence and establish more effective security for Iraq's population, Iraqi leaders could have an opportunity to begin the process of political compromise necessary for longer term stability, political process and economic recovery.

- Nevertheless, even if violence is diminished, given the current winner-take-all attitude and sectarian animosities infecting the political scene, Iraqi leaders will be hard pressed to achieve sustained political reconciliation in the time frame of this Estimate.

A number of identifiable developments could help to reverse the negative trends driving Iraq's current trajectory. They include:

- **Broader Sunni acceptance of the current political structure and federalism . . .**
- **Significant concessions by Shia and Kurds . . .**

A number of identifiable internal security and political triggering events, including sustained mass sectarian killings, assassination of major religious and political leaders, and a complete Sunni defection from the government have the potential to convulse severely Iraq's security environment.

Note: Bold and italics in original.
Source: Office of the Director of National Intelligence, *National Intelligence Estimate: Prospects for Iraq's Stability; A Challenging Road Ahead*, January 2007, https://www.fas.org/irp/dni/iraq020207.pdf.

Some Security Progress but Political Reconciliation Elusive, a title that suggested mixed success for the US strategy. This update used the January NIE as a "baseline" and examined prospects for security and national reconciliation for the next six to twelve months.[15]

Naturally, other NIEs have focused on the terrorist threat to the homeland. Also in 2007, the NIC produced a major NIE titled *The Terrorist Threat to the US Homeland*, which judged that the United States would face a "persistent and evolving terrorist threat over the next three years." In this estimate, the IC experts judged that "greatly increased counter-terrorism efforts over the past five years have constrained the ability of al-Qaida to attack the US homeland again and have led terrorist groups to perceive the homeland as a harder target to strike than on 9/11." Like other forward-looking NIEs, it forecast the "likely spread of radical—especially Salafi—Internet sites, increasingly aggressive anti-US rhetoric and actions, and a growing number of radical, self-generating cells in Western countries, indicating that the radical and violent segment of the West's Muslim population is expanding, including in the United States."[16] Again, these kinds of assessments bolstered the Bush administration's confidence that its efforts to combat terrorism abroad and tighten surveillance and border security at home were working, yet it also put Washington decision-makers on notice that radical Islamic extremism was spreading. Subsequent ISIS-inspired attacks in Europe and even the United States confirmed that al-Qaeda was not the only group that threatened US security.

Global Trends: An Atypical Strategic Assessment

A final example of relevant strategic intelligence is the NIC's practice of publishing a major unclassified report that amounts to a very speculative "estimate of the world." Its Global Trends series of strategic assessments discusses how key trends and uncertainties might shape the world over the next five to twenty years. It is designed to help policymakers consider longer-term developments as they develop their current strategies and policies. These publications are unlike almost every other intelligence product. First, unlike other NIC products, the Global Trends documents do not rely on secrets or classified information. To state the obvious, there is next to no classified information that focuses on the future as far out as twenty years. Second, the preparation of a Global Trends paper is not restricted to intelligence analysts and agencies alone. It is also not the result of the customary coordinated IC-drafting process. Rather, the NIC engages with a wide range of American and foreign experts on a wide range of topics that go well beyond what is normally considered a national security or intelligence topic. For instance, the Global Trends documents regularly assess the state and future impact of factors such as demographics, energy, climate change, biomedical advances and health, financial and business trends, and information technology. That requires the NIC to engage with anthropologists, sociologists, demographers, epidemiologists, and technologists as well as the usual security experts.

Last, unlike any other intelligence product, the Global Trends series has increasingly brought the "US role" into its speculative analysis. As is well understood, American intelligence analysts customarily do not analyze the United States, as their mission is to focus on foreign policy developments. However, when the United States is such a central actor and has such a huge influence over foreign adversaries' and allies' policies and behaviors, it is almost impossible not to consider how Washington's actions would shape other actors' future actions. So, Global Trends has made consideration of the US role one of the major "game changers," particularly now as it seems to be in a state of flux.[17] Also, including foreign participants' perceptions of current American policies is particularly relevant to the construction of provocative speculation about the future.

The NIC has now produced five editions of Global Trends, timing them to be available to each new administration as it takes office in January. The principal drafters commission studies by various think tanks and experts, schedule a series of conferences on multiple continents, and post online their preliminary reports and drafts for invited specialists to critique. The intent is to generate a variety of perspectives on what are the most significant known factors shaping the world today and tomorrow, as well as to highlight key uncertainties that might radically alter the current geopolitical environment. The result has been a series of thought-provoking and groundbreaking papers. For example,

- In 1997, *Global Trends 2010* forecast that the postwar international order was ending, leading to three major significant trends: conflicts would be largely internal, not state-to-state; weak states would fail, resulting in ethnic conflict and refugee flows; and even major powers would lose some control over their destinies by virtue of the advancing globalization process and technological revolution.
- In 2001, *Global Trends 2015: A Dialogue about the Future* highlighted global drivers of change (such as demographic trends, natural resources, globalization, and even the role of the United States) and described plausible alternative futures to describe the range of outcomes possible under very uncertain conditions.
- In 2004, *Global Trends 2020: Mapping the Global Future* deepened the practice of combining key uncertainties such as globalization and governance and presented fictional scenarios. A "Davos World" foresaw challenges in sustaining globalization's positive aspects, "Pax Americana" examined whether the American unipolar moment could continue, "A New Caliphate" illustrated the impact of new identity politics, and "Cycle of Fear" captured a perfect storm of WMD proliferation, international terrorism, and global power shifts.
- In 2008, *Global Trends 2025: A Transformed World* foresaw a multipolar world, with China, India, Brazil, Iran, and, perhaps, a resurgent Russia emerging as power blocs in contest with the United States. Postwar international institutions would no longer be effective or be seen as legitimate by newly rising powers, suggesting that major changes in the global order are needed.
- In 2012, *Global Trends 2030: Alternative Worlds* identified "megatrends" and "game-changers" (which includes the US role in the world) that could create four quite different scenarios. Increased empowerment, widely available technologies, more diffusion of power among nations, and urbanization

and youth bulges in less-developed countries could produce some very challenging international conditions. The paper further identified a dozen key emerging and disruptive technologies and their impact on world conditions.

With each new publication, the Global Trends series has experimented with different forms of consultation with the incoming national security team as well as with outside experts and use of online social media. These unclassified assessments had surprising impact on policymakers both in Washington and around the world. New administrations received these papers well in advance of their formal publication, and often they included some of the Global Trends thinking in the preparation of their own National Security Strategy documents. Former NIC chairman Thomas Fingar also noted that by involving hundreds of foreign participants in the preparation of the papers, it built up interest in using the publications in their own governments and translating the findings into foreign languages. Several North Atlantic Treaty Organization (NATO) allies adopted or echoed some of the findings and also began their own "futures" projects.[18]

The most recent version, *Global Trends: Paradox of Progress* (2017), is perhaps the most ambitious strategic analysis conducted by the NIC. It was a two-year process of commissioning outside research and testing assumptions and themes, with more than two thousand participants in thirty-five countries. Breaking new ground, it went beyond the customary think-tank experts and foreign officials to include focus groups with students, women's groups, and entrepreneurs in a number of countries. Unlike past Global Trends, this one focused on both a five-year and twenty-year time frame, believing that it would engage policymakers more to see the kinds of projections that might actually impact their policies and priorities as well as stimulate their thinking about how those same policies might shape the longer-term future. The paper laid out three key scenarios, summarized below, built on a set of key trends and implications outlines in the paper, shown in box 6.3. The three scenarios—described as "Islands," "Orbits," and "Communities"—are the result of responses made by key governments and other international actors to the near-term volatility projected to occur:

- *Islands* is a major restructuring of the global economy of slow or no growth that challenges states' responses to societal demands for both physical and economic security, where popular rejection of globalization and emerging technologies transform work and trade. Governments adopt protectionist policies and reduce support for multilateral cooperation.
- *Orbits* is a world of competing major powers seeking spheres of influence while maintaining stability at home, driven by rising nationalism, disruptive

technologies, and evolving forms of conflict that reduce global cooperation. It foresees possible use of nuclear weapons, which forces international stakeholders to rethink their actions.

• *Communities* reflects a world in which declining state capacity makes room for local governments and private nonstate actors to build networks of cooperation, even in the face of national government resistance. It imagines how information technology becomes a key enabler for companies, advocacy groups, and local governments to effectively deliver services and build support for their agendas.[19]

Admittedly, the Global Trends series is not a coordinated, classified NIE that has the gravitas of being endorsed by the ODNI and other heads of US intelligence agencies. However, it has introduced a new type of strategic analysis that is closer to being a "net assessment" of the interaction of US policies with the actions of foreign governments and future trends that the IC can imagine, although not predict. The NIC makes no apologies for "getting some things wrong" in terms of its projections, although it does conduct a self-review in preparation for each new project. Necessarily, such strategic speculation must be caveated as not representing the official views of the IC. Moreover, despite foreign experts' appreciation for inclusion in these Global Trends exercises, many are puzzled that the IC might prepare assessments that project a world that the United States does not wish to see or that might project a less powerful American role. The best one can say is that this strategic analysis abides by the adage of trying to imagine the future as best as one can understand it without making it fit policymakers' preferences.[20]

KEY ISSUES: IMPACT, ACCURACY, AND QUALITY

Strategic intelligence is a vital but not always widely appreciated function of the IC. Critics contend that strategic intelligence is less relevant to daily policy decisions and seldom critical to issues of war and peace. While there is some truth in these arguments, one needs to keep in mind that good strategic research is the foundation for providing good current intelligence and timely warning as well. If the IC's understanding of the strategic environment is flawed, most likely it will have a skewed view of current events and major threats as well. Hence, it would be foolish for policymakers to dismiss the importance of the NIC, CIA, DIA, and other agencies conducting good strategic intelligence, even if it does not always address all of their short-term intelligence needs. That said, it is important to examine several dimensions of this argument to have a more balanced appreciation for what strategic intelligence can and cannot provide policymakers.

Box 6.3 2017 Global Trends and Key Implications through 2035

The rich are aging, the poor are not. Working-age populations are shrinking in wealthy countries, China, and Russia but growing in developing, poorer countries, particularly in Africa and South Asia, increasing economic, employment, urbanization, and welfare pressures and spurring migration. Training and continuing education will be crucial in developed and developing countries alike.

The global economy is shifting. Weak economic growth will persist in the near term. Major economies will confront shrinking workforces and diminishing productivity gains while recovering from the 2008–09 financial crisis with high debt, weak demand, and doubts about globalization. China will attempt to shift to a consumer-driven economy from its longstanding export and investment focus. Lower growth will threaten poverty reduction in developing countries.

Technology is accelerating progress but causing discontinuities. Rapid technological advancements will increase the pace of change and create new opportunities but will aggravate divisions between winners and losers. Automation and artificial intelligence threaten to change industries faster than economies can adjust, potentially displacing workers and limiting the usual route for poor countries to develop. Biotechnologies such as genome editing will revolutionize medicine and other fields, while sharpening moral differences.

Ideas and Identities are driving a wave of exclusion. Growing global connectivity amid weak growth will increase tensions within and between societies. Populism will increase on the right and the left, threatening liberalism. Some leaders will use nationalism to shore up control. Religious influence will be increasingly consequential and more authoritative than many governments. Nearly all countries will see economic forces boost women's status and leadership roles, but backlash also will occur.

Governing is getting harder. Publics will demand governments deliver security and prosperity, but flat revenues, distrust, polarization, and a growing list of emerging issues will hamper government performance. Technology will expand the range of players who can block or circumvent political action. Managing global issues will become harder as actors multiply—to include NGOs, corporations, and empowered individuals—resulting in more ad hoc, fewer encompassing efforts.

The nature of conflict is changing. The risk of conflict will increase due to diverging interests among major powers, an expanding terror threat, continued instability in weak states, and the spread of lethal, disruptive technologies. Disrupting societies will become more common, with long-range precision weapons, cyber, and robotic systems to target infrastructure from afar, and more accessible technology to create weapons of mass destruction.

Climate change, environment, and health issues will demand attention. A range of global hazards pose imminent and longer-term threats that will require collective action to address—even as cooperation becomes harder. More extreme weather, water and soil stress, and food insecurity will disrupt societies. Sea-level rise, ocean acidification, glacial melt, and pollution will change living patterns. Tensions over climate change will grow. Increased travel and poor health infrastructure will make infectious diseases harder to manage.

Source: Excerpted from Office of the Director of National Intelligence, *Global Trends: Paradox of Progress*, January 2017, https://www.dni.gov/files/documents/nic/GT-Full-Report.pdf.

Does Strategic Intelligence Have Impact and Relevance?

Policymakers often do not heed US intelligence or even read important NIEs. This is not a new problem. Intelligence officials from the 1950s up to current times have lamented the difficulty of getting busy policymakers to read lengthy NIEs or other intelligence products. Often policymakers want the "bottom line" and then only if it reaffirms what they already believe to be true. Some intelligence studies scholars have concluded that in reality strategic intelligence has a very limited influence on national security decisions. According to intelligence scholar Stephen Marrin, "strategic intelligence has had less influence on American foreign policy than many would expect."[21] Marrin's principal argument is that policymakers are analysts too. Like analysts, they have their own cognitive biases and preferred sources of information; however, they also have a preference for greater certainty than intelligence analysts are prepared to give them. For all these reasons, then, policymakers will tend to favor their own world-views over those of the IC, particularly if the IC's findings are at odds with their own. In many respects, they are now empowered by the existence of widely differing ideological news sources. They can also use their access to raw intelligence reporting—further allowing them to be their own analysts—and pick and choose which reporting favors their current ideological perspective.

Numerous examples of policymakers' dismissal of strategic intelligence can readily be found. One former senior intelligence manager, Douglas MacEachin, detailed a number of cases where policymakers ignored strategic intelligence and suffered what could be termed "strategic surprises."[22] In this study, some common causes were

- a static policy mind-set that discourages alternative policy approaches,
- a decision-making process driven by a mind-set that ignores dissenting intelligence analysis or policy advice,
- lack of appreciation for on-the-ground expertise and reporting from the field,
- excessive compartmentalization of information that impedes the flow of intelligence to policymakers,
- organizational cultural imperatives that play down intelligence findings or distort the decision-making process, and
- time pressures that reduce attention to the intelligence findings and professional advice.

These findings suggest that strategic intelligence can be illuminating but nonetheless ignored for reasons that have little to do with its quality, accuracy, or relevance.

By the same token, strategic intelligence is often not credited as a contributing factor to decision-making if one is trying to link a specific intelligence product to a specific policy decision. As mentioned above, strategic intelligence on priority top-ics such as the Cold War–era Soviet military challenge or today's terrorism threats are being provided constantly in a variety of products and forums. Thus, there is more reason to believe that the totality of the intelligence provided has indirectly or even subconsciously shaped the policymakers' overall view of an international problem. Decision-makers throughout the Cold War were inundated with NIEs on the Soviet Union covering topics ranging from its strategic nuclear and conven-tional forces to its civilian and defense industries. This steady stream of informa-tion helped to shape successive administrations' views on how poorly that centrally planned economic system was performing and how large an economic burden the Soviet military was.

More recently, it has been alleged that the 2002 Iraq WMD estimate was irrelevant to the Bush administration's decision to invade Iraq.[23] Yet the 2005 Iraq WMD com-mission report also concluded that the IC had been providing essentially the same assessment of Iraq's programs to the Clinton administration in the late 1990s. This underlines the fact that the extant strategic intelligence had become part of most Washington policymakers'—not just the Bush administration's—mind-set regarding the threat posed by Saddam Hussein.[24] To say that the NIE did not drive the decision for invasion ignores the fact that its conclusions were already part of the conven-tional wisdom at the time. Indeed, many Bush administration officials did not believe an NIE was needed, for precisely those reasons, and it was produced only because the Senate Select Committee on Intelligence (SSCI) requested it prior to the vote to authorize the use of military force.[25] As other practitioners have pointed out, NIEs are often not the best or most useful vehicle for conveying strategic intelligence find-ings, since they usually reflect views that have become widely known through other means. As former NIC chairman Thomas Fingar has pointed out, "By the time most estimates are produced, decision makers working on the issue have already received a great deal of information on the subject, including both raw intelligence and analytic products but also including briefings from and conversations with the analysts with whom they interact on a regular basis."[26]

Suffice it to say, then, that strategic intelligence at a minimum is likely to stimulate discussion and debate, if not always lead to decisive action. As Kent argued back at the dawn of US intelligence, such analysis should be part of the conversation, but that does not necessarily mean policymakers will always agree or take actions that intelligence might warrant. Moreover, even if policymakers are indifferent to strategic intelligence, there are reasons why the IC would want to produce it. First, it records the IC's official views on important topics; indeed, it is often necessary to look back on previous estimates and decide if those judgments need to be reviewed for the sake of analytical rigor and integrity.[27] Such strategic assessments become a source for future inspections and postmortems on how the IC's judgments have evolved and a way to critique the quality of intelligence over time.

Second, NIEs may be very useful to policymakers who are not themselves experts on the subjects but wish to have a working knowledge of how the IC assesses a problem. In the author's experience, diplomats and military officers wishing to "get smart" on topics such as Iran, Iraq, and Afghanistan will very often read recent NIEs and other intelligence products to familiarize themselves with topics that might become important if they are assigned to a Middle Eastern embassy or a command in that part of the world. Likewise, new political appointees such as ambassadors are eager to read the latest NIE or other finished intelligence products to understand what challenges they will face when they are running US diplomacy from their foreign posts.

Finally, the IC has a selfish reason for developing strategic intelligence. Such work is necessary to develop analysts' skills at putting together cogent arguments, weighing evidence in a rigorous fashion, and challenging their own judgments by exposing them to peers' critiques and outside review. In regard to the latter, NIEs and other strategic-level analysis are usually exchanged with foreign intelligence services. It is common practice for the NIB to release sanitized versions (i.e., free of the most sensitive intelligence reporting) to the other Five Eyes services (Commonwealth countries) as well to those of other close NATO allies.[28] Such exchanges not only help American analysts to test their hypotheses against other perspectives but also can often help to shape a foreign government's views of an issue in ways that are advantageous to the United States.

How Accurate Must Strategic Intelligence Be?

Strategic intelligence is not focused on predictions but rather on reducing uncertainty to the extent possible. Yet many policymakers and outside critics of intelligence expect the IC to make forecasts with unrealistic precision. From a decision-maker's perspective, uncertainty complicates the ability to take action. If intelligence assessments are essentially saying an event is less than a 50 percent possibility, should policymakers plan for it, or not? If a less than 50 percent event does occur, has the IC "failed" to accurately forecast an event? Policymakers may not want to run the risk of a less than even chance that Iran could produce a nuclear weapon in three months to a year or that Russia would consider conducting hybrid warfare against one of the Baltic states. Even a 1 percent chance that Iraq might give a terrorist group access to a nuclear weapon led Vice President Cheney to recommend that the United States act as if it were a certainty and invade Iraq.[29] Policymakers crave certainty, which intelligence analysts are usually unable to give them. So how accurate and precise should strategic intelligence strive to be?

The term national intelligence *estimate* contains part of the answer. "Estimates" are not facts or predictions. The future is unknowable with any great certainty.

Estimates are informed judgments based on the best information available, but that knowledge is usually incomplete and often contains contradictory evidence. What facts do exist seldom allow for perfect certainty. As one former CIA deputy director noted, these judgments are "not chiseled in stone," never to be changed.[30] Rather they are subject to revision as new information is available that confirms, alters, or rejects those previous judgments.

Policymakers must recognize that, at best, estimates and intelligence judgments more generally must go beyond the few facts available and craft projections of how the future might look. They can be useful in laying out the key factors that might alter the future and preferably also suggest how a different plausible set of conditions might produce different outcomes. In so doing, strategic intelligence can educate policymakers about the relationship among political, economic, and military factors that they should be mindful of. Developing alternative outcomes can also prepare decision-makers for circumstances they had not previously considered. This can in turn allow military and civilian leaders to game out how US policies and actions might have to change to address those different scenarios as well as to highlight which factors are most problematic and might be susceptible to US preventive action.

How Good Is Strategic Intelligence?

The quality of strategic intelligence is always an important criterion of whether it can have impact and relevance. When the IC fails to provide good-quality analysis, it can not only impact important foreign policy decisions but also undermine the confidence policymakers will have in future intelligence assessments. The ill-conceived October 2002 Iraq WMD NIE is a case in point. Once it became known that the estimate was woefully off base, Congress and the public grew to distrust US intelligence and place much of the blame for the Iraq War on the CIA's poor analysis. Somewhat ironically, some Bush officials also tended to hide behind the flawed NIE even though their decisions preceded its publication. The fact is, however, that this particular NIE haunts the IC to this day for its poor examination of the evidence and its flawed argumentation.

Origins of the 2002 NIE

It is worth examining what went wrong in the 2002 Iraq WMD NIE because it highlights key challenges to preparing high-quality intelligence analysis. The 2005 Iraq WMD commission examined the ninety-plus-page NIE as well as other intelligence products and all the reporting used to prepare the estimate. Its findings were a devastating indictment of the quality of reporting and analysis used to put the estimate together. There are many lessons to be learned from the commission's report as well as from an SSCI inquiry that also focused on the NIE's flaws.[31]

This NIE was prepared at the mid-September request of the SSCI, which asked the NIC to produce a broad estimate on Iraq's WMD programs no later than October 1. The Senate wanted it prior to its October 3 vote to approve an "authorization for the use of military force" requested by the Bush administration. This "fast-track" NIE was produced in less than three weeks, which allowed for only one day's coordination of the estimate by the IC's WMD and Iraq experts. Moreover, the short-fuse estimate did not permit a bottom-up review of past reporting but essentially was a "cut-and-paste" cobbling of past intelligence judgments reached on Iraq's WMD programs. The NIE's key conclusions were the following:[32]

- Iraq was reconstituting its nuclear program and could have a nuclear device in the next few years.
- Iraq's biological weapons (BW) capability was larger and more advanced than before the 1991 Gulf War.
- Iraq had renewed its production of chemical weapons (CW) and had a stockpile of one hundred to five hundred metric tons of mustard, sarin, VX, and other dangerous neurotoxins.
- Iraq also had UAVs for delivering BW and ballistic missiles exceeding the 150-kilometer range banned by the United Nations.

Nearly all these key judgments proved to be wrong in most respects. Later inspectors of the Iraq Survey Group (ISG) found no evidence of CW or BW research or stockpiles and, most important, no active nuclear weapons research and development.[33] The UAVs were most likely not designed for dispersing biological toxins, and only some of the ballistic missiles found were capable of ranges exceeding 150 kilometers. Perhaps most shocking was the fact that the estimate had the temerity to attach "high confidence" and "moderate confidence" to many of these judgments, even though the evidence of any WMD activity proved to be so thin and mostly false.

How could the IC get this critical estimate so wrong? First, collection failed to provide significant and corroborated information on Saddam's WMD activities after UN inspectors were withdrawn from the country in 1998. The WMD commission concluded that the CIA had no dedicated HUMINT sources in Iraq, and the handful of assets it did have were not reliable. What little new information was collected, then, turned out to be false, exaggerated, or fabricated by sources with personal agendas. The ISG subsequently concluded that Saddam had unilaterally destroyed his WMD stocks in 1991.[34]

Second, in the absence of good information, analysts fell back on their assumptions that Saddam probably had WMDs and was very clever in hiding them from inspectors and the IC. Having underestimated Saddam's WMD capabilities in 1990, WMD analysts spent the next decade assuming Iraq was up to something, which the commission found to be no longer just a hypothesis but a firm conclusion.[35] As it reported, "Rather than weighing the evidence independently, analysts accepted information that fit the prevailing theory and rejected information that contradicted it."[36] Furthermore, analysts "layered" one judgment on top of another, so there was a cascading set of unproven assumptions masquerading as evidence; this layering effect disguised the fact that those previous judgments were also based on limited and uncertain information.[37]

Third, intelligence analysts did not do a good job of understanding the pressures the Saddam regime was under to curtail rather than restart its WMD programs. Weapons analysts were not regional Iraq specialists, and they simply did not consider how the political, cultural, and regional dynamics might play into Saddam's theatrical performance of inhibiting inspections of WMDs he no longer possessed. Analysts failed to entertain the idea that "Saddam was actually telling the truth" or to revisit earlier intelligence that suggested his programs had been dismantled.[38]

Finally, the estimate presented its findings without ever explaining its "high-to-moderate" confidence judgments. While there were numerous caveats sprinkled throughout the lengthy estimate underlining some of the intelligence gaps that existed, the key judgments themselves contained far fewer qualifiers. Thus, Congress and Bush administration officials had no way of knowing the basis on which they were reached. Unbeknown to the few readers of the estimate, analysts themselves had little information on the sources they were relying on, as collectors shielded that information from most analysts. Up to that time, a general need-to-know principle prevented HUMINT collectors from revealing the identity and other characteristics of sources to analysts. Thus, there was little information available to judge a source's reliability.[39]

Improvements to Strategic Intelligence

In the wake of the 2002 Iraq WMD estimate, many critics have argued for reforming the way strategic intelligence is prepared and disseminated. The 2005 WMD commission's lengthy report included a series of recommendations that not only led to the major organizational reforms that created the DNI and associated analysis centers but also instructed the IC to improve its collection-and-analysis process. Among those recommendations, five stand out:

- Embrace a **need-to-share** principle to avoid excessive compartmentalization of source information that analysts would have to assess the credibility of reporting.

- Emphasize strategic analysis and establish a long-term research and analysis unit under the NIC to lead interagency projects involving in-depth analysis and expanded contacts with outside experts.
- Institute community-wide career-long training programs for analysts and their managers.
- Encourage diverse and independent analysis throughout the IC by *encouraging* alternative hypothesis generation and by forming offices dedicated to independent analysis.
- Develop and integrate new tradecraft tools to assist analysts in processing and examining the huge volume of reporting.
- Ensure that analysts are engaging in competitive analysis, conducting routine examinations of finished intelligence, and incorporating "lessons learned" from postmortems into training programs.

The IC has made strides in all these areas, although more improvement is needed. The NIC initially established its Long-Range Assessment Group, which has been empowered to develop longer-term assessments of broad topics. This group—later renamed the Strategic Futures Group—has now largely taken over the responsibility for organizing and drafting the Global Trends series. Those efforts are perhaps the best example of extensive outreach to tap the knowledge of nonintelligence experts on broad national security issues. The IC has also committed itself to more in-depth training of analysts to ensure they understand the perils of poor analysis and can utilize more rigorous analytical methods to challenge their assumptions and judgments. Multiweek courses have been established that enable analysts to use more structured analytical techniques—some of which were described in chapter 5—that aim at uncovering key assumptions, critically examining reporting, and developing alternative hypotheses. Inculcating these so-called tradecraft tools has become a standard training objective at the CIA, DIA, and several other intelligence agencies. The CIA as well as the DIA also created lessons-learned centers, where classified postmortems are conducted on successes and failures of strategic analysis. These studies in turn are often used in IC training courses.

At the CIA and DIA, a number of Red Cell teams have been created, whose mission is to craft alternative analyses that challenge the conventional views held by analysts or to provide unconventional perspectives on key intelligence questions. As described in chapter 5, this technique helps analysts get out of their US mind-set. In this capacity, the Red Cell will design strategies to undermine US interests and thereby demonstrate how an enemy might react differently than the planners anticipate. The Red Cells found in the IC often are asked to play an adversary's "national security team" and fashion hypothetical decision memos and policies to illustrate to US policymakers how that enemy's plans and intentions might deviate from their own presumptions.

Finally, the DNI has taken a number of steps to improve the NIE process to ensure that mistakes made in the 2002 Iraq WMD estimate are not repeated. First, the DNI has instructed that collection agencies must review all sources used by analysts and stand by those sources' reliability and validity; at every NIB review of an NIE, collection agencies must address how their products were used in the final estimate. At the same time, the DNI has pressed HUMINT and SIGINT collectors to provide analysts more information on the nature and reliability of the sources they are using. Second, the DNI and the NIC have vowed to conduct future NIEs with an eye toward more zero-based reviews of intelligence problems and to avoid accepting past judgments as a starting point. The use of outside reviewers who can bring in different perspectives has also been revitalized. Moreover, alternative views of an intelligence problem are given equal treatment in the NIEs rather than being played down or minimized in a short dissenting footnote as in the past.

A third initiative by the DNI has been to issue several important interagency Intelligence Community Directives (ICDs) that have encouraged greater analytical rigor as well as more extensive academic outreach to nonintelligence experts. For example, in 2007, the DNI issued *Intelligence Directive 203: Analytical Standards*, which instructs that all IC products shall

- properly describe all sources, data, and methodologies;
- properly express and explain uncertainties associated with major analytical judgments;
- properly distinguish underlying information from analysts' assumptions and judgments;
- use clear and logical argumentation; and
- explain consistency to or change in analytical judgments.

Likewise, the DNI also promulgated in 2008 *Intelligence Community Directive 205: Academic Outreach*, which echoed the WMD commission's recommendation for more use of outside expertise:

- Analysts shall leverage outside expertise as part of their work.
- Each element of the IC shall establish a single academic outreach coordinator.
- The IC should use outside experts whenever possible to contribute to, critique, and challenge internal products and analysis and to provide alternative perspectives.[40]

These directives have helped set community goals, but agencies and senior managers are still in a position to encourage or resist such efforts. In the case of improved training, programs for integrating new tradecraft methods have continued, but some of these techniques remain untested as to whether they truly improve analytical performance or not.[41] Most alarming, however, IC budgets have been cut, and some of the previous tradecraft training has also been reduced. In terms of academic outreach, the intent of encouraging more analysts to reach out to their counterparts in think tanks, academia, and the private sector has not really grown. Indeed, the era of WikiLeaks and Edward Snowden has caused senior intelligence managers to be reluctant to expose their analysts to outside experts. Ironically, the outreach coordinators created by *ICD 205* became in some cases obstacles to greater academic exchanges, as they created so much red tape and anxiety for analysts that they often just abandoned efforts to contact nongovernment experts.[42]

When all is said and done, high-quality strategic intelligence rests on senior intelligence officials as well as analysts taking seriously the mission of providing timely, accurate, and cogently argued assessments within the limits of the information they are able to use. It is incumbent on analysts to remain self-aware of their own analytical biases as well as be willing to alter their assessments as new evidence requires. As senior intelligence officials such as Richard Kerr have argued, building and improving a strategic intelligence capability is not something achieved overnight: "Expertise building cannot be achieved quickly or easily. Analysis is a 'people's business' that requires hiring, training, and leading the best thinkers. CIA has sought people with area expertise, technical training, and linguistic skills to assemble the most complete knowledge of important security issues."[43]

In addition, efforts must be made to ensure that adequate priority is placed on conducting strategic analysis despite the constant policymaker demand for more current intelligence reporting. As another former senior CIA official, Douglas MacEachin, has argued, weaving together a "comprehensive, detailed tapestry should not, however, be treated as part of an 'either-or' tradeoff with the more concise products delivered to top policy officials." Strategic intelligence is more of a capital investment for the overall intelligence enterprise.[44]

USEFUL WEBSITES

CIA Center for the Study of Intelligence, https://www.cia.gov/library/center-for-the-study-of-intelligence
    Contains a number of declassified case studies and volumes of declassified NIEs and other strategic analysis.
ODNI, Global Trends website, https://www.dni.gov/index.php/global-trends-home
    Contains the latest Global Trends publications as well as past ones.
ODNI, National Intelligence Council, https://www.dni.gov/index.php/who-we-are/organizations/nic/nic-who-we-are
    Contains unclassified NIEs and other NIC products.

FURTHER READING

Richard Betts, *Enemies of Intelligence: Knowledge and Power in American National Security* (New York: Columbia University Press, 2007).

> A compilation of the author's critiques of strategic intelligence's role and inevitable failures.

Center for the Study of Intelligence, *Sherman Kent and the Board of National Estimates: Collected Essays* (Washington, DC: Center for the Study of Intelligence, 2007).

> Provides an excellent description of how Kent constructed the NIE process and how he viewed strategic intelligence.

Commission on the Intelligence Capabilities of the United States regarding Weapons of Mass Destruction, *Report to the President*, March 31, 2005.

> https://fas.org/irp/offdocs/wmd_report.pdf.

> Most complete postmortem of an intelligence failure on major strategic issues.

Thomas Fingar, *Reducing Uncertainty: Intelligence Analysis and National Security* (Stanford, CA: Stanford University Press, 2011).

> A practitioner's examination of how strategic intelligence informs policy, providing useful case histories.

Harold P. Ford, *Estimative Intelligence* (Washington, DC: Association of Former Intelligence Officers, 1993).

> A early description and assessment by a well-known senior CIA estimates officer of how national estimates were conducted.

Gregory F. Treverton, *Intelligence in the Age of Terror* (Cambridge: Cambridge University Press, 2009).

> A former senior official's view of how strategic intelligence has adjusted to the post-9/11 world.

NOTES

First epigraph: Sherman Kent, "Estimates and Influence," in Donald P. Steury, ed., *Sherman Kent and the Board of National Estimates: Collected Essays* (Washington, DC: Center for the Study of Intelligence, 1994), 34.

Second epigraph: Thomas Fingar, *Reducing Uncertainty: Intelligence Analysis and National Security* (Stanford CA: Stanford University Press, 2011), 72.

1. See an example of an intelligence assessment on climate change prepared by the NIC in ODNI, *Implications for National Security of Global Climate Change*, National Intelligence Council, September 2016, https://www.dni.gov/files/documents/Newsroom/Reports%20and%20Pubs/Implications_for_US_National_Security_of_Anticipated_Climate_Change.pdf.

2. ODNI, Statement for the Records, Worldwide Threat Assessment of the US Intelligence Community, May 11, 2017, Testimony before the Senate Select Intelligence Committee, https://www.dni.gov/files/documents/Newsroom/Testimonies/SSCI%20Unclassified%20SFR%20-%20Final.pdf.

3. These documents can be found at the National Security Archive, http://nsarchive.gwu
.edu/, as well as the Homeland Security Digital Library, https://www.hsdl.org/?collection
&id=4. Multiple dates in parentheses indicate that successive administrations have issued
national strategy documents on a similar topic. This highlights the enduring if evolving nature
of these international issues.

4. White House, *National Security Strategy to Combat Weapons of Mass Destruction*, September 17, 2002, https://fas.org/irp/offdocs/nspd/nspd-17.html. This short version was later
updated and expanded with the promulgation of the second *National Strategy for Combating Terrorism*, issued in February 2003, https://www.cia.gov/news-information/cia-the-war-on
-terrorism/Counter_Terrorism_Strategy.pdf.

5. Sherman Kent, "Estimates and Influence," *Studies in Intelligence* (Summer 1968), declassified in 2007, https://www.cia.gov/library/center-for-the-study-of-intelligence/csi-publications
/books-and-monographs/sherman-kent-and-the-board-of-national-estimates-collected-essays
/4estimates.html.

6. Donald P. Steury, *Sherman Kent and the Board of National Estimates* (Washington, DC:
Center for the Study of Intelligence, 1994), xxii.

7. Steury, *Sherman Kent*, xv. The ONE comprised the analysts and support staff, including
the much smaller and elitist BNE, on which sat Kent and a half dozen consultants drawn from
leading universities and think tanks.

8. Historically, CIA and DIA estimates of Soviet missile-production rates, missile accuracies, and the USSR's defense burden were the subject of continuing internal government
disagreements, which sometimes broke out into the public. In the 1980s, the DIA took the lead
in producing a series of unclassified reports titled *Soviet Military Power*, which the Pentagon
promoted to highlight the threat and make the case for larger American military programs
and budgets. See DOD, *Soviet Military Power*, 1981, http://edocs.nps.edu/2014/May/Soviet
MilPower1981.pdf.

9. Pub. L. No. 108–458, 118 Stat. 3657, 50 U.S.C. 403-3b.

10. Christopher A. Kojm, "Change and Continuity: The National Intelligence Council
2009–2014," *Studies in Intelligence* 59, no. 2 (June 2015): 7.

11. Kojm, 8.

12. ODNI, Intelligence Community Assessment, ICA-2017, *Assessing Russian Activities
and Intentions in Recent US Elections*, January 6, 2017, unclassified, https://www.dni.gov/files
/documents/ICA_2017_01.pdf.

13. Cited by Dr. Gregory Treverton, NIC chairman until 2017, in an address to a Center for
Strategic and International Studies audience, "Strategic Intelligence: A View from the NIC,"
March 4, 2016, https://www.csis.org/events/strategic-intelligence-view-national-intelligence
-council-nic.

14. President Gerald Ford, with the then CIA director George H. W. Bush, agreed to conduct
the so-called Team A / Team B exercise, which pitted a group of outside critics of CIA analysis
against the drafters of NIE 11/3–8 in an effort to expose different assumptions used to analyze
Soviet strategic programs. The exercise was generally judged a failure because it was clear
from the beginning that the opponents had their own firm views. For a more complete discussion, see *Intentions and Capabilities: Estimates on Soviet Strategic Forces, 1950–1983*, ed. Donald Steury (Washington, DC: Center for the Study of Intelligence, 1996), 335–36, https://www

.cia.gov/library/center-for-the-study-of-intelligence/csi-publications/books-and-monographs/Est%20on%20Soviet%20Strategic.pdf.

15. ODNI, *Prospects for Iraq's Stability: Some Security Progress but Political Reconciliation Elusive*, National Intelligence Estimate (Update to *NIE, Prospects for Iraq's Stability: A Challenging Road Ahead*), August 2007, https://www.dni.gov/files/documents/Newsroom/Press%20Releases/2007%20Press%20Releases/20070823_release.pdf.

16. ODNI, *The Terrorist Threat to the Homeland*, National Intelligence Estimate, July 2007, http://nsarchive2.gwu.edu//nukevault/ebb270/18.pdf.

17. According to one former NIC chairman, the NIC has tried to address the "US factor" in products in addition to the Global Trends series. Private email with a former senior official, June 2017.

18. Fingar, *Reducing Uncertainty*, 55.

19. See ODNI, *NIC Global Trends: Paradox of Progress*, January 2017, https://www.dni.gov/files/documents/nic/GT-Full-Report.pdf.

20. Former NIC chairman Thomas Fingar has also commented to the author that when foreign officials were asked to share their views of what the United States might do in the future, many were initially pleased to be asked but ultimately declined to provide any negative comments. Personal email, June 2017.

21. Stephen Marrin, "Why Strategic Intelligence Analysis Has Limited Influence on American Foreign Policy," *Intelligence and National Security* 32, no. 6 (2017): 725–42.

22. Douglas MacEachin and Janne Nolan, *Discourse, Dissent, and Strategic Surprise: Formulating US Security Policy in an Age of Uncertainty* (Washington, DC: Institute for the Study of Diplomacy, 2006). The cases examined include 1979 US policy toward Iran, 1998 threats to US embassies in East Africa, pre-1979 Soviet military preparations in Afghanistan, 1989 rise of the Afghan mujahideen ("holy warriors"), and the 1998 Asian financial crisis.

23. Paul Pillar, "Intelligence, Policy and the War in Iraq," *Foreign Affairs* 85, no. 2 (2006): 15–27.

24. If one wants further evidence of the commonly held view on Saddam's WMD programs driven by intelligence, review Kenneth Pollock, *The Threatening Storm: The Case for Invading Iraq* (New York: Random House, 2002), in which the former CIA analyst makes the case better than the Bush administration for why containing Saddam was not sufficient.

25. An interesting fact is that of the few senators who did read the NIE, almost all voted against the authorization to use military force, presumably because the full NIE contained a large number of caveats on its judgments as well as dissenting opinions from the intelligence analysts of the State Department and the Energy Department. This would suggest NIEs can have impact if they are actually read carefully.

26. Fingar, *Reducing Uncertainty*, 108.

27. Fingar, 85–87.

28. Based on defense and intelligence cooperation among the United States and British Commonwealth countries during World War II, the Five Eyes forum includes the US, the United Kingdom, Canada, Australia, and New Zealand. This forum is where multinational classified intelligence exchanges are the most frank and complete.

29. Ron Suskind, *The One Percent Doctrine* (New York: Simon & Schuster, 2006).

30. John McLaughlin, CNN interview, December 10, 2007.

31. See also SSCI, *Report on the Intelligence Community's Pre-war Assessments of Iraq WMD*, July 7, 2004, https://fas.org/irp/congress/2004_rpt/ssci_iraq.pdf.

32. Commission on the Intelligence Capabilities of the United States regarding Weapons of Mass Destruction, *Report to the President*, March 31, 2005, "Overview," 8–9, https://fas.org/irp/offdocs/wmd_report.pdf.

33. The ISG comprised fourteen hundred inspectors and support staff and issued a comprehensive final report on its findings. In three volumes, the ISG systematically assessed the Iraqi regime's intents and strategy as well as reviewed the state of Iraq's delivery systems and nuclear, chemical, and biological programs. See ISG, *Comprehensive Report of the Special Advisor to the DCI on Iraq's WMD; 30 September 2004*, https://www.cia.gov/library/reports/general-reports-1/iraq_wmd_2004/. It concluded that Saddam had abandoned his nuclear program in 1991, believing it was more important to get economic sanctions removed. Furthermore, it found no evidence of any CW or BW and concluded that Saddam wished to deceive his enemies into believing he retained some WMDs to deter them from attacking him.

34. ISG Comprehensive Report, 151.

35. ISG Comprehensive Report, 9.

36. ISG Comprehensive Report, 169.

37. ISG Comprehensive Report, 172.

38. ISG Comprehensive Report, 174.

39. ISG Comprehensive Report, 176.

40. *ICD 205* has been revised since 2008 but not made publicly available. Some intelligence officials have implied that the new version is more cautious than the original one.

41. See Steve Artner, Richard S. Girven, and James B. Bruce, *Assessing the Value of Structured Analytic Techniques to the U.S. Intelligence Community* (Washington, DC: RAND Corp. 2016), 1–15, https://www.rand.org/content/dam/rand/pubs/research_reports/RR1400/RR1408/RAND_RR1408.pdf.

42. See Susan Nelson, "Analytic Outreach: Pathway to Expertise Building and Professionalization," in Roger Z. George and James Bruce, *Analyzing Intelligence: National Security Practitioners' Perspectives* (Washington, DC: Georgetown University Press, 2014), 331. She highlights some of the challenges to conducting outreach and calls for a more balanced approach between counterintelligence concerns and analysts' desire for outside perspectives. For a more pessimistic view, see Roger Z. George, "Reflections on CIA Analysis: Is It Finished?," *Intelligence and National Security* 26 no. 1 (March 2011): 78, http://www.tandfonline.com/doi/abs/10.1080/02684527.2011.556360.

43. Richard J. Kerr and Michael Warner, "The Track Record of CIA," in George and Bruce, *Analyzing Intelligence*, 50–51.

44. Douglas MacEachin, "Analysis and Estimates," in *Transforming US Intelligence*, ed. Jennifer E. Sims and Burton Gerber (Washington, DC: Georgetown University Press, 2011), 126.

7

THE CHALLENGES OF WARNING

Successful warning is essentially a two-fold process; if warning is to be effective, not only must the alert be given, but the consumer of intelligence must accept the fact that he has in fact been warned.
—CIA director John McCone, 1962

After every crisis there surfaces in the press some obscure intelligence report or analyst purporting to have predicted it, only to have been foolishly ignored by policymakers. What these claims omit to mention is that when warnings become too routine they lose all significance; when reports are not called specifically to the attention of the top leadership they are lost in the bureaucratic background noise, particularly since for every admonitory report one can probably find also its opposite in the files.
—Henry Kissinger, *White House Years*, 1979

Warning has a special priority in American intelligence. Were it not for the 1941 Japanese attack on Pearl Harbor, it is debatable whether there would have been such urgency in establishing the CIA in 1947 or encouraging the growth of the huge intelligence enterprise that exists today. Without the "surprise attack" on December 7, American intelligence might have remained largely a military service function, with some diplomatic reporting provided by the Department of State. Instead, the growing fear of "another Pearl Harbor"—whether from Soviet strategic nuclear missiles in the Cold War, a catastrophic terrorist attack like 9/11, or a possible massive cyberattack against the US homeland's infrastructure—has made warning a major mission of the US intelligence community. This chapter will describe what **warning analysis** is and how the warning process is conducted and organized. In addition, it will present a short survey of major warning cases, which can then be analyzed for some general lessons learned and challenges for the future.

WHAT IS WARNING?

Not all strategic analyses contain a warning. However, warning invariably involves detailed examination of intelligence that leads analysts to conclusions that certain trends are moving in a dangerous direction. Historically, warning has been associated with a military threat. In fact, the best-known "strategic surprises"—for example, Pearl Harbor, Adolf Hitler's 1941 eastern offensive against Joseph Stalin's armies, the 1950 North Korean attack on the south, and the 1979 Soviet invasion of Afghanistan—are most often associated with direct military attacks. For much of the Cold War, American intelligence was focused heavily on the danger of a Soviet or Chinese conventional or nuclear attack on the United States or its allies in Europe or Asia. For example, in 1975 an authoritative definition of "strategic" warning issued by the director of central intelligence read, "Strategic warning is defined as the earliest possible warning that the Soviet Union, the Warsaw Pact, the PRC, or North Korea is considering military action by its armed forces beyond its borders, or is employing its military capabilities beyond its borders in ways that might threaten military confrontation with the United States."[1] Fear of a "bolt-from-the-blue" conventional attack or nuclear strike motivated American defense planners to argue for a rigorous warning system that could provide Washington a timely alert to evidence of Soviet preparations for war. Thus, the warning mission was foremost in the minds of both intelligence officials and decision-makers.

Like other forms of strategic analysis, there has to be a strong linkage between intelligence and policy. A longtime military intelligence analyst, Cynthia Grabo, wrote a major treatment on warning in the 1960s that remains relevant even today. In it she describes warning analysis as "the considered judgment of the finest analytic minds available, based on an exhaustive and objective review of all available indications, which is conveyed to the policy official in sufficiently convincing language that he is persuaded of its validity and takes appropriate action to protect the national interest."[2] Embedded in this citation, as well as in the two epigraphs that open this chapter, are three key characteristics of good warning: (1) exhaustive study of all available information, (2) development of a set of indicators that can alert warning analysts of an impending threat, and (3) successful and convincing communication of that threat to policymakers so they are in a position to take action. This seemingly simple description of warning process disguises an incredibly elusive result.

Warning in many respects remains the most difficult form of strategic analysis. First, it requires in-depth strategic intelligence conducted by analysts who understand what effective warning is. Warning intelligence is unique in that it is not just reporting the latest or most alarmist report received but rather is a careful sorting through—what Grabo and others describe as "exhaustive" study—of an adversary's capabilities and intentions. It requires careful understanding of past as well as current behavior. Most often this results in the development of **indicators** (unique and observable actions or behavior tied to hostile intent) that warning analysts monitor over time. As Grabo noted, "Rarely if ever will [the analyst] regard a single report or indication as a cause for alerting the community."[3]

Second, it requires a good understanding of what developments would conceivably damage US national interests in a significant way. In the Cold War, warning analysts understood how Soviet strategic missile forces operated and the Soviet strategic military doctrine on the use of nuclear weapons. Military analysts also had a good understanding of Soviet ground-force capabilities opposite NATO and what the USSR's war plans probably entailed. For nonmilitary situations such as political instability, financial crises, or ethnic conflicts, the indicators would be very different and in most cases harder to assess. Analysts both inside and outside government have tried to develop indicators that would help to anticipate higher chances of state failure or political instability. For a time, the CIA had a Political Instability Task Force, which attempted to develop a model for forecasting where the next government crisis or coup might occur in developing nations; these efforts focused on identifying "triggers" (events) that might lead to broader political unrest or key "vulnerabilities" that might tip weak states into a crisis.[4] Unlike military indicator methods, however, there seem to be far fewer highly predictive factors. Efforts to correlate economic performance, demographic shifts, unemployment trends, or abuses of power have not necessarily been good indicators of state failure. Looking at the grim statistics of North Korea's economic performance, quality of life, and human rights abuses, some experts have anticipated the regime's collapse for decades, yet it has not occurred. So, indicators might not work as well in the socioeconomic field as in the military domain.

Third, warning rests on analysts being able to convince policymakers that US interests are at risk. Here the challenge is presenting sufficient evidence that the plausible outcome would lead to an actual commencement of military hostilities, a military coup, government collapse, or economic setback to the United States and its interests. Such a message should not be buried in a lengthy assessment that can be too easily lost—it needs to be the headliner of the assessment or be part of a special warning memorandum that will grab the attention of the policymaker. To take a simple example, analysts have to present a cogent argument for why observed military activities are not merely training exercises or an attempt to blackmail an opponent. Then the argument has to lay out the consequences of this military operation. For instance, if the warning suggests that a limited military clash is possible rather than a precursor to a large-scale invasion, policymakers may not feel compelled to act. On the other hand, if the warning is that an adversary has marshaled sufficient forces to conduct a rapid invasion in a matter of days, it would presumably draw far more attention. There is always the danger that too many such warnings will be seen as "crying wolf" and thus will lose their impact with policymakers over time. Decision-makers can worry that intelligence will often provide a **"worst-case analysis"** and cause them to over-react in those cases.

And fourth, it requires that policymakers be convinced to take action that might avert or at least reduce the impact of such a development. Often policymakers will wish for more time to deliberate and for more confirming information before they are forced to take action. Good strategic warning sometimes involves telling policy-makers, "You've been warned, and we are not likely to be able to give you much tacti-cal warning." Senior officials or military commanders must have an appreciation for how quickly the situation they face might worsen if they do not act now. To take one recent example, NATO experts have said that a plausible Russian invasion of a Baltic state could occur quickly and be completed long before US or other NATO forces are able to reach the battlefield. Knowing that, policymakers have to weigh the merits of putting more NATO forces closer to the Baltics and/or raising the tempo and size of NATO forces that are temporarily rotated into the Baltic states to show the alliance's resolve in defending them.[5] In sum, warning provided too late is neither strategic nor helpful.

WARNING: TERMINOLOGY AND METHODOLOGY

There is a very unique terminology when talking about warning intelligence. First, one has to distinguish *strategic* warning from *tactical* warning. Intelligence professionals want to provide as much time as possible prior to a major shift in an adversary's hos-tile intent so that policymakers can act to build up US defenses or reposition them, or at least disperse them so as to blunt any possible military attack. Likewise, other types of strategic warning might alert policymakers to unfavorable economic or political trends in key countries that might be moderated by timely American actions. Tactical warning essentially is intelligence that announces that military hostilities or other dangerous events are now occurring and the United States must be ready to absorb whatever military shocks or politico-economic disruptions are underway. The lack of accurate or timely tactical warning is often the source of many strategic surprises, even if there has been demonstrable strategic warning given to decision-makers.

Strategic Warning's Characteristics

Strategic warning is perhaps the most difficult concept to define with any precision. This kind of intelligence has at least three significant dimensions. First, the word *strategic* suggests that the warning focuses on an event or trend that would have a major impact on US national interests in a physical way (such as a direct attack on the US homeland or forces or those of our close allies or partners) or would undermine American economic prosperity or political influence abroad. Second, analysts need to have sufficient information and also enough confidence to determine that the development has a reasonable probability of occurring within a given time frame that matters to policymakers. Third, such strategic warning needs to be given enough in advance so that policymakers are in a position to take actions designed to head off the danger or at least ameliorate the consequences of the event occurring.

All three characteristics are subject to great debate about what qualifies as a strategic threat, what is a reasonable probability that analysts and policymakers consider worrisome, and how much advance warning (i.e., time to prepare) must be given to allow policymakers to adopt measures to avert some disaster or negative trend. The simple answer to those questions is that it depends on the issue, the set of conditions surrounding it, and the current US policies and set of policymakers. Consider that during the Cold War, policymakers viewed our greatest threat to be a nuclear war with the Soviet Union; accordingly, they designed US military forces and intelligence systems around strategies that could give us maximum survivability and warning time in order to deter Moscow's consideration of a first-strike nuclear attack.[6] Analysts generally did not believe there was a high probability of a Soviet preemptive attack so long as the United States maintained a diversified set of nuclear systems, but even if the probability was low, the consequences were so high that adequate warning was considered critical to giving the president time for deciding whether to launch a US counterstrike. Today, the overriding importance of strategic warning of a Russian attack is lower but certainly not zero in the era of Vladimir Putin. Instead, the consequences of a military confrontation with North Korea or emergence of a nuclear Iran seem more threatening and more probable than another nuclear confrontation with Moscow.

Military threats are not the only ones requiring strategic warning. In today's world, there are a variety of plausible scenarios around which advanced warning needs to be provided:

1. Military attacks: Warning focuses on detecting a changing order of battle between adversarial states that indicates preparations for war. Typically, good indicators are based on analysis of past military exercises, redeployments, or doctrinal changes.
2. Military/scientific breakthroughs: These are announcements or forecasts of major military capabilities detected in weapon laboratories and at test facilities (e.g., nuclear detonations, missile tests, and antiballistic missile intercepts).

3. Internal instability: Alerts to a possible military coup, state failure, or lack of effective governance—such as forecasts of major outbreaks of violence, genocide, or ethnic-cleansing campaigns.

4. Transnational threats: Warning of terrorist plots and attacks, pandemic disease outbreaks, financial meltdowns, or cyberattacks against major infrastructure or financial institutions also constitute tough warning problems, given the paucity of good indicators.

Warning is easiest when there are easily observable indicators such as the movement or massing of large forces, clear battle lines, and large-scale operations that require time and large amounts of equipment and personnel. Those indicators are more easily observed by US reconnaissance satellites and SIGINT systems. The US intelligence system was largely based on a military type of **indications and warning (I&W)** analysis. Analysts would determine what kinds of military actions an adversary like the Soviet Union or now Russia and China might contemplate in Europe or Asia. This was based on observations of the kinds of military training exercises or actual combat those militaries have conducted. For example, Russia's war with Georgia in 2008 and its use of hybrid warfare against Ukraine have provided insights into the kinds of operations Russia might engage in vis-à-vis the Baltics as well as what steps it can take to mask or obscure its intentions or actual military presence in Eastern Ukraine.

I&W analysis amounted to studying how an adversary plans or has used its military forces. As Grabo defined it, an indicator list is a "compilation of projected, anticipated, or hypothetical actions which any nation might take in preparation for hostilities or other inimical actions.[7] These indications, however, have to be ones that are clearly linked to some planned actions as well as be visible or collectable. Typical indicators of possible military hostilities might include

- reallocation of civilian industrial production for military use,
- plans for rationing strategic goods (e.g., petroleum, medical supplies, food),
- sudden cancellation of military leave or mobilization of reserve forces,
- relocation or reinforcement of key military posts,
- heightened operational security around military facilities,
- abnormally high communications between field commanders and headquarters,
- higher alert levels for air-defense forces, or
- increased intelligence collection against specific military targets.[8]

For other categories, such as military/technological breakthroughs, the indicators may also be reasonably observable and reliable since they usually involve extensive research and development activities at known institutes or industrial facilities. A foreign military's own highly technical monitoring of those tests are themselves often detectable or collectable by American intelligence collectors. As one former senior CIA official noted, the track record of monitoring Soviet and Chinese military programs has been reasonably good. Few military or scientific developments are entirely missed, although the IC is often surprised when an adversary can achieve a military capability faster than anticipated.[9] As recent North Korean nuclear and missile tests show, with enough concealment and secrecy even a poor nation committed to gaining a military capability can complicate accurate forecasts of its programs.

Strategic warning of internal political instability—for example, state failure, civil wars, or genocide—often are less convincing or precise than military-technological threats. Knowing when a government or country has reached a "tipping point" toward chaos or a coup depends on understanding the unique characteristics of a foreign political culture and its leadership. Many intelligence estimates have forecast political challenges for governments that the United States was either supporting or opposing. In the former category, many pessimistic NIEs were written about the stability of the South Vietnamese government during the 1960s and 1970s. In 1979, however, intelligence failed to warn of the growing indecisiveness of the shah of Iran or his possible demise. In the case of adversaries, the CIA and IC generally is unfairly faulted for not having forecast (i.e., warned about) the possible collapse of the Soviet Union. More recently, the intelligence forecasts of Iraq and Afghanistan have been filled with warnings of sectarian and religious animosities, high levels of corruption, and waning popular support for governments that had only limited political legitimacy. Developing reliable indicators that would convince analysts, much less policymakers, that a government collapse or military coup is coming is far more difficult. Often analysts resort to describing a range of outcomes, including a fairly dire or worst-case scenario. In a few instances, a clear call has been made, but policymakers even then may choose not to act in a timely fashion.

The track record of the last warning category of transnational threats, which includes terrorism, financial crises, climate change, and pandemics, is even more dismal. One can argue that strategic warning of major terrorism threats has been reasonably good, even if tactical warning of actual plots has been much more mixed. In the case of financial crises, very few have been accurately forecast as there are far too many intervening variables to understand when a failing bank or investment house or a currency crisis will turn into a full-blown global financial meltdown. These fall into the realm of "black swans," a term popularized by Nassim Taleb to describe unique, hard-to-predict discontinuities that have huge consequences and appear to come out of nowhere with little warning.[10]

This notion of black swans also is so ill-defined that it is hard to generalize about the characteristics that might allow analysts to develop an I&W-style list of indicators. Terrorism might lend itself to such analysis, if the target is a large, multifaceted organization like al-Qaeda or the Islamic State of Iraq and Syria (ISIS).[11] In many respects, both operated more like military organizations—and their members considered themselves "soldiers"—which included having identifiable logistics experts, financiers, bomb makers, and commanders who used a variety of communication systems and locations. In the case of ISIS, it operated tanks and field artillery, had organized brigades in Syria and Iraq, and considered itself a state, not just an organization. Hence, monitoring via technical and human means might yield some indicators of plans and capabilities. Indeed, prior to the 9/11 attacks by al-Qaeda, CIA director George Tenet remarked that the "system was blinking red," meaning a lot of intercepted communications chatter was saying something big was coming.[12] On the other hand, small, self-radicalized cells or "lone wolf" individuals are much harder to monitor and forecast whether they have the intention and capability to attack unprotected targets. Naturally occurring events such as earthquakes, tsunamis, and pandemics are more like mysteries, for which no reliable method exists to forecast with any precision. Some would argue that Californians have been given strategic warning that the "big one" is overdue and so the only question is whether citizens are prepared and whether any better seismic-monitoring system might give them enough tactical warning to take cover.

Tactical Warning: Hard to Provide

While the track record of strategic warning shows as many successes as failures, tactical warning is far more difficult. As suggested above, if strategic warning has been given, the intelligence challenge becomes one of gathering enough information to answer the questions of "where, when, how, and who?" In many cases, the IC is not in a position to give high-confidence answers to those questions. Tactical surprise can occur, even when analysts and decision-makers know there is a general threat out there. Among the many causes for such failures, the following are most common:

1. *Collection gaps* frequently exist in how a threat will materialize, in what form, at what time, or where.
2. *Deception and denial* can magnify existing collection gaps if an adversary has maintained good operational security, spread disinformation to confuse analysts, and mastered other deception techniques that cloak its preparations.
3. *Misinterpretation* and *mind-sets* can cause analysts to miss signals or dismiss them as "noise" or disinformation because they do not fit their expectations of how an adversary would behave.

4. *Poor communication* of warning can mute or muddle the message so policy-makers do not realize they have been warned.

5. *Policymakers' wishful thinking* can lead them to dismiss warnings as indicative of the IC's worst-case or cry-wolf syndromes.

AN EVOLVING WARNING PHILOSOPHY

American intelligence has conducted warning in two fundamental ways—either through specialized warning staffs or by assigning the warning mission to every analyst; some mix of both has also been practiced. Simplistically put, during the Cold War, the emphasis was on the Soviet and Chinese military threats and associated conflicts that involved the US-Soviet bipolar competition. Faced with a standing threat of a nuclear or a large-scale land war in Europe or Asia, American intelligence established a set of special intelligence units dedicated to providing warning of possible attack. Over the decades, these groups carried a variety of names, such as the Watch Committee, the National Indications Center, and the National Warning Staff. But essentially their mission was to create a set of indicators that analysts would monitor to ensure that the Soviets and their allies were not making preparations for war. These groups could issue their own "alert memoranda" that laid out changed military conditions such as a higher military readiness on the part of an American adversary (e.g., the Soviet Union, China, North Vietnam, North Korea). These warnings might also be inserted into the daily intelligence publications, including the *President's Daily Brief*, fast-track special NIEs, or other sensitive daily publications produced by the CIA and DIA.

The Defense Department naturally puts special emphasis on warning of military attacks and historically has organized its own warning systems as part of a broader IC effort. Each combatant command (e.g., European Command, Pacific Command, Strategic Command) has maintained a warning staff, as has the Joint Staff J-2 (intelligence directorate) in the Pentagon. These staffs received information from SIGINT, IMINT, and other collectors on its specific set of indicators that would allow warning officers to determine if there had been significant change in enough factors that there might be a higher possibility of military hostilities. In the 1960s and 1970s, this system was called the Worldwide Indications and Warning System, which was replaced in 1990s with the Defense Indications and Warning System, which was again renamed in 2008 the Global Warning Enterprise and continues to this day.[13]

The NIC also has been involved in providing warning by issuing NIEs on adversaries' military capabilities and intentions. The annually updated estimates on Soviet strategic and conventional force developments were constantly describing new Soviet military capabilities and interpreting Soviet military doctrine regarding its war plans; these inherently carried important warnings. Special estimates such as the infamous 1962 special NIE on the Soviet military buildup in *Cuba* contained warnings that were insufficient to alert policymakers to Moscow's intentions regarding support to Fidel Castro's regime. The 2002 Iraq WMD NIE could also be categorized as a warning analysis regarding Saddam Hussein's intentions to resume his nuclear and other programs, even as flawed as it was.

The NIC became even more involved in the warning process when, in 1979, DCI Stansfield Turner created the national intelligence officer for warning (NIO/W). Following the strategic surprise of the shah's fall, he established this new position to head the national warning system that already existed. The NIO/W was now directly responsible for providing warning analysis to the DCI and to the policy community. Accordingly, these duties included becoming an advocate for warning across the community's analytical elements but also for improved collection to reduce intelligence gaps and to improve analysis. As a matter of course, this individual also would be responsible for overseeing the national warning system plus coordinating the warning activities of other regional and functional NIOs. Individual NIOs were in turn responsible for monitoring conditions in their areas of responsibility and would host monthly "warning meetings" at which agencies could raise concerns about developments that might lead to political instability, military conflicts, or other negative consequences. These NIO reports would be inputs to the NIO/W's own monthly report to the DCI. In addition, the NIO/W could independently raise concerns with other NIOs if he or she believed developments in their areas were occurring that needed more attention. In this way, the NIO/W could provide a "second opinion" or act as a "devil's advocate" when there might be too much consensus or complacency among analysts regarding a security issue. This, naturally, could create friction between the NIO/W and his counterparts who might view this intervention as crying wolf or micromanagement. Depending on the personality of the NIO/W, the relationship between his office and those of other NIOs could be collaborative or frosty.

This centralized system of an NIO/W running the national warning system ended in 2011 when DNI James Clapper eliminated the NIO/W position and directed that "every analyst is a warning analyst." The notion that warning constituted an important duty of every intelligence analyst was by no means new. Even during the Cold War and its centralized system of warning, there had been the mantra that every analyst must be writing assessments that highlight both threats and opportunities for policymakers. However, with the end of the bipolar military competition and the proliferation of many nonmilitary threats, the NIO/W seemed to be a legacy of a bygone era. The national warning system and its entire I&W methodology had been predicated on an enduring Soviet-American military competition. The NIO/W and the national warning staff were likewise seen as being more military analysts than experts in political instability, economic crises, or a host of other transnational challenges. Hence, intelligence officials came to believe that analysts responsible for each issue were in the best position to warn of any changes that would endanger US national interests.

That said, individual NIOs continue to be responsible for warning in their regional and functional areas. More than anything, however, the new mantra was "integration" of efforts to make the IC a single operation. Hence, holding out warning from other analytical and collection functions clashed with DNI Clapper's vision of a more integrated national intelligence enterprise. To accomplish this, he also established a new group of national intelligence managers (NIMs)—generally mirroring the separate regional and functional areas covered by NIOs—which were now responsible for ensuring that the IC's many functions, including warning, were integrated rather than operating separately from each other. As such, NIMs were responsible for ensuring that adequate collection as well as analytical resources were available to promote timely warning.

A MIXED TRACK RECORD ON WARNING

Having laid out the distinction between strategic and tactical warning and their characteristics and challenges, it is useful to consider some of the more prominent warning successes and failures. Having done that, the remainder of the chapter will assess what can be learned from them.

1941 Japanese Attack on Pearl Harbor

Japan's attack on the US Pacific Fleet based in Pearl Harbor is considered a classic warning failure that involved a "strategic surprise"—one that caused significant damage to the US military as well as a strong psychological blow to the American sense of invulnerability. Its causes are still debated by scholars. Early writers on the attack believed there was sufficient information to provide strategic warning that the Japanese might begin hostilities against the United States somewhere in the Pacific region, although this information was lost in the "noise" of other reporting and so was not picked up in a timely fashion.[14] Other scholars emphasize the mind-set held by most analysts and military leaders that the Japanese were inferior militarily, had not trained for attacking harbors like Pearl, and did not have torpedoes that could operate in such shallow waters. Many critiques also emphasized the poor coordination, information sharing, and dissemination of intelligence by the US Army and US Navy that contributed to policymakers and military commanders not appreciating the urgency of preparing for war. Another school believes that information was difficult to come by, given excellent Japanese military operational security.[15] In the end, one can say that tactical information on the where, when, and how was lacking regarding Japanese attack plans, so that even with the knowledge that a US-Japan conflict was unavoidable, few senior Washington officials and military commanders in Hawaii believed the war would begin there.

1950 North Korean Invasion of South Korea

The US forces in South Korea, led by Gen. Douglas MacArthur, had seen reports of possible invasion but tended to disregard them because they judged North Korean forces to be inferior. The CIA had reported a buildup of Kim Il-sung's forces that had the capability to attack, but the dominant analytical mind-set was that the North Korean leader could not unilaterally initiate hostilities without Soviet acquiescence. Most importantly, analysts doubted Stalin wanted to start a conflict with Washington, being convinced that Moscow was mostly focused on the Cold War crises in Germany and Central Europe. Overall, the evidence for an attack was spotty, and such intelligence reports were mostly nonspecific and obscured by the prevailing North Korean war rhetoric.[16] The CIA did somewhat better in alerting US policymakers and commanders to China's preparations to intervene on North Korea's behalf when General MacArthur advanced toward the Yalu River. However, as before, MacArthur dismissed those warnings until it was too late.

1962 Cuban Missile Crisis

The Cuban Missile Crisis has become the most widely discussed, dissected, and reexamined case of a failure to warn but also of ultimately successful crisis management with the aid of subsequent intelligence.[17] In September 1962, the Board of National Estimates issued its special NIE (SNIE 85-3-62) that concluded the Soviets would avoid the risky move of placing offensive nuclear missiles on the island for fear of provoking an American invasion. This reassuring message was in short order dashed by resumed U-2 imagery two weeks later showing advanced preparation for dozens of intermediate- and medium-range missiles. Postmortems later would emphasize that limited HUMINT and effective Soviet D&D (not to mention outright lying by senior Soviet diplomats to President John F. Kennedy) combined with a dominant analytical mind-set to suggest that such a move was inconsistent with past Soviet caution about deploying nuclear-armed missiles outside the USSR. Sherman Kent defended his analysts by suggesting that they could not be held accountable for Premier Nikita Khrushchev miscalculating on how the United States would react.[18] Policymakers were aware of the risks but generally agreed with analysts—the exception being CIA director John McCone—that Khrushchev would not dare to challenge the United States in its own backyard.

1967 Israeli Six-Days War against Arab States

A case of successful warning was CIA forecasting of an Israeli defeat of the Arab military coalition against it. Israel, having sensed a growing threat from the combined armies of Egypt, Syria, and Jordan, preempted what Israeli intelligence believed would be a combined Arab assault on its southern and eastern borders. Soviet arms deliveries prior to the war threatened the favorable military balance Israel held up to that time. Then, in May 1967, Egypt further escalated tensions by closing the Gulf of Aqaba, Israel's main access to the Red Sea. Israel (and the United States previously) had termed this an act of war.

The CIA had by then produced an assessment of the military balance, which forecast that Israel could "defend successfully against simultaneous Arab attacks." A second, joint CIA-DIA paper on the military capabilities of Israel and the Arab states forecast that Israel would need seven to nine days to reach the Suez Canal. When war broke out on June 5, President Lyndon Johnson already knew that the IC judged Israel would prevail, and hence he chose not to respond to the urgent request of Israeli prime minister Golda Meier for emergency military supplies, which the White House deemed unnecessary. This set of judgments was considered by then CIA director Richard Helms as "pretty much a triumph."[19] Credit was given to good intelligence on the state of Arab military preparedness and analysts' excellent understanding of the order of battle of the contending armies. This success also convinced many Middle East military analysts of Israeli's air-combat superiority, leading them to believe another war was unlikely until that military balance was dramatically altered.

1973 Egyptian Attack on Israel (Yom Kippur War)

In contrast to the previous case, the October 1973 Egyptian attack into the Sinai during the Yom Kippur holiday caught Israeli and US intelligence totally flat-footed. Previous warnings in 1972 and early 1973—derived from good HUMINT and SIGINT sources—had led to Israeli military mobilizations, and there had been no Egyptian attack. Based on good intelligence about Egyptian war plans, Israeli intelligence and military officials concluded that Egypt would not attack so long as it lacked sufficient air-defense systems needed to fend off a superior Israeli air force. Accordingly, Israeli officials allowed soldiers home leave for the holidays, even as Egyptian forces were preparing to attack. US intelligence estimates also were flat-out wrong as they accepted the Israeli analysis that there would be no war. This message was conveyed to National Security Adviser Henry Kissinger on the morning of October 6, just as the attack had commenced in the Sinai.

Official postmortems of what caused this warning failure focused not only on excellent Egyptian deception regarding large-scale exercises it was conducting but also on optimistic Israeli and American assumptions that Egypt would not start a war it could not win. Described by many such critiques as "the concept," this assumption of inferior Egyptian forces being incapable of attacking Israeli air bases or defending against Israeli air strikes combined with what were seen as past "false alarms" of Egyptian attacks to dissuade the Israeli military to mobilize again.[20] Such decisions led to the near defeat of Israel and a subsequent major reorganization of its intelligence services. Moreover, US and Israeli analysts failed to understand Egyptian president Anwar Sadat's motive for war: he did not presume he would win but that he could deal Israel a severe blow to its military prowess and sense of security, thereby regaining the diplomatic initiative. In the United States, the Yom Kippur War also was a reminder that relying too heavily on foreign governments' assessments could be dangerous—a problem that cropped up again in the 1990 Iraqi invasion of Kuwait.

1979 Soviet Invasion of Afghanistan

The Soviet full-scale military invasion of Afghanistan on Christmas 1979 shocked the Carter administration, which had dismissed the possibility, believing that Moscow would not wish to undermine a newly negotiated SALT II strategic agreement with Washington. Distracted by the Iran hostage crisis as well as the growing debate over Soviet deployment of intermediate-range nuclear missiles opposite NATO, senior officials engaged in wishful thinking. It also caught most US intelligence analysts by surprise. Nearly all had agreed that the Soviet military was in a position to intervene massively, as they monitored and reported a steady buildup of forces, but most analysts doubted Moscow would commit to a long-term, costly, and likely unsuccessful engagement in a faraway land. What warnings were provided forecast a modest and graduated injection of Soviet forces. According to a September 1979 interagency intelligence memorandum, the two options confronting Moscow were gradually increasing assistance, amounting to a "division or two" or a "commitment of large numbers of regular ground forces in a potentially open-ended operation."[21] As the Soviet buildup intensified in November and December, some Carter advisers became alarmed, but discussion of policy options was hampered by disagreement among them and preoccupation with other issues. Some participants lamented that the IC had not "predicted" an invasion in order to force the Carter administration to consider a firmer response that might have deterred Moscow from intervening.[22]

1990 Iraqi Invasion of Kuwait

IC failure to provide timing warning of Saddam Hussein's intention to invade Kuwait was an important reminder to analysts that sometimes a low-probability event can shift quickly. In assessing Iraq's military potential in 1989, CIA analysis suggested "diminished threats to the region," largely as a result of the mutually exhausting eight-year war between Iraq and Iran. Analysts perceived Iraq to be a war-weary state, deeply in debt as a result of loans it needed from Kuwait and other Gulf states to keep its war with Iran going. In assessing Saddam's views toward Kuwait, analysts agreed that he had territorial and financial grievances against the Kuwaiti monarchy but that his saber-rattling military buildups were more of a "shakedown" than war preparations. Ten days prior to Saddam's invasion of Kuwait, US policymakers as well as analysts were reassured by messages from key Gulf allies (especially Egyptian president Hosni Mubarak and Jordan's King Hussein) that Saddam was bluffing. George H. W. Bush administration officials appeared divided over the seriousness of the threat and inclined to study the problem rather than act. In mid-July 1990, DIA and CIA assessments separately said Iraq was unlikely to use "significant force" against Kuwait.[23]

However, as Saddam's buildup accelerated, some intelligence mind-sets, if not all, began to perceive that Saddam had the intention to invade if his demands for loan forgiveness and territorial concessions were not accepted. On July 25, the NIO/W alerted the White House to this danger, a week before Iraqi forces entered Kuwait. Other CIA analysts were slow to come around to this, perhaps explaining why the Bush administration had not made stronger statements or taken some preparatory actions to deter Saddam. However, Defense Secretary Dick Cheney, in defense of the administration, told senators, "All the reports we received from those most directly affected focused specifically on the proposition that Saddam Hussein will never invade Kuwait."[24]

Breakup of the Soviet Union and Coup Potential

As the Cold War ended, the IC wrestled with the problem of forecasting what would become of the Soviet Union. Throughout the 1980s, the IC had been monitoring the steady decline of the USSR's economy, its mounting social and political problems, and the restlessness of its Warsaw Pact allies, where dissidents in Poland, Hungary, and Czechoslovakia were pressing their communist governments for political and economic reforms. NIEs and CIA assessments were issuing numerous warnings of problems, even for a reformer such as Mikhail Gorbachev.[25] Preparing for his 1989 summit with Gorbachev in Malta, President George H. W. Bush remarked that a CIA paper has impressed him with the warning that his counterpart's economic and political reforms were enough to disrupt the old system but not strong enough to produce any benefits, thereby putting Gorbachev in some jeopardy.[26] A selection of titles from NIEs released from 1988 to 1990, when Gorbachev narrowly survived a failed coup, testify to the warnings embedded in numerous intelligence assessments:

- NIE 11-23-88, December 1988: *Gorbachev's Economic Programs: The Challenges Ahead*

- NIE 11-18-89, November 1989: *The Soviet System in Crisis: Prospects for the Next Two Years*
- NIE 11-18-90, November 1990: *The Deepening Crisis in the USSR: Prospects for the Next Year*

If fault can be laid on the IC's doorstep, perhaps it was its overwhelming focus on Moscow's economic problems and not imagining how the political system could be undone by them. Yet, in April 1991, the director of the Office of Soviet Analysis, George Kolt, prepared a prescient analysis laying out the possibility of political collapse, including a move by hardliners to remove reformers through force and restore a communist dictatorship. Titled "The Soviet Cauldron," the analysis warned that Gorbachev was in deep trouble and that civilian and military opponents of reform had already put steps in motion so that a military coup was possible. (See box 7.1 for a more complete set of intelligence findings.) Already alert to Gorbachev's precarious position, President Bush was less shocked by the announced August 1991 coup against this hapless reformer as he vacationed in Crimea. Bush stood by Gorbachev, having also been alerted to other reporting that suggested the coup plotters were poorly organized and not widely supported.

The 1990 Breakup of Yugoslavia

This warning "success" is a case of "we told you so, but you did not listen." As the Soviet Union was breaking apart and the George H. W. Bush administration was prosecuting the Gulf War, the IC was also monitoring the growing dissension among the ethnically diverse regions of the Socialist Federal Republic of Yugoslavia. Led by strongman Slobodan Milošević, the large Serbian Republic was battling with the Croatian, Slovenian, and Bosnian Republics to preserve and dominate the federal system that Marshal Josip Broz Tito had ruled until his death in 1979. In October 1990, the IC issued an unusually stark and precise warning that "Yugoslavia will cease to function as a federal state within one year and will probably dissolve within two" (see box 7.2 for full set of key points). It went on to conclude that the state could slide from sporadic ethnic violence into an inter-republic civil war. However, perhaps its most ominous and controversial statement was that "the United States will have little capacity to preserve Yugoslav unity."

At the time this estimate was released, the Bush administration was fully preoccupied with the USSR's breakup and had no interest in legitimizing another federal state's dissolution. There is little doubt that the warning message was received, but it drew little policy attention from an administration filled with senior officials who had served in Yugoslavia and knew the situation well.[27] Instead, the administration determined that it had no strategic interest at stake (e.g., Secretary of State James Baker declared "we had no dog in the fight") and relied on European allies who had

> ## Box 7.1   April 1991 CIA Analysis: The Soviet Cauldron (Excerpts)
>
> The economic crisis, independence aspirations, and anti-communist forces are breaking down the Soviet empire and system of governance.
>
> [Gorbachev]'s attempts to preserve the essence of a center-dominated union, Communist Party rule and a centrally-planned economy without the broad use of force, however, have driven him to tactical expedients that are not solving basic problems and are hindering but not preventing the development of a new system.
>
> Gorbachev has truly been faced with terrible choices in his effort to move the USSR away from the failed rigid old system. His expedients have so far kept him in office and changed that system irretrievably, but have also prolonged and complicated the agony of transition. . . .
>
> [A] pre-meditated, organized attempt to restore a full-fledged dictatorship would be the most fateful in that it would try to roll back newly acquired freedoms and be inherently destabilizing in the long term. Unfortunately, preparations for dictatorial rule have begun in two ways:
>
> - [M]ilitary, MVD, and KGB leaders are making preparations for a broad use of force in the political process.
> - A campaign to retire democratically inclined officers or at least move them out of key positions has been going on for some time.
>
> Any attempt to restore full-fledged dictatorship would start in Moscow with the arrest or assassination of Yeltsin and other democratic leaders. . . . The long-term prospects of such an enterprise are poor, and even short-term success is far from assured.
>
> Even a putsch is not likely to prevent the pluralistic forces from emerging in a dominant position before the end of this decade.
>
> The current Soviet situation and the various directions in which it could develop over the short term present us with three possible Soviet Unions over the next year:
>
> - Continuation of the current political stalemate would maintain the current Western dilemma of developing the proper mix of relationships with contending forces.
> - An attempt at the restoration of dictatorship would face the West with a repetition of Poland 1981 but almost certainly with more brutality and bloodshed.
> - An accelerated breakthrough by the pluralists would create the best prospects for internal and external stability based on cooperative arrangements.
>
> *Source:* Extracts from a ten-page assessment authored by George Kolt, "CIA Memo, The Soviet Cauldron," in Center for the Study of Intelligence, *At Cold War's End: US Intelligence on the Soviet Union and Eastern Europe, 1989-1991* (Washington, DC: Center for the Study of Intelligence, 1993), https://www.cia.gov/library/center-for-the-study-of-intelligence/csi-publications/books-and-monographs/at-cold-wars-end-us-intelligence-on-the-soviet-union-and-eastern-europe-1989-1991/art-1.html#rtoc7.

pledged to manage the crisis. The warning did not generate any major US policy initiative or shift. Subsequent national estimates on the possible outbreak of violence in Bosnia also elicited little policy response until after President Bill Clinton took office, when the Serbian-led ethnic-cleansing campaign shocked the conscience of the world and pressed the new administration to get more involved.

**Box 7.2   *NIE 15-90: Yugoslavia Transformed*, October 1990
(Key Points)**

- Yugoslavia will cease to function as a federal state within one year, and will prob-ably dissolve within two. Economic reform will not stave off the breakup.
- Serbia will block Slovene and Croat attempts to form an all-Yugoslavia federation.
- There will be a protracted armed uprising by Albanians in Kosovo. A full-scale, inter-republic war is unlikely, but serious intercommunal conflict will accompany the breakup and will continue afterward. The violence will be intractable and bitter.
- There is little the United States and its European allies can do to preserve Yugoslav unity. Yugoslavs will see such efforts as contradictory to advocacy of democracy and self-determination.

Source: DCI, NIE 15-90: Yugoslavia Transformed, October 18, 1990, iii.

In this case, then, the warning of political dissolution was accurate as was its ominous forecast of violence. However, it failed to move policymakers in a way that might have tried to head off the violence that lasted from 1991 to 1995. Some crit-ics believe that the NIE's presumption that the United States could not prevent the breakup was not only flawed but also verged into being policy-proscriptive. Others held the estimate up as an example of how pointless strategic warning analysis can be when an administration has already formed an opinion and is resistant to revisit-ing those views.

2001 al-Qaeda Attack

The stunning al-Qaeda airliner attack on the Twin Towers in New York City and the Pentagon was not the first intelligence failure regarding al-Qaeda–sponsored terror-ism against the United States. It was preceded by the 1993 failed attack on the Twin Towers, the 1998 US embassy bombings in East Africa, and the 2000 boat-borne explosives attack on the USS *Cole* in Yemen. Terrorism had become an important intelligence target and major warning concern by the mid-1990s. Indeed, CIA direc-tor George Tenet had declared in a 1998 memorandum to other IC agency heads, "We are at war with Al-Qaeda," and the Clinton administration had admonished the newly elected George W. Bush team that terrorism would constitute its most serious threat upon taking office.[28] Tenet has recounted numerous meetings at which senior intel-ligence officials conveyed their concerns to the new White House national security team. In July 2001, a senior operations officer briefed National Security Adviser Con-doleezza Rice of Osama bin Laden's intentions, saying, "There will be a significant terrorist attack in the coming weeks or months." The CIA did not know the specific day, but in the officer's words, "it will be spectacular," and multiple and simultaneous attacks are possible.[29]

In that sense, the IC had provided "strategic warning." Publications such as a 1995 NIE on terrorism had already forecast terrorist attacks, even in the United States.[30] The DCI's annual Worldwide Threat Assessment testimonies to Congress from 1998 onward had identified Bin Laden's shadowy organization as the number-one terrorist threat. Moreover, in August 2001, in response to a question from President George W. Bush, the *PDB* ran a lead item titled "Bin Laden Intent on Striking the U.S. Homeland" (see box 7.3). Following the attacks, the 9/11 Commission conducted an extensive investigation that concluded the IC had failed to apply its own warning methods to al-Qaeda, which contributed to a "failure of imagination." Also, the Commission credited poor information sharing by the CIA and FBI that might have identified some of the nineteen plotters who had already entered the country and were taking flying instructions.

The 9/11 Commission's findings remain controversial, as many intelligence experts defended the IC's performance in the face of vocal criticisms coming from the 9/11 victims' families and many in the public at large.[31] The fact that the CIA, its Counterterrorism Center (CTC),[32] and other agencies had repeatedly warned about

---

Box 7.3 President's Daily Brief, August 6, 2001, Regarding Bin Laden (Excerpts)

Clandestine, foreign government and media reports indicate Bin Ladin since 1997 has wanted to conduct terrorist attacks in the US. Bin Ladin implied in US television interviews in 1997 and 1998 that his followers would follow the example of the World Trade Center bomber Ramzi Yousef and "bring the fighting to America."

The millennium plotting in Canada in 1999 may have been part of Bin Laden's first serious attempt to implement a terrorist strike in the US.

Although Bin Ladin has not succeeded, his attacks against the US Embassies in Kenya and Tanzania in 1998 demonstrate that he prepares operations years in advance and is not deterred by setbacks.

Al-Qaida members—including some who are US citizens—have resided in or traveled to the US for years, and the group apparently maintains a support structure that could aid attacks.

We have not been able to corroborate some of the more sensational threat reporting, such as that from a [foreign intelligence] service in 1998 saying that Bin Ladin wanted to hijack a US aircraft to gain the release of "Blind Shaykh" Umar Abd al-Rahman and other US-held extremists.

Source: "Bin Ladin Determined to Strike the US," *President's Daily Brief*, August 6, 2001, https://nsarchive2.gwu .edu/NSAEBB/NSAEBB116/pdb8-6-2001.pdf.

Bin Laden's plans to attack US interests is seen by those defenders as evidence of the IC having provided strategic warning. They argue that seldom can intelligence collect sufficiently detailed information on the "where," "when," "who," and "how" to prevent such attacks.

The CIA in particular felt singled out unfairly for its failure to imagine such an audacious attack, when it was the one agency doing the most to capture or kill Bin Laden. Almost a dozen previous CTC plans to go after him were largely squelched by a Clinton administration worried about the uncertainty of the intelligence and possible blowback that such operations might have. Where some fault may lie is in the Bush administration's slowness in adopting a more rigorous counterterrorism strategy being recommended by then senior counterterrorism adviser Richard Clarke or in pushing other federal agencies (e.g., the Federal Aviation Administration, customs officials, and the FBI) to take more counterterrorism measures.

KEY LESSONS AND CHALLENGES TO WARNING

The list of successes and failures in warning tends to highlight some recurring patterns in how surprise happens, even when policymakers are warned. Among the most typical causes and challenges of effective warning are cognitive biases, organizational hurdles, and policymakers' resistance to accepting and acting on warning. However, a fourth lesson learned is that adversaries often can play on those weaknesses in the warning process by effective use of deception, disinformation, and denial.

Cognitive Bias: The Mind-set Problem

In many of the cases cited above, analysts—and often policymakers as well—were prone to dismiss existing evidence of a military attack or other challenges to American interests. In the case of Pearl Harbor, military analysts had a mind-set of an inferior enemy who would most likely go for an easy target in East Asia rather than challenge the US Pacific Fleet in its home waters. Likewise, Israeli and American analysts had a preconceived view that Arab armies were too weak to challenge the more powerful Israel Defense Forces. In the end, those analysts were correct about Israel's ultimate victory, but they failed to realize that Egypt had not expected it could defeat Israel but only aimed to deal Israel a shock that would force negotiations (which it did).

Mind-sets, it turns out, are hard to change, particularly when there is a paucity of information that challenges the conventional wisdom. So, US analysts reported in September 1962 that they were confident that the Soviets would not dare to place strategic missiles in Cuba, and there was almost no credible reporting that missiles were in place prior to the U-2 flights later in October. Overcoming cognitive biases like these takes much more positive information than is often available to the analysts or policymakers. In 2002, analysts warned that Saddam possessed substantial WMD stockpiles and might be making progress toward developing nuclear weapons. There was little real information that pointed to renewed WMD activities, but collectors also had not been providing any disconfirming information either. So, in the absence of good information, analysts will always fall back on their assumptions about how capable or devious an adversary is. Robert Jervis, a distinguished political scientist and frequent consultant to intelligence agencies, has famously written about the power of decision-makers' perceptions and misperceptions, which can be far off the mark.[33]

Doing good warning, then, requires that analysts and policymakers be aware of their own biases and unproven assumptions about the world and how it operates. Too often Americans presume that foreign leaders will operate and calculate the risks and benefits of taking certain actions much as Washington does. In such instances, analysts conclude that an adversary would not start a war it cannot win or take an action that would be too risky were it an American decision. Analysts must guard against such mirror-imaging. Understanding foreign leaders, who have been raised in very different cultures and for whom risk and benefit may be assessed differently, is perhaps the hardest job that analysts face. Historically, the IC has not done well anticipating how dictators such as Iraq's Saddam Hussein, Serbia's Slobodan Milošević, or North Korea's Kim Jong-un might behave. Warning of foreign leaders' erratic, or what some people might consider irrational, behavior poses real challenges without some resort to different cultural and psychological lenses. At the least, warning analysis needs to take advantage of structured analytical techniques—Red Cell analysis, **devil's advocacy**, or assumptions checks—that can challenge an American analytical mind-set.

Organizational Effects

Contributing to many successes and failures is the role that the IC's own operations and organizational cultures play in shaping warning. During the Cold War, a centrally directed warning system performed well enough that the United States never experienced a strategic surprise involving nuclear weapons. The national warning system was sufficiently reliable, and American nuclear forces were sufficiently survivable that the Soviets were convinced that a surprise "first strike" could not disarm the United States. National warning systems, including the sizable specialized warning staffs and the actions of the NIO/Ws, also were reasonably good at alerting policymakers to major military buildups. However, the CIA and DIA as organizations also tended to fall into recognizable and predictable camps regarding the nature of the Soviet threat. The CIA tended to take a more benign view of Soviet strategic programs, believing Moscow would reason that nuclear war was "unwinnable" and so achieving strategic parity with the United States was sufficient. On the other hand, the DIA and the military intelligence services tended to ascribe more ambitious goals, including achieving strategic superiority and "winning" a nuclear war, to the Soviet leadership. Neither got it exactly right. At times the CIA underestimated the Soviet strategic programs, while defense intelligence was generally regarded as taking a worst-case position.

Intelligence organizations also tend to develop a "party line" on warning issues. In 1973, the CIA was confident that Israel's superior military could not be defeated, so Egyptian president Sadat would not dare to attack Israel. The CIA also tended to defer to Israeli intelligence, which also had developed a "conception" that Egypt would not consider attacking Israel again until its military had vastly improved its air defenses. Once an analytical judgment has been pronounced within an agency, it takes on an important foundational basis for all future analysis. Few analysts are willing to contest a well-accepted office position. Hence, "linchpin" assumptions, as one senior CIA official termed them, go unchallenged because they reflect past conclusions that the agency's analysts feel obliged to defend. The accepted wisdom that "Saddam was hiding WMDs" or that "Egypt would not start a war it could not win" or that "the Soviets would not deploy offensive missiles in Cuba" would have been tough for any individual analyst to question, much less debunk.

Organizations also share information poorly, which can undermine effective warning. As seen in the 1941 attack on Pearl Harbor, the army and navy code-breakers were competing to provide deciphered messages to the few Washington officials privy to them, and bureaucratic infighting slowed down communication with policymakers. In the case of 9/11, there was information collected overseas on the plotters, which the CIA had and did not share with the FBI, and the FBI field offices also had collected information, which it had not provided to its Washington headquarters or the CIA. For a variety of reasons, each agency saw no reason it should pass its unique information to each other. This hampered analysts in building a complete picture of the threat, which had both domestic and international aspects. Since 9/11, there have been efforts to soften the long-standing need-to-know principle that compartments information inside organizations or even within an organization's separate divisions. The DNI's call for a "need to share" has helped to break down some of these organizational barriers, but it remains a challenge when so many intelligence organizations are now involved in monitoring a range of international threats.

It is worth considering whether the transition from a centrally directed warning system relying on warning specialists to one that places primary warning responsibility on all analysts is working. It presumes a solid understanding of what warning is and how it must be communicated to policy officials. Yet at the moment there is very little formal warning training, especially in civilian intelligence agencies such as the CIA. Moreover, it presumes that effective warning can be produced through the normal analytical production methods, when warning is as much an art as a science.[34] As troubling, the DNI's latest moves away from old-style warning to something now termed "anticipatory" intelligence has created a new concept in need of further definition. As articulated by the DNI, "anticipatory intelligence is the result of intelligence collection and analysis focused on trends, events, and changing conditions to identify and characterize potential or imminent discontinuities, significant events, substantial opportunities, or threats to U.S. national interests."[35]

To some analysts, anticipatory intelligence is nothing more than new jargon for what has long been called strategic and warning analysis. But that definition fails to highlight the need to provide advanced skills to analysts or to develop mechanisms for passing such anticipatory intelligence to policymakers who can take action. At a minimum, more needs to be done to foster the skills for such missions regardless of what one calls it. In partial recognition of the need to do more, the NIC now has a special adviser on warning, whose mission might appear to be advocating for more attention to warning issues. At the time of this writing, that adviser appears to lack the substantial staff or authority previously held by the NIO/W.

Policymakers' Wishful Thinking

In reviewing the many warnings provided to presidents and their national security teams, there emerges a pattern of some policymakers not wanting to believe the warnings that the IC issues. As Sherman Kent's comment at the opening of this chapter indicates, national security decision-makers can ignore intelligence. Partly policymakers are reluctant to make decisions on incomplete information that suggests there is some risk but no certainty that a postulated threat will actually occur. Usually taking steps to avert some disaster has its own consequences and costs. Today's dilemma of halting a North Korean nuclear program highlights the policymaker's set of bad choices. Strategic warning of an eventual North Korean capability to strike the United States with a nuclear-armed intercontinental ballistic missile has been delivered. Indeed, this warning has been provided to the White House ever since Bill Clinton was president. He and his successors all tried measures short of a preemptive attack—for example, use of sanctions as well as economic incentives to halt the program—in an effort to head off such a threat. Today, however, President Donald Trump faces some of the same unappealing choices of minimizing the threat or using economic sanctions to pressure Kim Jong-un to halt his program or considering a military course of action to destroy or at least retard that program. Such a military step would have huge consequences for South Korea and the United States, as well as other Asian allies and partners. Hence, acting on intelligence warnings is never as easy as it might appear.

Some of the aforementioned cases of warning also show that, confronted with growing evidence of possible military conflict (e.g., the 1979 Soviet invasion of Afghanistan) or ethnic violence in the former Yugoslavia (the 1990–95 breakup and the Bosnian War), neither the Carter administration nor the Bush administration wanted to take action. In the former case, it was the wishful thinking that Moscow would not want to jeopardize its relations with Washington; further, it would undermine a strategic arms treaty that Congress would most likely reject if the Soviets invaded. In the latter case, it was the Bush administration's hopes that Europeans would manage the Yugoslav crisis and that it could avoid involvement while it dealt with more pressing problems such as the dissolution of the Soviet Union and the Gulf War. In both cases, warning was provided but just not acted on. From the analysts' perspective, this might seem irresolute or even irresponsible. But from the policymakers' perspective, this is their choice to make. What often happens, however, is policymakers will later lament that the IC had not effectively communicated their concerns, had not highlighted the consequences, or had played down the probability of such dire events occurring.

The Adversary Gets a Say

Blaming failure to warn on either analysts or policymakers is not completely correct. Some credit is due to adversaries and their own efforts to confuse and surprise the United States. It is important to recognize that adversaries often are very clever in playing on the cognitive biases, organizational hurdles, and wishful thinking of American analysts and decision-makers. In many of the cases examined here, the adversary was able to use D&D techniques to hide their actual intentions and preparations or at least to play into the existing mind-sets of analysts and wishful thinking of policymakers. D&D had been used effectively by the Japanese prior to Pearl Harbor, so that the United States had no idea where the Japanese fleet was headed. The Soviets masked the nature of the military equipment being shipped to Cuba for months before it was finally detected by aerial reconnaissance flights. Egypt skillfully announced and conducted what first appeared to be routine annual military exercises around the time of the Yom Kippur holiday. And Saddam Hussein effectively hid his WMD programs from the United States prior to the 1990 Persian Gulf War.

In the military field, analysts must in particular be alert to the use of D&D to cover up what might be military preparations for attacks. Many adversaries have developed these concealment techniques to a fine art. Iran has built many of its nuclear-related facilities in underground locations, partly to hide them but also to make them less vulnerable to attack. Likewise, North Korea has put many of its military assets in either underground facilities or in caves where they cannot be observed, much less destroyed. The Russians continue to use a variety of techniques to mask their own military operations, whether it is "little green men" (soldiers wearing uniforms that bear no unit designations) or conducting hybrid warfare through the use of "volunteers."

Operational security—steps used to prevent the IC from intercepting sensitive communications—also has been a commonplace technique for hostile militaries but also for terrorist groups. The Japanese maintained radio silence between Tokyo and its fleet in the Pacific. The Soviet and Russian military have routinely encrypted communication systems to keep military plans secret and also routinely put out misinformation to disguise their true intentions. Even al-Qaeda and ISIS are wise to the ways of operational security. They learned to avoid using cell phones or any Internet sites that would be susceptible to American intelligence collection, opting instead for couriers and other low-tech methods of communication. Use of the "dark Web" and heavy encryption also can shield terrorist and other illicit operations from US intelligence and law enforcement. Likewise, if such groups suspect that the IC is listening, they will invoke euphemisms or code words to describe their planned activities. Terrorist cells and their networks are by their very nature decentralized, making it harder to uncover all of their plots by capturing a key leader or a terrorist cell's computers and mobile phones.

IS EFFECTIVE WARNING POSSIBLE?

When all is said and done, warning remains the most difficult but most important task for intelligence. As the previously discussed cases illustrate, the IC's record of warning successes and failures is mixed. Improving it has proven difficult, especially as the types of warning issues have moved from strictly military problems into transnational issues, where there are fewer secrets and more mysteries. Richard Betts, who has written widely on intelligence and strategic surprise, has concluded that "intelligence failures are inevitable." In his view, surprise occurs most often by policymakers' inability or unwillingness to accept warnings and act on them. So long as warning information remains ambiguous—that is less than certain—then policymakers will harbor the illusion that somehow intelligence should have been better or needs to be improved.[36] On the other hand, intelligence faults should not be excused entirely. Other scholars have argued that providing strategic warning is seldom enough to avoid strategic surprise.[37] But good strategic warning can alert the IC to devote more collection and analytical resources to develop tactical warning. Thus, specific measures to expand collection that reduces information gaps on strategic warning issues can be made; moreover, strategic warning should put analysts on notice that they also need to review their assumptions and mind-sets that may have lulled them into complacency.

At the same time, however, policymakers must be more attuned to what the IC is communicating and also to telling their intelligence counterparts which issues are of most concern to them, about which they need to be warned. As one seasoned intelligence analyst concluded, "To expect to predict or prevent any and all surprises is not reasonable. But it is unreasonable to expect that intelligence analysts will not make mistakes, just as policymakers have and will."[38]

USEFUL DOCUMENTS

Improving CIA Analytic Performance: Strategic Warning, 2002, https://www.cia.gov/library/center-for-the-study-of-intelligence/kent-csi/kent-vol1no1/html/v01n1p.htm
  A senior CIA intelligence adviser and training officer's assessment of how to avoid future intelligence failures.
Joint Military Intelligence College, *Intelligence Warning Terminology*, October 2001, https://archive.org/stream/JMICInteligencelwarnterminology/JMIC_intelligencewarnterminology_djvu.txt
  A useful collection of specialized warning concepts and terms as used in the Department of Defense.
The 9/11 Commission Report, https://www.9-11commission.gov/report/911Report.pdf
  A well-written description of how the 9/11 attacks occurred and what intelligence agencies were doing at the time.

FURTHER READING

Erik Dahl, *Intelligence and Surprise Attack: Failure and Success from Pearl Harbor to 9/11 and Beyond* (Washington, DC: Georgetown University Press, 2011).
  Author makes the case that tactical intelligence failed to provide sufficient warning in both cases.
John Gentry and Joseph Gordon, *Strategic Warning Intelligence: History, Challenges, and Prospects* (Washington, DC: Georgetown University Press, 2019).
  The most recent and definitive treatment of warning by two recognized warning practitioners.
Cynthia Grabo, *Anticipating Surprise: Analysis for Strategic Warning* (Lanham, MD: University Press of America, 2004).
  One of the earliest, and now declassified, treatments of the warning problem, which remains a classic.
Robert Jervis, *Why Intelligence Fails: Lessons from the Iranian Revolution and the Iraq War* (Ithaca, NY: Cornell University Press, 2010).
  Author compares warning failures of these two cases and analyzes their causes and impacts.
Janne Nolan and Douglas MacEachin, eds., *Discourse, Dissent, and Strategic Surprise: Formulating U.S. National Security Policy in an Age of Uncertainty* (Washington, DC: Georgetown University Institute for the Study of Diplomacy, 2006).

Authors review a series of lesser-known cases where intelligence warnings were provided but not heeded by policymakers.

Roberta Wohlstetter, *Pearl Harbor: Warning and Decision* (Stanford, CA: Stanford University Press, 1962).

Study remains the classic description of an intelligence warning failure, arguing that too much noise disguised available signals of a Japanese attack.

NOTES

First epigraph: John McCone quotation in the CIA's Historical Intelligence Collection, as cited in Charles E. Lathrop, *The Literary Spy: The Ultimate Source for Quotations on Espionage and Intelligence* (New Haven, CT: Yale University Press, 2004), 411.

Second epigraph: Henry Kissinger quotation from his memoir *White House Years*, cited in Lathrop, *Literary Spy*, 413.

1. US Intelligence Board, DCI Directive No. 1/5, "Strategic Warning," February 6, 1975, https://www.cia.gov/library/readingroom/docs/CIA-RDP91M00696R000600150012-2.pdf.

2. Cynthia Grabo, *Anticipating Surprise: Analysis for Strategic Warning* (Lanham, MD: University Press of America, 2004). An "indication" is new information that reveals an adversary's intentions for aggressive action. Usually it includes specific changes in behavior or capabilities that are defined as "indicators." For example, new imagery showing a transfer of forces along a contested border, a higher state of military readiness, or major buildup of ammunition depots could be indicators of an intent to commence military actions.

3. Grabo, 37.

4. J. Eli Margolis, "Estimating State Instabilty," *Studies in Intelligence* 56, no. 1 (March 2012): 13.

5. David Shlapak and Michael Johnson, *Reinforcing Deterrence on NATO's Eastern Flank*, RAND Paper 1200, 2016, https://www.rand.org/content/dam/rand/pubs/research_reports/RR1200/RR1253/RAND_RR1253.pdf.

6. Once the launch of Soviet intercontinental ballistic missiles has been detected, nuclear planners believed that a president would have no more than thirty minutes to make a decision to launch American missiles before the ICBMs could destroy American land-based nuclear missiles.

7. Grabo, *Anticipating Surprise*, 365.

8. These examples are drawn from a more comprehensive set of military indicators found in John Gentry and Joseph Gordon, *Strategic Warning Intelligence: History, Challenges, and Prospects* (Washington, DC: Georgetown University Press, 2019).

9. See Richard Kerr and Michael Warner, "The Track Record of CIA's Analysis," in Roger Z. George and James Bruce, eds., *Analyzing Intelligence: National Security Practitioners' Perspectives* (Washington, DC: Georgetown University Press, 2014), 41. One clear exception was the Soviet biological weapons program that was not discovered until a high-level defector revealed the extensive R&D conducted by Moscow in violation of its commitment to the BW convention.

10. Nassim Taleb, *The Black Swan: The Impact of the Highly Improbable* (London: Penguin, 2008).

11. Roger George and James Wirtz, "Warning in an Age of Uncertainty," in George and Bruce, *Analyzing Intelligence*, 225.

12. See George Tenet, *At the Center of the Storm: My Years at CIA* (New York: Harper-Collins, 2007), 133–74. Although a "hindsight" reflection, the chapter titled "They Are Coming Here" recounts the CIA director's unsuccessful efforts to draw attention to the grave danger of a major attack in the spring and fall of 2001. It illustrates that warning messages may not be convincing enough to produce action.

13. See the excellent description of the I&W methodology and strategic warning in John A. Gentry and Joseph S. Gordon, *Strategic Warning: History, Challenges, and Prospects* (Washington, DC: Georgetown University Press, 2019).

14. Roberta Wohlstetter, *Pearl Harbor: Warning and Decision* (Stanford, CA: Stanford University, 1962).

15. Erick Dahl, *Intelligence and Surprise Attack: Failure and Success from Pearl Harbor to 9/11 and Beyond* (Washington, DC: Georgetown University Press, 2013).

16. See Eric Dahl, "Testing the Argument: Classic Cases of Surprise Attack," in Dahl, *Intelligence and Surprise Attack*, 69–70.

17. The volume by Graham Allison and Phil Zelikow, *The Essence of Decision: Explaining the Cuban Missile Crisis* (New York: Longman, 1999), remains widely read and an authoritative treatment of how Kennedy and his advisers negotiated the removal of missiles during the thirteen-day crisis.

18. See his defense in Sherman Kent, "A Crucial Estimate Relived," *Studies in Intelligence* (Spring 1964), declassified, https://www.cia.gov/library/center-for-the-study-of-intelligence/csi-publications/books-and-monographs/sherman-kent-and-the-board-of-national-estimates-collected-essays/9crucial.html.

19. David S. Robarge, "CIA Analysis of the 1967 Arab-Israeli War," *Studies in Intelligence* 49, no. 1 (April 2007), https://www.cia.gov/library/center-for-the-study-of-intelligence/csi-publications/csi-studies/studies/vol49no1/html_files/arab_israeli_war_1.html.

20. See Ephraim Kahana, "Early Warning Concept: The Case of the Yom Kippur War 1973," *Intelligence and National Security* 17, no. 2 (2002): 81–104.

21. Extracted and quoted from *IIM Soviet Operations in Afghanistan*, found in Janne Nolan and Douglas MacEachin, eds., *Discourse, Dissent, and Strategic Surprise: Formulating U.S. National Security Policy in an Age of Uncertainty* (Washington, DC: Georgetown University Institute for the Study of Diplomacy, 2006), 55.

22. Nolan and MacEachin, 62–63.

23. CIA and DIA assessments are described in John Diamond, *The CIA and the Culture of Failure: U.S. Intelligence from the End of the Cold War to the Invasion of Iraq* (Stanford, CA: Stanford University Press, 2008), 141–56 and 126–27, respectively.

24. Diamond, *CIA and Culture of Failure*, 139–40.

25. For a defense of the CIA's record on tracking the Soviet decline, see Bruce Berkowitz, "Intelligence Estimates of the Soviet Collapse: Perception and Reality," *International Journal of Intelligence and Counterintelligence* 21 (2008): 237–50, https://www.cia.gov/library/readingroom/docs/20080229.pdf.

26. Cited in Jon Meacham, *Destiny and Power: The American Odyssey of George Herbert Walker Bush* (New York: Random House, 2015), 383.

27. National Security Adviser Brent Scowcroft, a retired US Air Force lieutenant general, had served as assistant air attaché in Yugoslavia in the early 1960s, and Deputy Secretary of State Lawrence Eagleburger had been ambassador there in the late 1970s.

28. See Tenet, *Center of the Storm.*

29. Tenet, 151–52.

30. 9/11 Commission, *Final Report of the National Commission on the Terrorist Attacks against the United States*, 341, https://www.9-11commission.gov/report/911Report.pdf.

31. See Paul Pillar's critique of the 9/11 Commission's work blaming the CIA and using the 9/11 attacks for justifying the unnecessary intelligence reforms that created the ODNI and the NCTC. Paul Pillar, *Intelligence and U.S. Foreign Policy: Iraq, 9/11, and Misguided Reform* (New York: Columbia University Press, 2011).

32. The CIA's Counterterrorism Center (CTC) is primarily focused on the collection of human intelligence on terrorist organizations and has a small number of targeting analysts assigned to it. The National Counterterrorism Center (NCTC), created in 2004 and run by the DNI, has overall responsibility for coordinating counterterrorism policies as well as for producing finished intelligence analysis on counterterrorism threats. As part of a major organizational modernization in 2015, the CTC was combined with elements of the directorate of operations and renamed the Mission Center for Counterterrorism.

33. Robert Jervis, *Perception and Misperception in International Politics* (Princeton, NJ: Princeton University Press, 1976).

34. See Gentry and Gordon, *Strategic Warning*, 82–89. The authors are generally critical of the abandonment of a national warning system in which trained "warning analysts" would devote their full attention to monitoring worrisome trends and for which formal training in warning methodologies as well as foreign D&D techniques were emphasized.

35. ODNI, *The National Intelligence Strategy of the United States*, February 2014, 7, https://www.dni.gov/files/2014_NIS_Publication.pdf.

36. Richard Betts, *Enemies of Intelligence: Knowledge and Power in American National Security* (New York: Columbia University Press, 2007), 19.

37. Dahl, *Intelligence and Surprise Attack*, 176.

38. John Hedley, "Learning from Intelligence Failures," *International Journal of Intelligence and Counterintelligence* 18, no. 2 (February 2007), 447.

8

INTELLIGENCE SUPPORT AS POLICY ENABLER

The ultimate objective of intelligence is to enable action to be optimized. The individual or body which has to decide on action needs information about its opponent as an ingredient likely to be vital in determining its decision; and this information may suggest that action should be taken on a larger or smaller scale than that which otherwise would be taken, or even that a different course of action would be better.
—R. V. Jones, "Intelligence and Command," 1989

Current operations intelligence includes the intelligence necessary to support time-sensitive needs of the military, diplomatic, homeland security and policy customers in times of conflict or crisis, but also provides opportunities to shape future operations and desired operational outcomes.
—National Intelligence Strategy of the United States, 2019

Compared to long-range strategic intelligence forecasting or urgent warning analysis, intelligence that is required for effective policy decisions or actions is far less visible or controversial. Yet in many respects this type of **policy support** is the lifeblood of intelligence. It is occurring constantly in the form of current intelligence reporting, analyst briefings, and interactions with policymakers in all national security departments on a wide range of topics. Thus, this chapter will review some of the major ways in which intelligence contributes not only to the development of national security policies but also to their actual implementation and operation. It will begin by examining the role of current intelligence but then broaden into a discussion of several unique forms of policy support to crisis management, diplomatic negotiations, and operational targeting. Providing such tactical support also raises some wicked choices about how to spread limited resources across a vast list of targets and how to satisfy both national and military intelligence users.

Once decision-makers have assessed a particular issue, considered the relevant intelligence, and evaluated their possible courses of action, they announce a policy or set in motion diplomatic, economic, or military actions. But intelligence is not finished supporting policy. In the case of North Korea, a presidential decision to pressure Pyongyang to stop and eventually give up its nuclear weapons program may include new diplomatic measures to isolate North Korea or to generate international agreement to impose new economic sanctions. It might also involve military measures to strengthen South Korean missile defenses or other measures short of war. In a worst case, a president might determine that some preemptive action is needed to avert North Korean achievement of an intercontinental-range nuclear weapon system that could directly threaten the United States homeland. Intelligence will play a role in all aspects of American actions vis-à-vis Pyongyang.

Looking at this one example, one can envision a wide variety of intelligence analysis or operations that can support different elements of an American strategy to contain and curtail North Korean nuclear proliferation threats. Table 8.1 lays out some of those types of direct intelligence support that policymakers might expect or ask for. In these ways, intelligence is an "enabler" of US policy instruments—diplomatic, military, economic, and informational. In the diplomatic field, intelligence can provide assessments of how key foreign governments might react to American proposals in international forums such as the UN Security Council and Asian regional security organizations. At the same time, intelligence might be asked to provide briefings or unclassified white papers (official reports not identified as written by intelligence agencies)[1] assessing North Korea's nuclear programs, which can be used with allied governments and publics as part of a "public diplomacy" campaign. As the international community, led by the United States, has imposed strenuous economic sanctions on North Korean trade and financial dealings, intelligence is expected to monitor and report on the impact those sanctions are having and whether any violations are occurring that need to be addressed. Potential military options will require the intelligence community to identify key nuclear and missile facilities, their vulnerabilities, and their susceptibility to military or potentially nonkinetic attacks (e.g., cyberattacks) designed to disable or destroy Pyongyang's nuclear and missile programs.

As will be discussed in the next chapter, some intelligence planning could potentially go into covert action operations designed to discredit or weaken the North Korean regime's stability or status as well as disrupt its military programs. In each case, intelligence can provide "opportunity" analysis that highlights the regime's

Table 8.1. Intelligence as Policy-Support "Enabler": Examples for North Korea

Diplomatic Policy	Economic Policy	Informational Policy	Military Policy
International Organizations • Prepare briefings to UN Security Council members • Support démarches on WMDs • Publish white papers	*Foreign Assistance* • Monitor illicit trafficking • Identify critical shortfalls	*Public Diplomacy* • Prepare white papers on WMDs • Review government statements/speeches • Monitor foreign media	*Coercive Actions* • Support WMD interdiction operations • Construct cyber actions • Plan covert operations
International Law • Report on human rights violations • Support extraditions/renditions	*Economic Sanctions* • Monitor border traffic • Report sanction violations • Assess regional impact	*Political Actions* • Identify political vulnerabilities/opportunities • Assist strategic communication plans	*Paramilitary Actions* • Support special operations forces' plans to capture WMD devices • Warn of / identify North Korean plans to attack South Korea
Alliances/Coalitions • Assess Japanese and South Korean plans/intentions • Forecast foreign public reactions to US actions	*International Trade Policies* • Monitor world markets • Support free-trade negotiations	*Intelligence Sharing* • Share information with International Atomic Energy Agency • Joint counterproliferation operations	*Force Short of War* • Map suspect WMD sites/facilities • Support intrusive inspection regimes
International Negotiations • Assess North Korean/Russian/Chinese negotiation style/posture • Inform US negotiating position	*Humanitarian Operations* • Monitor North Korean refugee flows to China • Forecast casualty figures in case of conflict	*Soft Power* • Assess North Korean public diplomacy campaigns • Monitor North Korean disinformation / cyber operations	*War Plans* • Provide target information • Conduct bomb-damage assessment

Note: This figure was adapted from one used by Dr. Robert Levine in teaching intelligence at the National War College. Used by permission.

military or economic vulnerabilities, internal pressure points, or poor relations with key partners that can be leveraged by US actions.

As table 8.1 makes clear, analysts are providing bits and pieces of information and analysis related to various policy actions, where the policymakers are trying to determine how best to use an instrument or which possible countermeasures an adversary might take if the United States were to initiate certain actions designed to increase US leverage. Few of these intelligence activities should be transparent to the outside observer, but they are critical contributions to enabling American policies to succeed.

In simple terms, intelligence analysis can enable decision-makers to choose the best course of action. Few writers outside the IC, however, recognize the wide range of analytical contributions to this phase in the policy process, which are less noticeable than a major intelligence warning or prescient strategic analysis of an important international development. As longtime intelligence professional and educator Jack Davis has noted, there are literally thousands of what he termed "transactions" between analyst and policymaker that fall into the category of policy support.[2] The list of such policy-support activities is almost endless, and the daily demands unending. IC analysts receive such requests, or "taskings," at interagency meetings as a result of a one-to-one briefing or at the end of an important telephone or email conversation with a policymaker. Here is where analysts are at their most objective and least likely to be regarded as undermining current policies with critical analysis. Analysts are being mostly instrumental in providing information, which "enables" current policy objectives, regardless of whether analysts think the policy is correct or likely to succeed.

CURRENT INTELLIGENCE

Current intelligence has been a steady staple of intelligence support to policymakers. In contrast to strategic analysis, discussed in chapter 5, current intelligence is focused more on the present than the future. But, if truth be told, most policymakers also operate more in the present than the future. Much of what the IC produces has to address the current set of issues facing policymakers each morning when they reach their offices or military headquarters. The virtue of current intelligence is that it can be produced quickly and focus on those specific issues that are on each decision-maker's short-term agenda. As mentioned earlier in this volume, the range of intelligence users and their intelligence needs is vast. Thus, current intelligence must be prepared by multiple agencies and in a variety of forms. To a large degree, each policy agency's departmental intelligence element produces such products that are tailored to the specific needs of their principal customers.

Large agencies such as the CIA and DIA produce their own unique current intelligence publications. The CIA in the early 1950s had an Office of Current Intelligence devoted to the production of daily publications. This office—as opposed to the Office of National Estimates—focused on fast-breaking events. Its *Current Intelligence Bulletin (CIB)* was produced for the president and senior officials. Over time, the OCI broadened the distribution of its daily publication while also writing a version—later known as the *President's Daily Briefing*—exclusively for the president. These *CIB* publications were notable for their brevity and lack of deep analysis; they were intended to be quick updates on breaking events, not strategic assessments of long-term trends. As box 8.1 illustrates, early current intelligence reports covered in a few pages a half dozen topics that summarized a day's events with only brief comments on their significance. In these excerpts on Korea, analysts reported on recent announcements by the Chinese government regarding termination of 1950-53 conflict. This would have been a high priority topic for President Eisenhower, who inherited the UN military operation from the outgoing Truman administration and had pledged to end it.

Such CIA current intelligence products got lengthier and more sophisticated over time as policymakers demanded coverage of more aspects of the Cold War. What began as the *CIB* evolved into the *National Intelligence Daily (NID)*, which was distributed to dozens of senior officials in the NSC, the State Department, and the Defense Department as well as to other intelligence agencies. The *NID* became for many decades the document of record regarding what CIA analysts were reporting on a daily basis. In the intervening years, the information technology revolution

---

Box 8.1   1954 *Current Intelligence Bulletin* (Excerpts on Korea)

September 17, 1954   **FAR EAST**

1. Chinese to permit neutral surveillance of troop withdrawal from Korea.

The Neutral National Inspection Team at Sinanju, North Korea, reported on 16 September that it had received official notification that seven Chinese Communist divisions would leave Korea starting next week. The movement, under the surveillance of the NNIT will consist of ten trains daily, each composed of from 20-24 cars.

Comment: Peiping's public announcement on 5 September of its intention to withdraw these divisions was a departure from its usual practice, and undoubtedly was intended to counteract the announcement of UN withdrawals. At the time of the announcement, it was not clear whether the Chinese intended to withdraw troops in addition to those which had previously returned to China unannounced.

By permitting NNIT surveillance for the first time, the Communists are attempting to strengthen their case in the UN General Assembly against expected moves to terminate the mission of the teams. If these divisions are infantry units, their withdrawal would reduce Chinese strength in Korea from 709,000 to 604,000.

Sources: CIA, Office of Current Intelligence, *Current Intelligence Bulletin*, approved for release January 16, 2004.

and decision-makers' need for rapid intelligence support pushed the transformation of the *NID* into a quicker publication called the *Senior Executive Intelligence Brief (SEIB)*; that then morphed into an even more sophisticated daily publication called the **Worldwide Intelligence Report**, or *WIRe*. As its acronym conveys, this is very user-friendly and electronically distributed to other civilian decision-makers, military commanders, and intelligence agencies across the government and overseas.

Other intelligence agencies, however, were also providing daily publications and briefings for their departmental customers. At the DIA, intelligence analysts prepare daily summaries of politico-military developments around the world. The DIA is responsible for supporting not only the secretary of defense and his civilian defense experts throughout the Pentagon but also for supporting the Joint Staff and the military combatant commanders around the globe. Short intelligence items, termed Defense Intelligence Notices (DINs), were compiled in two daily publications called the *Defense Intelligence Summary (DINSUM)* and the *Military Intelligence Digest (MID)*. These products aimed at providing "situational awareness" wherever US defense forces or interests were at risk; naturally, they primarily reported foreign military capabilities and threats as well as related political and economic developments that would impact US defense policies. In comparative terms, the *DINSUM* and the *MID* were equivalent to the CIA's *NID*, *SEIB*, and the later *WIRe* publications. Like the CIA, the DIA produced a more exclusive intelligence summary for the secretary of defense and chairman of the Joint Chiefs of Staff called the *Morning Summary*, which was not widely circulated and emulated the *PDB* in terms of its sensitivity and narrow distribution. The DIA also supported the J-2's daily *Chairman's Brief*, which was an oral presentation of the most important topics with PowerPoint slides that could be later circulated electronically to some other parts of the Pentagon.[3] The agency also set up a special office that provided direct support to senior customers in the Pentagon via a system of briefers.

These intelligence products could run more than two dozen pages as they attempted to update politico-military events wherever US defense interests were at stake; their customers might be officials in the Pentagon, on the Joint Staff, or overseas commanders in Europe, Asia, or the Middle East. Depending on the individual users' interests, some daily items had direct relevance, while other updates would be far outside a reader's area of responsibility. Given their broad distribution, they often did not contain the most sensitive defense information. The example provided in box 8.2 illustrates how the DIA was obliged in the 1960s to follow political events that might impact the US military campaign in Vietnam. Defense intelligence analysts were assessing how China would react to President Lyndon Johnson's decision to halt the bombing campaign against North Vietnam, and they concluded it would not result in any major Chinese shift in commitment to Hanoi or its defense production.

Box 8.2   1966 *Defense Intelligence Summary* (Excerpts on China)

January 3, 1966 DINSUM   **FAR EAST ASIA SECTION**

Developments in Communist China

No Chinese Communist military reaction to the pause in US air strikes in North Vietnam has been detected.

Peiping has, however, issued a stinging restatement of its position on Vietnam. An editorial in the authoritative Party organ, *People's Daily*, of 1 January asserted that the US was merely spreading a peace smokescreen to conceal preparations for an expanded war and that "unconditional discussions" meant "unconditional surrender." Chinese efforts to prevent any peace talks are, therefore, likely to continue.

A spate of year-end reports out of Peiping noted Chinese industrial achievements during 1965 and announced the beginning of the long-awaited Third Five-Year Plan on 1 January. . . . The Chinese expect progress to be slow and calculate it will take from 20 to 30 years for their economy to surpass those of "advanced countries."

The new plan shows some signs of being especially tailored to meet commitment in Vietnam and to a possible showdown with the US. *People's Daily* said on 31 December that national defense would be bolstered and basic industry, communications, and transport strengthened. . . . Chinese leaders indicated that they were still primarily concerned with economic priorities and feared that emphasis on military production would have adverse effects on food production.

Source: Freedom of Information Act release, *Defense Intelligence Summary*, #10–66, January 13, 1966.

While large intelligence agencies such as the DIA and CIA produce current products for their many customers on a diverse set of security topics, smaller intelligence agencies tend not to produce daily reports but rather issue current intelligence reports when developments warrant it or when tasked by specific policymakers to assess a particular topic they are following. For example, the State Department's Bureau of Intelligence and Research has adopted this model. For a time, INR struggled to produce a daily current intelligence product comparable to CIA and DIA publications; of course, it focused on a range of topics of interest to a secretary of state and the assistant secretaries responsible for regional diplomatic policies, negotiations, or other politico-military affairs. This document was known as the *Secretary's Morning Summary*. Like the *NID* and the *DINSUM*, it covered a dozen or more topics but had to do that in no more than a dozen pages. The *Secretary's Morning Summary* was welcomed by many secretaries of state because it addressed issues they cared about; however, in many ways it duplicated what was found in CIA publications. Moreover, INR has only a very small cadre of intelligence analysts and so its leadership decided in the early 2000s to discontinue producing a daily intelligence

---

Box 8.3   1994 State Department *Secretary's Morning Summary* (Excerpt on DPRK)

January 29, 1994 **DPRK: Reaction to Patriots**

> Precisely how Pyongyang reacts to reports of US plans to deploy Patriots in South Korea will be determined, in part, by what else happens in the days and weeks ahead. For now, the North is holding its options open.

First Reaction: The North's initial response to the news of Patriot deployments, an unattributed commentary issued yesterday, is typical of what Pyongyang does in the initial stages of a new situation: the North wants to record its strong opposition without committing itself to any line of action while it sorts out its options. A higher-level, more definitive response—a *NoDong Sinmum* editorial or a foreign ministry statement, for example—awaits leadership decisions that usually take several days.

Though mostly a pastiche of themes that have appeared in other commentaries over the past month, this first response to the Patriots is clearly intended to signal that, at least for now, there has been no decision to back away from diplomatic engagement with the United States on the nuclear issues.

Breathing space
The commentary notes that the Patriots have not yet arrived and that the deployment is still only a "plan." By portraying the process as in an early phase, the North has given itself room to maneuver. . . . The characterization of the plan to introduce Patriots as an "unpardonable grave military advantage," and the warning that pressure on the North may lead to a "catastrophe," are not unusual, especially in this sort of low-level, unattributed piece.

Source: State Department Review Authority, declassified August 11, 2008.

---

product and move toward more tailored intelligence reports for specific senior diplomatic officials. That said, it was not uncommon for some occupants of the White House to complain that they liked the writing style found in the *Secretary's Morning Summary* and learned more from it than they did from CIA publications. As box 8.3 demonstrates, this discontinued intelligence product might focus on coercive diplomatic efforts, such as the 1994 movement of US Patriot antimissile batteries to South Korea ("DPRK" referring to the Democratic People's Republic of Korea, or North Korea).

President's Daily Brief: Coin of the Realm

Having described broadly the range of current intelligence products produced and circulated widely among national security agencies, one should acknowledge that these publications were not intended to radically shape or alter major US policies. However, by contrast, the *President's Daily Brief* is likely the most influential and actionable current intelligence publication that the IC produces. This daily summary of current events designed for the president has been a feature of US intelligence since Harry Truman first requested a consolidated digest of intelligence drawn from all government sources. The CIA produced this first compilation of intelligence reporting, then called the *Daily Summary*, beginning on February 15, 1946. It was a simple, two-page document focused principally on Cold War issues emanating from Germany, Yugoslavia, Turkey, and China.[4] From then on, each successive president has received a daily summary of the most sensitive reporting on the world's hot spots that threaten US national security interests. In the early days, this daily publication carried a variety of names (e.g., *Current Intelligence Bulletin* and the *President's Intelligence Checklist*) and formats; it was not until 1964 when it became formally known as the *President's Daily Brief*. Given a president's crowded schedule, the document seldom exceeded more than a dozen pages. Former CIA director Allen Dulles termed it "snappy, short, but at the same time fairly comprehensive" in its effort to cover the past twenty-four hours of world events that mattered.[5] Until the 1980s, the existence of the *PDB* was not widely known.

The *PDB* began as an exclusively CIA publication, although periodically other agencies' analysts were invited to submit articles or to provide their own comments on and dissents to the CIA's analysis. After 2005, with the creation of the Director of National Intelligence, the DNI became responsible for preparing the *PDB*. Thus, the *PDB* is now a community product that can contain articles prepared by other analytical offices at INR, the DIA, and others. For many at the CIA, loss of exclusive control over the *PDB* to the DNI was an emotional blow, from which analysts have gradually recovered. In fact, CIA analysts continue to prepare most *PDB* items. In reality, most other agencies' analysts consider their department's officials, not the White House, to be their principal customers, and they dread the complicated and time-consuming *PDB* coordination process. Although the DNI oversees its preparation, the *PDB* is reviewed, edited, and assembled at CIA headquarters. Thus, in practical terms, the *PDB* remains a largely CIA product, and as former CIA director Robert Gates put it, "Writing for the *PDB* . . . was the reason for our existence."[6]

Several things distinguish the *PDB* from other current intelligence reporting. First, its exclusivity allows for the inclusion of extremely sensitive intelligence and more explanation of sources (including very restricted SIGINT and HUMINT reporting) than would otherwise be permitted in daily publications distributed broadly throughout the government. For more than a few decades, the very existence of the *PDB* was not disclosed beyond the Oval Office or the CIA. The document was considered so sensitive that it was sent via courier and retrieved after the president finished with it.

The *PDB* was truly the president's document. Accordingly, each president has established his own list of recipients. It is not unusual for that list to be extremely narrow at the beginning of an administration. In a few cases, only the president and his national security adviser have initially received the *PDB*. Vice presidents did not regularly see the *PDB* until Gerald Ford held that office. Typically, however, as a president's time in office lengthened, more recipients would be added. This becomes almost unavoidable, as items in the *PDB* could prompt a president to start a discussion with his secretaries of state and defense about an issue. Hence, it soon proved necessary to include those senior officials, in addition to the national security adviser.

As often as not, the eventual distribution list will include—in addition to the president, vice president, and national security adviser—the White House chief of staff, the secretary of state, the secretary of defense, and the chairman of the Joint Chiefs of Staff. In most instances, each of these officials' deputies (who attend the Deputies Committee meetings where presidential policies are often hashed out) will also receive the *PDB*. Hence, depending on a president's style and comfort with intelligence sharing, the list could range from a handful to a dozen or more senior officials across the government. Since 9/11 and the growing concern about terrorism, the *PDB* has been provided to the FBI director and the secretary of homeland security, as they now carry major national security responsibilities for protecting the homeland.

A second characteristic unique to the *PDB* is that it is redesigned to suit each president's own preferences. Formatting and length will change to suit a president who is a comfortable or uncomfortable reader. The use of graphics, maps, and photo imagery augment the attractiveness of the publication. For example, a typical *PDB* might show charts of increased Chinese military spending over time or photos of the latest North Korean missile launch site or nuclear test. If a president was particularly interested in a topic, the *PDB* might carry a special analysis or include raw clandestine or diplomatic reporting on that topic. In its latest iteration, the *PDB* is now provided on a classified iPad so that each of the articles is available electronically. Its virtues include good graphics and more storage so that additional reporting and other intelligence products can be loaded onto the iPad should a recipient have further questions raised by a *PDB* item.[7]

A third unique feature of the *PDB* is its production process and presentation. Each morning, analysts will review their message traffic and determine if a current intelligence item needs to be prepared; only a few of these current items are ever judged of "presidential level" interest. For example, President Trump is likely interested in statements issued by North Korean leader Kim Jong-un and how they should be interpreted or the latest missile tests conducted by Iran. Those items will receive much more extensive review by analysts and their supervisors, knowing that they must pass muster with senior intelligence officials before they will be included in the *PDB*. An analyst might spend a day or more writing, revising, and coordinating the article with other analysts across their agency and the IC more broadly. Once that is finished, *PDB* editors will examine the item to determine whether it would be of high-level interest and reflects critical information or analysis that would be new to the president. Even after the item is edited and approved by the editorial staff, the analyst's job is not yet done. Presuming that this article will appear in the next day's *PDB*, the analyst is obliged to arrive at the office in the early hours that next day to review any new information that came in during the night that might require revising the article.

In addition, the *PDB* has become the only current intelligence product that regularly is conveyed by a "briefer." Since the days when the *PDB* was transported via courier, those individuals have now become senior-level briefers of the *PDB* for the recipients. Depending on the president (and other recipients), the briefer may simply hand over the document, or the briefer might highlight or summarize orally the key items. That means the president (as well as other recipients) will have several analysts assigned to provide him his daily intelligence brief. Analysts selected for such assignments have to be more than just good analysts; indeed, they must be fast learners, well spoken, and have thick skins for tough feedback provided to them by demanding consumers. These briefing assignments are coveted positions, as they come to know what the president is interested in, how much information he has already received on any given topic, and what particular complaints or kudos he has for the *PDB*s he has received.

This daily feedback is very important for shaping the intelligence reporting to suit presidential needs. Equally important, it also motivates analysts to undertake the onerous *PDB* process for a president and other senior officials when they know their work has impact. Hence, the analyst drafting a *PDB* will be expected to meet the president's briefer on that early morning in order to prepare the briefer for follow-up questions that the president might have about the piece. Typically, *PDB* briefers also want to hear from the analyst how good the sourcing is, in case the president probes on "how we know something" or asks how confident the IC is in these judgments.

Early each morning, *PDB* briefers spread out across Washington, DC, to their respective recipients, prepared to hand over their documents, explain items, take follow-up questions, and return to their offices to debrief senior intelligence officials and analysts on how the *PDB* was received. In the case of the White House, *PDB* briefers will often provide separate briefings to the national security adviser and possibly the vice president prior to briefing the president, when those individuals and others such as the chief of staff might also be in attendance. A former *PDB* briefer for President George W. Bush, Michael Morell, described his preparation process in the following fashion:

> It was my job to deliver the PDB—five days a week during the transition and six days a week after the inauguration. I'd start work at 4 a.m., sifting

through the most critical pieces of current intelligence and analysis, deciding which ones to present and in what order, cramming additional information on each topic into my head in case the president or any of the
others in the room—almost always Vice President Dick Cheney, National
Security Adviser Condoleezza Rice, and White House Chief of Staff Andy
Card—had additional questions, as they almost always did. . . . It was like
preparing to orally defend several graduate school dissertations every day,
six days a week.[8]

A final educational feature of the *PDB* is worth mentioning. When incoming presidents receive their initial *PDB* briefing, it is often their first exposure to intelligence.
Traditionally, during election campaigns, major candidates will receive several general briefings; however, the president-elect will begin to get the full *PDB* only after the
election. Thus, the *PDB* process becomes a way of educating a president and other
recipients not only on the wide range of national security topics but also about what
the intelligence community can provide. Over a presidential term of four or possibly
eight years, presidential learning curves will flatten out, so material presented in the
PDB at the start of an administration is most likely far too general and unfocused for
a seasoned president. The president will become more knowledgeable about foreign
affairs and perhaps more demanding of intelligence as time goes on. In cases where
presidents receive the *PDB* briefer each day and develop a good working relationship,
they can push intelligence to provide far more insight than those who do not meet
regularly with their briefers.

The *PDB* process also educates the IC about presidential style and needs. It can
help to determine how much and what kind or forms of information a new president
wants. Sadly, this process takes some time before a new president can come to trust
the IC is working for him and not his predecessor. Even so, most cabinet officials privy
to the *PDB* feel obliged to review it since they know it is available to the president,
vice president, and the national security adviser. At the moment, it is far from clear
whether President Trump has developed a real relationship with the *PDB* briefer or
any familiarity with how this document can serve him. The few media reports on how
Trump approaches intelligence suggest that the *PDB* writers have tried to focus on
economic topics, using graphics as much as possible.[9]

SPECIALIZED TYPES OF POLICY SUPPORT

The *PDB* and National Intelligence Estimates garner the most attention of outside
observers of the IC's work, but there is much more specialized policy-support work
that seldom if ever is noticed or understood. These types of policy support range

from intelligence provided to diplomats for negotiations, to that used to support military and civilian crisis managers, to intelligence supporting ongoing operations to counter other threats, such as terrorism, proliferation, and drug trafficking. Describing a few such examples will illustrate how different these activities are from strategic analysis, warning, or current intelligence reporting.

Intelligence Support to Diplomatic Negotiations

Policy support might also be described as a kind of "scouting" function the analyst can provide to senior officials. In numerous negotiation arenas over the years, US diplomats have wanted to put themselves into the shoes of the adversary or ally to understand what their negotiating strategy might be. Analysts are often called on to imagine how the other party will behave in those negotiations, what their bottom lines will be, and what compromises they might be willing to strike. In other cases, they are providing technical analysis or assessments for arms control negotiations involving nuclear, chemical, or conventional weapons. As one former intelligence adviser to the US ambassador to the UN, Madeleine Albright, put it, "Intelligence is the silent partner in these diplomatic endeavors, rarely acknowledged or recognized. Intelligence is a support function to diplomacy, not a peer relationship."[10] Without suggesting what the United States should do, analysts—either as advisers to a US delegation or in written assessments—often can indirectly suggest how to play an issue to the best American advantage or provide information that can strengthen the US bargaining position.

Throughout the US-Soviet era of arms control negotiations, CIA analysts were part of the negotiating process. They brought their knowledge of the opposing Soviet military capabilities and past negotiating behavior along with an understanding of Kremlin politics to help shape an effective American strategy. In those bilateral diplomatic negotiations, military analysts could advise American diplomats on the composition and capabilities of Soviet forces—often providing surprisingly detailed facts about Soviet nuclear weapons that the Russian military had not shared with their own negotiators. Moreover, intelligence support had to also assess the implications of a strategic arms treaty's provisions. The first question was, Would the treaty improve Moscow's forces relative to the United States? Analysts had to forecast how Soviet forces would be able to modernize under the treaty terms. However, a second question for the IC always was whether it could adequately monitor an arms control treaty and detect any militarily significant treaty violations. In the 1970s, monitoring the major arms control agreements limiting each superpower's nuclear arsenal rested largely on the use of **national technical means (NTM)**.[11] In simple terms, it meant that each party's intelligence assets would be used to monitor compliance (see box 8.4). Much of the debate regarding those treaties had to do with whether

---

Box 8.4   National Technical Means

National technical means is the term referred to in many bilateral US-Soviet arms control agreements when referring to each country's reliance on its own national intelligence assets to monitor compliance with the SALT, ABM, INF, and START I Treaties' limitations. US reliance on its NTM practically means using its multidiscipline intelligence collection systems of all kinds. However, it has traditionally meant heavy reliance on nonintrusive overhead reconnaissance satellites that collect SIGINT and imagery of weapon sites, test ranges, production facilities, and other significant aspects of an opponent's military capabilities that are covered by a specific treaty. In fact, the design and deployment of overhead surveillance systems in the 1970s and 1980s essentially focused on monitoring Soviet capabilities and helped to make arms control agreements possible.

In some of those treaties, each party also agreed to certain "cooperative measures" that would allow NTM to monitor compliance with key treaty limitations. Some of these included banning the use of camouflage or coverings over missile sites or the encryption of telemetry information used by a party to monitor a weapon system's operational capabilities. Information exchanges were also called for in many agreements to facilitate verification of weapon numbers and locations.

Separate from NTM, some US-Soviet treaties also included a set number of on-site inspections to verify the destruction or removal of prohibited systems. Indeed, there is still an agreement in place that permits a small number of aerial overflights of Russia and the United States by each other's reconnaissance aircraft to verify aspects of some treaties that are still in effect.

Source: Amy Woolf, *Monitoring and Verification in Arms Control*, Congressional Research Service, December 23, 2011, https://fas.org/sgp/crs/nuke/R41201.pdf.

---

the IC could detect Soviet cheating. Administrations often had to commit to funding additional defense programs—including intelligence collection—to reassure skeptical senators that ratifying those treaties was in the best interest of the United States.

To support SALT negotiations, the CIA initially established a small team of military analysts called the "SALT support staff." When developing an interagency consensus on a proposed arms control negotiation, this staff and its larger successors were responsible for representing the IC's views on the agreements' impact on the respective US-Soviet military balance. Intelligence analysts would participate in the interagency process, providing briefings on Soviet force levels and plans as well as presenting the IC's views on which treaty provisions were most needed to be able to monitor a treaty. Many times these interagency "negotiations" over monitoring requirements were as important and fractious as those that had to be hammered out with the Soviets; when it came to on-site inspections, the IC would propose more intrusive measures on Soviet programs than the Pentagon would want to permit on American defense programs.[12]

Once the United States had developed its negotiating strategy, it was the job of this staff to provide updated intelligence assessments to the SALT negotiating teams meeting in Geneva. This SALT support staff was also made available to advise members of the US delegation. In preparing for the later SALT II Treaty ratification, the then CIA director Stansfield Turner further underlined the IC's role in three areas:

- assessing the size, capabilities, and future potential of the Soviet strategic forces to be limited by the agreement
- providing timely, responsive support to policymaking agencies and officials in the process of developing US positions and in negotiating the agreement
- providing assessments of the US capability to monitor proposed treaty provisions[13]

Regarding the monitoring responsibility, this activity included ensuring that intelligence-collection and analytical resources were adequately assigned to that mission in order to be able to report on Soviet compliance and support US officials who had to reach decisions regarding Soviet violations. Senior intelligence officials also had to testify before congressional armed services and foreign relations committees to explain how well the IC could monitor those agreements. Many expensive overhead reconnaissance programs were approved largely to ensure that arms control treaties could be adequately monitored and approved by the Senate.

Later, as arms control grew in importance in the 1980s—when the United States was engaged in multiple negotiations over strategic nuclear weapons and intermediate nuclear forces (INF) in Europe as well as the conventional forces in Europe (CFE) reduction talks in Vienna—this staff expanded and became known as the Arms Control Intelligence Staff (ACIS).[14] The ACIS became the IC's—not just the CIA's—clearinghouse for collection and analysis for answering negotiation team questions, monitoring and assessing treaty compliance, and briefing senior executive branch officials as well as congressional oversight committees on the intelligence implications of various arms control agreements. In the case of the INF and CFE treaty negotiations, ACIS was also actively briefing NATO allies regarding Soviet positions and on-site inspection provisions in order to build European support for American negotiation approaches. In this respect, intelligence was playing a direct diplomatic support role for US policies.

Likewise, today one finds many analysts working to support difficult negotiations vis-à-vis North Korea, Iran, and other states, whose intentions and actions require serious all-source analysis and deep expertise. At the CIA, the office most responsible for policy support for these issues through the 1990s and early 2000s was the Weapons Intelligence, Nonproliferation, and Arms Control Center (WINPAC). This office housed analysts knowledgeable about the processes involved in developing weapons of mass destruction, including nuclear, chemical, and biological programs. As the name implies, it also serviced the needs of policy agencies engaged in preventing the spread of WMD technologies, including negotiations that might be pursued to that end. During President Obama's terms of office, the then CIA director Leon Panetta reorganized WINPAC by combining most of its analytical elements with the separate Counterproliferation Center of the Directorate of Operations that was responsible for tracking and disrupting proliferation networks. This new Mission Center for Counterproliferation (previously known as the CTC) thus became the CIA's counterpart to the DNI's National Counterproliferation Center—similar to how the CIA's Mission Center for Counterterrorism (a combined operation by the Directorate of Analysis and the Directorate of Operations) complements the DNI-managed National Counterterrorism Center.

In the nonproliferation field, the United States has been an active participant in the Non-Proliferation Treaty (NPT) regime as well as the Chemical Weapons and Biological Weapons Conventions. In each case, when US diplomats enter into diplomatic discussions or formal negotiations, they can depend on the IC to support their intelligence needs. Thus, a prime example of the kinds of intelligence support to international negotiations can be seen in how the US delegation to the International Atomic Energy Agency (IAEA) operates in Vienna. The US ambassador to the IAEA heads the American delegation,[15] which—in addition to its role of assisting in the peaceful uses of nuclear power—is principally responsible for controlling and monitoring the nuclear activities of nonnuclear NPT member states.[16] In this capacity, the ambassador represents US views on suspected nuclear activities in such places as Iran, North Korea, and previously Syria. To do this effectively, the ambassador relies heavily on intelligence support provided by WMD analysts, some of whom are part of his team in Vienna.

The ambassador to the IAEA has had a unique and close arrangement with the IC. The United States has placed a high priority on monitoring nonproliferation threats and presenting compelling arguments to the IAEA board regarding the proliferation threats from countries such as Iran and North Korea. This makes intelligence support essential. Accordingly, the ambassador can rely on his or her intelligence team to highlight the latest intelligence—both raw and finished—that arrives daily via CIA support cables. Moreover, given the salience of Iran and North Korea's nuclear programs, the IAEA ambassador can reach back to Washington and talk to senior WMD intelligence experts there whenever additional or special kinds of intelligence support are needed. In addition to the small intelligence team in Vienna, other WMD analysts can be sent to the mission for short periods on special projects or to provide in-depth briefings to the US delegation and in some cases to foreign delegations at the IAEA.

Importantly, the IAEA is heavily dependent on member states such as the United States providing information to the organization in order to prepare its reports on compliance with NPT safeguards. Naturally, the United States has been a critically important partner for the IAEA in monitoring suspect activities in Iran and North Korea. In exchange, the US mission can also provide intelligence analysts with important insights into foreign governments' attitudes toward IAEA safeguards compliance and inspections of suspect sites. This two-way street illustrates how the intelligence-policy relationship is perhaps the most intimate and least fractious when focused on implementing US policies.

Target Analysis: An Expanding Mission

The chapter's earlier discussion about intelligence's enabling role noted that intelligence supports many US activities involving the threat or use of force. Historically, military intelligence organizations have been involved in developing target sets for foreign military production plants, bases, equipment, and the forces themselves. Military intelligence analysts working in the individual military services or later in the Defense Intelligence Agency were assigned the job of identifying military threats and any vulnerabilities in adversaries' military systems that could be exploited. For much of the Cold War, these skills were trained on the Soviet Union, Communist China, and their allies. In America's wars in Korea, Vietnam, and elsewhere, a form of **target analysis** was central to reducing the enemy's military production, logistics, and force concentration. In Vietnam, for example, there had to be extensive military target analysis to conduct the bombing campaigns over North Vietnam and to interdict Hanoi's supply routes into the south. More recently, military target analysis was used to identify key Bosnian and Serbian military targets for NATO's air strikes that were used to compel the warring parties to negotiate peace settlements in Bosnia and Kosovo.

Such targeting requires analysts to combine information gained from HUMINT, SIGINT, and open sources to identify and monitor a range of objects or even individuals. For many military operations, the work of defense intelligence organizations such as the NGA, NSA, and DIA has played a central role. But in large-scale operations, the CIA was also called on to provide such target analysis. For example, in the case of Bosnia, President Bill Clinton placed the highest intelligence priority on American "force protection," which practically meant that even the CIA was asked to identify possible Serbian targets. In addition, the CIA has also been involved in bomb damage assessment, requiring military analysts to examine targets attacked by US forces to determine whether they have been destroyed. But in the pre-9/11 period, the CIA considered target analysis to be a minor responsibility.

All of this changed after the September 2001 attacks. Within the CIA's Counterterrorism Center, there had been a small cadre of operators and analysts who were responsible for tracking terrorist networks. As early as 1995, a few analysts from CIA's DA joined some DO officers to begin working on Afghanistan and investigating a group that became known as al-Qaida (The Base). This CIA unit—known as Alec Station—became the core of the al-Qaeda target analysis team. It had prepared numerous reports on a little-known Saudi who had fought in Afghanistan against the Soviets and helped to finance the mujahideen. The team examined operational intelligence reporting and developed a good understanding of the al-Qaeda network's financing, recruitment, leadership, and operational capabilities. These few target analysts continued to write some *PDB* items and other longer reports for policymakers, but they were increasingly drawn into supporting DO operations to help track, locate, and apprehend known terrorists. Unlike most analysts in the CIA's DA who have little day-to-day contact with operations officers, target analysts were immersed in operational-level discussions with collectors. They knew their sources better than almost any other analytical group in the CIA.[17] Their numbers remained small, growing slowly after the 1998 bombings of the US embassies in Kenya and Tanzania but then expanding rapidly after the 9/11 attacks (see box 8.5).

In order to augment the few target analysts already in the CTC, the CIA turned to analysts in the agency's crime and counternarcotics center, who also were trained in following narco-traffickers and organized crime groups and assisting operations officers and law enforcement in apprehending them. Such skills transferred well to the counterterrorism operations that were scaled up at the CTC and later the NCTC. As a former chief of the counternarcotics center explained target analysis, "Rather than focusing on the preparation of analytic assessments to support the policy decision process, target analysts within the intelligence community seek to develop detailed understanding of individuals, networks, and organizations for operational purposes. Those operational objectives can range from developing plans to collect further

---

Box 8.5 Targeting Analysis: Bin Laden Raid

In the summer and early fall of 2010, I did not know that a small cell of analysts at CIA had acquired a lead on a courier thought to be in contact with Bin Laden. In the end, he would be found not through the $25 million reward or any help from the Pakistanis. Bin Laden was found through old-fashioned detective work and long, painstaking analysis by CIA experts. There would be a lot of heroes in the Bin Laden raid and even more people in Washington who would take credit for it, but without those extraordinary analysts at CIA, there would have been no raid.

—Robert Gates, former secretary of defense, 2014

Source: Robert M. Gates, *Duty: Memoirs of a Secretary of Defense* (New York: Knopf, 2014), 538–39.

intelligence on the persons or organizations involved to designing operations to disrupt their activities."[18]

Today target analysis is considered a major analytical discipline, on par with political, military, or economic analysis. Defense intelligence agencies as well as the CIA are recruiting and training analysts for these challenging assignments. Much of the training every analyst receives on weighing evidence and evaluating sources, ferreting out deception, filling intelligence gaps, and employing structured analytical techniques is very relevant. What distinguishes target analysis are the different data sets and sources, some of the specialized data-mining tools, and network-analysis techniques that are used against a range of targets. Thus, target analysis can be aimed at terrorism, WMD proliferation, insurgencies, narco-trafficking, and counterintelligence or cyber threats. While such analysts still write threat assessments for policymakers, they are much more engaged in providing close support to intelligence operators, the military, and law enforcement officials responsible for identifying and removing those threats.

Crisis Management: Task Force Reporting

Daily tactical intelligence support is perhaps most crucial during crises when senior officials are trying to understand fast-changing events in far-flung lands. To manage these crises, policymakers often require more than the customary intelligence reporting. Hence, when major events are unfolding, the CIA and other agencies will often establish special task forces of analysts drawn from different parts of their agencies to provide more in-depth and around-the-clock coverage of an issue. One early example of this was the CIA's coverage during the Cuban Missile Crisis. Having discovered Soviet missile shipments, the CIA quickly assembled a team to increase collection coverage and produce **situation reports** ("sit-reps") on developments in Moscow, in Havana, and in the waters around the island nation. During those famous thirteen days, overhead collection was resumed, and SIGINT coverage increased on Soviet vessels approaching the island and on Soviet missile crews at the suspected missile sites. HUMINT sources were debriefed for whatever information they could reveal about the state of readiness of those missiles. Analysts provided frequent updates, including imagery of the missile sites themselves.

In what was perhaps the most famous public use of highly classified U-2 photos, US ambassador Adlai Stevenson presented the evidence of Soviet missiles to the UN Security Council, proving that the United States had caught the Soviet Union redhanded. Military analysts briefed President John F. Kennedy's Executive Committee of the National Security Council frequently and were called on to make estimates of when those missiles might be operational. All of this information played directly into Kennedy's own calculation of how much time he had to negotiate their withdrawal.

Because of their resource demands, task forces are created only for short periods of time during the most acute crises. When there was the prospect or outbreak of war in the Middle East, task forces have been assembled. Similarly, when crises occurred within the Soviet sphere of influence—for example, during the Soviet suppression of the Prague Spring in 1968 or the Polish martial law was invoked in 1981—task forces were used to monitor and report on Soviet diplomatic and military moves.[19] Task forces are particularly useful when there is an urgent need for quick and coordinated responses to policy needs; they can bring together all the expertise on a problem, expedite collection requirements to the many different collectors, and ensure that intelligence is providing a coherent and common picture of a crisis situation.

One early example of this kind of policy support was the establishment of the Balkan Task Force (BTF), born out of the 1990 dissolution of Yugoslavia. Established in June 1992, it became the first and longest-lasting interagency task force in the IC's history. For more than thirty months, the BTF followed the breakup of Yugoslavia, which began during President George H. W. Bush's term and continued through most of President Clinton's first term. At the time, the then CIA director Robert Gates announced its creation to assist President Bush in managing what many feared would be a spreading instability in the entire Balkans region.[20] In practice, much of its work focused on the Bosnian War and anti-Serbian sanctions.

The BTF's organizational structure illustrates the wide range of policy-support functions that intelligence can provide to presidents and their civilian and military advisers. The BTF had three major functions: (1) to centralize and coordinate enhanced collection against the Balkans crisis, (2) to centralize and coordinate economic-sanctions monitoring on Serbia and its allies, and (3) to coordinate general and tactical military intelligence support to US policy. In practical terms, this led to the CIA's inclusion of senior collection representatives from the NSA, the DIA, and its own DO into the task force team in order to ensure higher intelligence-collection priorities that presidential decisions would need. The BTF also established three separate analytical groups to follow these activities and provide direct support to different aspects of US policy:

- Political Group: Prepared current-intelligence and longer-term assessments of political developments in the region as well as leadership analysis. It ultimately was producing both daily and weekly summaries of major events.
- Economic Group: Published a weekly sanctions-monitoring report that examined the impact sanctions were having and evaluated compliance by regional neighbors.
- Military Group: Provided tactical intelligence support to UN peacekeepers and later US forces in the form of general order-of-battle databases, military

assessments, and monitoring of arms flows into the former Yugoslavia. It also would produce weekly military update reports.[21]

These separate BTF analytical units were instrumental in providing policymakers in both the Bush and Clinton administrations with up-to-date assessments of the military conflict as well as direct assistance to enforcing the economic and arms embargoes against Serbia. Customers not only included executive branch officials but also key congressional committee members and their staffs, who were following the conflict and calling administration officials to testify on all aspects of the Balkans conflict. Less visible but no less important, the BTF assessments of the ethnic-cleansing campaigns in Croatia and Bosnia were instrumental in decisions to provide humanitarian assistance to displaced persons in Bosnia and for documenting war crimes charges that would eventually be brought against senior Bosnian Serb and other officials.[22] In a more traditional fashion, the BTF would produce articles for the *PDB* and *NID* daily publications; however, it also distributed electronically a sit-rep every eight to twelve hours for those senior officials responsible for US Balkans policies.

When the Clinton administration entered office, Bosnia was only one of several high priorities, but it quickly came to dominate the Clinton presidency. It convened its first two Principals Committee meetings devoted entirely to Bosnia, at which BTF military assessments were key intelligence products.[23] Senior Clinton officials also relied heavily on the BTF's assessment of Serbia's economic vulnerabilities in targeting certain sectors for sanctions; in many ways, the BTF was responsible having in place key assessments of how sanctions could be made most effective if they were made comprehensive and the administration engaged with all of Serbia's neighbors. As an example of real policy impact, the BTF's bleak assessment of the number of displaced persons (upward of one hundred thousand) in Bosnia during its upcoming harsh winter months led to a Deputies Committee decision to double US Air Force planned air-drops of tents, blankets, food, and fuel onto those locations. Such direct support was made easier by having the chief of the BTF attend NSC, PC, and DC meetings as the plus one to the CIA director.[24] As the US/NATO bombing of Bosnian Serb forces and joint Bosnian-Croatian military victories drove Belgrade to the negotiating table in 1995, the BTF was also instrumental in informing US negotiators regarding the parties' negotiating redlines and complications in any settlement. Balkans analysts were able to provide a more historical perspective to the policymakers' question of whether a cease-fire would hold (see box 8.6).

The scope and size of the BTF, involving multiple agencies and dozens of analysts over nearly three years of operation, was highly unusual. However, the use of task forces of various durations and scale is normal whenever political instability or extreme violence occurs around the world. A more recent variant on the ad hoc task

---

Box 8.6   Balkan Task Force Assessment, September 1995 (Excerpt)

DCI Interagency Balkan Task Force
27 September 1995

Ceasefires in the Balkans: A Historical Overview

The previous country-wide cease-fires that have lasted the longest have done so either because the warring parties had some mutual interest in temporarily reducing the level of violence or because weather would have limited fighting in any event. The presence of peacekeeping forces probably has influenced somewhat the longevity of cease-fires, but has not been decisive.

UN forces in Bosnia are adequate to monitor implementation of an in-place cease-fire as long as they enjoy complete freedom of movement. They are not, however, to deter any of the warring parties from deciding to abandon the peace process.

Some incentive for both sides to comply with a cease-fire—possibly including a desire to build up forces prior to renewed fighting—has been the key factor in cease-fire maintenance. The "successful" cease-fires to date have codified a willingness to cease offensive actions when none of the factions would benefit from them. . . .

If the negotiating parties entered into a cease-fire agreement in good faith, the UN could monitor compliance relatively quickly using existing peacekeepers and military observers. Large numbers of outside forces would not be needed immediately so long as observers already in the country enjoyed freedom of movement and the terms of the peace agreement—such as demilitarized zones, limitations on training and maneuvers and on-site inspections of heavy weapons at declared sites were designed to simplify verification of compliance.

Source: Bosnia, Intelligence and the Clinton Presidency: The Role of Intelligence and Political Leadership in Ending the Bosnian War, CIA Library, https://www.cia.gov/library/readingroom/collection/bosnia-intelligence-and-clinton-presidency; boldface and italics in original.

---

force phenomenon is the growth in close tactical military and counterinsurgency support that is now provided by the CIA and DIA to warfighters in the Middle East and South Asia. The DIA as a combat-support element of the DOD has always had a role in providing support to military commanders in the field. The CIA, typically, has not always been a major contributor to military operations in the field. However, criticism of the CIA's performance in the 1990 Gulf War led to a rethinking of how it might support the military and resulted in the CIA establishing an Office for Military Affairs, headed by a two-star general officer who could enhance cooperation and information flow between the CIA and the military. The CIA also began assigning senior analysts to each unified and specified command as well as a senior CIA representative to the JCS chairman's office to ensure close agency support to the military.

In the almost two-decades-long wars in Afghanistan and Iraq, intelligence support to combatant commands has grown tremendously. Today there are large numbers of CIA and DIA analysts deployed to the field to provide a range of services from target analysis to assessments of local and regional politico-military developments. These analysts, in turn, develop regional expertise as well as send reports back to their respective headquarters that can be included in both current and longer-term assessments for Washington-based officials.

Policy Rotations: On the Desk Support

A discussion of the types of intelligence support provided to decision-makers would not be complete without mention of the practice of loaning mid- to senior-level analysts and sometimes operations officers to serve in key policy agencies. The best example of this can be found at the NSC, where intelligence officers are asked to spend a tour of one to two years working in one of the regional or functional directorates. One reason intelligence officers are valued at the NSC is that they come with no policy or agency bias—that is, as intelligence officers they are trained not to advocate policy. So, unlike career diplomats or military officers, they are not viewed as carrying State or DOD policy preferences into the White House. Another advantage is their expertise. Most of the intelligence officers serving at the NSC have worked on their regional or technical issues for many years and are well-known experts in their own right. One prime example is former CIA China analyst and senior manager Dennis Wilder, who served in George W. Bush's NSC. A PhD in Chinese area studies, Wilder was centrally involved in numerous crises, including the downing in 2001 of an American surveillance aircraft and tricky negotiations for the return of the plane and its crew.[25]

Policy rotations to the Department of State and the DOD are also routine. As former CIA deputy director John McLaughlin notes, these are highly valued by both the policy agency and the intelligence organization.[26] On the one hand, State or the DOD gets the services of a well-regarded intelligence expert on whatever policy issue he or she is assigned. The rotation can allow policy officials to more directly reach back to the IC with intelligence questions and tasking. On the other hand, career intelligence officers get a bird's-eye view of the policy process, can develop a network of policy contacts that can serve them well later in their careers, and receive greater insight into what kinds of intelligence would be useful to those policy agencies.

As often happens, an officer who has performed well in such a policy rotation often is promoted further, as his or her understanding of the policy process and connections with senior policymakers are judged to be valuable. In the author's case, a policy rotation at the Department of State led to his selection as a national intelligence officer, a position that depended heavily on having a good reputation with senior officials at the NSC, the State Department, and the DOD, where he was already a known quantity. John McLaughlin, who served earlier in his career at the State Department, also credits some of his career success to being more aware of how the policy process operates, having proven himself to senior policy officials and then helping the CIA develop a better relationship with a wide range of customers downtown.

KEY CHALLENGES: BALANCING COMPETING INTELLIGENCE PRIORITIES

As this chapter demonstrates, intelligence support to decision-makers' formulation and execution of policy comes in many forms, depending on who the customers are and what their specific needs are. As mentioned in earlier chapters, intelligence is a finite resource, and some trade-offs inevitably are made when the demands exceed the supply of information and analysis. In the collection field, there is at least a National Intelligence Priorities Framework that theoretically orders by rankings (1 to 5) the immediate and long-term needs of policy users; in practice of course, the immediate and urgent needs tend to crowd out other important priorities. This certainly is true of analytical resources, which are also finite and have to be distributed across an equally broad set of intelligence topics and policy needs. Among the many challenges the IC faces, the trade-offs are most obvious between current versus strategic analysis, global coverage versus specific threats, and military versus national intelligence needs. Unfortunately, these are never easy choices in what are usually zero-sum circumstances.

Current versus Longer-Term Analysis

As this chapter demonstrates, current intelligence support has become a multifaceted set of activities. Historically, this was not the case, as the CIA placed a great deal of emphasis on so-called strategic research (and had an office dedicated to it). Alongside this Office of Strategic Research was the Office of Current Intelligence. They coexisted for more than a decade until the CIA's Directorate of Analysis was reorganized into a set of regional and functional offices. Over time, and especially with the end of the Cold War and the advent of the global war on terrorism, a new emphasis was placed on providing timely, actionable intelligence (i.e., information that can be acted on quickly). The epitome of this was the rising stature of the *PDB*. This became the symbol of the CIA's and later the DNI's relevance to the president and his advisers. The long-standing criticism of NIEs and other long-term assessments was and continues to be that they take too long to produce, are ponderous, and were seldom read. One example of this is the well-known fact that the flawed 2002 NIE on Iraq's WMD program was read by only a half-dozen senators prior to the Senate's vote to authorize the use of force against Saddam; ironically, it was the

Senate Select Committee on Intelligence that had requested this estimate. Other critics often complain that longer-term assessments seldom are focused on their immediate agendas. Hence, there has been a risky trend to play down longer-term, in-depth assessments in favor of more current intelligence products such as the *PDB* and the *WIRe*.

While it might seem obvious that intelligence should produce timely and concise reports that are useful to policymakers, prioritizing short-term production ignores the importance of conducting longer-term research that is necessary to build expertise among intelligence analysts. The in-depth understanding of an intelligence issue and the ability to look over the horizon at potential shifts or new trends enables analysts to bring attention to emerging issues when policymakers can take timely action. One of the critiques of the CIA and IC after 9/11 was that they had not produced any NIEs on terrorism or al-Qaeda specifically since 1995, suggesting that long-term research into Bin Laden had suffered because analysts were too busy supporting current targeting operations conducted by the CTC.

One of the recommendations of the 9/11 Commission's report was to reestablish an intelligence unit inside the National Intelligence Council to conduct longer-term research on subjects that might not get attention by offices more focused on producing *PDB*s and other intelligence products. As mentioned in chapter 6, this unit is now largely responsible for preparing the NIC's Global Trends series as well as other special projects that might be considered out of the normal range of intelligence topics. The CIA's Senior Analytical Service (SAS) was designed shortly prior to 9/11 to offer analysts the opportunity to remain specialists in their preferred region or technical fields precisely to enhance in-depth expertise on the highest-priority topics. This SAS is a cadre of several hundred senior officers who are often called on to guide complex analytical challenges and conduct "deep-dive" discussions with a president or cabinet officer on topics such as Russia, China, or Iran.

But the question remains whether enough analysts—especially at the CIA and DIA—are conducting longer-term research in order to sharpen their expertise for when those topics demand deeper understanding. Given that most analysts' career tracks move them among various offices and intelligence targets, there is now a tendency to devalue deep expertise over a generalist's skill set. This may create intelligence gaps if senior intelligence managers do not make sure that sufficient analytical resources are placed on issues that might one day become more significant.

Global Coverage versus Specific Threats

US intelligence prides itself on being a global intelligence enterprise. Given the far-flung American interests across the globe, there is a tendency to presume that the IC must follow every single country, target, and topic that any policymaker might conceivably wish to learn about. That is a goal that even the large IC cannot easily meet. Often the decision about so-called global coverage revolves around how much collection to require. Specific threats such as Iran and North Korea tend to produce insatiable demands for information and analysis. Thus, justifying higher intelligence priorities on many developing countries where US interests seem remote is hard. For example, during the budgetary and personnel build-down of the IC in the early 1990s, collection was cut, with defense attaché offices and CIA stations closed in parts of Africa. Then, in 1994, the Rwanda genocide occurred, which dramatically highlighted the relatively poor collection and coverage of what was going on in Central Africa. While there was some diplomatic reporting, it did not get the proper attention it deserved until large-scale massacres had already occurred.[27]

In many cases, when a topic is placed in the global-coverage category, it remains without much coverage at all. Often the instinct is to delegate those low priorities to the Open Source Enterprise to collect materials such as radio and television broadcasts and blogs from online media. When relying on such open sources, however, it may then be difficult to quickly ramp up other collection efforts that require reporting from defense attachés, diplomats, or CIA case officers. When a country is judged to be a low priority, it also usually means that few analysts are left to watch developments there. Historically, for example, the CIA has usually had many more analysts following large targets such as China, Russia, and Iran, while leaving only a few to cover large parts of Africa and Latin America. This often then requires a sudden surge of collection efforts and assignment of additional analysts to a problem like Rwanda, or other hot spots, in order to respond to the uptick in intelligence requests. A more recent example of this problem may have been the limited coverage given to Tunisia, where violence and rebellion against an autocratic regime exploded in 2010 and began what became known as the Arab Spring.

There are no quick fixes for this trade-off, as too many developing countries can easily tip into a state of instability or failure. The 2017 case of Zimbabwe's toppling of longtime head of state Robert Mugabe makes the point that seemingly stable situations can quickly deteriorate and demand more intelligence attention. Efforts to retain deeper knowledge on lower-priority intelligence topics sometimes have to include use of outside experts at universities or former intelligence specialists working at consulting firms. Realistically, the IC will have to be flexible and resilient enough to quickly shift its attention to newly arising problems, either in the form of task forces or more current intelligence coverage than was previously thought necessary.

Military versus National Intelligence Needs

Closely related to the above challenges is the issue of how much attention the IC should give to military users as opposed to senior civilian leaders. Their intelligence needs overlap but often diverge. Since the DOD controls a large share of intelli-gence resources, there has been a tendency to favor military users over the national intelligence priorities of civilian intelligence agencies and policymakers in other departments. Specifically, the DOD controls the major overhead satellite collection systems (run by the NRO and exploited by the NGA) as well as the SIGINT activi-ties of the NSA. A strong argument can be made, and has been repeatedly, that sup-port to the warfighter must be the highest intelligence priority. This proved to be the case during Operation Desert Shield and Operation Desert Storm in 1990–91, the Balkans wars of the mid-1990s, and the Iraq and Afghanistan wars of the 2000s and 2010s. One of the lessons learned from the Gulf War was that commanders need the national IC to contribute even more to the intelligence requirements in the field. For example, commanders often complained that the CIA's analysis often was so highly classified that it could not be provided to field commanders lacking the proper clearances. Today the process of downgrading military intelligence for use in the field is much more efficient because the wars in Afghanistan and Iraq have put more analysts in the forward operating areas who can quickly determine what information is needed.

That said, the CIA has long worried that DOD intelligence priorities would ignore its interest in other political and economic information of high interest to Washington policymakers but of less salience to military customers. One of the reasons why the 2004 IRTPA legislation was so controversial was that early recommendations from the **President's Intelligence Advisory Board (PIAB)** called for placing the NSA and NRO under the leadership of a strengthened DCI.[28] Members of the Senate Armed Services Committee—along with Defense Secretary Donald Rumsfeld—argued stren-uously against this recommendation, and so those agencies remain combat-support elements of the DOD.[29] However, it highlights how sensitive the issue of turf can be among intelligence agencies.

Looking to the future, US intelligence is likely to remain confronted with difficult decisions regarding the need to balance all the competing demands for its finite collection and analytical resources. It is difficult to imagine major shifts in the focus on current intelligence as well as military intelligence needs so long as the United States remains engaged in so many international problems around the globe. For a stopgap, the IC will inevitably have to resort to placing its bets on where the next hot spot or crisis is likely to be and try to develop workforces and intelligence-collection systems that are flexible enough to surge to wherever information and analysis is needed. The practice of standing up new crisis task forces is also likely to remain an important tool for ensuring adequate intelligence for decision-makers confronted with new decisions and the call for action.

USEFUL DOCUMENTS

Bosnia, Intelligence and the Clinton Presidency: The Role of Intelligence and Political Leadership in Ending the Bosnian War, CIA Library, https://www.cia.gov/library/readingroom/collection/bosnia-intelligence-and-clinton-presidency
   The best compilation of declassified policy documents and intelligence assessments of a major crisis where intelligence played a major role.
President's Daily Brief: Nixon and Ford PDBs Released in 2016, CIA Library, https://www.cia.gov/library/readingroom/presidents-daily-brief
   A recent volume that includes redacted *PDB* items reflecting the intelligence priorities of the Nixon and Ford presidencies.

FURTHER READING

Peter Bergen, *Manhunt: The Ten-Year Search for Bin Laden from 9/11 to Abbottabad* (New York: Broadway, 2012).
   A leading counterterrorism expert's review of how the CIA tracked and eventually targeted Osama bin Laden.
Ellen Laipson, *Intelligence: A Key Partner to Diplomacy*, Case 337, Institute for the Study of Diplomacy Case Study Series (Washington, DC: Georgetown University, 2017).
   A former official's assessment of the role intelligence plays in major negotiations.
Michael Morell, *The Great War of Our Time: The CIA's Fight against Terrorism—from al Qa'ida to ISIS* (New York: Hachette, 2016).
   A former *PDB* briefer and later senior official recounts how daily actionable intelligence was provided to and used by presidents.
David Priess, *The President's Book of Secrets: The Untold Story of Intelligence Briefings to America's Presidents from Kennedy to Obama* (New York: Public Affairs, 2016).
   A practitioner's history and assessment of the *PDB*'s central role.

NOTES

First epigraph: R. V. Jones, "Intelligence and Command," *Intelligence and National Security* 3, no. 3 (July 1988): 288.

Second epigraph: ODNI, *National Intelligence Strategy of the United States: 2019*, 10, https://www.dni.gov/files/ODNI/documents/National_Intelligence_Strategy_2019.pdf.

   1. Some examples include the white paper that distilled the unclassified findings of the 2002 Iraq WMD estimate, and the series of DIA-prepared white papers on Soviet military power in the 1980s, and the more recent DIA white paper focused on China's military power. See DIA, *China Military Power: Modernizing a Force to Fight and Win 2019*, www.dia.mil/Military-Power-Publications.
   2. Jack Davis, "Facts, Findings, Forecasting, and Fortune-Telling," *Studies in Intelligence* 39, no. 3 (1995): 25–30.

3. Author's November 2017 email correspondence with a former senior DIA official involved in current and long-term analysis.

4. David Priess, *The President's Book of Secrets: The Untold Story of Intelligence Briefings to America's Presidents* (New York: PublicAffairs, 2016), 5. This is perhaps the most comprehensive examination of the *PDB*, written by a former CIA historian who has interviewed *PDB* briefers and reviewed many *PDBs* as part of his research.

5. Priess, 25.

6. Priess, 54.

7. Priess, 283.

8. Michael Morell, *The Great War of Our Time: The CIA's Fight against Terrorism—From al Qa'ida to ISIS* (New York: Hachette, 2016), 32.

9. Julian E. Barnes and Michael S. Schmidt, "To Woo a Skeptical Trump, Intelligence Chiefs Talk Economics Instead of Spies," *New York Times*, March 3, 2019, https://www.nytimes .com/2019/03/03/us/politics/trump-daily-intelligence-briefing.html?smid=nytcore-ios-share.

10. Ellen Laipson, *Intelligence: A Key Partner to Diplomacy*, Case 337, Institute for the Study of Diplomacy Case Study Series (Washington, DC: Georgetown University, 2017).

11. For more complete description of the current US-Russian nuclear arms control negotiations and monitoring provisions, see Amy Woolf, *The New START Treaty: Central Limits and Key Provisions*, Congressional Research Service, October 5, 2017, https://fas.org/sgp/crs/nuke /R41219.pdf. Recent American approaches rely primarily on NTM, data exchanges and notifications, and scheduled and short-notice on-site inspections of deployed systems to confirm the accuracy of the data exchanges.

12. The Defense Department in 1987 established a new On-Site Inspection Agency that was responsible to manage the DOD's treaty-implementation responsibilities under various treaties; it later became part of the Defense Threat Reduction Agency, which commands almost $3 billion annually to implement US obligations under numerous arms control treaties and WMD agreements.

13. See CIA, "Memorandum for the Record, Admiral Turner's Contribution to SALT, January 21, 1981," approved for release July 3, 2003, https://www.cia.gov/library/readingroom /docs/CIA-RDP86B00269R000800040001–8.pdf.

14. This discussion has been aided by communications with former senior analysts who were directly responsible for overseeing the ACIS's activities during the 1980s.

15. The US mission in Vienna is formally called the UN Mission to International Organizations in Vienna, which represents the United States to the IAEA but also to a number of other UN-related international organizations such as the Comprehensive Test Ban Organization and the International Narcotics Control Board.

16. The IAEA, established in 1957 by the UN, has become the foremost scientific and technical organization for fostering peaceful uses of nuclear energy as well as for developing safeguards to verify that nations are not diverting their nuclear energy programs for military purposes. As such, it has a Department of Safeguards responsible for verifying the peaceful uses of nuclear power. The IAEA can demand documentation and on-site inspection by its teams of technical inspectors to verify that nuclear facilities in member states are not violating the NPT obligations.

17. This information is based on communications with two former target analysts who worked in the CTC from 1995 until 2013.

18. John Kringen, "Serving the Senior Military Consumer: A National Agency Perspective," in Roger Z. George and James Bruce, *Analyzing Intelligence: National Security Practitioners' Perspectives* (Washington, DC: Georgetown University Press, 2014), 108.

19. According to former military analysts interviewed by the author, more informal office-level task forces were often established to enhance reporting on things as diverse as the Falklands War between Argentina and the United Kingdom, the Cuban involvement in Angola, and various Taiwan Straits crises involving the People's Republic of China and the Republic of China.

20. See Deputy DCI, Memorandum to National Foreign Intelligence Board, "Establishment of the Interagency Balkan Task Force," June 12, 1992, in *Bosnia, Intelligence and the Clinton Presidency: The Role of Intelligence and Political Leadership in Ending the Bosnian War*, CIA Library, https://www.cia.gov/library/readingroom/collection/bosnia-intelligence-and-clinton -presidency.

21. Deputy DCI, Memorandum to National Foreign Intelligence Board, 33. Leadership analysis is focused on describing individual foreign leaders' personalities, decision-making styles, and ideological or political convictions. They are highly valued by diplomats and military commanders who negotiate with foreign officials.

22. As a result of the BTF's work, the CIA established its own war crimes team, which collected eyewitness accounts via intelligence reporting and debriefing of émigrés that was later part of the State Department's program to support the work of the International Criminal Tribunal for the Former Yugoslavia, which brought to justice such well-known figures as Serbian president Slobodan Milošević, Bosnian Serb politician Radovan Karadžić, and the Bosnian Serb military leader Ratko Mladić.

23. Daniel Wagner, "Year One of the DCI Interagency Balkan Task Force," in *Bosnia, Intelligence and the Clinton Presidency*, 18. According to the BTF's senior manager, these first meetings focused on the news that Bosnian Serbs were holding Muslims in detention camps, and the BTF had already produced a map showing suspected camps.

24. A. Norman Schindler, "Reflections on the DCI Interagency Balkan Task Force," in *Bosnia, Intelligence and the Clinton Presidency*, 25.

25. Wilder served as the NSC senior director for East Asia during the incident in which a US Navy EC-3 was damaged by a Chinese fighter (which crashed, killing its pilot) and had to land on Hainan Island, where it was seized and its crew detained. There were extended negotiations during which he was one of the key experts advising President Bush on how to respond to the challenge. Wilder went on to become a senior office director at the CIA, later also running the critical preparation of the *PDB*, from which he retired to teach at Georgetown University. For one view of his centrality, see Chris Nelson, "America's China Brigade," *International Economy*, Spring 2007, http://www.international-economy.com/TIE_Sp07_Nelson.pdf.

26. John McLaughlin, "Serving the National Policymaker," in George and Bruce, *Analyzing Intelligence*, 81–92.

27. For a detailed look at the reporting that came out of the Rwanda crisis, see the National Security Archive, which includes some declassified current intelligence reporting on the crisis as it unfolded. See, e.g., William Ferragiaro, "The United States and the Genocide in Rwanda 1994: Information, Intelligence, and the U.S. Response," March 24, 2004, National Security Archive, https://nsarchive2.gwu.edu/NSAEBB/NSAEBB117/.

28. Brent Scowcroft, who headed the PIAB under President George W. Bush, reportedly had made this recommendation but faced stiff opposition from Defense Secretary Donald Rumsfeld. See Philip Zelikow, "The Evolution of the Intelligence Reform: A Personal Reflections," *Studies in Intelligence* 56, no. 3 (2012): 6–9, https://www.cia.gov/library/center-for-the-study-of-intelligence/csi-publications/csi-studies/studies/vol.-56-no.-3/pdfs/Studies56-3-September 2012-18Sep2012-Web.pdf.

29. See the excellent discussion of intelligence-defense turf questions in Michael Allen, *Blinking Red: Crisis and Compromise in American Intelligence after 9/11* (Dulles, VA: Potomac Books, 2013), esp. 14–15.

9

COVERT ACTION AS POLICY SUPPORT

Meddling secretly in other people's internal politics is distasteful; it is so much at odds with our domestic arrangements and values. On the other hand, however much Americans might like it otherwise, the world frequently *is* a nasty place. If we are to compete, it often seems, we may have to be just as nasty as our adversaries.
—Gregory Treverton, *Covert Action*

It is true that the CIA's biggest mistakes involved covert action. But it is also true that these mistakes, without exception, also involved operations carried out at the behest of presidents pursuing flawed policies. And for every covert action that failed spectacularly, there have been others that enabled presidents and policymakers to achieve ends in the nation's interest with an unseen hand, which is almost always preferable to a heavy footprint.
—Jack Devine, former CIA senior official responsible for numerous covert operations

This chapter will explore the CIA's role as a policy implementer, when it conducts covert action in support of special operations at the direction of the president. Often described as the "third way" between inaction and the use of military force, covert action is another policy instrument at the disposal of the president and the NSC. Covert action is the one area in which the CIA participates as an influential decision-maker that executes policy, which gives it a special stake in how policy is fashioned. At the same time, the CIA operates under strict guidelines, requiring far more presidential involvement and congressional notification than is required for the US military when it conducts its own special operations. This chapter will examine the purposes, scope, and processes involved in covert action. In particular, it will examine the roles the president, the NSC, and Congress play in providing accountability and oversight. Some of the major successes and failures, along with lessons learned, will be examined. Finally, the chapter will highlight special challenges that covert action presents for the CIA and the US government more generally.

WHAT IS COVERT ACTION?

Covert action, in the American context, has evolved over time to describe a range of measures taken by the US government in which its role is designed to be hidden or deniable. According to section 503 (e) of the National Security Act of 1947, covert action is "an activity or activities of the United States Government to influence political, economic, or military conditions abroad, where it is intended that the role of the United States Government will not be apparent or acknowledged publicly." As will be detailed later, such operations can be long- or short-term, of a military, diplomatic, or economic character, and involve very little or very large amounts of resources and people. It all depends on the goals set out by the president and his or her advisers.

When the Cold War broke out in the late 1940s, President Truman and his advisers were much concerned about Soviet subversion taking place in Europe. Moscow's involvement in the 1946–49 Greek Civil War, the Soviet-sponsored coup overthrowing the Czechoslovak government in 1948, and the rising influence of communist parties in Western Europe prompted Washington to find countermeasures. George Kennan, the father of the emerging US containment policy as well as a drafter of the Marshall Plan for Europe, was among those recommending immediate political warfare. Hand in hand with the publicly announced Marshall Plan to aid weak European economies, Truman approved NSC-4/A, a directive that authorized secret "psychological warfare" by the CIA as a government "service of common concern." Among other things, the CIA provided funds to Christian Democratic parties in Italy and France to support their electoral campaigns to defeat resurgent communist parties in the 1948 elections.

A year later this mandate was expanded to a broader range of activities known as "covert" action. A new directive, titled NSC-10/2, instructed elements in the CIA to undertake operations "which are conducted or sponsored by this Government against hostile foreign states or groups or in support of friendly foreign states or groups but which are so planned and executed that any US Government responsibility for them is not evident to unauthorized persons and that if uncovered the US Government can plausibly disclaim any responsibility for them."[1] Thus was born the notion that covert actions would be measures taken secretly that could be plausibly denied, even if used in conjunction with overt programs such as the Marshall

Plan to bolster weak democratic institutions in postwar Europe. As Kennan himself described it, covert action should be "preventive direct action," including sabotage, subversion against hostile states, assistance to resistance movements and guerrillas, and support of indigenous anticommunist elements.[2]

Although covert action was seen as essential to counter Moscow's subversion, from the beginning it was controversial. First, there was concern about officially giving this responsibility to the CIA, which might prove to be too independent and expand such operations beyond what might be approved by the State Department or might undermine US foreign policy objectives. These objections were partly overcome by assigning Kennan himself to be the State Department's first representative to the interagency oversight group—called the Senior Consultants to the Office of Policy Coordination (OPC)—that would review any CIA plans for covert action.[3] A second concern was whether the CIA was the appropriate place for "paramilitary operations," which the CIA initially questioned but Kennan seemed to insist on. Given the CIA's origins in the OSS, the prospect of it conducting quasi-military operations might seem logical, but the OSS's wartime performance had not been that impressive. Defense Department officials were not keen to have "cowboys" operating outside its control. This issue has continued to be a source of friction between the DOD and CIA over the years and will be touched on later in the chapter.

However, other factors argued for assigning covert action to the CIA. First, the insistence on "plausible deniability" required secrecy, a capacity best suited to the new CIA. It could operate more quietly than either the State or Defense Departments; moreover, its budgets and programs were entirely cloaked in secrecy, unlike other national security operations. Second, a wide range of covert actions were best centralized in one place, rather than distributed across different agencies depending on whether they were essentially political, economic, or military measures. Again, the CIA was the logical location. Third, the CIA was forging close liaison relationships with other intelligence services throughout the world. Thus, it was building a global overseas presence and had officers who ran agents, spoke the local languages, and were most aware of any counterintelligence threats. Finally, since the director of central intelligence reported directly to the president, this would ensure that the commander in chief could be fully in charge of all covert operations.

Throughout the early phases of the Cold War, presidents from Truman through Johnson utilized covert action extensively. According to one scholar, by 1952 there were more than forty covert action programs in Central Europe alone.[4] Another declassified study reports that the CIA conducted over 80 operations during the Truman administration, over 100 during the Eisenhower years, approximately 160 during the brief Kennedy administration, and over 140 during Johnson's term. While the scale and duration of those operations varied widely, it is nonetheless impressive that they totaled in the hundreds.[5]

WHAT FORMS DOES IT TAKE?

Covert action is indeed an instrument of policy. Unlike the usual set of overt political, military, economic, or informational tools of statecraft, it is designed to remain secret. Simply stated, covert action encompasses all the instruments of statecraft when used covertly and run by the CIA under the auspices of the president. Hence, the range of covert action can be quite broad. Whether large or small, those operations can apply one or blend several of the usual tools of American statecraft. Some forms of covert actions might include the following:

- *Political*: paying or pressuring foreign officials to take pro-US positions; supporting or influencing political parties, unions, or other interest groups; sponsoring pro- or antigovernment demonstrations; supporting coup plotting
- *Economic*: providing funds to enable groups to undertake actions deemed favorable to the United States; conducting economic sabotage of foreign military or industrial production; disrupting a hostile government's or organization's financial transactions
- *Military*: sponsoring pro-US factions within a foreign military; providing arms and training to rebels or governments favorable to the United States; fielding paramilitary groups fighting a US opponent; covertly weakening or destroying an enemy's military capabilities
- *Informational*: conducting covert psychological warfare or propaganda; paying foreign journalists to promote favorable views of US policies; placing media stories in foreign newspapers; sponsoring radio broadcasts into "denied" areas; conducting cyber operations against an adversary

The early use of covert action in Western Europe in the late 1940s illustrates some of these forms of covert action. In 1947, as the threat of communist control of Western European governments rose, the United States began secretly providing money to selected prodemocracy groups in several European countries.[6] In addition to the well-known Truman Doctrine of openly aiding governments opposed to communist subversion, the CIA sponsored so-called black propaganda in the form of widely distributed pamphlets that publicized the Red Army's brutal tactics during the war and the dismal conditions in communist-led countries.[7] Much of the focus was on the 1948 Italian elections. However, similar covert assistance was also provided to the Greek government by the CIA.

Most of the above-mentioned forms of covert action were primarily responses to Soviet subversion. Yet the Truman administration also wished to take some cautiously proactive actions. For instance, the June 1948 Soviet-Yugoslav split (when Stalin expelled Yugoslavia from the Soviet-sponsored Comintern [Communist International] for its failure to defer to Moscow) opened an opportunity for the United States—through the CIA—to offer Belgrade secret aid to enhance its ability to withstand a possible Soviet attack.[8] Subsequent decisions by the Truman administration included not only overt trade assistance to Tito's fragile economy but also secret CIA liaison with Yugoslav military intelligence.[9] Moreover, the NSC approved at least two secret shipments of military equipment—orchestrated by CIA covert action director Frank Wisner—to bolster the Yugoslavian army's morale.[10] More broadly, the Truman administration wished to conduct psychological warfare against the Soviet Union by broadcasting news into Eastern Europe. For this purpose, the CIA sponsored the National Committee for a Free Europe, which set up Radio Free Europe (RFE), a service that broadcast news into Czechoslovakia beginning in 1950, and eventually a separate service, Radio Liberty (RL), that broadcast into the Soviet Union itself. The CIA secretly funded both RFE and RL until 1971, when its sponsorship was revealed and the function was transferred to the State Department as part of its overt public diplomacy programs.[11]

Covert action programs are sized to suit specific US political objectives, the feasibility and cost of covert action options, and the risk and damage that failure or disclosure of such operations might hold for the United States. The least risky is the use of propaganda, which can range from "white" to "gray" to "black" operations (see box 9.1). Political action is usually taken when more rapid results are desired and the United States is prepared to run higher risks. The least-used but most controversial are paramilitary operations, which tend to be costly, lengthy, and hard to keep secret. Usually such paramilitary operations become known if not openly acknowledged by the United States. For example, by the early 1980s, it became impossible for the expanded scope of US support to the Afghan mujahideen fighters to be disguised; deniability was maintained in name only. The United States understood that the Soviets knew who was supplying US-manufactured Stinger antiaircraft missiles to the Afghans.[12]

WHAT MAKES FOR SUCCESSFUL OR FAILED COVERT ACTION?

Covert action has had a mixed reputation, at least in terms of what is known or believed by the public. In reality, most covert action operations remain unknown. From the hundreds (now probably thousands) of operations approved by presidents since 1945, only a small percentage have been publicly revealed or acknowledged. Of

Box 9.1   Types of Covert Action

Propaganda: Most often used form of covert action requiring few resources. Often takes longer to have impact, if only indirectly. Variants:
- "White": Usually advertised as being produced by a US government agency, such as the former US Information Agency; it is overt and usually truthful. Voice of America radio broadcasting is a good example of US efforts to provide truthful information.
- "Gray": Usually hides the fact of a US source, but sponsorship is often known by experts to be backed by the United States. The information is often accurate, if spun to a favorable view of the United States. Radio Free Europe and Radio Liberty were initially examples of gray propaganda.
- "Black": Usually well-hidden sources that are providing disinformation designed to discredit an adversary or undermine an opponent. Forged documents are a classic form of black propaganda that alleges some horrific action by an adversary. For example, Soviet disinformation placed in Indian newspapers claimed the CIA had produced the AIDS virus.

Political action: Used to directly influence a foreign government's policies and actions; designed to have more immediate impact on decision-makers. For example, developing agents of influence who are able to work inside a foreign government or institution:
- supporting media: buying or subsidizing newspapers or other foreign media for the purpose of developing inroads into foreign public opinion and government decisions
- supporting civil society organizations: funding special-interest groups that are hostile to an anti-US regime; providing resources for their activities
- supporting political parties: funding their officials and campaigns as well as providing them with information, political expertise, or campaign supplies that are in short supply
- influencing elections: supporting activities that can shift electoral support for or against particular candidates or parties through propaganda, demonstrations, or covert interference in electoral processes

Economic: Covert use of economic tools (money, financial manipulation, or sabotage) to directly support groups working against a US adversary or alternatively to weaken it economically:
- provision of money and other resources to political groups fighting against authoritarian governments
- use of sabotage against the economic or industrial capacity of a foreign government
- manipulation of monetary and financial transactions of a hostile actor involving freezing bank funds or transfers

Paramilitary: Unacknowledged military assistance or actual use of force to weaken or remove a hostile government or actor; least often employed as it usually requires more resources, has far more consequences, and is often hard to disguise the US role:
- supplying of weapons, ammunition, and other matériel (e.g., radios, medical supplies) that can be readily used by a rebel group, often types that are not clearly of US manufacture

- providing military training of rebel or guerrilla groups to improve their military effectiveness
- providing intelligence to assist paramilitary operations to target high-value targets of a hostile government

Lethal military: Political assassination is prohibited by law, but the use of lethal military force by covert means is authorized in certain war zones and regions of terrorist activities:
- targeted attacks on known terrorists by armed drones
- special covert military operations conducted in conjunction with the US military's special operations forces to eliminate known terrorists

course, the most publicized are those that fail or possibly involved wrongdoing. Some lessons can be drawn from some of the most infamous and celebrated cases: the 1953 coup in Iran, the 1961 Bay of Pigs operation, the 1986 Iran-Contra scandal, and the 1980–88 program to aid Afghans fighting the Soviets.

The 1953 Coup in Iran: Lucky, Short-Term Success?

The CIA helped to engineer the coup that put the shah back on the throne in Tehran. This operation has been responsible for much of the myth regarding the agency's ability to topple governments. The facts show that in 1953, the CIA's efforts in what was initially a British-backed effort to remove Prime Minister Mohammad Mosaddegh almost failed. The prime minister's nationalization of the Anglo-Persian Oil Company and his increasing reliance on the Soviet-backed Tudeh Party had made him very unpopular in the West. The British and American governments were both convinced that he was becoming susceptible to Soviet influence, if not a communist himself. The British had removed their petroleum engineers, making it impossible for Iran to operate its oil fields, and the Eisenhower government prevented international institutions from providing Iran with loans until Tehran reversed its decision on nationalization. These measures alone brought on a severe financial crisis in the country.

British and American early plans to have the young Reza Shah remove Mosaddegh, however, were dashed when he fled to Paris, fearing the growing political instability. For a time, the prospects of removing the prime minister seemed remote. However, his government was already highly unpopular, having lost the support of the clerics and the military. His increasingly autocratic behavior, such as his decision to dissolve the parliament, and his inability to control the streets were proving to be real liabilities, on which a second CIA covert operation (code name AJAX) was built. Through the secret funding and organization of antigovernment demonstrations and negative press articles, the CIA was able to convince the shah to return; thereafter, his loyal military removed Mosaddegh, and a more pliable prime minister was appointed.

Kermit Roosevelt, one of the architects of this operation, remarked on what conditions need to be present: If "we are ever going to try something like this again, we must be absolutely sure that people and the army want what we want."[13]

The Iranian coup—despite its primarily indigenous causes—became a model for subsequent efforts to use psychological and propaganda operations to force other anti-American leaders from office. The removal of Guatemalan leader Jacobo Árbenz in 1954 followed this pattern. Like Mosaddegh, Árbenz had shown a willingness to resist Washington, expropriate American companies, and toy with the idea of accepting aid from Moscow. Through the use of very modest amounts of money and people, the US operation (code-named PBSuccess) was able to fool Árbenz into thinking that a major counterrevolution was occurring. Using two planes, dropping a single large bomb on a large military parade ground, and issuing radio broadcasts reporting columns of soldiers marching to the capital, the CIA frightened Árbenz into resigning and seeking asylum at the Mexican embassy.

Again, a small operation had led to surprising results. But, unfortunately, the lesson learned was that the CIA could easily pull off such coups without major costs. By one estimate, the Iran operation lasted less than six months, involved a handful of CIA officers, and cost around a million dollars.[14] At the time, the operation was judged a huge success, and the shah's strong support for US policies, including his anti-Soviet and pro-Israeli leanings, made his government a major pillar of US Middle East policies. Less appreciated at the time was the prospect that installing the shah by stealth would make the United States the "Great Satan" to many Iranians who would later resent the shah's Westernization plans and his vicious security service, SAVAK. The 1953 coup has remained a key element of the grievances and strong anti-American attitudes of the post-1979 governments of the Islamic Republic of Iran. Likewise, toppling the Árbenz government was a relatively minor paramilitary operation, but it too did not lead to better governance but rather decades of repressive authoritarian rule, albeit one that was more anticommunist in tone.

The 1961 Bay of Pigs Fiasco: Wishful Thinking

The story behind the Bay of Pigs highlights the dangers of inadequate—but not nonexistent—oversight by the president of covert operations for which he will be held responsible. The 1959 Cuban Revolution ousted the reviled dictator President Fulgencio Batista in favor of the young, charismatic revolutionary Fidel Castro. Rising animosity between the Castro government and the Eisenhower administration caused Havana to embrace Moscow's patronage by 1960. At that point President Eisenhower asked CIA director Allen Dulles for a covert action plan to bring down the Castro regime. Near the end of his term, a few senior CIA officials had developed an elaborate paramilitary plan (code-named Operation Zapata) to place fifteen hundred trained and armed exiles onto the island, who would be the vanguard to an expected mass uprising against the supposedly unpopular Castro. President Kennedy insisted that the US role remain invisible and would not approve sufficient air support to the beach landing that some military advisers believed was necessary.[15] Dulles and his head of covert operations, Richard Bissell, downplayed this requirement in conversations with President Kennedy and his brother, Attorney General Robert Kennedy, and believed that the president would be forced to authorize more overt force if the invasion started to go badly. It did go badly almost immediately, but Kennedy would not approve more than one hour's sortie of six bombers, which could not turn the tide.

Thus, the exiles soon found themselves on an inhospitable beachhead (known as the Bay of Pigs). The few unmarked aircraft allowed to bomb the Cuban airfields were not successful in destroying the Cuban air force jets that would quickly attack the beach landings. Cuban ground forces numbering nearly twenty thousand and armed with tanks easily defeated and killed or captured the exiles. As postmortems would testify, the covert action plan suffered from wishful thinking that Castro was unpopular and that a general uprising would spontaneously occur; moreover, the operation itself was not a secret, as Latin American newspapers had been reporting the training of an exile force that would mount an invasion. Finally, the strict compartmentalization of the operation inside the CIA had prevented any true country experts from questioning the operational assumptions and details. In the end, however, President Kennedy admitted it was his mistake to depend so heavily on a few senior CIA officers who were so committed to the operation that they could not be objective about its chances for success.

The abject failure of this operation convinced President Kennedy that he needed much more oversight of future operations. He did not give up on anti-Castro covert action, but he did deputize his brother to oversee future plans to ensure no new failures. Much has been written about other, more multifaceted CIA plans to remove Castro (under what became known as Operation Mongoose). While that program focused on economic sabotage, it did include assassination plots—none of which were ever executed.[16]

The 1986 Iran-Contra Operation: The NSC Goes Rogue

The Iran-Contra affair arose out of the Reagan administration's simultaneous efforts to free hostages held by Iran-backed Hezbollah in 1985 while running a major paramilitary operation in Central America. In both cases, the administration faced some political and legal impediments. In the first case, it was US policy not to negotiate with terrorists for hostages. At the time, Hezbollah held seven Americans in Lebanon, and President Reagan was eager to get them back. In the second case, the Reagan administration had been running a CIA-backed paramilitary operation that was no longer popular with Congress and sought ways to circumvent legislative restrictions.

President Reagan earlier had approved a covert action plan for the CIA to fund anti-Sandinista rebels (the "Contras") to harass the Nicaraguan government, which was seen as a pro-Cuban foothold in Central America. Following some missteps by the CIA (including the illegal mining of harbors in Nicaragua), Congress had steadily limited the agency's backing of the Contras by allowing only nonlethal aid, then putting funding limits on the aid and eventually banning it entirely in 1985 through the Boland Amendment. US Marine Corps lieutenant colonel Oliver North, assigned to the NSC, was put in charge of finding new ways to fund the Contras. He succeeded in soliciting monies from "third countries" (largely from the Middle East) but soon began funneling the profits from the sale of arms to Iran to aid the Contras—both actions that would later been seen as circumventing congressional intent if not the law.

Unbeknown to most CIA officials as well as large parts of the US national security bureaucracy, North concocted this elaborate illegal covert plan (called "the Enterprise") with CIA director William Casey and a few others. Senior CIA officers, including its then deputy director, opposed CIA involvement in the plan. In essence, the NSC now was running a covert action program. North along with the then national security adviser, Vice Adm. John Poindexter, were largely responsible for planning and running the operation, enlisting individual officers from the NSA and CIA for logistical support as needed. Most significantly, the operation was conducted without any clear presidential approval. Poindexter later admitted a presidential directive was approved only retroactively, which included the proviso that the CIA not inform Congress, but Reagan never actually signed it.[17] Following lengthy congressional and a special prosecutor's investigations, North, Poindexter, and other NSC, military, and CIA officers were indicted on a range of charges including obstruction of justice, destroying evidence, and lying to or withholding evidence from Congress. Many were later pardoned by President George H. W. Bush.

This scandal highlighted the need for more executive and legislative control over covert action. In addition, President Reagan empowered a special presidential review board (named the Tower Commission after its chairman, Sen. John Tower) to investigate how the NSC found itself at the center of this failed operation. The Tower Commission's recommendations also became instrumental in reforming the role of the NSC system that Reagan's successor, George H. W. Bush, established. As some former officials noted at the time, "the report reached important conclusions that the covert action on the sale of arms to Iran did not comply with U.S. law prior to a written finding. The executive branch did not comply with legal requirements that Congress be notified of covert actions in a 'timely' manner."[18] In other respects it let the Reagan administration off gently by suggesting Iran-Contra was an "aberration." That said, it was clear that the NSC system under Reagan—which saw a revolving door of six national security advisers in eight years—had proven to be one of the least well managed.

1980–88 Afghanistan: Successful but Hardly Covert

As one participant termed it, the Reagan plan to reverse the 1979 Soviet invasion of Afghanistan proved to be the largest and last covert action of the Cold War.[19] Initiated by President Carter, what President Reagan inherited was a very small operation. Designed to merely "harass" the Soviets, not defeat them, it amounted to a few million dollars to purchase bolt-action Lee-Enfield rifles and transfer them via Pakistan to anti-Soviet mujahideen. Upon taking office, however, President Reagan and his advisers determined they were prepared to expand their objectives to inflict heavy political and military costs on the Soviets.[20] The program grew from $120 million in 1981 to over $700 million in 1988, when the program ended by successfully pushing the Red Army out of Afghanistan.[21] What began as the procurement of a few rifles and mortars became a massive transfer of sophisticated weapons and ammunition to support 120,000 mujahideen. The end result was the death of thousands of Russian soldiers, a major headache for the Kremlin at home, and the eventual withdrawal of Soviet forces in 1988. One important feature of this successful operation was the strong congressional support it had elicited from the beginning. Indeed, a few proponents, such as Congressman Charlie Wilson, became well known publicly and closely associated with this supposedly secret war against the Kremlin.[22]

One by-product of this success, however, was greater difficulty in maintaining any plausible deniability. At the height of the program, the Afghan task force of CIA officers numbered over a hundred. The program had initially relied mostly on Egyptian- and Chinese-manufactured weaponry. However, the Soviet introduction of heavily armed M-24 Hind helicopters had made the arduous transport of weapons through mountain passes costly. After some deliberation, the CIA elected to arm the mujahideen with advanced, US-manufactured, shoulder-fired Stinger surface-to-air missiles. These weapons proved effective in pushing Soviet helicopters beyond the range of their own weapons, so they were unable to staunch the resupply of Afghan fighters from Pakistan. The problem, of course, was that the sophistication of these weapons undermined the already thin veneer of plausible deniability with which the program had begun. By the late 1980s, however, the Reagan administration was less concerned about US sponsorship remaining secret and more convinced that such a forceful covert action program had dealt the Soviets a serious setback that should be trumpeted.

LESSONS THAT SHOULD BE LEARNED

Decades and hundreds of operations later, there are clear lessons that one can learn from the successes and failures of presidentially directed covert action. First, covert action should never be either the "first or last resort." That means covert action is best conducted as part of a comprehensive set of policy actions, of which it is only one small piece. It is not a replacement for good statecraft and overt diplomacy, nor can it substitute for the absence of any other good options. The adage of covert action being a "third option" between doing nothing or going to war misrepresents the kind of leverage it can realistically produce.

Second, as a rule covert action is most effective when it remains small and discreet. The use of propaganda and some modest political action can help to reinforce overt US political, economic, and military actions. With covert action kept modest and secret, the chances it will be disclosed and possibly discredit American foreign policies remain low. Also, setting modest objectives with limited resources increases the prospects of its success.

Third, covert action works best if it has bipartisan congressional support. If that is lacking, there may be good reasons why a president should rethink the feasibility or value of an operation. Where there is serious congressional opposition, there may be a deeper foreign policy disagreement than simply the use of covert action. Significant opposition in Congress or perhaps even within the national security enterprise also increases the risks of whistleblower leaks to the media that can defeat such programs.

Fourth, good covert action requires good intelligence and rigorous analysis. A poor understanding of the geopolitical context in which an operation is to be conducted is a recipe for failure. Moreover, optimistic appraisals by committed proponents of an operation should be tested by other experts both inside the CIA and by national security officials with no stake in the game.

Last and most important, covert action proposals need to balance their ethical and legal aspects against the purported political benefits of such operations. There needs to be proportionality in how much the United States will risk in terms of its moral and political standing in the world against the short-term gains a covert action program might produce. In many cases, the unintended consequences of success may well carry greater costs than those near-term benefits. Like the overt use of military force, however, covert action should be directed only against serious external threats for the purpose of protecting the United States and its institutions as well as its people. Thus, some practitioners, such as former senior British intelligence official Sir David Omand, have suggested applying a set of principles—"just intelligence" (*jus intelligentia*)—that mirrors the just war doctrine applied to the use of lethal military force. Accordingly, those principles would involve

- a sufficient and enduring cause (significant threat or opportunity),
- an integrity of motive (US actions are legitimate and moral),
- proportionate methods (US actions are reasonable and limited in effect),
- a legitimate authority (presidential authorization and congressional notification),

- a reasonable prospect of success (US actions are well conceived/planned), and
- reliance as a last resort (other options have been judged insufficient and require such additional methods).[23]

If these principles were applied to covert action decisions, a president would have to weigh the nature of a threat, the legitimacy and morality of a US covert operation, its chances of success, and its likely longer-term consequences, as well as whether other less risky options might achieve similar or better results.

HOW HAS COVERT ACTION BEEN MANAGED?

For the first three decades of the CIA's existence, covert action was conducted with few formal restrictions or regulations and uneven oversight. Presidents from Truman to Carter varied in the degree to which they wished to oversee the CIA's covert action programs, although each established an NSC committee to oversee and provide advice on covert action programs. Those committees took a variety of names, often carrying cryptic titles (e.g., "Special Coordination Group" under Eisenhower, "Special Group" under Kennedy) or were given numbers (e.g., "40 Committee" under Nixon/ Ford, "303 Committee" under Johnson).[24] Those NSC groups typically included CIA covert action managers plus representatives from the State and Defense Departments, along with an NSC staff member representing the president.

It was common for presidents to issue NSC decision documents authorizing the CIA to conduct covert actions aimed at some general political objectives without necessarily reviewing all the details of the plans. Naturally, for large and highly risky or sensitive operations, such as the 1953 Iran coup and the 1962 Bay of Pigs operation, presidents took a more prominent role. Partly presidents distanced themselves from the operational details in order to preserve plausible deniability. In fact, for many of the smaller, less controversial covert programs, the CIA director could essentially authorize them without formal presidential approval, so long as the NSC oversight committee considered them to be consistent with American foreign policy objectives. In some administrations, operations that involved costs under $25,000 and were presumed to be less risky were left to the CIA director's discretion.

Legislative oversight of covert action was virtually nonexistent until the creation of the intelligence oversight committees in the mid-1970s. Up to then, subcommittees of the Armed Services and Appropriations Committees of both houses signed off on CIA budget authorization and appropriations, including covert action programs. In the early days, Congress was especially wary of knowing too much about covert action. The Armed Service and Appropriations Subcommittees were mainly concerned about the CIA having sufficient resources to fight communism, and less interested in overseeing its operations. The few congressional initiatives to establish real oversight in the 1950s and 1960s—such as calls to create a joint oversight committee—never garnered much support. For the most part, oversight consisted of private, informal conversations between the CIA director and individual powerful committee chairmen, who typically did not wish to know too much.[25]

CURRENT LEGISLATIVE OVERSIGHT

A series of events and revelations led to what is today's congressional oversight of intelligence activities, especially covert action. First, in the aftermath of the Vietnam War, Congress determined that President Nixon had conducted secret wars in Laos and Cambodia without informing Congress, partly through the use of CIA covert action capabilities. So, in 1974, Congress passed the Hughes-Ryan Amendment to the Foreign Assistance Act, which compelled the president to approve a finding for each covert action program and required that those findings be "notified" to the select members of the armed services and appropriations committees prior to the operation. This measure did not give Congress a veto on any program, but it did prevent future presidents from denying their involvement should an operation be exposed. Subsequent legislation in 1980 (the Intelligence Oversight Act) strengthened the original Hughes-Ryan Amendment's insistence on "advance" notification to demand "timely" notification.

Second, the Watergate hearings that revealed significant ill-advised and in some cases illegal activities by the CIA, NSA, and FBI against anti–Vietnam War activists led in 1975 to the hearings of the Senate Select Committee to Study Governmental Operations with Respect to Intelligence Activities. Among other things, this so-called Church Committee (named after its chairman, Sen. Frank Church) explored CIA covert action programs extensively. It criticized presidents for not ruling out some of the more extreme plans, such as the one to assassinate Fidel Castro. Senator Church famously warned during the hearings that the CIA was a "rogue elephant," yet the final conclusions of the year-long investigations essentially disproved the allegation that the CIA had conducted covert operations without presidential approval. Although some of the operations may have been misguided, poorly implemented, or illegal, it became clear that all had the blessing of President Nixon or President Johnson. At the conclusion of the hearings, Congress did establish separate Senate and House intelligence committees, with the expectation that they would be briefed on the CIA's covert action programs more completely than in the past.

The third event was the Iran-Contra scandal of 1986, which moved congressional oversight of covert action to an even higher level. As Congress became less and less enthusiastic for the funding of the Contras' war against communists in Nicaragua, it passed key legislation that added new requirements on presidential notifications of major covert action programs to the oversight committees. In particular, the 1988 and 1991 intelligence legislation insisted the president notify congressional committees within forty-eight hours, that there be a written finding signed by the president, that it not be issued retroactively (as occurred in the Iran-Contra case), and that the president list all involved US government agencies (such as the Department of State or Department of Defense) as well as any foreign entities. Most of these new restrictions were aimed at heading off another circumvention of congressional intent as occurred in the Iran-Contra affair.[26]

As a practical matter, congressional notification of covert action findings does not prevent the president from going forward. However, it does impose a degree of discipline on what an administration attempts to do covertly, when it runs the risk of congressional condemnation. At worst, the oversight committees might refuse funding in the next year's appropriations for a covert action program they did not support or put strict funding or operational limits on a program. On the positive side, a president benefits from having congressional assent to its covert action programs, particularly if they prove to be controversial or possibly fail; in such circumstances, the White House can at least spread responsibility down Pennsylvania Avenue. And finally, outside critiques can in some instances head off ill-advised proposals or warn a president of political controversy a program could entail that had not been raised by Executive Branch advisers.

CURRENT PROCEDURES FOR APPROVING COVERT ACTION

In the post-1990 period, covert action programs have been reviewed and approved using the long-established interagency process described in earlier chapters. Like other policy decisions, a covert action proposal will often emerge from the White House or other NSC discussions. Most administrations produce a classified national security directive outlining the interagency process by which it planned to propose, review, and approve covert action. While each administration since 1990 has modified that process in some ways, each has had a much more deliberate process that ensures covert actions are rigorously reviewed internally by the CIA as well as by the NSC, fully briefed to and duly authorized by the president, and, finally, notified to the appropriate congressional oversight authorities.

As an illustration of this elaborate vetting process, the following describes how covert action was handled during George W. Bush's tenure.[27] At the request of President Bush, the national security adviser would typically draft a memo to the CIA director (and after 2005, the director of national intelligence). Almost without exception, no CIA planning would begin without NSC authorization. Then, the CIA's

---

Box 9.2   Typical Covert Action Authorization Process

1. Presidential request for covert action options (memo from the national security adviser to the CIA).
2. CIA covert action staff develops options (e.g., the scope, methods, costs, and risks) with regional operations division and agency legal counsel.
3. Interagency legal group from the CIA, the NSC, and the State, Justice, and Defense Departments approves the legal basis and appropriateness of covert action proposals.
4. Special Principals Committee and Deputies Committee group reviews and approves covert action proposals prior to transmittal to the president.
5. President reviews, then approves, disapproves, or modifies a presidential finding.
6. White House "notifies" congressional oversight committees of a presidential finding.

Directorate of Operations would assign the appropriate regional or functional operations division (or, after 2015, the appropriate mission center) to prepare proposals (see box 9.2). For instance, it would be natural that any covert action dealing with a Middle Eastern country would be developed within the CIA's regional mission center covering Middle Eastern countries or that a counterterrorist covert action would emanate from the Mission Center for Counterterrorism.

In virtually all cases, lawyers are extensively involved in planning and overseeing covert operations to ensure they are conducted within the bounds of the intelligence community's standing regulations, executive orders, and US law. The CIA's Office of General Counsel will have to sign off on any proposals before they are reviewed by the NSC's legal counsel as well as by the interagency NSC Lawyers Group (LG), chaired by the NSC's legal counsel and including lawyers from the Department of State, Department of Defense, and Department of Justice.

The LG also participates in the interagency annual review of every ongoing covert action program. Based on this review, the president would then send a report to the congressional intelligence oversight committees that indicated which programs would be continued, modified, or terminated in the coming year. This elaborate process, if anything, dispels the notion that the CIA can independently launch secret operations without the knowledge or approval of the president and his senior policy advisers.

A CIA covert action proposal would normally consider a number of possible options that might achieve the proposed policy objectives. Each would be evaluated in terms of

- resources (personnel required, funds for assets or equipment),
- operational methods and scope,
- operational and human risks,

- prospects for success and/or compromise, and
- degree of involvement of other agencies or foreign intelligence services.

The CIA might present a set of options or make a recommendation on the most promising one that it believes meets the president's objective. Once the covert action proposal has met with the approval of the Directorate of Operations, a cross-directorate review group reporting to the CIA director (i.e., the Covert Action Review Group) would review, amend, or approve the proposal. If the CIA director approves the plan, it would be forwarded to the White House for interagency review.[28]

At the White House, the NSC's senior director for intelligence (typically a CIA officer assigned to the NSC) would chair a special interagency policy committee that reviews covert action plans. Attendance would be limited to the specially cleared representatives from the State Department, the Defense Department, and the Joint Staff, along with the LG representatives.[29] The White House contingent would typically include NSC senior directors responsible for the region or focus of the covert action, a senior representative of the vice president's office, the NSC's legal counsel, and a senior deputy from the Office of Management and Budget. On occasion, a Treasury representative might be included if the covert action involves financial transactions.

The IPC would focus on the obvious questions about a program's costs, benefits, risks, chances of success, and legality. The State Department's Bureau of Intelligence and Research would also be attuned to how the covert action would fit with and impact existing diplomatic policies and how ambassadors in the region of the operation might react or be affected. It might take several meetings and drafts of a potential finding before it is ready to be transmitted to the Deputies Committee and eventually the Principals Committee for approval and signature by the president. By law, once the president has signed a finding, it has to be transmitted to the congressional oversight committees. That is usually accomplished within forty-eight hours unless there are special circumstances. In highly sensitive and fragile operations, such notification can also be limited to the so-called Gang of Eight—the majority and minority leaders of the House and Senate, as well as the majority and minority leaders of the two intelligence oversight committees.[30]

KEY COVERT ACTION ISSUES IN A POST 9/11 ERA

The 9/11 attacks have once again elevated covert action to an important instrument of national security policy. One measure of this is the huge increases in the CIA's budget that are partly explained by the use of covert action applied to the global war against terrorism across multiple presidential administrations in countries such as Iraq, Afghanistan, and Syria. Those operations depended much more on new forms of covert action, including renditions, interrogations, and armed drone operations. The earlier question of where paramilitary operations rightfully belong—at the CIA or the DOD—has also risen again. And there is now the rising concern about foreign intelligence services employing cyber operations not only for espionage purposes but also for covert information operations against the United States and other democracies.

Rendition, Detention, and Interrogation

In the wake of the 9/11 tragedy and the fear of follow-on attacks, President George W. Bush authorized the CIA to conduct covert action not just to disrupt terrorism plots but also to detain and interrogate alleged al-Qaeda members, who might have information regarding any future plots.[31] These covert activities amounted to a sensitive collection operation that did not fit neatly under the definition and interagency review procedures for covert actions. Those authorities, which the DOJ approved at the time, included secret renditions from theaters of combat and harsh interrogations at undisclosed overseas locations. Slightly more than a hundred detainees were captured on the battlefield, held at these sites, and interrogated. President Bush publicly acknowledged the program of detention and transfer of some detainees to Guantanamo Bay Naval Base, Cuba, on September 6, 2006.

As described by former CIA director Michael Hayden, **enhanced interrogation techniques (EITs)**—including sleep deprivation, stress positions, body slaps, water dousing, and in a few cases "waterboarding"—were used on about one-third of the detainees. Director Hayden claims that roughly half of what the CIA knew about al-Qaeda came from detainees.[32] Other officials—including President Obama's first DNI, retired admiral Dennis Blair—were less convinced that EITs were effective, legal, or ethical.[33] Obama's first CIA director, Leon Panetta, also had testified at his nomination hearing that he believed waterboarding constituted torture, and President Obama issued an executive order shortly after taking office that limited interrogation techniques to those found in the then existing army field manual on interrogation, and he specifically prohibited waterboarding.[34]

The interrogation program's effectiveness and appropriateness remains a debatable proposition. An extensive six-thousand-page Senate Select Committee on Intelligence review of the interrogation program—including a declassified six-hundred-page summary—claimed that the CIA's program was deeply flawed. Specifically, it charged that it was poorly run, harsher than described to either White House officials or the leadership of the congressional oversight committees, and did not produce the intelligence claimed to justify its existence.[35] CIA director John Brennan took issue with some of the report's findings but agreed that waterboarding was not appropriate.[36]

As with many controversial covert action programs, the CIA has taken the brunt of the criticism. Asked by President Bush shortly after the brutal airliner attacks in 2001, the CIA took action to use whatever means necessary to ensure that other plots were not about to unfold. The CIA has acknowledged that the initial phase of the interrogation program was not well managed; its revelation in the press has also caused the CIA to lose credibility and possibly the support of other intelligence partners who had agreed to host "secret prisons" where some of the EITs were conducted. Overall, a president's sense of urgency overrode caution about whether a program could be both effective and ethical. And, not surprisingly, journalists began reporting that there had been concerns that the CIA would once again be "scapegoated" once the political winds shifted.[37]

Early in his term, President Donald Trump had hinted that he might consider restoring some of the harsher interrogation techniques, but his then secretary of defense, James Mattis, said he did not believe they were necessary or effective. Other former intelligence officials, including Michael Hayden, have stated that any reintroduction of waterboarding would force military officers to refuse an "illegal order," as prescribed by the Uniform Code of Military Justice. So far, there has not been any sign of the Trump administration returning to such covert collection operations.

Drones and Targeted Killings

A second new dimension to post-9/11 covert action has been the advent of armed unmanned aerial vehicles—commonly called drones. Since the Balkan crises of the 1990s, the CIA has operated UAVs for intelligence-collection purposes—for example, surveillance of battlefields and tracking military movements. Those surveillance programs have become a standard part of the CIA's mission for identifying and tracking suspected terrorists and other battlefield combatants. Following the al-Qaeda attacks on the US embassies in Africa and the USS *Cole*, the Bill Clinton White House urgently pressed to begin arming some UAVs for possible covert action operations. Shortly before the 9/11 attacks, high-level discussions between the White House, the Pentagon, and the CIA focused on the merits of arming the current Predator UAV for the purpose of targeting Osama bin Laden. As former CIA director George Tenet described those decisions in the late 1990s, "the National Security Council authorized us [CIA] to begin deploying the Predator by September 1, in either an armed or unarmed reconnaissance mode.... We preferred that the next time it was over Afghanistan that it be equipped to take immediate action if we spotted UBL."[38] Although targeted killings had long been the practice by the US ally Israel, it constituted a new policy for the United States. Following the 9/11 attacks, any hesitation about arming the Predator evaporated.

Drone attacks began in earnest during the Bush administration. The US Air Force conducted those battlefield operations in Afghanistan, but of course it relied extensively on intelligence provided by the CIA and other agencies. When President Obama took office, he markedly increased drone strikes, which some observers believed were designed to shift from a boots-on-the-ground strategy toward a counterterrorism strategy. At the same time as drone strikes were escalating, outside observers believed that collateral damage caused by them was also rising. Several reports claimed that the civilian casualties might be as low as 250 or as high as 400 to 900.[39] Later, CIA director Brennan publicly defended the Agency's claims that there had been no civilian deaths caused by any classified drone programs, because President Obama instituted a much more rigorous process that called for near certainty before approving a strike.[40] Skeptics remain unconvinced regarding a nearly perfect record of drone strikes, and the debate over whether drones attacks are effective continues. Proponents argue they are far more precise and less risky to the US military than aerial bombing raids or ground operations; moreover, drone attacks are also less visible. Opponents argue that drone strikes create a moral hazard of encouraging more attacks on less important targets because they pose no major risk to US personnel. They also believe that collateral damage is higher than the US government is willing to acknowledge and that civilian deaths result in increased recruitment to terrorist organizations.

According to press reports, the Obama administration eventually reduced drone strikes, partly due to its successful elimination of key targets. In July 2016, President Obama also moved to quell allegations of substantial civilian casualties by issuing an executive order that required agencies to develop more precise rules of engagement and target selection.[41] This was accompanied by an annual report from the DNI on the number of strikes in areas outside active hostilities, the number of combatant and noncombatant casualties, and the reasons for any discrepancies between noncombatant drone casualty estimates by nongovernmental organizations and the US government. In 2018, there had also been some hints that the Trump administration might be considering shifting such drone operations to Afghanistan. In any case, US use of armed drones and targeted killings has set a precedent that other countries may eventually use to justify their own lethal drone operations. Even now, there are reportedly cases of Syrian opposition forces attempting to attack the main Russian military bases there through armed drones.[42]

Paramilitary Operations: CIA or DOD?

The wars in Afghanistan and Iraq have revived a long-standing question of whether the US military or the CIA should be principally responsible for major paramilitary operations. When 9/11 occurred, the CIA was ready with a plan to insert CIA officers into Afghanistan to work with the Northern Alliance to build a military campaign against the Taliban. The CIA had the foreign intelligence as well as an intelligence network in Afghanistan and could operate covertly and quickly to put this in place. Yet Defense Secretary Donald Rumsfeld was not comfortable with the CIA leading the operation and insisted there be some agreement about how the CIA's covert action role and the United States Central Command's operations would be coordinated. There was a memorandum of understanding that laid out the terms of the two organizations' operating areas and responsibilities, including a commitment to collaborate as well as deconflict their operations.[43]

While this division of effort seemed to work in Afghanistan, it never fully settled the issue. Periodically there have been efforts by the DOD to gain more control over paramilitary activities. In 1995, when former deputy secretary of defense John Deutch became DCI and CIA director, he tried unsuccessfully to allow more military control over CIA operations. His assistant DCI for military support, Adm. Dennis Blair (later DNI under President Obama) also believed the military should be running any covert paramilitary operations.[44] However, their efforts failed to gain much White House or congressional support. Following the 9/11 attacks, many Pentagon officials and advisers believed the department needed to get more involved in the covert side of the war on terrorism, recommending large increases in special operations forces and expanded missions.[45] Defense Secretary Rumsfeld tried to expand military operations to include measures that smacked of covert political-influence operations as well as covert HUMINT operations that had not been approved by Congress.[46]

The reality is that the CIA and DOD seem to be conducting similar activities with many of the same goals and results but under very different authorities. CIA operations are covered under Title 50 of the United States Code. Among other aspects of war, it specifies that any covert actions—as distinguished from its intelligence-collection mission—be approved by the president in a written finding and notified to the congressional oversight committees. Such covert actions are conducted with the expectation that the United States will deny official responsibility and that CIA personnel have none of the legal protections that uniformed military officers would normally have.

Under Title 10 of the United States Code, traditional military activities include kinetic (lethal) action in the form of unconventional warfare and special operations necessary in preparation of the battlefield environment. DOD special operations thus fall under these statutes. In most instances, however, military personnel are in uniform, are protected by the Geneva Accords if captured, and must follow the rules of war. Typically they are operating only in declared war zones such as Afghanistan and Iraq and usually with some form of congressional authorization for the use of force. Most important, the United States Special Operations Command is not under any obligation to prenotify Congress of these special operations. Figure 9.1 illustrates the different chains of command used in Title 10 and Title 50.

The May 2011 killing of Osama bin Laden has considerably blurred the above distinction. CIA director Leon Panetta announced the successful operation as being

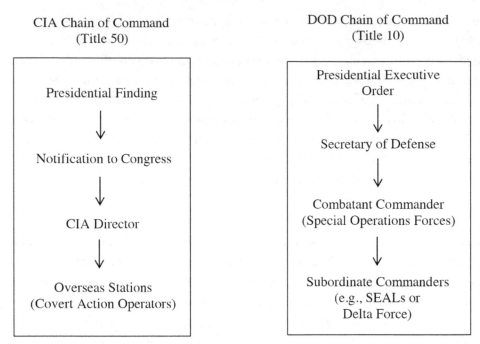

Figure 9.1. CIA and DOD Covert Operations Compared

conducted under Title 50 authorities, in which he had overall responsibility for the covert action. At the same time, he and President Obama acknowledged that special operations forces, under the command of Vice Adm. William McRaven, had conducted the covert strike action. A number of national security legal specialists had noted that the modern battlefield has led to a greater synthesis of intelligence and military operations than ever before, blurring any clear lines between the two functions: "As a matter of law, the President may authorize any agency to conduct a covert action via presidential finding. Alternatively, the President must justify the use of force under traditional military activities under *jus ad bellum* doctrines in domestic and international law."[47]

Another example of blurred lines has been the paramilitary activities conducted in the Syrian conflict. In 2013, President Obama was reluctant to intervene in what many believed to be a messy civil war, choosing instead to encourage regional states such as Turkey and Saudi Arabia to take a larger role in supporting the opposition to Syrian president Bashar al-Assad. Observers believed that Obama was trying to end the Iraq conflict, not get the US military involved in neighboring Syria. As recounted in several memoirs by former senior Obama advisers, they were urging the president to support opposition groups in Syria openly as well as covertly. Part of the explanation for multiple programs lay in the changing nature of the conflict. Once ISIS had become a bigger threat to Iraq, the Obama administration was obliged to adopt an overt military effort to defeat it rather than rely solely on other covert means of pressuring Assad to relinquish power. The Pentagon's program was designed to bolster Iraqi forces fighting ISIS rather than strengthen Syrian opposition forces. But having simultaneous and ultimately unsuccessful programs running within the same country, under very different authorities, merely highlights the unclear lines separating military and intelligence operations (under Title 10 and Title 50, respectively).

If future presidents consider more joint military-intelligence operations, then those distinctions may become less and less clear, and perhaps there will need to be new executive orders or legislation that create a new category of covert joint military-intelligence operations. Without it, there will be concerns that DOD clandestine operations might suffer from a lack of presidential and congressional oversight of special military activities. Shortly after taking office, President Trump gave Secretary of Defense Mattis wider authority for conducting military operations against terrorism, after the Obama administration had been accused of overly cautious "micro-management."[48] Since then, several special operations have suffered some notable casualties, including a US Navy SEAL lost in a botched operation in Yemen and four US Army Special Forces troops ambushed in Niger in 2017. The loss of the personnel in Niger has raised new concerns about the preparedness of the DOD to conduct such special activities, which had not been previously approved at the highest levels in the executive branch or by congressional oversight committees. President Trump reacted to that event by noting he had given his generals more leeway and had not specifically authorized this mission.[49] Congressional investigations into these events may well lead to more debate over whether the DOD or the CIA is best suited for covert paramilitary activities or whether some better mix of those organizations' capabilities should be found.

Future Covert Action: Cyber Operations

Covert action in the future will also increasingly involve cyberspace. Although unacknowledged, it is likely that recent US presidents have already authorized some covert operations designed to attack adversaries' information systems and the military programs run by them. The IC has long had the intelligence-collection mission of penetrating and exploiting adversaries' critical information systems. That collection mission has put the CIA and other intelligence agencies such as the NSA in a position to go further, if directed, to conduct operations that could disrupt or destroy an enemy's military capabilities. Naturally, the DOD is also involved in cyber operations. In the past few years, senior defense officials have acknowledged that the United States is prepared not just to conduct defensive cyber operations to protect military information systems but also to consider conducting offensive cyber operations.[50]

Little is known, correctly so, about the nature and extent of US covert cyber operations. United States Cyber Command is responsible for shielding DOD information systems from attacks and for conducting military cyber operations. At the moment, however, the four-star officer leading the NSA is also responsible for running CYBERCOM. The current arrangement where a single senior military officer is dual hatted, running a major intelligence organization as well as a separate military command, further blurs the lines between intelligence and military operations. The Obama administration had considered separating the two responsibilities, and that might still occur in the future.

The CIA, on the other hand, has been involved in so-called information operations as part of its own intelligence mission. It established a Directorate of Digital Innovation as part of a 2015 modernization of the agency's organizational structure. That directorate collects cyber-related intelligence as well as manages the increasingly important exploitation of "big data."[51] At the same time, the CIA may well be called on to develop covert actions that involve the use of cyber operations. Some press reporting has indicated that small cyber operations may have been launched against the personal computers of key al-Qaeda members.[52]

Given the growing importance of cyberspace to most governments' civilian sectors and military programs, it seems inevitable that cyber operations will be a significant new form of covert action. Where once the United States focused on economic or military "sabotage" or "political influence" conducted through newspaper placements and black broadcasting, now there can be cyber options. This has been amply demonstrated by the North Korean cyber operation against Sony Pictures in 2014, which penetrated the American entertainment company's computer system, published its emails, and also destroyed some data. The 2010 attack on Iran's nuclear program has also been analyzed by private security firms to be so sophisticated that it was more likely conducted by a government than any individual or hacker group. Likewise, the 2019 DNI's Worldwide Threat Assessment identified Beijing as posing a persistent cyber threat to the United States' military and critical infrastructure systems.[53]

The Russian interference in the 2016 US presidential campaign has become an example of how covert use of cyberspace to penetrate electoral computer systems and to manipulate social media websites to produce bogus news stories can influence voters. A joint NSA-CIA-FBI-DNI assessment characterized the Russian political-influence campaign as an officially sanctioned and highly organized effort to use covert cyber operations, along with overt Russian media, third parties, and social media bloggers, to undermine the Hillary Clinton campaign in favor of Donald Trump's.[54] Other examples are likely to emerge over time, suggesting that this will be a potential tool for the United States as well as its adversaries.

To summarize, then, covert action is likely to remain a potent tool for future presidents but also one that contains a number of operational, political, and legal-ethical risks. As former official Gregory Treverton's comments at the beginning of this chapter note, Americans do not want to think of their government as conducting dirty tricks, but the fact that governments hostile to the United States will do so tempts any president or senior US official to reply in kind. Adopting a set of principles such as cited by Sir David Omand earlier in this chapter would be one way to ensure that covert actions remain within the bounds of what would be acceptable to the American people.

USEFUL DOCUMENTS

Marshall Curtis Erwin, *Covert Action: Legislative Actions and Possible Policy Questions*, Congressional Research Service, https://fas.org/sgp/crs/intel/RL33715.pdf

Office of the Director of National Intelligence, *Background to "Assessing Russian Activities and Intentions in Recent US Elections": The Analytic Process and Cyber Incident Attribution*, January 6, 2017, at URL: https://www.dni.gov/files/documents/ICA_2017_01.pdf

United States Senate, Select Committee on Intelligence, "Executive Summary," *Committee Study of the Central Intelligence Agency's Detention and Interrogation Program*, https://fas.org/irp/congress/2014_rpt/ssci-rdi.pdf

FURTHER READING

William Daugherty, *Executive Secrets: Covert Action and the Presidency* (Lexington: University Press of Kentucky, 2004).
>   Provides a practitioner's view of earlier covert actions, which defends its uses when properly authorized and executed.

Jack Devine, *Good Hunting: An American Spymaster's Story* (New York: Farrar, Strauss and Giroux, 2014).
>   Describes the career of a CIA practitioner of covert action and his principal lessons learned from both successes and failures.

Roy Godson, *Dirty Tricks or Trump Cards: US Covert Action and Counterintelligence* (New Brunswick, NJ: Transaction, 2001).
>   Presents a typology of covert actions and some of the pros and cons of its uses since 1945.

Richard Immerman, *The Hidden Hand: A Brief History of the CIA* (New York: Wiley, 2014).
>   Provides a good discussion of the early decisions regarding covert action and some of the major successes and failures throughout the CIA's history.

Jennifer D. Kibbe, "Covert Action," *Oxford Research Encyclopedias*, http://internationalstudies.oxfordre.com/view/10.1093/acrefore/9780190846626.001.0001/acrefore-9780190846626-e-135.
>   Provides an extensive review of the covert action literature and highlights some of its challenges.

Peter Kornbluh, *Bay of Pigs Declassified: The Secret CIA Report on the Invasion of Cuba* (New York: New Press, 1998).

> Recounts the most often cited failure of CIA-sponsored covert action.

Gregory Treverton, *Covert Action: The Limits of Intervention in the Postwar World* (New York: Basic Books, 1987).

> A former staff member of the 1975 Church Committee provides his perspective on the CIA's secret operations up until those hearings.

NOTES

First epigraph: Gregory Treverton, *Covert Action: The Limits of Intervention in the Postwar World* (New York: Basic Books, 1987), 11.

Second epigraph: Jack Devine, *Good Hunting: An American Spymaster's Story* (New York: Farrar, Strauss and Giroux, 2014), 5.

1. See Office of the Historian, "Notes on Covert Action," in *Foreign Relations of the United States, 1964-48; Western Europe*, vol. 12, https://history.state.gov/historicaldocuments/frus 1964-68v12/actionsstatement.

2. See Richard Immerman, *The Hidden Hand: A Brief History of the CIA* (New York: Wiley, 2014), 19-29.

3. The OPC was the element within the CIA where covert action was centralized. The Senior Consultants included representatives from the Departments of State and Defense and the Joint Chiefs of staff.

4. Treverton, *Covert Action*, 38.

5. See "History of Evolution," *Coordination and Approval of Covert Operations*, February 23, 1967, CIA Library, declassified May 2002, https://www.cia.gov/library/readingroom /docs/DOC_0000790232.pdf.

6. See James Callanan, *Covert Action in the Cold War: US Policy, Intelligence and CIA Operations* (London: I. B. Tauris, 2010), 37-38.

7. Callanan, 41.

8. At the time, the CIA was assessing this split as the most significant division in the Soviet sphere of influence and was alert to the possibility of Stalin considering attacking Yugoslavia to force it back into the fold.

9. See Coleman Mehta, "The CIA Confronts the Tito-Stalin Split," *Cold War Studies* 13, no. 1 (Winter 2011): 101-45.

10. Mehta.

11. John Prados, *CIA's Secret Wars* (New York: William Morrow, 1986), 17, 312-13.

12. Devine, *Good Hunting*.

13. Quoted in William Daugherty, *Executive Secrets: Covert Action and the Presidency* (Lexington: University Press of Kentucky, 2004), 138.

14. Treverton, *Covert Action*, 45.

15. The US military had more elaborate plans for the invasion of Cuba and believed nothing short of a major operation would dislodge Castro. However, it was content to let the CIA continue its plans, believing in the end that Kennedy would have to provide more military

support and thereby be open to its more overt plans for invasion. This was an important backdrop to the military's thinking that invasion was necessary during the Cuban Missile Crisis.

16. Daugherty, *Executive Secrets*, 154.

17. Treverton, *Covert Action*, 226.

18. Former Secretary of State Cyrus Vance, quoted in the *New York Times*, March 1, 1987.

19. Devine, *Good Hunting*, 25–42, provides an eyewitness account of the operation by the former Afghan task force chief of the covert action program against the Soviet occupation.

20. On March 27, 1985, "National Security Decision Directive 166: U.S. Policy, Programs, and Strategy in Afghanistan" stipulated that "our covert program will deny Afghanistan to the Soviets as a secure base from which to project power further in the region."

21. Daugherty, *Executive Action*, 206. Another feature of the program's funding was that Saudi Arabia had pledged matching funds to whatever the US Congress was prepared to appropriate.

22. Some media, along with a book and movie, have characterized the Afghan operation as "Charlie Wilson's war" in view of his strong advocacy for the program.

23. Adapted from Sir David Omand, "Ethical Guidelines in Using Secret Intelligence for Public Security," *Cambridge Review of International Affairs* 19, no. 4 (2006): 613–28. Text in parentheses mine.

24. Each president usually issued a national security memorandum detailing the responsibilities and representation on covert action oversight groups. NSDM 40 (Nixon) became the title of the NSC subgroup assigned to review and approve covert action proposals.

25. Treverton, *Covert Action*, 232.

26. Daugherty, *Executive Action*, 100.

27. The author is indebted to a former senior NSC official responsible for overseeing covert action who explained the Bush process in some detail.

28. Daugherty, *Executive Action*, 103–4.

29. Attendance might expand depending on the topic and region. If other agencies, such as the FBI, DEA, or Department of Commerce had equities at stake, they might also be included.

30. According to one former NSC participant in covert action decisions, a senior congressional official might strongly object to a proposed finding, which raised the risk of a leak if the president went ahead with the operation.

31. CIA, Office of the Inspector General, *Unauthorized Interrogation Techniques*, October 29, 2003, https://www.cia.gov/library/readingroom/docs/0006541525.pdf.

32. Michael Hayden, *Playing to the Edge: American Intelligence in the Age of Terror* (New York: Penguin, 2016), 223–25.

33. Hayden, 223–25. Hayden and other former officials have noted that the full list of ten techniques has not been revealed, but once the existence of the interrogation program and waterboarding had leaked, the list was cut down and waterboarding was eliminated.

34. The United States ratified in 1994 the UN Convention on Torture and Other Cruel, Inhuman or Degrading Treatment or Punishment, which defines torture as "any act by which severe pain or suffering, whether physical or mental, is intentionally inflicted on a person." In August 2002, the DOJ produced a legal memorandum for President Bush that approved a wide range of techniques, concluding that "while many of these techniques may amount to cruel, inhuman or degrading treatment, they do not produce pain or suffering of the necessary intensity to meet the definition of torture."

35. Senate Select Committee on Intelligence, *Committee's Study of the CIA's Detention and Interrogation Program*, Executive Summary and Key Findings, and Declassified Revisions December 3, 2014, https://www.feinstein.senate.gov/public/_cache/files/7/c/7c85429a-ec38 -4bb5-968f-289799bf6d0e/D87288C34A6D9FF736F9459ABCF83210.sscistudy1.pdf.

36. "Statement from Director Brennan on the SSCI Study on the Former Detention and Interrogation Report," December 9, 2014, https://www.cia.gov/news-information/press-releases -statements/2014-press-releases-statements/statement-from-director-brennan-on-ssci-study -on-detention-interrogation-program.html.

37. Mark Mazzetti, *The Way of the Knife: The CIA, a Secret Army, and a War at the Ends of the Earth* (New York: Penguin, 2013), 120.

38. George Tenet, *At the Center of the Storm: My Years at the CIA* (New York: Harper-Collins, 2007), 158.

39. The New America Foundation claims that, by 2017, the United States had conducted over four hundred strikes in Pakistan, causing anywhere from 245 to 303 civilian casualties out of a total casualty range of 2,359 to 3,685. See New America Foundation, "America's CounterTerrorism Wars: Drone Strikes Pakistan," https://www.newamerica.org/in-depth /americas-counterterrorism-wars/pakistan/. The Bureau for Investigative Journalism reports that there were 429 confirmed strikes in Pakistan, resulting in 2,514 to 4,023 deaths, of which 424 to 926 were civilian deaths. See Bureau for Investigative Journalism, "Strikes in Pakistan," accessed January 5, 2017, https://www.thebureauinvestigates.com/drone-war/data/pakistan -covert-us-reported-actions-2017.

40. Scott Shane, "CIA Is Disputed on Civilian Toll in Drone Strikes," *New York Times*, August 11, 2011, http://www.nytimes.com/2011/08/12/world/asia/12drones.html.

41. See "Executive Order: United States Policy on Pre- and Post-Strike Measures to Address Civilian Casualties in U.S. Operations Involving the Use of Force," July 1, 2016.

42. Neil MacFarquhar, "Russia Says Its Syria Bases Beat Back an Attack by 13 Drones," *New York Times*, January 8, 2018, https://www.nytimes.com/2018/01/08/world/middleeast/syria -russia-drones.htm.

43. Tenet, *At the Center of the Storm*, 216.

44. Daugherty, *Executive Secrets*, 65–68.

45. Greg Miller, "Wider Pentagon Spy Role Urged," *The Nation*, October 26, 2002, http:// www.washingtonpost.com/wp-dyn/articles/A29414-2005Jan22.html.

46. Barton Gellman, "Secret Unit Expands Rumsfeld's Domain," *Washington Post*, January 23, 2005, http://www.washingtonpost.com/wp-dyn/articles/A29414-2005Jan22.html.

47. See Jeff Mustin and Harvey Rishikof, "Projecting Force in the 21st Century: Legitimacy and the Rule of Law; Title 50, Title 10, Title 18, and Art. 75," *Rutgers Law Review* 68 (Summer 2011): 1251.

48. Jim Michaels, "Trump Gives Defense Chief Mattis Running Room in War-Fighting," *USA Today*, April 5, 2017, https://www.usatoday.com/story/news/world/2017/04/05/mattis-trump -syria-iraq-yemen-isis/100016758/.

49. John Haltiwanger, "Trump Blames Generals for Ambush That Got Four Servicemen Killed," *Newsweek*, October 25, 2017, http://www.newsweek.com/trump-blames-generals-niger -ambush-four-us-soldiers-killed-693227.

50. See Joint Staff, *Cyberspace Operations*, Joint Publication-3–12, February 5, 2013, II-2, https://fas.org/irp/doddir/dod/jp3_12r.pdf, which lays out how cyberspace operations are to be conducted, including mention of "offensive operations."

51. "Big data" typically refers to extremely large and complex data sets that require sophisticated software to analyze and exploit the information found there. For intelligence purposes, big data analysis can reveal trends, patterns, or relationships hidden within these huge amounts of information gleaned from websites, blogs, or social media sources.

52. David Sanger, "Obama Order Sped Up Wave of Cyberattacks against Iran," *New York Times*, June 1, 2012.

53. ODNI, *Worldwide Threat Assessment of the US Intelligence Community*, January 29, 2019, 5.

54. ODNI, "Key Judgments," *Assessing Russian Activities and Intentions in the Recent U.S. Presidential Elections*, ICA 2017–01D, January 6, 2017, https://www.dni.gov/files/documents /ICA_2017_01.pdf. See also the Mueller Report, formally known as the *Report on the Investigation into Russian Interference in the 2016 Presidential Election*, volumes 1 and 2, submitted by Special Counsel Robert S. Mueller III, March 2019, https://www.justice.gov/storage /report.pdf.

10

THE CHALLENGES OF THE INTELLIGENCE-POLICY RELATIONSHIP

> Presidents and their national security teams usually are ill-informed about intelligence capabilities; therefore they often have unrealistic expectations of what intelligence can do for them, especially when they hear about the genuinely extraordinary capabilities of U.S. intelligence for collecting and processing information.
> —Robert Gates, former CIA director, 1989

> Often we feel the desire to influence policy and ... to wish simply for influence can, and upon occasion does, get intelligence to the place where it can have no influence whatever. By striving too hard in this direction, intelligence may come to seem just another policy voice, and an unwanted one at that.
> —Sherman Kent, *Estimates and Influence*, 1968

American intelligence has provided presidents and national security teams with an amazing amount of information and insight into a bewildering array of international challenges. As the preceding chapters make clear, intelligence has played a part in the shaping and execution of foreign and security policies at both the strategic and tactical levels; moreover, intelligence at times has to implement policies in the form of covert action. That said, the relationship between intelligence and policy has remained contentious and unpredictable. While policymakers and intelligence officers share the same national security enterprise, they sometimes appear to be coexisting in parallel universes. Policymakers and intelligence officers are driven by different sets of political interests and bureaucratic imperatives. This chapter will explain how the relationship has evolved but remains full of friction. In particular, it will examine how "politicization" of intelligence occurs, spotlighting some major cases and raising some issues about the future of the intelligence-policy relationship.

OPPOSING TRIBES: POLICY AND INTELLIGENCE

Early in the US intelligence community's formation, a clear distinction was made between those officials responsible for policymaking and others carrying the responsibility of presenting intelligence for a national security team's use. As the 1947 National Security Act makes clear, the director of central intelligence (and after the 2004 intelligence reform legislation, the director of national intelligence) was not a policymaking official but rather an "intelligence adviser." This signified a clear line between those empowered to make national security decisions and others who were merely providing inputs from their respective areas of expertise; intelligence, like military advice, was more an instrument for policymakers than policy itself. The CIA director and later the DNI were to bring the best information and analysis to the president and his senior policy officials. In a formal sense, no intelligence official would have a say in determining what US national security policy would be. This clearly separated the policy and intelligence communities.

As chapter 3 made clear, the policy advisers and their agencies are responsible for determining how to develop strategies for advancing US national interests and develop responses to major threats and opportunities to those interests. The policy "lane" is clearly distinguishable from the provision of information and analysis constructed in the intelligence "lane." Policymakers are always sensitive to intelligence usurping or at least complicating their roles by presenting national intelligence estimates and other assessments that might undermine the assumptions behind their preferred policies or suggest that a selected course of action might not have the desired results. Policymakers are above all else protective of their "decision space," which in the best of all worlds means not having any constraints on their freedom of action.

Many presidents and senior policy officials come from the worlds of politics, law, and business and are people of action. They are highly confident of their own abilities and firm in their own beliefs. As such, they are inclined to be optimists and bridle at any suggestion that their policies might be ineffective, unsustainable, or too risky. As political scientist and intelligence scholar Robert Jervis has noted, policymakers have to oversell their policies to domestic and foreign audiences, and that leads inevitably to distortion of intelligence and thus clashes with the IC.[1] A further demand of policymakers is the desire for "certainty" regarding future important events. They fear surprise and any unanticipated complications to their policy agendas.[2]

In contrast, intelligence officers by their very nature are more cautious if not skeptical about the feasibility of ambitious policy initiatives and wary of providing high-confidence judgments or predictions regarding the future. "It's complicated" would capture the essence of the intelligence world. Analysts in particular tend to see the world in shades of gray rather than black-and-white terms. Uncertainty can be bounded but not reduced to zero. Above all else, intelligence is designed to be "policy neutral," or free of any particular policy agenda. Indeed, the whole purpose of having an independent intelligence community is to assure that the most comprehensive set of facts and analysis can be brought to bear on very complex foreign policy issues. At best, that information might present policymakers with inconvenient facts and alternative assessments of an adversary's capabilities, intentions, or reactions to American policies; at worst, intelligence might raise questions about the underlying premises or conclusions of a policy decision. However, for intelligence officers, presenting the facts is more important than seeking approval from their policy masters.

ALTERNATIVE INTELLIGENCE-POLICY MODELS: KENT VERSUS GATES

At the outset of the Cold War, intelligence as a discipline was poorly understood, and the clear lines between policy and intelligence were not so carefully defined. However, a senior intelligence expert in the OSS (the CIA's precursor), and later a key official in the early estimates process at the CIA, laid out the ground rules for the IC's operation in the policy process. In his 1949 book *Strategic Intelligence for an American World Policy*, Sherman Kent enunciated the basic principle that intelligence should "raise the level of discussion" around the policymaking tables. In Kent's view, intelligence should *not* advocate a specific policy position; instead, it should inform policy. Intelligence analysts should be cognizant of, but detached from, any specific policy agenda. Kent knew that lively debates would tempt strong-willed policymakers to manipulate intelligence findings. Thus, intelligence analysts had to strive to present information objectively without regard to whether it was pleasing to senior officials.

Stating this principle, however, was not to say it would be easy to achieve in practice. Nor were intelligence assessments uncontroversial when matters of war or peace were to be based partly on these findings. Over the decades, US intelligence has been faulted for not only being incorrect at times but also of being biased against presidential policies. Intelligence frequently became embroiled in debates over strategy and was sometimes accused, rightly or wrongly, of becoming "politicized" (i.e., distorted by political agendas).

The Kent model of a kind of "arm's-length" approach to policymakers was designed to avoid becoming entangled in such political debates. However, it also tended to instill an attitude among analysts that they could write what they wished and that policymakers could take or leave their analysis. This "ivory-tower" intelligence attitude toward policy could at times verge on hubris. Policymakers would accuse analysts of indulging in faintly disguised criticism of policies with which they did not agree. Moreover, the CIA often conducted analysis on topics as much to sharpen the skills of its own analysts and deepen their expertise as to inform a specific policy discussion. Hence, periodically policymakers have complained that intelligence was not relevant to their policy needs. In the early days, intelligence assessments tended to be lengthy, excessively detailed, and hard to digest for harried policymakers. Indeed, the CIA and other agencies always considered themselves as much the audience for intelligence products as the policy agencies themselves.[3]

The end of the Cold War and demise of the Soviet Union found the IC less prepared to justify its huge operations than ever before. Some critics, citing the CIA's failure to forecast the collapse of the Soviet Union, asserted that there was no need for the agency at all if the principal threat was gone. Sen. Daniel Moynihan famously proposed in the early 1990s to either fold the CIA into the State Department or abolish it entirely.[4] Even before this time, however, senior officials, including Robert Gates, began to articulate a different intelligence-policy model that highlighted "relevance" in the place where "objectivity" once had pride of place. As a Soviet analyst, Gates had served in several presidents' National Security Council staffs, and he made the observation that too often analysis was not addressing current policy agendas. He wrote that while intelligence prided itself on understanding how foreign governments worked, few analysts understood how the US government worked or seemed aware of the policy processes that drove American foreign policy.[5] As deputy director for intelligence in the 1980s, he instructed his senior managers and analysts to spend more time "downtown" in interagency meetings and in the offices of NSC, State Department, and Defense Department policymakers.[6] Only then could analysts understand what the true intelligence needs of the government were.

From then on and up to the present, the CIA in particular has aimed to be close to policymakers in order to understand what policies are being considered and thereby tailor intelligence to the issues that most mattered. Senior analysts increasingly took rotational assignments to policy agencies in order to get close to policy discussions and to help provide direct intelligence support. The author was himself assigned to the State Department's policy planning staff in 1989–91 in order to help bring intelligence to some of Secretary of State James Baker's closest advisers.[7] The crafting of a *President's Daily Brief* (explained in detail in chapter 8) is perhaps the best example of the Gates model in action, as it explicitly focuses on presidential intelligence requirements. As the *PDB* became the key intelligence product, assignment as a *PDB* briefer was sought after by rising analysts, who were frequently promoted to become senior managers on the basis of their performance as briefers to the president or other cabinet officers. For example, Michael Morell, who was one of President George W. Bush's *PDB* briefers, went on to become a senior office manager, executive director (the number-three position), and eventually CIA deputy director. In practice, a briefer's exposure to senior policy officials gave them insight into how the interagency policy process ran and the types of intelligence questions being posed by senior officials. In addition, they gained personal credibility with their counterparts in the White House and State and Defense Departments, which built up important intelligence-policy relationships for the future.

Less apparent, however, was the inherent risk that this model presented to maintaining intelligence's analytical objectivity and integrity. By virtue of being close to policy, was there not a danger of analysts becoming inadvertently biased toward the policy preferences of the current occupant of the White House? As Richard Betts noted, "Packaging intelligence to be more productive makes it harder to draw sharp lines between what is relevant and what supports a particular policy choice."[8] Robert Gates, who had been deputy director of the CIA during the Reagan years, became the target of vicious accusations of "skewing" analysis in ways favorable to the hawkish views of CIA director William Casey and President Reagan (see box 10.1). The tendency for presidents also to pick their CIA directors from among personal advisers

---

Box 10.1   The Gates Confirmation Hearings and Charges of Politicization

In the fall of 1991, Robert Gates was nominated to become George H. W. Bush's CIA director. During the nomination hearings before the Senate Select Committee on Intelligence, several senior CIA analysts accused Gates of forcing analysts to rewrite analysis of the Soviet Union to bolster the Reagan administration's skeptical perceptions of Mikhail Gorbachev's so-called New Thinking. Those analysts claimed that as deputy director of intelligence, Gates had dismissed the Gorbachev phenomenon as mere tactics, exaggerated the Soviet military threat, and played down instability in the USSR.

Gates's own defense was primarily focused on his review responsibilities that CIA analysis be as rigorous and analytically defensible as possible. He acknowledged that he criticized some assessments as "flabby and complacent" and some analysts as being "closed-minded, smug, [and providing] arrogant responses to legitimate questions."* In his own memoir of the 1990s, he also admitted that he had significant differences with the then secretary of state George Shultz, who complained that Gates was using his position as CIA director to question Gorbachev's abilities and indirectly Shultz's diplomatic overtures toward Gorbachev.†

* Elaine Sciolino, "The Gates Hearings: Bush's C.I.A. Choice in Counterattack at Senate Hearing," *New York Times*, October 4, 1991, http://www.nytimes.com/1991/10/04/us/the-gates-hearings-bush-s-cia-choice-in-counterattack-at-senate-hearing.html?pagewanted=all.
† Robert Gates, *From the Shadows: The Ultimate Insider's Story of Five Presidents and How They Won the Cold War* (New York: Simon & Schuster, 1996), 443–47.

and political supporters rather than careerists also increased concerns that intelligence might become more prone to **politicization**.

PRESIDENTS AND THEIR INTELLIGENCE ADVISERS

Given that the assigned role of CIA directors and later directors of national intelligence is to be the principal intelligence adviser to presidents and the NSC, their relationships with their presidents has often become critical to the broader intelligence-policy relationship. Those presidents who had a better understanding of and valued intelligence tended to establish strong bonds with their intelligence advisers, while those less familiar or comfortable with intelligence kept a more arm's-length attitude toward those individuals and their agencies.

Among the presidents who held the most sophisticated views of intelligence, Dwight Eisenhower and George H. W. Bush stand out. As a military commander, Eisenhower had used intelligence throughout his wartime campaigns and saw it as a force multiplier in the struggle against communism during the Cold War. He was responsible for the development of some of the earliest overhead imagery programs (the U-2 "spyplane" and the first satellite programs). Moreover, as a military commander, he had been comfortable exploiting secret operations and later eagerly used covert action programs crafted by his CIA director, Allen Dulles. Eisenhower placed great confidence in Dulles, who had conducted OSS wartime operations overseas, and he boosted the agency's covert action programs.

George H. W. Bush was another president with a unique understanding of intelligence, as he served as CIA director under Gerald Ford. He came to this position with substantial international experience, having served as US ambassador to the UN and as first US envoy to the People's Republic of China. Later, as vice president during the Reagan presidency, he was authorized to read the *PDB* and enjoyed the interactions with his personal briefer. Hence, when he became president in 1988, he made it a practice to read the *PDB* every day, elevating the status of the document more than any previous president. "When I was president," he told the CIA history staff, "one of my favorite times of the day was when I would sit down with a briefer and read through the *PDB*."[9] He also decided to retain President Reagan's CIA director, former FBI director William Webster, who had replaced the controversial William Casey. Bush had failed to retain his own CIA directorship when President Carter came into office, so he also wanted to send the message that the job should be nonpolitical.[10]

Many presidents have been far less knowledgeable, supportive, or comfortable with intelligence. Christopher Andrew, the British intelligence historian, has described Harry Truman as "almost totally ignorant" of intelligence when he took office.[11] Truman also famously worried about creating a CIA that could become an American

Gestapo but eagerly wanted a single organization to collate and provide him infor-mation. John F. Kennedy came into office largely ignorant of intelligence operations but trusting and relying on careerists such as Allen Dulles. However, the Bay of Pigs fiasco quickly dispelled this confidence, and he designated his brother, Attorney General Robert Kennedy, to watch over the CIA to make sure it did not get him into trouble. Lyndon Johnson was perhaps the earthiest in reflecting on his problems with intelligence: "One day, I'd worked hard and gotten a full pail of milk, but I wasn't pay-ing attention, and old Bessie swung her s—smeared tail through the bucket of milk. Now, you know that's what these intelligence guys do. You work hard and get a good program or policy going, and they swing a s—smeared tail through it."[12]

As Johnson's quote makes clear, presidents are often frustrated by intelligence assessments that do not support their policy agendas. In particular, Richard Nixon suspected the CIA was opposed to his presidency, believing the agency was somehow involved in his defeat in the presidential election of 1960 and filled with "Georgetown liberals" who despised him and his conservative views.[13] In general, new occupants to the office are wary of the CIA, given its attention to presidential intelligence needs. They often suspect that the CIA and the IC more generally have been working so long for their predecessors (often from the opposing party) that they have become cap-tives of, if not advocates for, that former president's policies. During the postelection transition period prior to taking office, the president-elect begins to meet with senior intelligence officials and might see their first *PDB*s. They begin to take the measure of the current intelligence officials and their views. Likewise, those senior intelligence officials are anxious to prove their ability to work for the new president, regardless of party or policy views, and to get a sense of the new president's intelligence priorities. That "shake-down cruise" is sometimes smooth but often very bumpy.

The transition from George H. W. Bush to Bill Clinton was clearly a bumpy one. President Clinton appointed James Woolsey, who had been a prominent defense official in previous Democratic administrations. However, Clinton had never met Woolsey, and the two men proved unable to forge a close relationship. Clinton never became an avid reader of the *PDB* or comfortable with his intelligence advisers. Wool-sey became the victim of political cartoons showing him failing to get access to the Oval Office, and he eventually departed in frustration. Clinton's efforts to appoint his first national security adviser, Anthony Lake, as the next CIA director—in order to have someone with whom he did have a good relationship—foundered in the nomination process, and he eventually selected Deputy Secretary of Defense John Deutch, who had a similarly checkered and short tenure at the CIA. George Tenet, once Clinton's NSC senior director for intelligence and then the deputy DCI, would eventually take the number-one position. He proved to be a better fit for Clinton and clever enough to be retained during the first years of George W. Bush's presidency.[14] Throughout his presidency, however, Clinton seldom saw a *PDB* briefer, content to allow his national security advisers to read the *PDB* and remind him of the important articles he should read. While acknowledging the importance of intelligence, Clinton never took a particular interest in it.

The transition to the George W. Bush presidency saw the IC and its leadership having to prove itself once again to an occupant who had very little foreign policy experience or interest. He surrounded himself, however, with a skilled team of senior advisers who did have significant experience and strong opinions regarding intelligence. Secretary of State Colin Powell was supportive but skeptical at times, while Vice President Dick Cheney and Secretary of Defense Donald Rumsfeld were suspicious and often critical of the CIA's intelligence judgments. Bush, however, had an open mind and was encouraged by his father's positive experience working at and with the CIA. During early intelligence briefings at his "Texas White House," the president-elect remarked that he hoped when he was finally in office, he would be able to get the "good stuff!"[15] This remark put the CIA into a state of high anxiety, believing it already was providing the best intelligence it could. However, the then CIA director George Tenet decided to brief the president himself in order to sensitize him to the spectacular sources and methods the CIA employed as well as cement a solid personal relationship with the new president. That relationship survived the disastrous 9/11 attacks, but ultimately Tenet was a casualty of the Iraq WMD estimate's flawed findings.

His successor, Congressman Porter Goss, had even less success in building rapport with the president or his own workforce. In addition, the creation of the position of director of national intelligence demoted CIA director Goss's status and often put him at odds with the first DNI, John Negroponte. Goss left shortly thereafter, having unsuccessfully challenged Negroponte's authority to redirect some of the CIA's counterterrorism activities.[16] As the Iraq War bogged down into a protracted civil war, the Bush administration was tempted to let the CIA's flawed 2002 estimate carry a large share of the blame for the failing policies. The White House also did little to shield the CIA from congressional criticism for conducting presidentially approved secret detention and interrogation programs. US Air Force general Michael Hayden's selection as CIA director helped to quiet the uproar over the CIA's role in "torture," as he pledged to take the agency off the front pages. His longtime intelligence background and service as NSA director made him a suitable partner with DNI Negroponte. Most important, he formed a good relationship with President Bush.

Intelligence under President Obama began with its own share of controversy. His appointment of Leon Panetta—who had considerable political experience and clout but no intelligence background—struck many as puzzling if not risky. President Obama had publicly condemned the Bush administration's Iraq policies and its counterterrorism policy of using enhanced interrogation techniques. This led to a chilly relationship between the president and CIA professionals initially. Panetta, however, proved to be a skilled bureaucratic leader who had the president's ear. In short order, he restored morale at the agency and also its credibility with the White House.

If anything, Panetta overshadowed Obama's first DNI, retired admiral Dennis Blair, who managed to clash repeatedly with the CIA—especially over overseas assignment of chiefs of station—and lose the confidence of the White House. His replacement by James Clapper—a career military intelligence professional—proved to be a stroke of genius in terms of crafting an effective partnership among senior intelligence officials. Along with NSC senior director for counterterrorism and intelligence John Brennan, the intelligence leadership formed an effective team that gained the president's confidence. Obama came to appreciate intelligence, particularly the use of covert action and special operations, which led to the killing of Osama bin Laden. Obama also proved to be an exceptionally good reader of intelligence, requesting that his *PDB* be delivered via a classified electronic tablet that he regularly read. When he decided to shuffle his cabinet in his second term, he chose Brennan to become CIA director. By placing at Langley a former senior NSC adviser and seasoned intelligence professional, Obama ensured he had someone who could deliver tough intelligence assessments, oversee both active counterterrorism and covert action programs, and work with his defense, intelligence, and law enforcement counterparts.

Those positives, however, were overshadowed by the impact of Edward Snowden's stunning leak of highly sensitive electronic surveillance efforts by the NSA. The IC had to explain long-standing programs designed to collect metadata of millions of American citizens from major Internet and phone providers, which the IC could comb through to track down possible links to foreign terrorist organizations. In addition, this massive release of NSA intercept programs revealed collection efforts against key allied leaders, most notably German chancellor Angela Merkel. The diplomatic fallout from the Snowden leaks damaged not only US credibility but also strained the White House relationship with some intelligence officials. The administration was obliged to ratchet back those programs and establish new policies regarding collection against key allies. A presidentially appointed commission found that those NSA programs had probably overreached and did not in fact surface enough valuable information to justify the intrusion into Americans' personal communications. The Obama administration subsequently directed that the NSA would not collect that data but that Internet providers would have to archive that information in case a FISA warrant were issued allowing IC to access an individual user's metadata. (See chapter 11 for more details.)

In the most recent presidential transition, it became clear that president-elect Donald Trump would not readily accept the joint CIA, NSA, FBI, and DNI assessment that the Russian government had covertly interfered in the 2016 elections in an effort to undermine his opponent's candidacy. To President Trump, these assessments diminished his confidence in the intelligence leadership and the community's non-political nature. During the 2016 presidential campaign, the Trump campaign had mocked IC findings as speculation, stating, "These are the same people that said Saddam had weapons of mass destruction."[17] Throughout the campaign and even after taking office, he expressed skepticism about the Russian hacking episode; moreover, unlike any previous president, he attacked the independence and credibility of the FBI's efforts to uncover the Russian "active measures" program.[18] Like many presidents before him, President Trump wanted to have people leading intelligence agencies who shared his views and who were loyal to him. His selection of Republican congressman Mike Pompeo to be his first CIA director fit this mold of having political appointees. Likewise, the appointment of former diplomat John Bolton as President Trump's third national security adviser also raised alarm bells regarding politicization driven by a strong policy advocate with a record of misrepresenting intelligence.[19]

On the positive side, the appointment of a competent if controversial professional intelligence officer, Gina Haspel, as the first female CIA director likely will have a mixed impact on the policy-intelligence relationship.[20] Her nomination hearings were clouded by criticism of her involvement in the discredited CIA "torture" program and senatorial complaints that she might not stand up to President Trump's seeming attraction to harsher interrogation methods. Yet she pledged as a professional to speak truth to power and seemed to demonstrate this in the 2019 Worldwide Threat Assessment hearings, when she and DNI Dan Coats laid out IC assessments on Russia, Iran, North Korea, and ISIS that the media characterized as being at odds with the president's own views.[21] Periodic presidential dissatisfaction with his intelligence and law enforcement leaders now appears almost predictable, if they are asked to set the record straight.

President Trump has also proven to be an indifferent reader of the *PDB*. According to numerous press reports, he does not enjoy reading it and is content to be briefed orally on intelligence topics. While he receives the *PDB* daily, it is clear he is not overly focused on using an intelligence briefing to shape his agenda.[22] Some CIA careerists defend this practice as not being a huge deviation from some past presidents who also did not read every item or who preferred oral briefings; they note that other presidents also relied on their national security advisers to tell them which intelligence reports were significant.[23] From what reporters have learned, the president's national security adviser and other key White House officers remain readers of the *PDB*.

INTELLIGENCE AT THE CENTER OF POLICY DISPUTES

Policy disputes in which intelligence assessments play a role are often a reason for presidential distrust of and disregard for intelligence. As mentioned earlier, policymakers have their policy agendas and their own worldviews. When intelligence challenges either of those, conflict is sure to erupt. Because intelligence brings facts and uniquely secret information into a policy discussion, it can play an incredibly powerful role in supporting or opposing presidential decisions. A longtime scholar of the intelligence-policy relationship, Joshua Rovner, has noted that normal friction between intelligence and policy results when the two hold different assessments about the quality, objectivity, and implications of intelligence assessments. In such circumstances, well-informed policymakers have every right to challenge intelligence assessments and to demand the IC explain and prove its case. However, politicization most often occurs when policy officials try to manipulate or cherry-pick intelligence to suit their policy preferences.[24] Those instances tend to be ones where policymakers are so committed to a set of policies that any hint that intelligence might question their basis would be extremely damaging politically. Sometimes those instances reflect a genuine disconnect between policies and the intelligence that might undergird them. In others, policymakers accuse intelligence officials of producing estimates specifically to challenge policies with which they disagree.

The specific motivations for and forms of politicization are many, and Rovner's scholarship suggests they can be found in the policy assumptions and agendas, bureaucratic parochialism and organizational processes, and partisan and scapegoating tactics embedded in the intelligence-policy relationship (see box 10.2).

Box 10.2 Rovner's Taxonomy of Politicization Varieties

Embedded assumptions: Analysts may embrace political and social assumptions held by policymakers that limit their exploration of intelligence issues. These may be driven by conventional wisdom.

Intelligence parochialism: Analysts may unconsciously or consciously shade their analysis to suit policy preferences, to satisfy the desires of their superiors, and to receive more positive feedback and possible promotion.

Bureaucratic parochialism: Intelligence agencies interested in promoting their bureaucratic interest in budgets and personnel can be tempted to skew intelligence assessments in ways that will benefit their own organizational interests.

Partisan intelligence: Political parties can align themselves with or criticize intelligence for partisan political gain. This can distort the work of intelligence agencies, leading them to be more closely associated with particular political factions.

Intelligence as scapegoat: Intelligence assessments are regularly blamed for failed policies. According to the "Washington Rule," there are only policy successes and intelligence failures.

Source: Derived from a lengthy appendix in Joshua Rovner, *Fixing the Facts: National Security Politics of Intelligence* (Ithaca, NY: Cornell University Press, 2011), 207–9. Used with author's permission.

Blatant manipulation of intelligence judgments is relatively rare but nonetheless occurs. Many times politicization is more subtle and subject to debate about its intention and scope. The cases that follow represent varying degrees and forms of politicization. Sometimes it can be obvious or subtle; sometimes it is primarily driven by policymakers' assumptions and preferences, but it can also be the result of intelligence's skepticism about policy choices or driven by bureaucratic and organizational processes.

Vietnam War Estimates in the Johnson Administration

The mid-1960s CIA estimates on the conduct of the war in Vietnam were overwhelmingly pessimistic, at a time when the Johnson administration was making the case that the United States was winning. In its political assessments, the IC raised serious doubts about the political stability of the South Vietnamese governments, which were seen as inept, out of touch with important segments of the population, and increasingly corrupt.[25] Somewhat ironically, Secretary of Defense Robert McNamara was touting successful military operations while also approving increasing numbers of US forces to bolster the South Vietnamese army. DCI John A. McCone was aware of this discrepancy and of Johnson administration disapproval of CIA assessments, and he directed the Board of National Estimates to rewrite its assessments to be more in line with the views coming out of the US embassy and military command in Saigon.[26]

The clash between policy and intelligence, however, escalated further with a series of national military estimates from 1965 to 1967, when CIA military analysts disputed the military intelligence's order-of-battle tables.[27] The military intelligence assessments coming out of Saigon showed much lower numbers of "irregular" fighters (100,000 to 120,000) and were supportive of the view that the United States was gradually reducing the enemy's strength by attrition. In contrast, CIA military analysts used a different methodology,[28] and they were convinced that there were far larger irregular forces (250,000 to 300,000) than defense intelligence acknowledged. Efforts to arrive at a consensus proved unsuccessful, and senior military commanders demanded that the CIA agree to the lower DIA-approved numbers in the NIEs. The senior CIA representative reported to the then CIA director Richard Helms that the "rationale for the lower number seems to be that any higher figure would generate an unacceptable level of criticism from the press."[29] After much hand-wringing, Helms ordered this official to agree with the lower numbers, arguing that the CIA had made its case to the military and the White House and that it was now time to let the military have its way. CIA analysts believed that Helms caved to administration pressure, and several remained "renegades" who eventually went public with their charges that the CIA had acquiesced to the politicization of intelligence by the US military.[30]

In retrospect, senior CIA officials have documented how their warnings of deteriorating political conditions in South Vietnam had been provided through field reporting, CIA assessments, and NIEs, which President Johnson and Secretary McNamara dismissed as too pessimistic and politically inconvenient. Only much later did the former defense secretary acknowledge in his own memoirs that those intelligence assessments were correct and he had been "wrong, terribly wrong."[31]

Soviet Estimates in the Nixon and Ford Administrations

In 1969, President Richard Nixon and his national security adviser, Henry Kissinger, embarked on a series of ambitious arms control agreements with the Soviet Union. Simultaneously Nixon pressed forward on the development of antiballistic missile (ABM) defense systems, partly as a bargaining chip in what became the Strategic Arms Limitation Talks. During these negotiations, the CIA and the IC were also continuing to produce the famous NIE 11–8 series on Soviet strategic nuclear programs. Those annual estimates updated existing and projected Soviet offensive strategic forces in terms of their launcher numbers, warhead loads, and targeting accuracies.

The 1968 version in the series, NIE 11-8-68, directly contradicted the Nixon administration's argument that the ABM defenses were needed to counter a more powerful Soviet SS-9 missile system. According to the IC, this system could not give the Russians the "first-strike" capability that the DOD was citing to justify building the Safeguard ABM system. In angry response, Kissinger proposed a special review panel to examine the intelligence in hopes it could pressure the CIA to alter its assessments. According to Joshua Rovner's extensive study of politicization, the administration promoted leaks designed to support the White House and blame the CIA for political bias.[32] Steady pressure from the White House and the Pentagon succeeded in changing the 1969 NIE 11–8, in which CIA director Helms agreed to remove language that disputed the SS-9's MIRV (multiple independently targetable reentry vehicle) capability.[33] Like the Vietnam OOB dispute, Helms justified his altering of intelligence judgments on the claim that the CIA would maintain its separate analytical position and allow the Pentagon to have its own way.[34]

Kissinger's dispute with the IC was largely driven by his wish to conclude the 1972 SALT and ABM treaties as a key element of the Nixon administration's détente policies. Those policies, however, came under vicious attacks during the Ford presidency, when Republican and hawkish Democratic senators attacked the agreements as conceding Soviet nuclear superiority based on the alleged détente bias of CIA estimates. In 1975, those critics compelled President Ford and CIA director George H. W. Bush to agree to an outside review (known later as the **Team A / Team B exercise**) to examine the CIA's estimates of Soviet strategic programs. Well-known and outspoken critics of the CIA, such as Albert Wohlstetter and Paul Nitze, believed CIA estimates had failed to forecast the continued buildup of Soviet strategic forces because of the agency's support for détente and a mistaken belief that the Soviet Union subscribed to American views of mutual deterrence.[35] Team B, made up of those subscribing to the Wohlstetter-Nitze view, naturally concluded that CIA analysts (Team A) had used incorrect assumptions in forecasting Soviet force projections, which reflected a bias for the Kissinger policies of détente. Later examinations of the entire Team A / Team B exercise concluded that its findings were hardly objective or independent of bias themselves.[36]

A more balanced critique by the then chairman of the House Armed Services Committee, Les Aspin, concluded that CIA estimators had used incorrect assumptions about how Soviet planners would retire older weapon systems. CIA analysts may also have fallen prey to mirror-imaging in presuming that Soviet planners would favor eliminating obsolete weapons and favor quality over quantity by producing fewer missile launchers carrying more warheads; however, political bias was not the basis of those calculations.[37]

2002 Intelligence about Iraq during the Bush Administration

Much has been written about the ill-fated 2002 NIE on Iraq's WMD programs and its role in the Iraq invasion. In that estimate, the IC concluded, wrongly, that Saddam Hussein had restarted his nuclear, biological, and chemical programs and might be able to have a nuclear capability within the decade (see chapter 6 for more details). Critics of the Iraq War blamed the IC for developing "intelligence to please" for a Bush administration intent on toppling Saddam. But, in fact, the IC's analysis of Saddam's WMD programs shows surprisingly strong consistency from the Clinton to the Bush presidencies. The IC's conventional wisdom reflected a deep-seated belief that Saddam was hiding weapons as he had previously, and analysts had a poor understanding of why Saddam would prevent UN inspectors from confirming the absence of WMDs. In 2004, the Iraq Survey Group documented in an extensive report (known as the Duelfer Report) how secretive Saddam was in preserving the fact that he had terminated virtually all of his nuclear, chemical, and biological weapons work but tried to preserve the appearance of having programs in waiting to deter his enemies, such as Israel and Iran.[38]

Importantly, the October 2002 NIE was written well *after* President Bush had decided in early August on an invasion, and he had secretly instructed the Pentagon to develop an operational plan without a formal meeting at which senior intelligence officials were present.[39] So, it is somewhat illogical to conclude that the NIE drove the decision to invade. However, critics nonetheless believe the NIE was used to justify the invasion with Congress and the public, even if the IC did not produce it for that reason. Indeed, it was prepared at the request of the Democratic chairman of the Senate Select Committee on Intelligence, Bob Graham. He and other Democrats expected a lively Senate debate over giving President Bush an authorization to use force. That only a half dozen senators bothered to read the classified and lengthy estimate also suggests it was not a critical determinant of the congressional decision to go to war.

In evaluating whether politicization occurred or not, the subsequent 2004 Robb-Silberman WMD commission concluded that there was no evidence of blatant pressure on the CIA to alter intelligence judgments to support the Bush administration's policies. The commission did not evaluate how the Bush administration used intelligence. And this, in fact, is where some former intelligence officials centrally involved in the assessments regarding Iraq believed politicization occurred. Paul Pillar, the national intelligence officer for the Middle East and one of the authors of the 2002 NIE, contends that Bush officials "pocketed" the flawed judgments on Saddam's WMD programs because they helped build the case; moreover, White House officials went further in knocking down any intelligence judgments that conflicted with the campaign to sell the war's legitimacy.[40]

Pillar's argument is that senior Bush officials conspired to selectively cite intelligence reporting they liked, dismiss or discredit analysis they did not like, and encourage alternative intelligence assessments that favored their own views of Iraq's involvement in terrorism. Senior officials such as Vice President Cheney and Secretary Rumsfeld regularly appeared before congressional committees or on major TV programs, citing often uncorroborated intelligence reports that they characterized as providing absolute certainty that Saddam had a nuclear program. Simultaneously, some officials were actively discrediting anyone who had presented disconfirming evidence. In particular, Cheney's chief of staff had tried to punish former ambassador Joseph Wilson, who had confirmed to the CIA that reporting on Iraq's purchase of "yellow cake" uranium ore from Niger was entirely bogus. Finally, Rumsfeld's deputies had set up an in-house Pentagon unit for producing alternative intelligence assessments aimed at finding links between Iraq and al-Qaeda, which the CIA had largely dismissed. Known as the Policy Counter Terrorism Evaluation Group, its mission was to collect as much information as possible of those possible links for use with the public but also to undermine IC assessments that dismissed this linkage.

In view of these less visible forms of politicization and a steady stream of official requests for only information that confirmed prowar positions, Pillar believes that there was a not so subtle message to analysts: "Intelligence officers also did not need explicit threats or pressure to be all too aware of the ways in which producing what policymakers did not want to hear would make the officers' professional lives unpleasant but producing what was wanted would reduce the unpleasantness."[41]

A final fault line in the intelligence-policy relationship over Iraq occurred as the war was about to be launched. NIO Pillar had commissioned two interagency assessments on the impact of Saddam's removal on regional stability and Iraq's domestic future. Requested by Colin Powell's policy planning director, Richard Haass, both reports were generally pessimistic about the impact the war would have on the region and Iraq's future. One suggested that an invasion could bolster anti-American sentiment as a result of the occupation and generate support for al-Qaeda. The other warned that Iraq had little prospect for representative democracy because it was a society deeply divided among Sunni, Shia, and Kurdish factions and faced a huge economic recovery problem.[42] "No one who accepted and reflected on these assessments' conclusions," as Pillar recounts, "could possibly think the war was a good idea."[43] Not surprisingly, the Bush administration paid no heed to these assessments, largely ignoring the implications that the United States would have to shoulder a much larger and longer role in providing security and economic assistance to guarantee Iraq's recovery.

November 2007 Iran Nuclear NIE in the Bush Administration

Even as it struggled with the Iraq War, the Bush administration also was embarking on a new campaign to pressure Iran over its violations of the IAEA nuclear safeguards program requiring declarations of facilities and on-site inspections. In 2005, the IAEA had complained about Iran's failure to report on its activities and concluded Tehran had displayed a "pattern of concealment." That same year, the IC also was monitoring two undeclared nuclear facilities and had issued an intelligence memorandum stating that Iran was determined to develop nuclear weapons despite its international obligations. However, the flaws in the 2002 Iraq WMD estimate made it incumbent on the IC to restore its credibility for producing accurate and rigorously prepared assessments. Accordingly, the newly created DNI began in early 2005 to put in place a new set of analytical standards and processes for producing NIEs. Those analytical changes included more rigorous testing of assumptions, new standards for assigning confidence levels to evidence, and regular use of Red Cell teams to challenge and validate the judgments of intelligence estimators.[44]

One of the first tests of this new system was the call for an updated NIE on Iran's nuclear programs. The National Intelligence Council oversaw this project, which the administration expected would reaffirm the earlier 2005 conclusions. In fact, as the NIC was about to issue a new estimate, additional information was received that not only delayed publication of the NIE but also altered a small but significant portion of the estimate's findings. When the NIE was published in November 2007, it began its first key judgment with "We judge with high confidence that in fall 2003, Tehran halted its nuclear weapons program."[45]

Lost in translation was an important footnote to this judgment clarifying that the estimators meant that only the "weapons design" aspects of the nuclear program had been halted, not the covert, large-scale uranium enrichment necessary to produce weapons-grade fuel. Also, the IC concluded in the later parts of the key judgments that Tehran's agreement to sign an additional safeguards protocol was the result of "international scrutiny and pressure resulting from exposure of Iran's previously undeclared nuclear work." In essence, the IC believed it was confirming that the Bush administration's efforts to pressure Iran were working. In preparing these new findings, the then DNI Michael McConnell also promised the White House, and later announced to the press, a new policy of not releasing declassified key judgments as had occurred with the 2002 Iraq NIE.

The reaction from policymakers was quite different. First, the White House reached the conclusion that the key judgments were so different in tone from those in 2005 that they were likely to leak selectively and would draw fire from Congress. So, President Bush directed that the entire key judgments be declassified to show how much of the Iranian program was unaffected. Second, the administration found itself caught in a dilemma of explaining why more pressure on Iran was needed, if indeed a major part of Tehran's weaponization program had been halted. It was in the process of urging European allies, Russia, and China to join in additional sanctions measures. The release of the estimate's key judgments would most likely weaken support among those countries, and indeed it did. State and DOD defenders of the Bush actions against Iran accused the IC of political bias and trying to stymie the White House plans to threaten Iran with harsher measures, even possible military strikes.[46] Voices in Congress concluded that the military option was off the table and that allies would be less likely to back more hawkish moves against Iran.[47] While the White House attempted to put the best spin on the NIE, it was unhappy about the tenor and timing of this estimate, about which the IC had not warned the president.

Charges of analysts infusing their political bias into this estimate were unfounded, and intelligence professionals defended the NIE for its careful weighing of evidence and the genuine surprise that they felt in receiving new information confirming a halt in the weaponization process.[48] Senior intelligence officials did wonder if the key judgments' prose that was released would be easily understood by outsiders without knowledge or clearances. This example of intelligence-policy differences highlights just how different the two tribes' perspectives can be. By 2007, senior policymakers were well acquainted with Iran's nuclear program and did not need a general tutorial of how the IC had covered Iran in the past, allowing the IC to go directly to what had changed. On the other hand, the public and Congress would not read the estimate in the same fashion, and they would not appreciate that the estimate was referring only to one part of the nuclear program, while other parts (e.g., the production of fissile materials and testing of ballistic missiles) continued unchanged.

Assessments of Russian Interference in the 2016 Elections

The growing body of evidence that the Russian government directed a sophisticated social media campaign to shape American voters' views of the candidates and favor Donald Trump's candidacy posed a huge challenge for American intelligence and law enforcement agencies. The fact that the Soviet Union and now Russia were capable of and likely to use active measures to weaken or distort American foreign policies was not at all new. There are numerous examples of Soviet-era active measures designed to attribute a variety of negative actions to the United States and its allies. Those techniques included use of front organizations, manipulation of press reporting, forgeries, clandestine broadcasts, and exploitation of unwitting foreign academics or businesspeople.[49] What distinguished the 2016 campaign was not only its scale and sophistication and the speedy manipulation of social media but also its focus on undermining the very political institutions on which American democracy depends. Intelligence agencies have no difficulty informing senior US officials and Congress about Russian covert operations aimed at undermining American foreign policy; however, reporting on efforts to interfere with a US presidential election thrust US law enforcement and intelligence directly into domestic and partisan politics.

Recognizing the political sensitivity of these findings, the IC was cautious in publicly announcing its suspicions in the run-up to the election. However, as the evidence grew, it became impossible for agencies to avoid raising alarms. The first public indication that Moscow was meddling in domestic US politics came in the fall of 2015, when the FBI quietly notified the Democratic National Committee that there was evidence that Russian hackers were trying to access its data. Then, once the presidential election campaigns were in full swing, there was a series of WikiLeaks-related postings of Hillary Clinton's personal emails, which the Russian-backed Guccifer 2.0 group had obtained. The WikiLeaks posting of twenty thousand stolen emails was closely timed to the July convention when Clinton would be nominated as the Democratic Party's candidate. At this point, the FBI launched a full-scale investigation into the hacking of the DNC website.

By early fall 2016, unnamed law enforcement officials were hinting to news outlets that the Russian government was suspected. These hints were followed shortly by a joint statement from the Department of Homeland Security and the DNI pointing directly at the Russian government: "The US Intelligence Community (USIC) is confident that the Russian Government directed the recent compromises of e-mails from US persons and institutions, including from US political organizations. The recent disclosures of alleged hacked emails on sites like DCLeaks.com and WikiLeaks and by the Guccifer 2.0 online persona are consistent with the methods and motivations of Russian-directed efforts."[50]

This was only part of the IC's assessment. Once the election was over, the IC reported that in addition to the cyberattacks on the Democratic candidate and party organization and selected state electoral systems, the shadowy Internet Research Agency in Russia had run a massive disinformation and propaganda campaign. According to various media reports, this social media campaign involved hundreds of individuals, costing millions of dollars; more important, it may have reached over a hundred and twenty-five million Americans via a variety of social media websites. The combined effect of the hacking and social media campaigns raised serious questions about the results of the presidential election that was determined by fewer than eighty thousand votes across three states key to the Electoral College's tally.

After briefing both President Obama and president-elect Trump, the IC issued a joint CIA, FBI, NSA, and DNI report in January 2017 (see box 10.3). Looking back to the campaign, an observer can raise a number of questions. First, should President Obama and his administration have intervened more actively during the campaign to alert Americans about Russian meddling? Would the public perceive such action as a sitting Democratic president, in essence, intervening in an ongoing presidential

---

Box 10.3 *Assessing Russian Activities and Intentions in Recent US Elections* (Excerpts from Key Judgments)

Russian efforts to influence the 2016 US presidential election represent the most recent expression of Moscow's longstanding desire to undermine the US-led liberal democratic order, but these activities demonstrated a significant escalation in directness, level of activity, and scope of effort compared to previous operations.

We assess Russian President Vladimir Putin ordered an influence campaign in 2016 aimed at the US presidential election. Russia's goals were to undermine public faith in the US democratic process, denigrate Secretary Clinton, and harm her electability and potential presidency. We further assess Putin and the Russian Government developed a clear preference for President-elect Trump. . . .

We also assess Putin and the Russian Government aspired to help President-elect Trump's election chances when possible by discrediting Secretary Clinton and publicly contrasting her unfavorably to him. . . .

We assess Moscow will apply lessons learned from its Putin-ordered campaign aimed at the US presidential election to future influence efforts worldwide, including against US allies and their elections.

Source: ODNI, *Assessing Russian Activities and Intentions in Recent US Elections, Intelligence Community Assessment*, January 2017, https://www.dni.gov/files/documents/ICA_2017_01.pdf.

election that might sway voters in a favorable direction? Related to that, should intelligence agencies have spoken out more publicly as well? On the one hand, intelligence is not supposed to get involved in political matters; on the other hand, to avoid alerting the American public of the Russian interference might itself have helped determine the election's outcome.

An equally vexing question is how would a newly elected president, whose victory might well have benefited from Russian interference, respond to the intelligence assessment provided to him by his intelligence advisers? President Trump's campaign posture had been to deny any connection to the Russian government and to assert that the IC was merely speculating that the Russian government was behind the email leaks. Once in office and officially briefed, President Trump remained ambivalent regarding the veracity of the intelligence assessments when he mused that it might have been Russia or it might have been someone else; however, he was adamant that those activities had not affected the election. Moreover, he repeatedly misrepresented the intelligence assessments and the results of the 2018 House intelligence committee investigations by saying they confirmed that the Russian activities had not helped him or had any connection to his campaign.[51] In both cases, he misstated what the IC and congressional committee had concluded. Hence, President Trump was fudging the intelligence he received, for his own political and personal advantage.

Like no other president—except perhaps Richard Nixon—Donald Trump has formed a hostile perception of the law enforcement and intelligence communities. He acts as if he believes that they are intentionally disloyal if they present evidence of Russian behavior that suggests he may have personally benefited from those actions. This places the IC in an exceedingly awkward position of trying to present objective judgments on ongoing counterintelligence threats to an unwilling audience. While this particular set of circumstances is unique in American history, it highlights the inherent danger when intelligence officials attempt to present inconvenient truths to senior policy officials. The result is often that policymakers will attempt to discredit the reports, as well as the agencies presenting them, in order to rescue their policies or personal reputations. In such cases, intelligence agencies have little ability to defend themselves. Only Congress, which can also act on the basis of intelligence, has the power to correct the record publicly, but it too is presently polarized and in a poor position to give a more objective review of the IC's performance.

ISSUES FACING THE INTELLIGENCE-POLICY RELATIONSHIP

The foregoing cases of politicization of intelligence suggest that it can occur for a variety of reasons and be committed by both the policymaker and the intelligence officer. Blatant politicization, as seen in the case of the Vietnam War estimates and the Nixon-era disputes over strategic nuclear assessments, happens less often than generally appreciated. Subtler forms of politicization are usually at work, when "high politics" are in play. In the Iraq case, policymakers used intelligence selectively to win support but ignored and dismissed other assessments that would undermine their public diplomacy. This cherry-picking of intelligence happens regularly, often simply when informal policy discussions ensue. However, sometimes this practice can force senior officials—as in the case of the 2007 Iran NIE—to get the full story out by declassifying assessments they otherwise would prefer to keep secret. Finally, there is a natural tendency for those running programs to assess their operations more favorably than intelligence agencies with no direct responsibility for them. In those few instances where military intelligence is slanted toward more positive assessments, they are often a matter of opinion and highly subjective. One person's slanted intelligence is another person's more rigorous analysis. For all these reasons, a friction-free intelligence-policy relationship free from politicization is not likely to emerge.

Is Intelligence Becoming More Politicized?

In the current polarized American political environment, many observers worry that intelligence is becoming more politicized. Signs of this are seen in the manner in which intelligence is used or misused by senior White House and congressional members to win political arguments. Over the past several decades, more and more intelligence has been drawn into public discussions of national security policies. On the one hand, this can inform the debate if used appropriately. However, in some instances intelligence has become the scapegoat for mistaken policies (for example, in the case of the Iraq War) or has been accused of having its own political agendas (for example, the recent charges of an FBI that is politically corrupt and biased against President Trump).

Adding to this highly charged and polarized political environment is the erosion of nonpartisan congressional oversight. Scholars have noted that this less effective intelligence oversight has been developing since the mid-1980s.[52] The 2003 Iraq invasion and its aftermath caused a major new schism between Democrats and Republicans, which accelerated this trend toward more partisan sparring over intelligence. It erupted again during President Obama's tenure, when Sen. Dianne Feinstein released a six-hundred-page declassified summary of the Senate intelligence committee staff's findings that criticized the CIA's use of extreme interrogation methods as "torture."[53] This generated a strongly critical Republican minority report claiming the program had saved lives and that the Democratic staff had misrepresented the facts in its findings.[54]

In 2016, the tables were turned as Republicans controlled both houses of Congress. This time it was House Permanent Select Committee on Intelligence investigations into Russian interference in recent US elections that has been stymied by sharp disagreements between its ranking Republican and Democratic members.[55] Separate majority and minority reports were issued, which disagreed on whether these investigations uncovered Trump campaign collusion with Russia. Much of this played out on television as leading Democratic members of the House attacked the Republican report as a whitewash, and Republicans called for a speedy end to the many investigations underway. At the time of this writing, the congressional battles with the Trump White House and the Justice Department over the just-released Mueller Report promise to ignite another round of partisan debates over the quality and integrity of intelligence and law enforcement activities.

The other feature that is alarming is the more open commentary on national security topics by former senior intelligence officials. Heretofore, most departing directors and deputy directors avoided directly engaging in partisan debates. They were mostly content to write memoirs about their past service or sit on boards of major corporations or think tanks. With few exceptions, they were satisfied if asked to provide advice privately to legislators or executive branch officials. The 2016 elections have seemingly changed this. A number of former Bush and Obama intelligence officials have become regular commentators on CNN, MSNBC, and Fox News. This follows news outlets' earlier use of retired senior military officers to comment on ongoing national security issues. Some of these officers have also decided to become strong backers or critics of presidential candidates; in 2016, retired general John Allen spoke at the Democratic convention on behalf of Hillary Clinton, and retired general Michael Flynn gave a rousing speech for Donald Trump at the Republican convention. In response, former JCS chairman Martin Dempsey has admonished such behavior, as it can give the appearance of a military that is itself politicized and less professional.[56]

In late 2016, former CIA directors Michael Hayden and John Brennan and DNI James Clapper challenged President Trump's attacks on the IC (especially the CIA and FBI) as well as criticized his admiring comments about Vladimir Putin. Since leaving office, Brennan and Clapper have gone well beyond defending the IC to criticizing Trump's statements or actions as dangerous. They have also hinted that the president himself may have personal and unpatriotic motives for discrediting intelligence and refusing to admonish Russian behavior.[57] In response, President Trump has gone beyond just attacking these individuals publicly to terminating John Brennan's security clearance and threatening to do the same for other former officials criticizing him or his actions. Both these former officials' actions and the president's response are almost unprecedented and reveal a deep division between intelligence and the president it serves.

While these former officials have the right to exercise free speech, their statements also give the appearance of an IC that is prepared to engage in politics. If this becomes more widespread, there is a danger that the comments of former senior officials could undermine the public's view that intelligence agencies are above party politics when issuing their findings. Likewise, the president's broad attack on some past and even current leaders of the intelligence and law enforcement communities will spark further politicization charges and undermine public trust in the nonpolitical nature of intelligence activities.

How Can Intelligence Shield Itself from Politicization?

As the preceding discussion suggests, politicization remains a serious challenge, particularly when major party and policy disagreements exist in Washington. The remedies for politicization are relatively few. First, as many scholars have pointed out, policymakers have a right to question intelligence and to ignore it if they firmly believe it is incorrect. Second, identifying politicization is often a very subjective process; anything other than blatant pressure on the IC to alter its judgments can be as easily attributed to an honest analytical disagreement about how the IC relied on certain analytical assumptions, weighed the available evidence, and drew up its findings. Third, when policy matters—especially in issues of war and peace—political leaders naturally are going to want to have intelligence on their side. To expect that intelligence would not be drawn into a policy debate is to suggest it is irrelevant to those decisions, which would be tantamount to saying there is no reason for intelligence to exist.

In most cases, the best remedy for avoiding politicization is to conduct analysis in as rigorous and transparent a fashion as possible. A former senior CIA official, following the disastrous Iraq WMD estimate, addressed an audience of analysts to warn them, "If we don't conduct self-criticism effectively, someone else will."[58] The use of more rigorous analytical tradecraft methods—discussed in chapter 5—provides analysts with a way to make their analysis more transparent to policymakers so as to demonstrate how judgments were reached, based on certain evidence and key assumptions. Such exercises, along with the use of Red Cell alternative analysis of important intelligence issues, can help analysts avoid mind-sets arising from hidden political or analytical bias. Equally important, providing this kind of transparency to policymakers critical of intelligence findings may well head off charges of political bias on analysts' part.

A second structural check is the existence of multiple intelligence agencies that examine intelligence from their own perspectives and can deliver independent judgments that diverge from a consensus view. For all its flaws, the 2002 Iraq WMD estimate contained important dissents by the State Department's Bureau of Intelligence and Research and the Department of Energy's intelligence office, which doubted that Saddam had reconstituted his nuclear program or had acquired the proper steel cylinders for fashioning nuclear centrifuges. Procedures adopted since that estimate have also encouraged more sharing of views across the community, more rigorous drafting of key judgments to reflect only the actual text that follows, and inclusion in key judgments all dissents or minority views held in the IC.[59]

Improving the Intelligence-Policy Relationship

The foregoing discussion leaves one relatively pessimistic that much can be done to improve the intelligence-policy relationship. As some scholars have concluded, "There are reasons to expect that intelligence will play a smaller role in strategy and policy over time, and that the quality of the intelligence-policy relationship will steadily decline."[60] In most cases, that relationship will remain subject to the future idiosyncrasies of the president and his key advisers as well as the particular policy and intelligence issues they face. That said, there are some lessons learned from past experience that might help to improve those relationships.

First, the role and value of intelligence is enhanced when the national security decision-making process itself is transparent and conducted in ways that provide an opportunity for intelligence to make its legitimate contribution. When informal decision-making processes or presidential impulses drive decisions, there is less room for intelligence to perform its role of informing and warning policymakers of the consequences of their decisions. The IC has left behind the Sherman Kent arm's-length model and moved so much closer to policy debates to be relevant. That requires that the IC be more vigilant to the dangers of politicization. It means the intelligence world must respect the policymaker's world and a president's agenda without self-censoring itself or producing slanted findings. At the same time, policymakers must understand that inclusion does not mean "loyalty" to their worldviews or policies. Policymakers retain the right to disagree with intelligence assessments and ultimately be wrong in some cases. But they must respect the independence and analytical integrity of the IC if they are to gain the kind of support they need.

Second, given the limited understanding that many policymakers have of intelligence when they enter government service, the IC would benefit by providing more opportunities for tutoring presidents-elect and other senior officials on how the intelligence process works, how analysis is conducted, and what the strengths and weaknesses of intelligence are. Intelligence literacy is extremely uneven and generally low among policymakers. At the moment, IC training programs focus on educating analysts about the policy process, and many IC agencies strive to give their stronger analysts opportunities to serve in policy agencies to broaden their understanding of how policymakers operate. A comparable effort to educate policymakers on the IC does not exist. The sole opportunity for this at the moment is the presidential transition process, when intelligence officials can meet with the president-elect and his or her likely key advisers to begin a dialogue. This is a time when a future president and his or her team might be most susceptible to understanding how the IC is postured to meet the new administration's information needs. The briefers should not only cover the latest intelligence but should also conduct a high-level tutorial on intelligence, particularly for those officials who had not served previously in government and perhaps have never held a security clearance or seen classified information.

A third lesson is that selecting senior intelligence officials who have both the subject-matter competence and the confidence of the White House can dramatically shape the intelligence-policy relationship. There is no single recipe for successful intelligence leadership. Seemingly well-informed former military and civilian officials have failed as CIA directors and DNIs. Others with little practical experience in intelligence but great political skills have succeeded without overly politicizing intelligence. Whoever a president selects for intelligence advisers should, however, understand the role he or she is to play and the red lines between intelligence and policy. As intelligence has become such an integral part of the policymaking process, the senior-most positions in the IC are just as important as selecting a national security adviser or secretaries of state and defense. Some scholars have recommended those positions come with a set term of office, like the FBI director's, in order to make those assignments less political. That has merit but only if a president and those advisers can develop a trusting relationship.

Finally, it is unreasonable and unlikely to expect the IC could return to a Kent-style model of arm's-length advising, given the need for rapid and constant intelligence support. As one scholar notes, it was possible in the Cold War to rely on such a model when the dominant strategy was "deterrence" of a low-probability Soviet nuclear strike.[61] In the twenty-first-century world of quickly emerging transnational threats, intelligence must be at the elbow of policymakers and run the risk that its role can become politicized. Few would argue that a less forward-leaning IC would have prevented the Russian interference into the 2016 elections. Likewise, the increasing openness in discussing intelligence as part of American foreign policy debates is also not likely to decline. The challenge will be to establish the correct balance between keeping intelligence secret so it can provide decision-advantage to policymakers and still providing enough information for an informed congressional and public debate over critical national security decisions.

USEFUL DOCUMENTS

Iraq's Continuing Program for Weapons of Mass Destruction: Key Judgments (from October 2002 NIE), https://www.dni.gov/files/documents/Iraq_NIE_Excerpts_2003.pdf

National Intelligence Council, *Iran: Nuclear Intentions and Capabilities*, 2007 NIE, https://www.dni.gov/files/documents/Newsroom/Press%20Releases/2007%20Press%20Releases/20071203_release.pdf

ODNI and DNI, *Background to "Assessing Russian Activities and Intentions in Recent US Elections": The Analytic Process and Cyber Incident Attribution*, January 6, 2017, https://www.dni.gov/files/documents/ICA_2017_01.pdf

Special Counsel Robert S. Mueller, *Report on the Investigation into Russian Interference in the 2016 Presidential Election*, vols. 1 and 2, March 2019, https://www.justice.gov/storage/report.pdf

FURTHER READING

Richard Betts, *Enemies of Intelligence: Knowledge and Power in American National Security* (New York: Columbia University Press, 2011).

> A compilation of this intelligence scholar's views on intelligence analysis, politicization, and the intelligence-policy relationship.

James Clapper, *Facts and Fears: Hard Truths from a Life in Intelligence* (New York: Penguin / Random House, 2018).

> Recounts a former DNI's experiences dealing with policymakers, including presidents unwilling to accept intelligence judgments.

Thomas Fingar, *Reducing Uncertainty: Intelligence Analysis and National Security* (Stanford, CA: Stanford University Press, 2011).

> Describes the lessons learned from working closely with policymakers and how intelligence was used and misunderstood by various administrations.

John L. Helgerson, *Getting to Know the President: Intelligence Briefings of the Presidents, 1952–2004* (Washington, DC: Center for the Study of Intelligence, 2012).

> Provides a senior agency officer's study of how the CIA has provided intelligence during the transitions and terms of most recent presidents.

Paul Pillar, *Intelligence and U.S. Foreign Policy: Iraq, 9/11, and Misguided Reform* (New York: Columbia University Press, 2011).

> A practitioner's critique of the intelligence-policy relationship that examines how intelligence has not been the cause of failed policy choices but nonetheless suffers from politicization to suit policy preferences.

Joshua Rovner, *Fixing the Facts: National Security and the Politics of Intelligence* (Ithaca, NY: Cornell University Press, 2011).

> The most serious study of politicization, using a series of case studies to argue that the phenomenon should be expected when intelligence touches on high-stakes policy issues.

Gregory F. Treverton, "Intelligence Analysis: Between 'Politicization' and Irrelevance," in *Analyzing Intelligence: Origins, Obstacles, and Innovations*, 1st ed., ed. Roger Z. George and James Bruce (Washington, DC: Georgetown University Press, 2008).

Focuses on the types of politicization that can occur and the methods for countering them.

NOTES

First epigraph: Robert Gates, *From the Shadows: The Ultimate Insider's Story of Five Presidents and How They Won the Cold War* (New York: Simon & Schuster, 1996), 567.

Second epigraph: Sherman Kent, "Estimates and Influence," in Don Steury, Sherman Kent, and the Board of National Estimates, *Collected Essays* (Washington, DC: Center for the Study of Intelligence, 1994), 42.

1. Robert Jervis, "Why Intelligence and Policymakers Clash," *Political Science Quarterly* 125, no. 2 (Summer 2010): 185–204.

2. James Steinberg, "The Policymaker's Perspective: Transparency and Partnership, in Roger Z. George and James Bruce, *Analyzing Intelligence: National Security Practitioners' Perspectives* (Washington, DC: Georgetown University Press, 2014), 2nd ed., 94.

3. The author as analyst recalls having examined numerous dissemination lists of assessments he prepared and found that far more copies were distributed among other intelligence agencies' analysts than were turned over to policy agencies.

4. Richard Immerman, *The Hidden Hand: A Brief History of the CIA* (New York: John Wiley, 2014), 150.

5. Robert Gates, *From the Shadows: The Ultimate Insider's Story of Five Presidents and How They Won the Cold War* (New York: Simon & Schuster, 1996), 56. Gates also recounts that senior managers discouraged him from taking an NSC assignment as it was not considered career enhancing, exactly the opposite of what he came to believe after serving on the Nixon, Carter, and Reagan NSC staffs.

6. According to John McLaughlin, a former deputy director of the CIA, Gates insisted that any analyst who wished to compete for a senior management job serve a tour in a policy agency before being promoted. See John McLaughlin, "Serving the National Policymaker," in George and Bruce, *Analyzing Intelligence*, 2nd ed., 84.

7. As a member of the policy planning staff, the author was able to direct intelligence requirements to CIA offices and get quick responses to State Department counselor Robert Zoellick and policy planning director Dennis Ross, for whom he worked. This assignment also involved organizing senior intelligence briefings for these officials.

8. Richard K. Betts, *Enemies of Intelligence: Knowledge and Power in American National Security* (New York: Columbia University Press, 2009), 77.

9. Cited in David Priess, *The President's Book of Secret: The Untold Story of Intelligence Briefings to America's Presidents from Kennedy to Obama* (New York: PublicAffairs, 2016), 165.

10. Bush laments that when Jimmy Carter became president, he did not keep him on in order to depoliticize the CIA director's job. He urged his son later to keep CIA director George Tenet, partly to dispel the notion that the CIA job was a political assignment.

11. Christopher Andrew, *For the President's Eyes Only: Secret Intelligence and the American Presidency from Washington to Bush* (New York: Harper Perennial, 1996), 3.

12. Quoted in Robert Gates, "An Opportunity Unfulfilled: The Use and Perceptions of Intelligence at the White House," *Washington Quarterly*, Winter 1989, 42.

13. See Evan Thomas, "Why Nixon Hated Georgetown," *Politico*, June 4, 2015, https://www.politico.com/magazine/story/2015/06/richard-nixon-georgetown-set-118607.

14. John L. Helgerson, *Getting to Know the President: Intelligence Briefings of the Presidents, 1952–2004* (Washington, DC: Center for the Study of Intelligence, 2012), 170–71, https://www.cia.gov/library/center-for-the-study-of-intelligence/csi-publications/books-and-monographs/getting-to-know-the-president/pdfs/U-%20Book-Getting%20to%20Know%20the%20President.pdf.

15. Priess, *President's Book of Secrets*, 227.

16. David Stout, "CIA Director Goss Resigns," *New York Times*, May 6, 2006, https://www.nytimes.com/2006/05/05/washington/05cnd-cia.html.

17. Linda Qiu, "How Trump Has Flip-Flopped on Intelligence Agencies," *New York Times*, December 7, 2017, https://www.nytimes.com/2017/12/07/us/politics/trump-reversals-fbi-intelligence-agencies.html.

18. Qiu. "Active measures" is the term applied to Soviet/Russian covert political warfare designed to increase Moscow's influence over world events and diminish US and other Western powers' influence.

19. See former deputy secretary of state Anthony Blinken's *New York Times* op-ed that lays out the numerous charges made against John Bolton when he was a senior State Department official during the Bush administration. The story recounts how Bolton misused intelligence and employed blatant pressure and threats to force changes in intelligence judgments. Anthony Blinken, "When Republicans Rejected Bolton," *New York Times*, March 23, 2018, https://www.nytimes.com/2018/03/23/opinion/john-bolton-republicans.html.

20. Director Haspel has also selected a career analyst and senior manager, Vaughn Bishop, as her deputy director, which could further insulate the agency from political pressures that a White House might like to exert in the future.

21. Jaqueline Thomsen, "Trump Strain with Intel Chiefs Spills into the Public," *The Hill*, February 2, 2019, https://thehill.com/policy/national-security/428157-trumps-strain-with-intel-chiefs-spills-into-public.

22. Carol Leonnig, Shane Harris, and Greg Jaffe, "Breaking with Tradition, Trump Skips Reading President's Written Intelligence Report for Oral Briefings," *Washington Post*, February 9, 2018, https://www.washingtonpost.com/politics/breaking-with-tradition-trump-skips-presidents-written-intelligence-report-for-oral-briefings/2018/02/09/b7ba569e-0c52-11e8-95a5-c396801049ef_story.html?utm_term=.694e7cd2b642.

23. David Priess, "CIA Tailors Its Briefing So It Doesn't Anger Trump; That's Good," *Washington Post*, December 14, 2017, https://www.washingtonpost.com/news/posteverything/wp/2017/12/14/the-cia-tailors-its-briefings-so-it-doesnt-anger-trump-thats-good/?utm_term=.0f099c5983be.

24. Joshua Rovner, *Fixing the Facts: National Security and the Politics of Intelligence* (Ithaca, NY: Cornell University Press, 2011), 29.

25. See Harold Ford, *CIA and the Vietnam Policymakers: Three Episodes, 1962–1968* (Washington, DC: Center for the Study of Intelligence, 1991), https://www.cia.gov/library/center-for-the-study-of-intelligence/csi-publications/books-and-monographs/cia-and-the-vietnam-policymakers-three-episodes-1962-1968/.

26. Ford, *CIA and the Vietnam Policymakers*, episode 1, https://www.cia.gov/library/center-for-the-study-of-intelligence/csi-publications/books-and-monographs/cia-and-the-vietnam-policymakers-three-episodes-1962–1968/epis1.html.

27. The OOB analysis in this case was assessing the numbers and organization of both regular North Vietnamese military units and the irregular forces (i.e., part-time fighters not assigned to specific military units) that constituted the Viet Cong.

28. CIA methodology involved analysis of captured enemy documents, which an enterprising military analyst, Sam Adams, used to calculate much higher (and more accurate) numbers of Viet Cong, which he believed should have alerted the United States to the forthcoming 1968 Tet Offensive.

29. Ford, *CIA and the Vietnam Policymakers*, episode 3, https://www.cia.gov/library/center-for-the-study-of-intelligence/csi-publications/books-and-monographs/cia-and-the-vietnam-policymakers-three-episodes-1962–1968/epis3.html.

30. Helms recounts that a particularly zealous, self-assured analyst, Sam Adams, continued to dispute the military OOB and conducted what Helms described as a "crusade" that led to television appearances and a libel suit against Gen. William Westmoreland. See Richard Helms, *A Look over My Shoulder: A Life in the Central Intelligence Agency* (New York: Random House, 2003), 326–27.

31. Harold P. Ford, "Why CIA Analysts Were So Doubtful about Vietnam," *Studies in Intelligence* 40, no. 5: 87, https://www.cia.gov/library/center-for-the-study-of-intelligence/kent-csi/vol40no5/pdf/v40i5a10p.pdf.

32. Rovner, *Fixing the Facts*, 100. Rovner's study goes into detail on this particular episode, noting that CIA director Helms chose to remain silent during critical Senate Foreign Relations Committee hearings, where Secretary of Defense Melvin Laird made the case that the DOD viewed the SS-9 as a first-strike weapon.

33. Rovner, 101. MIRV capability allowed a single missile to attack multiple targets simultaneously.

34. Helms, *Look over My Shoulder*, 386–87.

35. Wohlstetter was a towering figure in the strategic studies community as a longtime RAND Corporation specialist. He published a series of critiques of NIEs found in *Foreign Policy* magazine in 1974. See Albert Wohlstetter, "Is There a Strategic Arms Race?," *Foreign Policy* 15 (Summer 1974): 3–20.

36. Ann H. Cahn, *Killing Détente: The Right Attacks the CIA* (University Park: Pennsylvania State Press, 1998). Her view was that the exercise was "concocted by conservative cold warriors determined to bury détente and the SALT process."

37. Les Aspin, "The Debate over Soviet Strategic Forces: A Mixed Review," *Strategic Review* 8, no. 3 (Summer 1980): 22–59.

38. After the war, DCI Tenet commissioned former State Department official Charles Duelfer to lead a large US team of inspectors to determine whether Saddam had restarted his WMD programs. Called the Iraq Survey, it spent months inspecting Iraqi facilities, examining captured documents, and interviewing former Iraqi scientists, which resulted in a three-volume report laying out how Saddam and his regime had disposed of the WMD programs and how he kept his own senior officials unaware of exactly what capabilities he retained. See *Comprehensive Report of the Special Advisor to the DCI on Iraq's WMD*, September 2004, https://www.cia.gov/library/reports/general-reports-1/iraq_wmd_2004/.

39. CIA director George Tenet recounts that a "presidential decision on going to war was always alluded to by the NSC in hypothetical terms, as though it were still up in the air and the conferees were merely discussing contingencies." See George Tenet, *Center of the Storm: My Years at CIA* (New York: HarperCollins, 2007), 308.

40. Paul R. Pillar, *Intelligence and U.S. Foreign Policy: Iraq, 9/11, and Misguided Reform* (New York: Columbia University Press, 2011), 140.

41. Pillar, 155.

42. See National Intelligence Council, *Regional Consequences of Regime Change in Iraq*, Intelligence Community Assessment, January 2003, https://www.cia.gov/library/readingroom /docs/DOC_0005299385.pdf; and National Intelligence Council, *Principal Challenges of a Post-Saddam Iraq*, Intelligence Community Assessment, January 2003, https://www.cia.gov /library/readingroom/docs/DOC_0005674817.pdf.

43. Pillar, *Intelligence and U.S. Foreign Policy*, 58.

44. See Gregory Treverton, *Support to Policymakers: The 2007 NIE on Iran's Nuclear Intentions and Capabilities* (Washington, DC: Center for the Study of Intelligence, 2013). This case study provides a comprehensive look at the intelligence-policy friction surrounding this estimate.

45. ODNI, *Iran: Nuclear Intentions and Capabilities*, National Estimate, November 2007, https://www.dni.gov/files/documents/Newsroom/Press%20Releases/2007%20Press%20 Releases/20071203_release.pdf.

46. John Bolton, "Flaws in the Iran Report," *Washington Post*, December 6, 2007, http:// www.washingtonpost.com/wp-dyn/content/article/2007/12/05/AR2007120502234.html.

47. Steven Lee Meyers, "An Assessment Jars Foreign Policy Debate on Iran," *New York Times*, December 2007, https://www.nytimes.com/2007/12/04/washington/04assess.html.

48. See Thomas Fingar, "It's Complicated," *American Interest* (May/June 2013): 31–35, https://www.the-american-interest.com/2013/04/12/its-complicated/.

49. See US State Department, *Soviet Active Measures: Forgery, Disinformation, and Political Operations*, Special Issue No. 88, October 1981, https://www.cia.gov/library/readingroom /docs/CIA-RDP84B00049R001303150031–0.pdf.

50. Department of Homeland Security, *Joint Statement of the Department of Homeland Security and Office of the Director of National Intelligence on Election Security*, October 2017, https://www.dhs.gov/news/2016/10/07/joint-statement-department-homeland-security-and -office-director-national.

51. Greg Miller, Greg Jaffe, and Philip Rucker, "Doubting the Intelligence, Trump Pursues Putin and Leaves a Russian Threat Unchecked," *Washington Post*, December 14, 2017, https:// www.washingtonpost.com/graphics/2017/world/national-security/donald-trump-pursues -vladimir-putin-russian-election-hacking/?utm_term=.4af26317f918; Greg Megerian, "Trump Praises House Republicans Who Found No Evidence of Russian Collusion," *Los Angeles Times*, March 13, 2018, http://www.latimes.com/politics/la-na-pol-essential-washington-updates -president-trump-praises-house-1520952667-htmlstory.html.

52. Marvin Ott, "Partisanship and the Decline of Intelligence Oversight," *International Journal of Intelligence and CounterIntelligence* 16 (2003): 69–94.

53. Senator Feinstein as chairperson initiated in 2009 a massive, years-long investigation into the CIA's use of enhanced interrogation techniques, which concluded the program was poorly run, caused the death of some detainees, and failed to elicit claimed information

that resulted in foiled terrorist plots. See US Senate, Senate Select Committee on Intelligence, *Staff Study on the CIA's Detention and Interrogation Program*, December 2014, https://www .feinstein.senate.gov/public/_cache/files/7/c/7c85429a-ec38-4bb5-968f-289799bf6d0e /D87288C34A6D9FF736F9459ABCF83210.sscistudy1.pdf.

54. Jonathan Topaz, "GOP Senators Defend CIA in Alternative Report," *Politico*, December 9, 2014, https://www.politico.com/story/2014/12/gop-senators-defend-cia-alternate-report -113434.

55. As of this writing, the Senate Select Committee on Intelligence's investigation into the Russian hacking appear to be operating much better, largely because of the comity between the ranking Democratic senator, Mark Warner, and Republican chairman Richard Burr. The Senate's investigations had not yet been released when this chapter was completed.

56. Martin Dempsey, "Military Leaders Do Not Belong at Political Conventions," letter to the editor, *Washington Post*, July 30, 2016, https://www.washingtonpost.com/opinions/military -leaders-do-not-belong-at-political-conventions/2016/07/30/0e06fc16–568b-11e6-b652 -315ae5d4d4dd_story.html?utm_term=.a200eb158f2c.

57. See, e.g., Harriet Sinclair, "Trump Finances May Be the Next Shoe to Drop in Russia Probe," *Newsweek*, February 18, 2018, http://www.newsweek.com/james-clapper-donald-trump -russia-probe-810357; and Matthew Rosenberg, "Ex-CIA Chief Says Putin May Have Compromising Material on Trump," *New York Times*, March 21, 2018, https://www.nytimes.com/2018 /03/21/us/politics/john-brennan-trump-putin.html.

58. The author was present when the then deputy director of intelligence John Kringen addressed senior analysts at the CIA auditorium on the issue of analytical tradecraft.

59. Fingar, "It's Complicated," 32–33.

60. Rovner, *Fixing the Facts*, 199.

61. Gregory F. Treverton, "Intelligence Analysis: Between 'Politicization' and Irrelevance," in *Analyzing Intelligence: Origins, Obstacles, and Innovations*, 1st ed., ed. Roger George and James Bruce (Washington, DC: Georgetown University Press, 2008), 101.

11

INTELLIGENCE AND
AMERICAN DEMOCRACY

If angels were to govern men, neither external nor internal controls on government would be necessary. In framing a government which is to be administered by men over men, the great difficulty lies in this; you must first enable the government to control the governed; and in the next place oblige it to control itself.
  —Federalist No. 51 (James Madison)

Oversight is designed to look into every nook and cranny of governmental affairs, expose misconduct, and put the light of publicity to it. Oversight can protect the country from the imperial presidency and from bureaucratic arrogance.
  —Former congressman Lee Hamilton, cochair of the 9/11
  Commission

We are responsible stewards of the public trust; we use intelligence authorities and resources prudently, protect intelligence sources and methods diligently, report wrongdoing through appropriate channels; and remain accountable to ourselves, our oversight institutions, and through those institutions, ultimately to the American people.
  —Principles of Professional Ethics for the Intelligence
  Community

In democracies the role of intelligence remains controversial and at times problematic. On the one hand, democracies thrive on openness and transparency. On the other hand, they also face international and domestic threats that require protection by all elements of national power, including intelligence. Like the military instrument, intelligence requires careful supervision, and its use must be consistent with the US Constitution and federal law. This chapter will examine the challenges that intelligence poses to democratic principles in its efforts to safeguard national security. The executive, legislative, and judicial mechanisms for oversight will be described and analyzed. Finally, the chapter will examine issues related to post-9/11 intelligence operations and their impact on American democracy. Today the practice of intelligence has become more complex, and the existing oversight framework that balances security and liberty have been severely tested.

IS INTELLIGENCE ETHICAL?

There is an argument that intelligence and democracy are so antithetical to each other that there should be no place for intelligence at all. This proposition, like pacifism, rests on an idealistic notion of peaceful and nonthreatening relations among states. Before the Cold War, American leaders were also very wary of creating permanent intelligence organizations. Clearly, most of today's American policymakers and politicians do not share this view but instead believe intelligence—like the military instrument—is a legitimate tool for protecting a democracy. In this view, it would be unethical not to seek or to withhold important intelligence needed to make better policy decisions or to protect the security of the homeland. Who would argue that the United States should decide on war or peace in an information vacuum? Even the United Nations has recognized the utility of member states providing intelligence for use in UN Security Council deliberations. As a practical matter, the International Atomic Energy Agency's monitoring of suspect WMD facilities also is aided by member states' contributions of their national information for that purpose. In the Cold War, the United States and the former Soviet Union cautiously revealed intelligence data for the purpose of negotiating and implementing major nuclear arms control negotiations. In this case, intelligence can be credited with helping to prevent a major nuclear confrontation by applying national technical means for verifying compliance with those agreements. And the ongoing US and international efforts to head off further development of nuclear weapons by Iran and North Korea depend in part on a robust intelligence capability.

The ethical issues notwithstanding, the CIA and other intelligence collectors have the authority under US law to break the laws of other countries by recruiting foreign nationals to spy or by stealing secrets by other technical means. (Of course, the target country sees these activities as illegal and will take steps to stop them.) For the purpose of protecting and enhancing a state's security, presidents, prime ministers, and monarchs have all used human as well as technical intelligence to know the plans, intentions, and military capabilities of their adversaries. The Russian and Chinese foreign intelligence services as well as most US European allies' foreign intelligence agencies recruit foreign agents. They and the CIA use a variety of techniques to spot, develop, recruit, and run agents. The CIA historically has used American "soft power" to attract foreign officials and influential private citizens to volunteer (as so-called walk-ins). In these cases, spies volunteer to assist the United States because of their distaste for the despotism of their own governments and a wish to bring about long-term positive changes to their societies. In other instances, the CIA can recruit such agents because of their need for money, revenge, or greater self-esteem or status. For some, playing on the weaknesses or vulnerabilities of such agents seems reprehensible. Yet the United States' interest in knowing more about Vladimir Putin's Russia or Kim Jong-un's North Korea overrules individual morality that would discourage the exploitation of human frailties.

Likewise, the NSA is authorized to collect the electronic communications of foreign governments and foreign citizens. These broad authorities have necessitated high levels of secrecy to enable collectors to conduct their operations without detection and to provide the United States with plausible deniability. As is sometimes acknowledged, foreign governments know that US intelligence is breaking their laws and diplomatic codes, intercepting their communications, and recruiting their citizens to spy for the United States. This is tolerated so long as it remains shrouded in secrecy and because many of those same governments are using similar methods to gather intelligence on the United States.[1]

Collection of intelligence also raises another ethical issue seldom appreciated by those outside the intelligence community—namely, given the risks of secretly breaking the laws of foreign governments, US intelligence has a moral and practical obligation to protect its sources and methods. In cases of human intelligence, a case officer is promising to protect the anonymity of a foreign national committing treason from exposure, prison, and possible death. It is no light matter to ask a person to risk his freedom and possibly his life to spy for the United States. Hence, US intelligence officers must weigh the benefits of what a foreign spy can provide against the risks that person faces if caught. As a rule of thumb, the case officer should not ask any asset to collect what is already known or easily acquired through less risky means. In the 1990s, when the issue of whether the US IC should be collecting economic intelligence, senior Treasury officials such as Lawrence Summers challenged the CIA's collection and analysis of international monetary data, when as deputy secretary he could phone any head of a foreign central bank for that same information. Likewise, deputy director of the CIA Robert Gates noted at that time he would not ask a CIA officer to spy for General Motors. His point was that intelligence should be collected to benefit US national security, not American companies, even if such practices were found among some foreign intelligence services.

Intelligence analysis raises different ethical questions. First, speaking truth to power, as the saying goes, is the first obligation of the analytical profession. Analysts are schooled in the belief that their analysis must be as objective as possible, present all the relevant facts, and lay out significant implications for US policies regardless of how inconvenient to policymakers. Following the embarrassing 2002 Iraqi WMD estimate, the director of national intelligence issued "Intelligence Community Directive 203," which laid out the central ethical elements of the analytical profession:

> Analysts must perform their functions with objectivity and with awareness of their own assumptions and reasoning. They must employ reasoning techniques and practical mechanisms that reveal and mitigate bias. Analysts must be alert to influence by existing analytic positions or judgments and must consider alternative perspectives and contrary information. . . . Analytic assessments must not be distorted by, nor shaped for, advocacy of a particular audience, agenda, or policy viewpoint. Analytic judgments must not be influenced by the force or preference for a particular policy.[2]

A second ethical issue for intelligence analysis involves providing its judgments on a confidential basis to policymakers. To have maximum benefit and give policymakers a decision advantage, analytical judgments should remain secret and available only to those decision-makers with a need to know. This maxim has encouraged the IC to classify virtually everything it produces as SECRET or TOP SECRET, depending on its sensitivity. Revealing what US intelligence knows about a foreign government's military plans and capabilities reduces policymakers' ability to take advantage of known vulnerabilities and to avoid an adversary's strengths. Intelligence analysts thus prepare assessments on the assumption that their judgments will remain secret, so they can be as candid and objective as possible regarding a foreign government's behavior. If analysts believe their analysis will be leaked to the press, they would most likely have to hold back on some assessments for fear of their impact on US diplomacy.

As discussed in chapter 10, the selective leaking or misrepresentation of intelligence judgments can alter the political debate on important issues. This can politicize intelligence in ways that do not serve the country well. Even the approved release of controversial NIEs' key judgments—such as the 2007 Iran nuclear estimate—can produce huge political repercussions and generate subsequent regret on the part of some senior intelligence officials regarding how they wrote those judgments. Current ODNI policy is that there will be no future release of estimates or their key judgments, but whether that stated policy will withstand future political pressure remains to be seen. Unauthorized leaks, which have caused huge damage to US foreign policy and intelligence performance, will remain a major threat, particularly with the rising occurrence of the so-called insider threat (i.e., a government employee or contractor with access to intelligence who knowingly releases classified materials to the public).

Finally, the ethics of conducting covert operations continues to be controversial. As described in chapter 9, there are now elaborate executive branch procedures for proposing, approving, and notifying Congress about covert action programs. Nonetheless, justifying one democracy's interference in the internal affairs of other governments seems contradictory.[3] Yet presidents from both major parties have always wanted to have a third way other than doing nothing or going to war. Should Americans feel comfortable that their government is influencing—without acknowledging it—a foreign government's behavior? For example, should Americans embrace the use of covert action to weaken an autocratic regime that is repressing its people or perhaps to disrupt a proliferation network that is operating in a number of countries, including those of American allies? Which is the greater evil—doing nothing to stop actions that threaten US interests and values or interfering in a sovereign government's internal affairs? The United States is not alone in conducting such interference, as we know from the recent Russian hacking activities.

One standard that has some merit is insisting that any proposed intelligence operation must pass the *"Washington Post* test"—namely, if an activity were to be revealed in that major newspaper, would the American people find those actions acceptable or reject them? On that basis, some operations might never have been considered in the first place, while others might be easily justified. Consider for example, the difference between conducting a covert action aimed at subverting a democratic election in Chile in the 1970s versus operations to sabotage the Iranian or North Korean nuclear programs. Likewise, most Americans might readily accept the clandestine collection of information against a well-known autocrat like Russia's Vladimir Putin but might well question the same tactics used against a democratically elected leader like German chancellor Angela Merkel.

IS SECRECY NECESSARY?

To many scholars and practitioners of intelligence, secrecy is the central concept that distinguishes intelligence from other information used by national security decision-makers. This is, to be sure, too narrow a definition of intelligence, but it is a starting point for discussing the unique role intelligence plays in American democracy. Americans have long been wary of secrecy as a tool of statecraft, bemoaning the Old World's reliance on secret alliances and treaties used to carve up much of the globe and plot wars. Woodrow Wilson's principle of "open covenants, openly arrived at" during the Treaty of Versailles negotiations of 1919 captured the American ethos that somehow the United States would operate differently from other nation-states.

Yet in reality the United States has had to rely on secret intelligence from the time it declared its independence—with Gen. George Washington presiding as essentially the country's first spymaster. Nonetheless, there has been discomfort with espionage, surveillance, and reliance on secret information throughout US history. Secret intelligence and spying were reluctantly deemed appropriate when the country was at war but discontinued when peace ensued.

The solution to the dilemma of conducting secret intelligence in a democracy was to ensure that there was proper governmental guidance on the purposes for which it was conducted, the kinds of information that could be collected, and with whom it could be shared. While the 1947 National Security Act was extremely vague on the operation of the CIA and the authorities granted to the DCI (later the DNI), it did charge this official with the protection of sources and methods used to collect secret intelligence. The 1949 Central Intelligence Agency Act also authorized the agency to protect (i.e., classify) the names and numbers of its employees. From the beginning, the IC's budget remained classified, hidden within the much larger Defense Department's appropriation. Only recently has the DNI agreed to publish the "top-line" (total figure) of the IC's spending as a nod to greater transparency.

Presidential executive orders have also laid out the IC's responsibility to protect secrets. However, they directed that these authorities could not be used to hide violations of law, administrative errors, or personal embarrassment of US agencies or officials. The IC was permitted only to classify information that was needed for national security purposes in the following categories:

- military plans, weapon systems, or operations
- foreign government information
- intelligence activities (including covert action), intelligence sources or methods, or cryptology
- foreign relations or foreign activities of the United States, including confidential sources
- scientific, technological, or economic matters relating to national security
- government programs for safeguarding nuclear materials or facilities
- vulnerabilities or capabilities of systems, installations, infrastructures, projects, plans or protection services relating to national security
- the development, production, or use of WMDs[4]

That said, there is tendency toward "overclassification" of information in the US government generally and the IC more specifically. The CIA and other agencies have programs to declassify documents after twenty-five years unless there is a compelling "sources and methods" reason for continued secrecy. Most of these efforts are slow and considered inadequate by historians and intelligence scholars eager to know more about the IC's past activities. The 1966 Freedom of Information Act (FOIA) mandates that federal executive agencies respond to citizen's requests for information that no longer needs to remain classified. A number of volumes have been published by the CIA's History Staff focused on the Bay of Pigs, the Cuban Missile Crisis, the Vietnam War, and other major international crises; volumes on past CIA analysis on the Soviet Union, China, and Yugoslavia are also available to scholars. Most recently, the CIA released a voluminous collection of *President's Daily Briefs* from 1969 to 1977, the first such glimpse into what these sensitive documents covered during the Nixon, Ford, and Carter presidencies.[5]

PROTECTING PRIVACY RIGHTS—UP TO A POINT

By definition, a liberal democracy is one that protects individual privacy while demanding government transparency. In a narrow sense, intelligence collected on its citizens secretly is antithetical to democracy. Governments should leave citizens alone and not be allowed to monitor their thoughts or beliefs so long as they do not lead to criminal acts. But individual privacy, like government secrecy, has its limits. Often the statement is made that Americans must choose between personal liberty and public safety; in fact, this is a false dichotomy. As intelligence scholar Richard Betts notes, there is a trade-off, but it is seldom an either/or choice between collective national security and individual civil liberties: "There is no need to compromise the more important elements of civil liberties having to do with freedom of speech, political organization, religion, or especially the right to due process of law—freedom from arbitrary arrest and incarceration without a chance to contest one's guilt. Having one's phone tapped without proper cause is not as damaging as being imprisoned for years without trial."[6] Compromises between individual privacy and public safety can be reasonably made. Intercepting an individual's phone conversations in an effort to protect the public's safety is hardly a severe overreach by the federal government, provided it has reasonable cause to believe that individual is working for a foreign power or is part of a terrorist organization whose goals are to attack innocent American citizens. None of these concerns necessarily breaches the First Amendment rights of free speech, assembly, or religion.

It is important to distinguish between an individual's privacy rights and his broader civil liberties. During the Cold War, those individual privacy rights could justifiably be infringed only if there was evidence of criminal behavior or a genuine counterintelligence threat. Under United States Code, law enforcement agencies such as the FBI could monitor citizens for the purpose of gathering evidence of a crime having been committed. Those searches and seizures usually required a court order or warrant showing "probable cause" (meaning a high standard of evidence), and often the individual was made aware of those warrants when a physical search was being conducted. Under the 1978 **Foreign Intelligence Surveillance Act (FISA)**, however, law enforcement and intelligence agencies also could conduct clandestine surveillance if there was thought to be a counterintelligence threat in which the target was "a foreign power" or an "agent of a foreign power" (discussed in more detail later in this chapter). In these cases, according to the act, law enforcement could maintain such secret surveillance *without* a court order for up to a year so long as the attorney general of the United States certified to the **Foreign Intelligence Surveillance Court (FISC)** that there was minimal risk of turning up information on innocent US citizens. Suffice it to say that protecting individual privacy in the information and social media age has become a complicated domain in which civil libertarians, Internet and social media companies, and law enforcement officials all have competing equities.

THE ROLE OF OVERSIGHT

Given the tremendous powers that the IC has to collect and analyze secret information, as well as conduct covert operations, there must be a system of oversight and control to ensure that such authorities are not abused. Within the US government, there is an elaborate framework of legislative, executive, and judicial review of intelligence activities. It is complicated and far from perfect but probably the most comprehensive oversight system of any democratic government in the world. It was created over time to reflect the growing scale and complexity of US intelligence operations as well as a result of intelligence failures and abuses that occurred along the way.

Many of these checks on US intelligence activities reflect lessons learned from painful mistakes made by intelligence agencies as well as a failure of effective executive and congressional oversight in the past. In particular, the current system is the result of the Vietnam War protests of the 1960s and 1970s, which prompted the Nixon White House to resort to extralegal surveillance of civil rights and antiwar activists. On the heels of President Nixon's resignation in 1974, revelations of CIA, NSA, and FBI illegal surveillance of Americans led to the House and Senate investigations (later known as the Pike and Church hearings, respectively) of wrongdoings and intelligence failures.[7] This series of public hearings produced massive reporting on previously unknown plans, some of which had proposed illegal opening of mail, wiretaps, and home entries. It also confirmed the existence of a seven-hundred-page dossier of the CIA's "Family Jewels"—a compilation of agency missteps that included failed assassination attempts on Fidel Castro, mind-altering drug experimentation programs, and involvement in coup attempts.[8] These hearings gave the appearance of the CIA operating as a "rogue elephant," as Sen. Frank Church once characterized it, and called for further controls on intelligence agencies.[9]

Legislative Oversight

As a result of the Pike and Church hearings, both houses of Congress established select committees on intelligence in the late 1970s.[10] These two committees have slightly different mandates (see box 11.1). The House Permanent Select Committee on Intelligence (HPSCI) has exclusive jurisdiction over the national intelligence program and shares jurisdiction over tactical military intelligence and budgets with the House Armed Services Committee. The Senate Select Committee on Intelligence has sole jurisdiction only over the CIA and the DNI and its various subelements (e.g., the NIC, NCTC, and NCPC). At the same time, the Senate Armed Services Committee essentially retains oversight of the much larger defense intelligence programs and budgets of the NSA, NRO, NGA, and DIA. Although these two oversight committees carry out the bulk of the oversight responsibilities, it should be noted that the armed services, judiciary, homeland security, and appropriations committees do retain substantial leverage when it comes to defense intelligence (roughly 70 percent of the IC's budget), FBI and DHS intelligence activities, and any intelligence appropriations.

Box 11.1 House and Senate Intelligence Oversight Committees

The House Permanent Select Intelligence Committee (HPSCI) was established in 1977, and its size has fluctuated from twenty to twenty-two members. The majority-minority ratio is roughly comparable that found in the full House but generally is no more than a 3:2 ratio. At least one member must be drawn from the membership of the House Appropriations, Armed Services, Judiciary and Foreign Affairs Committees. The HPSCI has jurisdiction over the National Intelligence Program and the Military Intelligence Program. Jurisdiction over the FBI and DHS is shared with other committees of the judiciary and homeland security.

The Senate Select Committee on Intelligence (SSCI) was established in 1976 and is currently composed of fifteen senators. By custom, the majority party always has eight members and the minority has seven members, regardless of the full Senate composition. In a sign of bipartisanship, the SSCI also has a vice chairman representing the minority party. At least one member is drawn from the armed services, foreign relations, appropriations, and judiciary committees. The chairman and ranking minority member of the Senate Armed Services Committee are also ex officio members of the SSCI. The SSCI has jurisdiction only over the National Intelligence Program budget, including the CIA and the Office of the DNI. Otherwise, it has limited jurisdiction over DOD, DHS, Treasury, and Justice Department entities with the corresponding committees of the Senate.

For reassuring the public's confidence in intelligence, the SSCI has the responsibility for confirming the appointment of the DNI, the CIA director, and all other directors of the National Intelligence Program, including those within the Department of Defense, such as the NSA and DIA. This lends the SSCI the power to hold public hearings and grill those officials on their views prior to confirming them. This can be a platform from which to express critical views and concerns regarding the operation of intelligence as well as to extract promises of greater transparency and truthfulness regarding the IC's performance. As was demonstrated in early 2018, the nomination of Gina Haspel as CIA director allowed for a robust congressional and public debate over past CIA conduct regarding secret detention camps and enhanced interrogation techniques. Her pledge to speak truth to power in dealing with President Trump as well as to never to employ "torture" again were conditions on which her nomination was narrowly approved.

The earlier chapter on covert action described in great detail the procedures for sharing presidential findings with Congress. However, it is worth underlining the key role the intelligence oversight committees play in reviewing and commenting on highly classified CIA operations. The 1980 law requires that the CIA share presidential findings with both House and Senate oversight committees in a timely manner (see box 11.2). While these committees have no power to stop or modify those operations, hypothetically they could encourage the passage of legislation to prevent their future funding or alter their scope. Having that kind of power tends to discourage ill-advised or highly risky operations. When a covert action is considered extremely sensitive, the president may decide to delay notification beyond the normal forty-eight-hour period. Alternatively, the president may elect to brief only a select group of congressional leaders. Often, the so-called **Gang of Eight**—the Senate majority leader and the House speaker, along with their ranking minority leaders and the chairmen

---

Box 11.2   1980 Intelligence Oversight Act

The 1980 Intelligence Oversight Act requires the CIA director to keep the intelligence oversight committees "fully and currently informed of all intelligence activities, including any significant anticipated intelligence activity." It requires timely notification of any significant illegalities or intelligence failures. Importantly, it supersedes the Hughes-Ryan Amendment in providing that the president notify the intelligence oversight committees of any decision for a planned covert action and lays out the procedures and timelines for such notification. In exchange for eliminating the requirement that the CIA report significant intelligence operations to up to eight separate congressional committees, it reduced that requirement to only the two intelligence oversight committees and demanded a set of detailed procedures (later known as "findings" and "notifications") for informing those committees of presidentially approved covert actions.

and ranking minority members of the two oversight committees—is employed to keep congressional knowledge to a minimum. This has become a more controversial method, as it is sometimes seen more as an excuse to limit possible congressional criticism than a protection against possible leaks.

As with any other congressional committee, the intelligence oversight committees have power of the purse over intelligence programs and budgets, including the authority to disapprove or approve spending on specific programs. Each oversight committee—as well counterpart appropriations committees in both houses—maintains large audit staffs that are continuously reviewing the IC budgets and spending to ensure they are adhering to legislative guidance and priorities. They will examine the annual consolidated intelligence budget request prepared by the DNI—contained in thick, highly classified congressional budget justification books (CBJBs)—that has already been reviewed and approved by the Office of Management and Budget (see box 11.3). Senate and House congressional committee budgetary experts will pick apart and question these spending requests, often requesting further information or briefings. Typically the DNI and heads of individual agencies will testify before the committees to answer questions and defend these budget requests.

Committees will frequently question spending or proposed additional funding for programs they wish to see advanced or protected. In the 1980s, for example, the SSCI prohibited the CIA from spending money to provide lethal aid to the Contras in Nicaragua, which the Reagan administration wanted to use to undermine the Cuban-backed Sandinista government. Subsequent legislation demanded that any covert action program be "notified" to the oversight committees prior to its initiation. Additional legislation followed that set out an elaborate procedure for presidential findings (see chapter 9) of covert action to ensure proper authorization and notification within both the executive and legislative branches. In another sensational case, the SSCI's audit team, according to a *Washington Post* story, discovered that the National

---

Box 11.3   Congressional Budget Justification Book

"The CBJB is the annual report to Congress that describes in detail the full extent of intelligence capabilities, essentially detailing what we'd done with the money that had been allocated to us and justifying our requests for the following year. It went into specifics about many programs—how they worked, what results they produced, and the effect they had on national security. It covered how we protected our forces from insurgent attacks and how we assessed adversarial leaders' intentions. It explained how we monitored proliferation of weapons of mass destruction, including in Iran, North Korea, and Syria. It contained, in short, the full expanse of how the US conducts intelligence."

Source: James Clapper, *Facts and Fears: Hard Truth from a Life in Intelligence* (New York: Viking, 2018), 240.

Reconnaissance Office had not spent previously appropriated and designated funds and later reprogrammed some monies for its headquarters building in Northern Virginia. The NRO had never briefed these plans to Congress. Needless to say, the committee's chairman held hearings and demanded an explanation and ultimately a resignation of a senior NRO official.[11]

Congressional oversight via its hearings and independent investigations can also constrain and shape intelligence activities. In the wake of the 2002 Iraqi WMD NIE scandal, both oversight committees undertook their own investigations into what went wrong. They reviewed intelligence documents, interviewed analysts and managers, and reached a series of critical findings regarding CIA and IC analytical tradecraft practices. Similarly, in 2011, at the behest of the then chairperson Dianne Feinstein, a two-year staff investigation focused on the CIA's secret detention and interrogation program. A massive classified final report outlining the program's flaws and false claims—including a redacted six-hundred-page summary—was prepared to underline the committee majority's belief that the program was misguided and should never be repeated. More contemporary examples have been the separate House and Senate committee investigations into the Russian interference in the 2016 elections, which are not yet completed at the time of writing.

Executive Branch Oversight

Long before Congress established more focused committee attention to intelligence activities, the executive branch held the principal responsibility to supervise and direct the IC. As made clear in earlier discussions of the national security decision-making process, the IC reports to the president and the NSC, giving them more daily contact over and control of intelligence matters. In addition to the various NSC bodies established by presidents to set intelligence requirements, approve budgets, and authorize covert actions, presidents have relied on advisory bodies to review the performance of the IC.

President's Intelligence Advisory Board

One of the earliest tools of presidential oversight has been the President's Intelligence Advisory Board (PIAB). Created in 1956 by President Eisenhower, its purpose was to provide him with outside recommendations on how to improve intelligence on the growing Soviet military program. In his executive order, Eisenhower noted that he sought out the best advice from the scientific, military, and business communities. His relatively small board of six to eight acknowledged experts provided him influential views on developing overhead reconnaissance programs, devising a new technical directorate for the CIA, and proposing a new Defense Intelligence Agency to centralize military intelligence functions.[12] Later presidents would also ask the PIAB to perform postmortems on intelligence failures and examine the effectiveness of implemented intelligence reforms. For example, President George W. Bush's NSC staff engaged the PIAB during the 2008 revisions to the FISA. President Obama also reportedly directed his PIAB to examine the intelligence failure surrounding the "Underwear Bomber's" nearly successful downing of an airliner in 2009; the board also proposed ways to manage the expanding volume of data on the Internet and investigate what the government can do about WikiLeaks types of disclosures.

The PIAB has fluctuated in size and significance, depending on each president's personal involvement in intelligence matters and relationship with the board and its chairman. A president typically issues an executive order laying out the size, duties, and scope of this advisory group. During the Eisenhower and Kennedy years, the body was instrumental for some major organizational innovations at a time when the IC was still taking shape. Other presidents have relied on it far less. Indeed, President Carter chose not to create a PIAB, as the new congressional oversight committees had just been established and he believed they would be sufficient oversight of a function in which he had little interest. During those times when the PIAB was little used—as in the Clinton presidency—it became largely a ceremonial body, where presidential friends or party stalwarts could occupy a seemingly lofty position.

In most cases, the PIAB's operations are seldom known and remain noncontroversial. One exception was during the Ford administration, when the body urged the creation of the Team A / Team B exercise that attacked the CIA's estimates of Soviet strategic programs. A more recent exception occurred during George W. Bush's first term, when his PIAB chairman, Brent Scowcroft, reportedly recommended that post-9/11 intelligence reforms include moving the NSA and NRO out from under the secretary of defense in order to give the then director of central intelligence more authority. This recommendation was never officially released and was reportedly strongly opposed by Defense Secretary Donald Rumsfeld. This dispute, combined with Scowcroft's open letter criticizing the administration's invasion of Iraq, led to his removal from the PIAB after 2004.

Intelligence Oversight Board

In 1976, President Gerald Ford signed an executive order (EO 11905) outlining steps to prevent intelligence abuses or infringement on Americans' civil liberties as occurred during the Nixon administration. This responded not only to the findings of the Pike and Church hearings into the CIA's and other agencies' illegal activities but also a separate presidential commission (called the Rockefeller Commission).[13] In the executive order, President Ford banned political assassinations (a prohibition that remains in force through subsequent presidential executive orders) and created a small (three to five members) **Intelligence Oversight Board (IOB),** which would investigate and report to the attorney general and Department of Justice any illegal activities by the CIA or other intelligence agencies. The IOB serves as a subcommittee to the PIAB itself and thus ultimately reports to the president. Intelligence agencies and their inspectors general (IGs) are responsible for making any and all information available to the IOB for them to conduct their independent investigations.

Inspectors General

By law and executive order, many of the national intelligence agencies must maintain an Office of the Inspector General.[14] At the CIA, for example, the Office of the Inspector General was established in 1953 but later made fully autonomous in 1989 by a separate statute. The president nominates an individual who must then be confirmed by the Senate Select Committee on Intelligence; only the president can remove the IG, making him or her more independent of the current CIA leadership.

By statute, an IG is charged with conducting routine audits and inspections of units and programs within an executive department as well as performing special investigations to ensure the efficiency, effectiveness, and legality of the organization's activities. In the CIA, audits focus on financial transactions and accounting practices, while inspections can examine the performance of specific agency components or crosscutting programs. Investigations can be launched to uncover alleged fraud, waste, mismanagement, or violations of laws and government regulations. These reports are sent to the CIA director for his or her review and possible further administrative actions. Such reports can focus on employees' fraudulent submission of time cards and misuse of government property or funds, all the way up to illegal covert actions, alleged detainee abuse, or unauthorized destruction of detainee interrogation methods videos.[15] IG reports involving possible criminal activity must be reported to the attorney general, while those investigating significant intelligence failures or problems must be shared with the congressional oversight committees. In this way, IGs often assist in the legislative branch performing its own oversight responsibilities.

While most reports and investigations are used to determine internal administrative actions—such as reprimands or dismissals for inappropriate and unethical behavior or legal wrongdoing—occasionally an IG report becomes a public issue. In 2001, Inspector General John Helgerson, a senior career CIA analyst, produced a report critical of the CIA Counterterrorism Center's performance prior to 9/11, which recommended forming an accountability board to reprimand individuals for their mistakes. This angered the CIA leadership and also demoralized some CTC analysts. Helgerson's office also later issued a 2004 study that claimed the secret CIA detention and interrogation program very likely violated the United Nations Convention against Torture. This made it harder for the Bush administration to brush aside civil libertarian organizations' criticisms of the secret prisons and harsh treatment of detainees and led the SSCI to commence its own separate investigation.[16] Director Michael Hayden reportedly was unhappy at the time and authorized a study of the IG's operations by the CIA's general counsel. That report led Hayden to install an ombudsman over the IG to ensure quality control and to keep the agency managers informed as to its activities. Reportedly, Helgerson agreed to these changes, but he was not made available to comment to the media on these changes.

The DNI also established his own statutory IG, created by the Intelligence Authorization Act for Fiscal Year 2010. This IC IG, also accountable to Congress, conducts inspections, audits, and investigations across the entire sixteen-member IC. This office is also designed to provide leadership, training, and coordination of the other IGs across the community. Other agencies, such as the DIA, NSA, and NGA, maintain IGs to monitor these organizations' performance for efficiency as well as ethical standards.

Judicial Oversight: Foreign Intelligence Surveillance Court

The judicial branch has broad authority to interpret national security laws passed by Congress and implemented by the executive branch. In this oversight capacity, the courts have the power to restrict intelligence activities desired by a president and demand some procedures be in place for justifying the secret collection of information. In these ways, federal courts all the way up to the Supreme Court can place checks on how US intelligence operates. The Supreme Court has often served as a brake on presidential authority and an interpreter of legislation related to national security and intelligence. In the post-9/11 era, Supreme Court decisions have placed limits on presidential actions aimed at detainee operations at Guantanamo Bay Naval Base, in particular. In the 2006 *Hamdan v. Rumsfeld* case, the court ruled that the George W. Bush administration's military commissions at Guantanamo violated US and international law; it also ruled that Article 3 of the Geneva Conventions ("minimal protections") applied to detainees as well.[17] In a subsequent 2008 case, the court further ruled that the military commissions violated the Constitution by not providing detainees the same rights of habeas corpus petition as US citizens.[18] In general, the Supreme Court's rulings have tended to extend more protections to non-US citizens than presidents are inclined to confer.

The best-known judicial oversight activity is the Foreign Intelligence Surveillance Court. Established under the 1978 FISA, this court was seen as one remedy to the Church committee's recommendations for more oversight of the executive branch's use of intelligence. The FISC would review requests for search warrants to allow electronic (and later physical) surveillance in national security cases. This special court would operate in secret and comprise eleven federal judges drawn from different

---

Box 11.4   Foreign Intelligence Surveillance Act

The 1978 Foreign Intelligence Surveillance Act (FISA) created the Foreign Intelligence Surveillance Court (FISC), which reviews and approves requests from law enforcement and
intelligence agencies for physical and electronic surveillance of persons suspected of "being
foreign agents for foreign powers" of espionage or terrorism. Section 702 of the FISA allows
law enforcement and intelligence agencies to obtain emails and telephone communications
of foreigners outside the United States without a warrant.

Significantly, it strictly defines the procedures under which a federal warrant for electronic (and later physical) surveillance can be conducted. The primary purpose must be to
protect against a foreign power's or its agent's efforts to engage in an attack, sabotage,
international terrorism, or clandestine intelligence activities. If the intelligence information
concerns a "United States person," the information must be necessary to prevent an attack,
sabotage, or act of terrorism or espionage.

Subsequent interpretation and Justice Department procedures led to a restriction ("The
Wall") on allowing law enforcement and intelligence agencies to coordinate and share information for fear of tainting criminal proceedings. Essentially, a FISA warrant cannot be used
to get around the Fourth Amendment's "due process" protections for American citizens.

---

federal court districts around the country. The FISA instructed the court to review
search warrant requests of communications intercepts of foreign targets operating
outside the United States in order to prevent or at least "minimize" the intercept of
American citizens' communications.[19] The act requires that the DOJ apply for a warrant in order to collect communications transmissions on foreign targets that are collected in the United States. The department must provide probable cause that the
target is a "foreign power" or "agent of a foreign power" (see box 11.4).

The FISA was renewed and amended in 2008 amid considerable debate regarding the NSA's domestic surveillance programs, later revealed by Edward Snowden. At
that time, the IC was adamant that it needed certain provisions found in Section 702
that permitted the NSA to collect—with court supervision—communications of non-
US persons operating outside the United States who might be involved in terrorism.
According to legal scholars, the law had previously always distinguished between US
citizens and non-US citizens as well as between domestic and foreign locations. The
FISA essentially eliminated both distinctions if the government could show probable
cause that an individual was an "agent" of a foreign power.[20]

Following the Snowden leaks, which revealed extensive collection of Americans'
Internet and telephone metadata, DNI James Clapper and other senior intelligence
officials tried to dispel congressional concerns that this provision was being misused
to spy on innocent American citizens. Clapper maintained that when the IC monitored the communications overseas of a non-US person who was speaking to a US
citizen, such "incidental collection" would be deleted if it had no foreign intelligence

value.[21] There have been continuing press reports that the NSA's ability to carefully track only non-US persons communications is far from perfect. The New America Foundation's analysis of ODNI semiannual reports on Section 702 reveal that the law's complexity as well as the NSA's vast collection capabilities means that inadvertent collection of Americans' phone messages and emails continues because of human error and poor tasking instructions.[22] The **Privacy and Civil Liberties Oversight Board (PCLOB)**—created by the 2004 intelligence legislation—also investigated the use of Section 702 and concluded that while the error rate was low, given the size and complexity of the collection programs, mistakes were inevitable. In its defense, the IC has duly reported these errors and has modified training of signals analysts to reduce these incidents.

POST-9/11 INTELLIGENCE CHALLENGES

At the end of the Cold War, it may have appeared that the United States could wind down its defense commitments and intelligence efforts. However, the attacks of September 11, 2001, put security back on the front burner. Moreover, it made more apparent the dilemmas of security versus liberty. More intrusive surveillance and interrogation techniques, as well as the resort to intelligence-led targeted killings, have led to questions regarding the adequacy of executive and legislative oversight. In addition, the need to share intelligence more widely within the IC and with foreign partners to aid counterterrorism has come at a time when unauthorized disclosures of classified intelligence programs have undermined America's trustworthiness in the eyes of some partners. Current and future US policymakers will have to wrestle with these issues in order to restore US credibility both at home and abroad.

Harsh and Intrusive Intelligence Collection

The global war on terrorism ushered in a new set of intelligence tasks designed to take down international terrorist organizations such as al-Qaeda, the Taliban, and most recently ISIS. Shortly after the 9/11 attacks, President George W. Bush authorized the CIA to conduct its most extensive covert action programs to disrupt future terrorist plots and destroy al-Qaeda. These included not just paramilitary operations in Afghanistan but also secret renditions and interrogations of captured fighters held at undisclosed camps outside the United States. These measures allowed the CIA to conduct very harsh interrogations it felt necessary to elicit information that could reveal plans for future attacks. This was done despite the United States being a signatory party to the United Nations Convention against Torture,[23] which bans "any act by which severe pain or suffering, whether physical or mental, is intentionally inflicted on a person for such purposes as obtaining from him or a third party information or a confession."[24] It further bans what it calls cruel, inhuman, or degrading treatment of prisoners of war.

At the time, the president and his closest advisers believed that it was urgent to prevent follow-on attacks at any cost. Authorizing the use of EITs—including the waterboarding of detainees that simulated drowning—on known al-Qaeda members seemed legitimate. Accordingly, White House counsel Alberto Gonzales in January 2002 had already announced that the Bush administration did not believe that al-Qaeda and Taliban fighters deserved protections under the Geneva Conventions as they were judged to be "unlawful combatants" rather than prisoners of war.[25] However, the CIA wanted more reassurance of the legality of its program and so requested and received in August 2002 a DOJ legal memorandum that judged those measures to fall short of the definition of torture. In that memo, DOJ lawyers argued that the president as commander in chief had the authority to conduct operations to protect the United States (the so-called necessity defense) and that United States Code regarding the UN Convention against Torture proscribed only the most extreme acts that inflicted severe pain or mental suffering:

> We conclude that for an act to constitute torture as defined in [United States Code,] Section 2340, it must inflict pain that is difficult to endure. Physical pain amounting to torture must be equivalent in intensity to the pain accompanying serious physical injury, such as organ failure, impairment of bodily function, or even death. For purely mental pain or suffering to amount to torture under Section 2340, it must result in significant psychological harm of significant duration, e.g., lasting for months or even years.[26]

By this definition, the DOJ set the bar very high before any charges of torture could be brought against any CIA staff or contract employee involved in the program.

The executive branch also believed it had covered itself by informing a few key members of Congress regarding the broad nature of the rendition and interrogation program. In September 2002, CIA officials briefed the ranking majority and minority members of the House intelligence committee—Porter Goss (later CIA director) and Nancy Pelosi (at the time, the House minority leader). Additional briefings were subsequently provided to a few more congressional oversight committee members, but the program was not briefed to the full committees until two years later. According to Bush administration and CIA officials, those few congressional leaders expressed no qualms at the time. The *Washington Post* revelation of the secret prisons and harsh interrogations program prompted the CIA to defend the program without providing any details, but it ultimately terminated it.[27] Later Pelosi alleged she had been lied to about the character and extent of the interrogation techniques. In particular, she claimed never to have been told about waterboarding, a claim that CIA officials strongly disputed. More broadly, this controversy not only raised questions about the practice of briefing only a small number of congressional figures rather than full committees, but it also suggested that CIA officials could not be trusted to volunteer information unless congressional oversight committee members posed direct questions to them.[28] In sum, the intelligence oversight function was seen to have proven inadequate to guaranteeing proper review of an ethically and legally questionable program.

The use of roughly a dozen coercive techniques continued until the program of secret prisons was leaked to the press in the fall of 2005. While never fully revealed, they appeared to include isolation, stress positions, faked executions, harsh slaps, sensory deprivation, dietary adjustments, extreme temperature changes, removal of clothing, and in three cases waterboarding. Once the program became exposed in 2005, President Bush and his advisers were forced to consider modifications, and Director Goss suspended the techniques in late 2005. Later in 2009, President Obama went further and prohibited them by executive order, limiting any US interrogations to following the existing US Army field manual that specifically prohibited waterboarding among other coercive methods.

American intelligence leaders have publicly disagreed on the extent to which these techniques actually produced actionable intelligence. Hayden and those involved in the program remain convinced they did produce useful intelligence that even contributed eventually to finding Bin Laden. Former CIA director John Brennan, on the other hand, has been more critical of the methods and equivocal about whether the CIA could prove they were decisive in preventing other attacks. What is known is that their use remains an ethical stain on America's reputation as a liberal democracy governed by the rule of law. The UN and most allied governments considered those measures to be torture and denounced them. Combined with the shocking photos of the military interrogations conducted at Abu Ghraib prison in Afghanistan, the United States had lost considerable credibility. It may have also cost the US future cooperation from some allied intelligence services. In sum, it appeared that a president gave a compliant CIA license to conduct an ill-advised and poorly improvised coercive program, justified by a DOJ only too willing to please an administration driven by fear.

Equally problematic was the Bush administration's secret approval of extensive electronic surveillance of foreign and domestic communications for the purpose of detecting new terrorist threats. In October 2001, President Bush determined that the extraordinary emergency facing the United States from al-Qaeda justified the NSA's electronic surveillance of both foreign and domestic Internet and phone communications *without* a court order. The NSA could collect metadata for a period of thirty to sixty days, and this authority was repeatedly renewed for nearly five years.[29] The NSA was then able to analyze the metadata and report it to the FBI and CIA as well as to other counterterrorism organizations. As was revealed later by Edward Snowden, one such technical collection program was code-named Prism. It involved the NSA collecting and storing millions of records from major Internet service providers, including Microsoft, Yahoo, Google, Facebook, YouTube, AOL, Skype, and Apple. As much of the world's Internet traffic passes through the United States via the "backbone" of major Internet providers, it was a simple matter for the US government to secretly get them to give the NSA access to receive and store such metadata records.

According to a 2009 report to President Obama by the IGs of the DOD, DOJ, CIA, NSA, and ODNI, NSA director Michael Hayden had briefed the HPSCI in October 2001 that under pre-9/11 FISA rules, the NSA would not have been able to adequately detect new terrorism threats.[30] FISA requirements for a court order would be too slow and cumbersome to ensure timely interception of phone or email traffic. In his view, however, collecting only the metadata without individual court orders raised fewer constitutional issues—such as Fourth Amendment protections against "unreasonable searches and seizures"—than collecting the content of those communications. After the administration successfully lobbied Congress for a freer hand in the way it conducted surveillance, Congress approved the 2001 USA PATRIOT Act. It allowed law enforcement to use the same electronic tools available against organized crime and drug traffickers (such as "roving wiretaps" and access to business records) to investigate terrorists. Most importantly, Section 215 of this act permitted the NSA to store telephone metadata provided by major Internet and phone companies. At the time, few in Congress understood how broadly this authority would be interpreted. Indeed, according to released records later, the more expansive NSA surveillance programs were not briefed to congressional leaders—and then only to the Gang of Eight—more than two years after the programs commenced.

This President's Surveillance Program (PSP) was given legal justification in a series of DOJ memoranda prepared by the Office of Legal Counsel. Their author, the only official given access to this highly classified program, was conservative legal scholar John Yoo, who had also authored the controversial "torture memos" justifying the CIA's secret interrogation program. Yoo's memoranda quickly dismissed Fourth Amendment concerns as not relevant to the collection of electronic communications on non-US persons. Regarding electronic surveillance of US persons, he opined that Fourth Amendment protections applied solely to law enforcement activities, which should not be construed to obstruct "direct support to military operations" duly authorized by the president as commander in chief.[31] Later, when other DOJ lawyers were allowed access to the PSP, they came to question Yoo's legal analysis that a president's wartime powers were excluded from FISA limits.[32] They warned Attorney General John

Ashcroft that the PSP might be based on unsound legal arguments. When then deputy attorney general, James Comey, was briefed on the PSP and its legal basis, he too was concerned about the legal arguments that appeared to ignore an act of Congress and failed to notify congressional leaders of this opinion.

Later DOJ legal opinions argued for revisions in the program following a March 2004 comprehensive briefing of the Gang of Eight. At that time congressional leaders expressed concerns about the surveillance program but did not oppose its continuation. In 2008, Congress passed FISA amendments that allowed the NSA to collect electronic communications inside the United States of non-US citizens believed to be involved in terrorism activities. This legislation gave the government even broader authority to intercept international communications than did the provisions of the presidential authorizations governing the NSA's activities begun in 2002.

In sum, 9/11 caused considerable expansion of electronic intelligence operations within the United States on the presumption that such authorities were critical to protecting American citizens. In practice, some individual privacy rights had to give way to public safely. Yet the effectiveness of this extensive surveillance program remains at best very ambiguous. The 2009 joint IGs report notes that it was difficult to assess or quantify the overall effectiveness of the PSP program because it was highly compartmentalized and hard to interview participants involved. With that limitation in mind, the DOJ's IG concluded that "although PSP-derived information had value in some counterterrorism investigations, it generally played a limited role in the FBI's overall counterterrorism efforts."[33] According to the same report, CIA and NCTC analysts were somewhat more positive, noting that the PSP-derived information had contributed; however, the program's effectiveness was difficult to assess because of its sensitivity and in the end proved no more useful than other streams of intelligence.[34]

The question in 2009 was whether the expansion of the NSA's surveillance authorities to find a few suspected terrorists was worth the cost of appearing to compromise *all* Americans' privacy protections. President Obama decided in 2010 that such an expansion of surveillance was unwarranted. His presidential commission on this matter reviewed the program and concluded that there were less intrusive ways to access these sources of information without jeopardizing American public safety. President Obama accepted the commission's recommendations that the NSA curtail bulk metadata collection and instead require that phone and Internet providers store their customers' metadata, which could be accessed by law enforcement and intelligence agencies with a request to the FISC. Congress also subsequently reinforced this presidential decision with new legislation that effectively replaced the PATRIOT Act's loose authorities granted the NSA with the US Freedom Act (see box 11.5). This 2015 law essentially forbids the NSA from retaining metadata and also requires the executive

---

Box 11.5   USA Freedom Act

The 2015 USA Freedom Act bans the George W. Bush-era bulk collection of metadata and requires that a government surveillance request "specifically identify a person, account, address, or personal device," which limits as much as possible the scope of the information sought to the purpose of the investigation. Furthermore, it directs the government to adopt "minimization" procedures to protect American citizens' privacy rights and allows FISC judges to direct additional minimization procedures concerning any nonconsenting persons. It also requires the US attorney general to submit to Congress an annual report of how many warrant requests were made to the FISA court, how many were granted but modified, and how many were rejected.

---

branch to issue annual reports that revealed how many FISA requests were made to the FISC, in order to provide more transparency to Congress and the American public.

One lesson from these various episodes is that 9/11 produced a sense of fear and urgency, conditions that encouraged loosening the restrictions on intelligence-collection practices at the expense of American civil liberties; moreover, this same sense of fear and urgency also tempered proper oversight by both the executive and legislative branches of government. These experiences should be remembered if there comes another major attack on the United States so that proper oversight can be exercised. A second lesson is that the IC cannot resort to simply staying "within the law" as interpreted by an administration's own lawyers. As one scholar put it, compliance with the law is not sufficient if those activities are not likely to be viewed as legitimate and ethical.[35]

Need for More Professionalism and Transparency

The foregoing discussion highlights how challenging it is for effective oversight of a secretive IC. The post-9/11 surveillance controversies have been proven to be nearly as damaging to US intelligence as the post-Watergate 1970s. The revelations of secret renditions and prisons, the use of extreme interrogation bordering on torture, and the extensive warrantless monitoring of Americans' phone, email, and social media communications have led to a deep cynicism and diminished public trust regarding the IC.

To rebuild public trust, the IC has pledged a renewed commitment to a set of ethical principles as well as greater transparency. First, the IC did some soul-searching about its practices and determined that a community-wide set of professional principles was needed. In 2012, the DNI announced those principles as being ones that cover the full scope of intelligence activities across the sixteen agencies:

1. Mission. We serve the American people, and understand that our mission requires selfless dedication to the security of our Nation.

2. Truth. We seek the truth; speak truth to power; and obtain, analyze, and provide intelligence objectively.

3. Lawfulness. We support and defend the Constitution, and comply with the laws of the United States, ensuring that we carry out our mission in a manner that respects privacy, civil liberties, and human rights obligations.

4. Integrity. We demonstrate integrity in our conduct, mindful that all our actions, whether public or not, should reflect positively on the Intelligence Community at large.

5. Stewardship. We are responsible stewards of the public trust; we use intelligence authorities and resources prudently, protect intelligence sources and methods diligently, report wrongdoing through appropriate channels; and remain accountable to ourselves, our oversight institutions, and through those institutions, ultimately to the American people.

6. Excellence. We seek to improve our performance and our craft continuously, share information responsibly, collaborate with our colleagues, and demonstrate innovation and agility when meeting new challenges.

7. Diversity. We embrace the diversity of our Nation, promote diversity and inclusion in our work force, and encourage diversity in our thinking.[36]

These seemingly obvious principles are important, if only because they commit the IC's agencies and individuals to weigh the ethics of their practices. These principles demand that officials authorizing collection operations, covert action, or analysis be cognizant that their efforts must serve the nation, respect American laws and civil liberties, speak truth to power, and remain accountable to oversight institutions and the American people.

Second, the IC has created new "Principles of Transparency," including the establishment of a community-wide Intelligence Transparency Council.[37] Its mandate is to work toward greater release of information so that the public can know more about intelligence missions, authorities, and oversight mechanisms. The four broad transparency principles attempt to strike a balance between encouraging more release of information that can inform the public and at the same time protecting what are absolutely essential sources and methods (see box 11.6). They seem to acknowledge that the IC must do better in only classifying what truly would cause major harm to national security and make a concerted effort to get more information declassified.

Third, the IC needs to talk up what successful contributions it does make to national security and public safety when it can do so without damaging intelligence collection or analysis. When DNI James Clapper announced this initiative, he also encouraged the individual agencies to speak more openly to the public about how

---

Box 11.6   Principles of Intelligence Transparency

1. Provide appropriate transparency to enhance public understanding about:
   a. the IC's mission and what the IC does to accomplish it (including its structure and effectiveness);
   b. the laws, directive, authorities, and policies that govern the IC's activities; and
   c. the compliance and oversight framework that ensures intelligence activities are conducted in accordance with applicable rules.

2. Be proactive and clear in making information publicly available through authorized channels, including taking affirmative steps to:
   a. provide timely transparency on matters of public interest;
   b. prepare information with sufficient clarity and context, so that it is readily understandable;
   c. make information accessible to the public through a range of communications channels, such as those enabled by new technology. . . .

3. In protecting information about intelligence sources, methods, and activities from unauthorized disclosure, ensure that IC professionals consistently and diligently execute their responsibilities to:
   a. classify only that information which, if disclosed without authorization, could be expected to cause identifiable or describable damage to the national security;
   b. never classify information to conceal violations of law, inefficiency, or administrative error, or to prevent embarrassment. . . .
   c. consider the public interest to the maximum extent feasible when making classification determinations, while continuing to protect information as necessary to maintain intelligence effectiveness, protect the safety of those who work for or with the IC or otherwise protect national security.

4. Align IC roles, resources, processes, and policies to support robust implementation of these principles, consistent with applicable laws, executive orders, and directives.

Source: ODNI, "Principles of Intelligence Transparency for the Intelligence Community," https://www.dni.gov/files/documents/ppd-28/FINAL%20Transparency_poster%20v1.pdf.

---

they contributed to the public's security. In a 2016 speech, he noted the significant role that the NRO and NGA had played in providing essential information to the first responders to a variety of natural disasters, such as hurricanes Rita and Katrina, as well as manmade ones, such as the BP oil spill in the Gulf of Mexico. On top of that, he and other senior intelligence officials have made more efforts to make public addresses when possible. In addressing one large audience, however, he hinted at how hard this was going to be for a community raised in a culture of secrecy to come from the shadows: "I admit, because of my experience growing up in the SIGINT business and my decades of intelligence work, the kind of transparency we're engaged in now feels almost genetically antithetical to me. . . . I think Air Force 2nd Lt. Jim

Clapper, from 1963, would be shocked by the level of detail with which we talk about SIGINT specifically and intelligence activities in general in 2015."[38]

Fourth, the IC needs to remind the public about its commitment to safeguarding their civil liberties at home. Within the ODNI, the PCLOB was established as part of the 2004 intelligence reforms. It comprises four part-time members and a full-time chairman, who are responsible for reviewing executive branch counterterrorism actions to ensure that those actions are balanced with the need to protect privacy and civil liberties. The board is also there to ensure any future development of laws, agency regulations, or policies are consistent with American civil liberties. In this latter case, it was instrumental in issuing recommendations following the Snowden revelations that shaped the USA Freedom Act and curtailed aspects of the NSA's surveillance programs. Its 2014 report on Section 215 and Section 702 of the 2008 FISA Amendments Act proved very influential in shifting congressional and executive branch thinking on electronic surveillance. All of the board's recommendations regarding these programs have been implemented in part or in full.

Moreover, those reports were public documents, allowing Americans to read more about their IC's surveillance activities than ever before. The PCLOB can and should provide status reports on how its recommendations are being implemented. It can hold public hearings and can involve outside experts and organizations in its deliberations, creating an indirect connection between the secretive IC and the American public. At the moment, the board's jurisdiction is limited to the IC's counterterrorism programs; however, civil liberties advocates strongly endorse broadening the PCLOB's mandate to cover a fuller range of intelligence-collection programs.[39] How effective this board will be under President Trump remains to be seen. In the past few years, it has been less highly regarded by Congress in particular, and its membership has dropped. In 2018, President Trump had named several new members, giving it the minimum of three necessary for a quorum.[40] Those supporters of an active board have recommended that the PCLOB be empowered to issue an annual report to Congress on how current intelligence practices and policies have impacted Americans' civil liberties. Efforts to pass such legislation failed in the last Congress, and it is uncertain whether it might be revisited any time soon. That said, should there be new threats to America's security that generate additional intelligence surveillance programs, it would be desirable to have an effective board that can ensure that Americans' civil liberties are not unduly infringed upon.

Whether the IC can regain American public trust is obviously a work in progress. While there are few public opinion polls on intelligence, what is available suggests the public is suspicious of intelligence yet regards its missions are vital. A 2015 Pew Research poll reported that following the Snowden affair, two-thirds of respondents "do not trust" intelligence agencies regarding its information collection and data privacy.[41] In a 2017 study, polls showed that a slight majority (55 percent) consider the IC "plays a vital role in warning against foreign threats and contributes to national security." Only a small minority (12 percent) felt the IC posed a threat to civil liberties. While those figures might be reassuring, other findings were less so:

- Millennials (individuals born after 1982) were least likely to believe the IC is vital and were less well informed about the IC.
- Almost a majority of those crediting the IC with a vital role said they had little knowledge of its missions.
- Nearly 60 percent of those responding to the question rated the IC's ability to protect privacy as "not very effective" or "not effective at all."[42]

At this juncture, one has to remain hopeful that the IC will do more to explain its role in the national security enterprise and its commitment to balancing security with protecting Americans' privacy. One of the purposes of this book has been to make the contribution of the IC more transparent to students of American national security. It has laid out the complexity of the national security enterprise as well as the diversity and secretive nature of the huge US IC. That said, much of what the IC provides to American policymakers will remain known only to those inside the government. As we enter a new decade with rising peer rivals and resurgent ones such as China and Russia as well as rogue states such as Iran and North Korea, intelligence will be as important as ever. Add to that the unpredictable nature of the digital and cyber worlds, and there is every reason to believe that intelligence will have many challenges to providing actionable information to protect Americans' safety while safeguarding US institutions and values.

USEFUL DOCUMENTS

Executive Order 12333 (as amended), https://fas.org/irp/offdocs/eo/eo-12333-2008.pdf
　　The key document authorizing and controlling US intelligence activities.
Foreign Intelligence Surveillance Act (as amended in 2008), https://www.gpo.gov/fdsys/pkg/PLAW-110publ261/pdf/PLAW-110publ261.pdf
　　The major legislation creating secret judicial review of sensitive US intelligence activities involving US persons.
President's Review Group on Intelligence and Communications Technologies, *Liberty and Security in a Changing World*, 2013, https://obamawhitehouse.archives.gov/sites/default/files/docs/2013-12-12_rg_final_report.pdf
　　President Obama's commission that reviewed the NSA surveillance programs and recommended major changes.
USA Freedom Act of 2015, https://www.congress.gov/114/bills/hr2048/BILLS-114hr2048enr.pdf

Current law that restricts the NSA's domestic surveillance programs that must be reviewed and reauthorized by the end of 2019.

FURTHER READING

Kenneth Absher, Michael Desch, and Roman Popadiuk, *Privileged and Confidential: The Secret History of the President's Intelligence Advisory Board* (Lexington: University Press of Kentucky, 2012).

> Provides the most authoritative descriptions of this highly secretive presidential advisory group.

Ross Bellaby, "What's the Harm? Ethics of Intelligence Collection," *Intelligence and National Security* 27, no. 1 (February 2012): 93–117.

> Describes the arguments for a "just intelligence" set of principles to guide post-9/11 intelligence collection.

James Clapper, *Facts and Fears: Hard Truths from a Life in Intelligence* (New York: Viking, 2018).

> Lays out some of the challenges a career intelligence officer faced in balancing the public's right to know and the IC's need for secrecy.

Genevieve Lester, *When Should State Secrets Stay Secret? Accountability, Democratic Governance, and Intelligence* (Cambridge: Cambridge University Press, 2015).

> Provides an analytical framework for critiquing intelligence's internal and external mechanisms for oversight, concluding ironically that creating more oversight mechanisms have actually reduced their overall effectiveness.

Steven Slick and Joshua Busby, "Glasnost for US Intelligence: Will Greater Transparency Lead to Increased Public Trust?," Chicago Council on Global Affairs, May 24, 2018, https://www.thechicagocouncil.org/publication/glasnost-us-intelligence-will-transparency-lead-increased-public-trust.

> Summarizes what little recent opinion polling exists on public attitudes toward the IC.

L. Britt Snider, *The Agency and the Hill: CIA's Relationship with Congress, 1946–2004* (Washington, DC: Center for the Study of Intelligence, 2008).

> Documents the CIA's stormy oversight relationship with Congress, as told by a former senior CIA legislative affairs official.

NOTES

First epigraph: James Madison, "The Structure of Government Must Furnish the Proper Checks and Balances between Different Departments," *Federalist Paper* no. 51, February 6, 1788, http://constitution.org/fed/federa51.htm.

Second epigraph: Lee Hamilton, "Oversight vs. Glitzy Investigation," *Christian Science Monitor*, July 15, 1999, https://www.csmonitor.com/1999/0715/p11s1.html.

1. Among US allies, only Canada claims to not maintain a clandestine HUMINT capability, instead relying solely on its diplomatic reporting. That said, within the Five Eyes intelligence sharing, Canada has access to American and British information; moreover, Canada does maintain a SIGINT capability of its own.

2. ODNI, "Intelligence Directive 203: Analytic Standards," June 21, 2007, https://www.dni.gov/files/documents/ICD/ICD%20203%20Analytic%20Standards.pdf.

3. Dov Levin of Carnegie Mellon University has compared American and Soviet electoral interventions and found that the United States conducted more than 70 percent of over a hundred instances of foreign interferences in other states' elections. According to Levin, the United States has regularly attempted to interfere in foreign elections in Latin America, the Middle East, and Asia; in many cases, this was done secretly. See Dov H. Levin, "Datasets," http://dovhlevin.com/datasets.

4. Executive Order 13526 / Intelligence Community Directive 710, "Classification Management and Control Markings System," https://www.dni.gov/files/documents/ICD/ICD_710.pdf.

5. See "President's Daily Brief 1969–1977," CIA's FOIA Electronic Reading Room, https://www.cia.gov/library/readingroom/collection/presidents-daily-brief-1969-1977.

6. Richard Betts, *Enemies of Intelligence: Knowledge and Power in American National Security* (New York: Columbia University Press, 2007), 163.

7. The House committee was headed by Rep. Otis Pike and the Senate committee by Sen. Frank Church.

8. The CIA director of security compiled the list of questionable ("flap potential") activities at the direction of CIA director James Schlesinger, and later CIA director William Colby felt compelled to release the study to the Pike and Church oversight committees. A redacted version is available through a FOIA request. See "Memorandum for the Executive Director, Subject: Family Jewels, May 16, 1973," https://www.cia.gov/library/readingroom/docs/DOC_0001451843.pdf.

9. Senator Church would eventually retract his statement, as the hearings revealed that the CIA and other intelligence agencies were largely operating under the direct or indirect instructions of the White House. But the public relations damage to the CIA and the IC was done.

10. A select committee is composed of legislators drawn from other standing committees. In the case of both intelligence committees, members are selected from the foreign affairs, armed services, judiciary, homeland security, and appropriations committees.

11. The SSCI held hearings on the NRO building in 1994, demanding that the NRO's director, Marty Faga, explain how the committee did not receive any information regarding the construction of a classified headquarters costing $300 million or more. See Senate Select Committee on Intelligence, Hearing on NRO Headquarters Project, August 10, 1994, https://www.intelligence.senate.gov/sites/default/files/hearings/103997.pdf.

12. Cynthia Nolan, "PIAB: Presidents and Their Foreign Intelligence Boards," *International Journal of Intelligence and Counterintelligence* 23 (2010): 27–60.

13. President Ford created the Commission on CIA Activities within the United States in January 1975 to determine whether any domestic CIA activities exceeded the agency's statutory authority. It concluded that some of the CIA's domestic activities were approved either directly or indirectly by presidents and fell into a gray area, while in a few cases CIA activities were "plainly unlawful and constituted improper invasions of the rights of Americans. See *Report to the President by the Commission on CIA Activities within the United States*, June 6, 1975, https://www.fordlibrarymuseum.gov/library/document/0005/1561495.pdf.

14. The Inspector General Act of 1978 has mandated the creation of such positions in more than sixty federal agencies. Some IGs are "statutory," meaning they are required by law and

have responsibilities to inform Congress as well as their agency heads of any major legal or ethical problems. Nonstatutory IGs report only to their agency heads and thus can be removed without congressional involvement.

15. For a list of exemplary titles of CIA IG reports, see "Agency Inspector General Reports and Investigations," *The Black Vault*, http://www.theblackvault.com/documentarchive/agency -inspector-general-reports-and-investigations/#.

16. John Warrick, "CIA Sets Changes to IG's Oversight, Adds Ombudsman," *Washington Post*, February 2, 2008, http://www.washingtonpost.com/wp-dyn/content/article/2008/02/01 /AR2008020103150.html?noredirect=on.

17. See Harvey Rishikof, "The Supreme Court: The Cult of the Robe in the National Security Enterprise," in Roger Z. George and Harvey Rishikof, *The National Security Enterprise: Navigating the Labryinth*, 2nd ed. (Washington, DC: Georgetown University Press, 2016) 312.

18. Rishikof, 313.

19. "Minimization" refers to the practice of removing the name of an American citizen from any intercepted communication and replacing it with a designation (e.g., "US person #1") in any signals intelligence report.

20. Rishikof, "Supreme Court," 315.

21. James Clapper, *Facts and Fears: Hard Truths from a Life in Intelligence* (New York: Viking, 2018), 198–99.

22. See Robyn Greene, "Unintentional Non-compliance and the Need for Section 702 Reform," *Lawfare* (blog), October 5, 2017, https://www.lawfareblog.com/unintentional -noncompliance-and-need-section-702-reform.

23. The full title is "Convention against Torture and Other Cruel, Inhuman or Degrading Treatment or Punishment." The United States is a party to the convention, which came into effect in 1987 and commits each state party to uphold these principles, not to transport individuals to states where they might be subject to such practices, to investigate suspected cases, and to compensate victims of such practices.

24. UN, *Convention against Torture and Other Cruel, Inhuman or Degrading Treatment or Punishment*, entry into force June 26, 1987, https://www.ohchr.org/EN/ProfessionalInterest /Pages/CAT.aspx.

25. According to the 2006 Military Commissions Act, an "unlawful combatant" is a person who has engaged in hostilities or who has purposefully and materially supported hostilities against the United States or its cobelligerents. Lawful combatants are only persons who are "members of regular forces of a state party" or "members of a militia, volunteer corps or organized resistance movement belonging to a State party engaged in hostilities, which are under responsible command, wear a fixed distinctive sign recognizable at a distance, carry their arms openly and abide by the law of war."

26. See "Memorandum for Attorney General Alberto R. Gonzalez, Counsel to the President, *Re: Conduct for Interrogations under 18 U.S.C. §§ 2340-2340A*," August 1, 2002, https://www .justice.gov/olc/file/886061/download.

27. Dana Priest, "CIA Holds Terror Suspects in Secret Prisons," *Washington Post*, November 2, 2005.

28. Paul Kane, "CIA Says Pelosi Was Briefed on Use of 'Enhanced Interrogations,'" *Washington Post*, May 7, 2009, http://thehill.com/homenews/house/65111-dems-say-cia-may-have -misled-congress-5-times.

29. Metadata is typically understood to be the records that commercial carriers routinely collect that are associated with individual phone calls, text messages, or emails. They can include the time and date of the transmission, the phone number, the email address and/or the Internet provider's address, the duration of the phone call, and the location of the phone call or email address. It does not include the content of the phone call or the email message.

30. See Offices of the Inspectors General of the DOD, DOJ, CIA, NSA, and ODNI, *Unclassified Report on the President's Surveillance Program*, July 10, 2009, https://oig.justice.gov/special /s0907.pdf.

31. Offices of the Inspectors General, 12.

32. Offices of the Inspectors General, 20. Senior DOJ lawyer Jack Goldsmith reviewed the Yoo memo in 2003 and noted that it had omitted any reference to the FISA provision allowing interception of electronic communications without a warrant for a period of fifteen days following a congressional declaration of war. This provision would seem to directly contradict Yoo's argument that Congress had never considered FISA applying in wartime. See 50 U.S.C. § 1811.

33. Offices of the Inspectors General, 32.

34. Offices of the Inspectors General, 34.

35. Zachary K. Goldman, "The Emergence of Intelligence Governance," in *Global Intelligence Oversight: Governing Security in the Twenty-First Century*, ed. Zachary K. Goldman and Samuel J. Raschoff (Oxford: Oxford University Press, 2016), 220.

36. ODNI, *Principles of Professional Ethics for the Intelligence Community*, January 2012, https://www.dni.gov/files/documents/CLPO/Principles%20of%20Professional%20Ethics %20for%20the%20IC.pdf.

37. ODNI, *The Intelligence Transparency Council*, April 5, 2016, https://fas.org/sgp /othergov/intel/dni-itc.pdf.

38. James Clapper, "Remarks on Transparency in Intelligence at AFCEA/INSA National Security and Intelligence Summit," September 9, 2015, https://www.dni.gov/index.php/news room/speeches-interviews/speeches-interviews-2015/item/1250-remarks-as-delivered-by-the -honorable-dni-james-r-clapper-transparency-in-intelligence-with-great-power-comes-great -responsibility-at-the-afcea-insa-national-security-and-intelligence-summit.

39. Daphna Renan, "The FISC's Stealth Administrative Law," in Goldman and Raschoff, *Global Intelligence Oversight*, 140.

40. Matthew Kahn, "Trump Nominates Two New Members to Privacy and Civil Liberties Oversight Board," *Lawfare* (blog), March 13, 2018, https://www.lawfareblog.com/trump -nominates-two-new-members-privacy-and-civil-liberties-oversight-board.

41. Mary Madden and Lee Rainie, "Americans' Attitudes about Privacy, Security and Surveillance," Pew Research Center, May 20, 2015, http://www.pewinternet.org/2015/05/20 /americans-attitudes-about-privacy-security-and surveillance/.

42. Steven Slick and Joshua Busby, "Glasnost for US Intelligence: Will Transparency Lead to Increased Public Trust?," Chicago Council on Global Affairs, May 2018, https://www.the chicagocouncil.org/publication/glasnost-us-intelligence-will-transparency-lead-increased -public-trust. It reports on a survey of a thousand Americans taken in May and June 2017. The survey provides a benchmark for future surveys on a range of questions regarding Americans' attitudes toward intelligence and democracy.

Glossary

Intelligence Terms

actionable intelligence. Intelligence that can lead to quick decisions or actions is often termed *actionable* to connote that it is highly valued as being timely and detailed enough to give decision-makers a decision advantage in being able to act quickly in ways that can mitigate risks or take advantage of opportunities.

all-source analysis. All-source analysis is based on the best reporting available from all sources, including HUMINT, IMINT, SIGINT, and open sources. All-source analysts are those experts able to access both classified and unclassified sources who are not working solely with a single source of information, as are IMINT or SIGINT analysts.

alternative analysis. Alternative analysis is the term often applied to a range of structured analytical techniques used to challenge conventional thinking on an analytical problem. The word *alternative* is used to underline the importance of using various techniques—such as devil's advocacy, Team A / Team B analysis, or analysis of competing hypotheses—to surface alternative interpretations of available information.

analysis. In intelligence, analysis is a cognitive and empirical activity combining reasoning and evidence in order to produce judgments, insights, and forecasts intended to enhance understanding and reduce uncertainty for national security policymakers. Analysts prepare "finished" assessments spanning current intelligence or more strategic research issues addressing the information requirements of government officials. Analysis includes understanding and tasking collectors, assessing both open-source and classified information, generating and evaluating hypotheses about events or developments, and identifying their implications for US security policies.

analytical assumption. An analytical assumption is any hypothesis that analysts have accepted to be true and that forms the basis of their assessments. The use of assumptions is part of the analytical process, but it is often difficult for analysts to identify these hypotheses in advance. Implicit assumptions can drive an analytical argument without ever having been articulated or examined.

analytical tradecraft. Analytical tradecraft is the term used to describe the principles and tools used by analysts to instill rigor in their thinking and prevent cognitive biases from skewing their analytical judgments. Through the use of so-called structured analytical techniques, analysts make their argumentation and logic more transparent and subject to further investigation. The term *tradecraft* originated with the Directorate of Operations term for techniques used to avoid counter-intelligence detection and to successfully recruit and run agents.

anchoring bias. A form of cognitive bias, anchoring bias occurs when a previous analysis of a subject prevents analysts from reassessing their judgments and allows for only incremental change in their forecasts. In essence, the initial judgment acts as an anchor, making the final estimate closer to the original one than should be the case, given the new information available to analysts.

basic intelligence. Basic intelligence is the fundamental and factual reference material on a country or issue that forms the foundation on which analysts can base current and estimative analysis. Examples include economic statistics, topographic and geographic information, and documentary information on a country's form of government, rules of law, and electoral procedures and patterns. The CIA's *World Factbook* is a product containing basic information on major countries of the world.

caveat. A caveat is a term used within the analytical community to suggest analysts are qualifying their judgments because of a problem in sourcing or in interpreting available information regarding an intelligence topic. Caveats include the use of qualifying statements, such as "we believe" or "we estimate," which indicate that analysts are reaching judgments, not stating facts.

clandestine. In intelligence terms, clandestine refers to the manner of acquiring information on a target in such a way as to conceal the collection operation itself as well as the identity of the source. It differs from *covert* in that a covert operation is observable but the US government is able to plausibly deny it had conducted the operation.

classified intelligence. Classified intelligence information requires special, expensive, or risky methods to collect, either by technical systems or humans, which must be protected. The risk of compromising these sources and methods is given a security classification (confidential, secret, or top secret). Classified intelligence is then shared only with those individuals who have a "need to know" this information. Analysts use this information in written assessments, which carry classification markings according to the sensitivity of the information used.

cognitive bias. Cognitive biases are mental errors caused by unconscious and simplified information-processing strategies. The human mind's natural tendency to develop patterns of thinking, or mind-sets, often distorts, exaggerates, or dismisses new information in ways that produce errors in judgment or thinking. Forms of cognitive bias can include mirror-imaging, anchoring bias, confirmation bias, and hindsight bias, to name a few.

collection. Gathering of raw information through specialized methods and systems used by intelligence agencies. Collection methods can be clandestine as well as overt and range from technical systems to human sources recruited to spy for the United States. Collection along with analysis are key elements in the *intelligence cycle*.

collection gap. Analysts identify shortfalls in their knowledge on a subject, and these collection gaps become "requirements" for future collection efforts. Identifying important collection gaps not only aids collectors but also sensitizes analysts to the need to qualify, or caveat, their judgments or set more modest levels of confidence in reaching their analytical conclusions.

collector. The organizations that operate a variety of technical systems or espionage units are collectors. They are part of the US intelligence community and are tasked by analysts through the development of complex sets of "collection requirements." For example, the National Security Agency is the principal SIGINT collector, while the CIA's Directorate of Operations is the principal HUMINT collector.

combat-support agency. The Department of Defense designates certain intelligence agencies as responsible for directly supporting department-level as well as tactical military combat operations. Such combat-support agencies include the Defense Intelligence Agency, the National Security Agency, the National Reconnaissance Office, and the National Geospatial-Intelligence Agency.

communications intelligence (COMINT). COMINT is information gathered from the electronic gathering of foreign communications of individuals or organizations, including from telephone, fax, and Internet systems, that can indicate the plans, intentions, and capabilities of foreign actors. It is part of the signals intelligence technical collection system.

competitive analysis. Competitive analysis refers to the explicit use of competing sets of analysts or analytical units to reach judgments on the same intelligence subject. The goal is to determine whether competing analysis will uncover different sets of assumptions, use of evidence, or contrasting perspectives, which would enhance analysts' understanding of an important topic. Historically, the CIA and the Defense Intelligence Agency provided competing analysis of Soviet military developments, often based on different assumptions about Soviet behavior.

confirmation bias. Confirmation bias is the human tendency to search for or interpret information in a way that confirms a preconception. Analysts will often seek out or give more weight to evidence that confirms a current hypothesis or the "conventional wisdom" while dismissing or devaluing disconfirming information.

congressional notification. The process by which the executive branch will inform the congressional intelligence oversight committees of any covert action or anticipated significant intelligence activity. Typically notification must be delivered in written form prior to the activity and is shared either with the full committees or with a smaller "Group of Eight," representing the majority and minority leaders of the House and the Senate and their respective intelligence committees.

coordination process. Many analysts or units often review an assessment because it may discuss aspects covered by more than one expert. The lead analyst or unit will share or "coordinate" an assessment with other experts across the agency or even with experts in other analytical agencies. This coordination process produces a "corporate" product that reflects the collective views of an agency or the entire intelligence community rather than the individual view of the principal drafter. Coordination is sometimes blamed for watering down judgments to a lowest common denominator. Conversely, coordination ensures analytical accountability because many analysts and mangers have checked sourcing, language precision, and the quality of a product.

counterespionage. As part of a counterintelligence effort, counterespionage seeks to penetrate foreign intelligence entities to assess their capabilities, exploit their vulnerabilities, and disrupt their hostile activities aimed at the United States.

counterintelligence (CI). CI is the gathering and analysis of information as well as the activities conducted to counter hostile foreign intelligence efforts to penetrate US national security and intelligence systems. It aims to identify foreign intelligence threats in order to counter or neutralize them.

covert action. Covert action describes operations conducted to influence foreign actors that remain secret so that the United States can plausibly deny its role. Covert action differs from clandestine action in that the former makes little attempt to conceal the operation but focuses instead on keeping the US role secret.

current intelligence. Current intelligence (also often called current analysis) is reporting on developments of immediate interest that is disseminated daily or even more frequently, allowing for little time for evaluation or further research. Current analysis appears in the daily products such as the *President's Daily Brief* (*PDB*) and the *Worldwide Intelligence Report* (*WIRe*) as well as other departmental intelligence products.

deception. Deception refers to the manipulation of intelligence by introducing false, misleading, or even true but tailored information into intelligence-collection channels with the intent of influencing analytical judgments and those who use them in decision making. Deception is used in conjunction with denial (together referred to as D&D) by both state and nonstate actors to gain advantage by reducing collection effectiveness, manipulating information, or otherwise attempting to manage perceptions by targeting intelligence producers and, through them, their consumers (e.g., policymakers and warfighters). Classic intelligence failures such as Pearl Harbor, the invasion of Normandy, and the Yom Kippur War involved deception.

denial. Denial describes activities and programs by an intelligence target intended to eliminate, impair, degrade, or neutralize the effectiveness of intelligence collection against the target, within and across human and technical collection disciplines. Examples of denial include communications encryption for SIGINT, camouflage and concealment for IMINT, surveillance detection for HUMINT, and rigorous operational security for all collection disciplines. Successful denial causes intelligence gaps, and the resulting missing information often degrades analysis.

departmental intelligence. Departmental intelligence is distinguished from national intelligence in that the former is produced within a single department and is largely for the use of that department's senior officials. For example, the State Department's Bureau of Intelligence and Research produces departmental intelligence principally for the use of the secretary of state and other senior State Department officials, as does the Defense Intelligence Agency for the Defense Department.

Deputies Committee (DC). The DC is a subgroup of the National Security Council made up of the deputy secretaries of state, defense, homeland security, and treasury, with the vice chairman of the Joint Chiefs of Staff and deputy director of national intelligence as military and intelligence advisers. Additional deputy cabinet officers will be invited if issues related to their departments are to be discussed. The DC reviews the work of lower-level interagency policy committees (IPCs) and forwards any policy issues and recommendations to the Principals Committee. The DC is also responsible for monitoring the implementation of presidential decisions taken after NSC and DC discussions.

devil's advocacy. Devil's advocacy is an analytical technique designed to challenge a consensus view held on an intelligence topic by developing a contrary case. Such contrarian analysis focuses on questioning the key assumptions or the evidence used by analysts holding to the conventional wisdom. Designed more as a test of current thinking than a true alternative to it, devil's advocacy has been used by some intelligence agencies on those issues said to be life-or-death matters.

Directorate of Analysis (DA). The DA is the major branch of the CIA in which all-source analysis is conducted on both regional and functional topics. Within the DA there are analysts and managers responsible for Europe/Russia, Asia, Africa and Latin America, the Near East, and South Asia as well as for analyzing transnational issues such as weapon developments, proliferation, and terrorism.

Directorate of Operations (DO). Formerly known as the National Clandestine Service, the DO is responsible for directing all HUMINT operations across the US

government, including the FBI and Department of Defense, for conducting foreign
intelligence collection and covert action abroad. The director of the DO reports to
the director of the CIA. As such, the DO is the principal "collection" manager—like
the National Security Agency for SIGINT—for human intelligence.

director of central intelligence (DCI). Prior to 2004, the DCI headed both the
CIA and the intelligence community and was the president's and the National
Security Council's senior intelligence adviser. The position was abolished and
replaced by the director of national intelligence as part of the 2004 intelligence
reforms.

director of national intelligence (DNI). The DNI serves as the head of the US Intelligence Community. The DNI also acts as the principal adviser to the president,
the National Security Council, and the Homeland Security Council for intelligence
matters related to national security. He or she also oversees and directs the implementation of the National Intelligence Program.

drones. Drones is the term given to unmanned airborne vehicles (UAVs) that were
originally deployed to collect imagery and electronic intelligence over battlefields.
They have more recently been armed with standoff missiles, allowing operators to
target suspected terrorists on a real-time basis.

electronic intelligence (ELINT). ELINT is intelligence gathered from technical
collectors that reveals the existence and characteristics of foreign electronic systems such as radars, air defense systems, and other military electronic systems.
It assists traffic analysis that identifies the location, frequency, and strength of
electronic warfare systems.

enhanced interrogation techniques (EITs). EITs are measures that cause distress,
confusion, and compliance in order to elicit uniquely valuable information from
suspected terrorists who have been captured or rendered into US custody. Waterboarding is the most well-known and controversial of those measures.

estimative intelligence. Finished intelligence assessments that are focused on
longer-term and inherently unknowable events are termed estimative intelligence
to convey that these analytical judgments rest on incomplete or sometimes nonexistent evidence. Assessing the future actions, behavior, or military potential of
known adversaries is by definition estimative. The best-known form of estimative intelligence is the National Intelligence Estimate, which is produced by the
National Intelligence Council.

executive order. An executive order is a memorandum or document issued by a president that instructs federal agencies to abide by regulations contained in those
memoranda or documents. So long as Congress has not issued any legislation
that would contradict those executive orders, they have the force of law. Executive

Order 12333, which was first issued by President Ronald Reagan and revised in 2008, governs overall US intelligence activities.

finished intelligence. Finished intelligence refers to the written assessments produced by all-source analysts, who evaluate raw intelligence reporting and prepare reports that are then disseminated to other US government agencies. Examples of finished intelligence include the *President's Daily Brief*, the *National Intelligence Daily* (now called the *WIRe*), and the Defense Intelligence Agency's *Military Intelligence Digest*—all of which are produced daily. Such analysis also includes longer-term assessments such as National Intelligence Estimates.

forecast. A forecast is an intelligence judgment concerning the future. In analysis, such estimative or predictive statements aim to reduce or bound uncertainty about a developing or uncertain situation and highlight the implications for policymakers. Forecasts are accompanied by probability statements ranging, for example, from "highly likely" to "very unlikely" or numerical odds that an outcome will or will not happen.

foreign instrumentation signals intelligence (FISINT). FISINT is part of the SIGINT technical collection system, which primarily monitors foreign military and scientific testing and tracking systems. TELINT (telemetry) is one such category of missile test data used for monitoring foreign military activities, which contributes to national technical means.

Foreign Intelligence Surveillance Act (FISA). The 1978 FISA established procedures for the electronic and physical surveillance and collection of information regarding "foreign powers" and "agents of foreign powers" suspected of espionage or terrorism. It established the Foreign Intelligence Surveillance Court (FISC) to review and approve federal warrants to monitor the activities of non-US persons suspected of planning espionage or terrorism. As amended in 2008, FISA requires "minimizing" the chances of inadvertent collection of information on US citizens.

Foreign Intelligence Surveillance Court (FISC). The FISC came into existence in 1978 and oversees federal requests from law enforcement and intelligence agencies for monitoring the activities of non-US persons suspected of conducting espionage or planning terrorist acts. It meets in secret and grants, denies, or requires modifications of any federal warrants. FISC consists of eleven federal judges selected by the Supreme Court chief justice from around the country who serve for a term of seven years.

Gang of Eight. The Group of Eight comprises the senior congressional leaders often first briefed on the most sensitive covert actions. They include the Senate majority and minority leaders, the speaker of the House and the House minority leader, and the chairmen and ranking minority members of the House and Senate intelligence oversight committees. Presidents resort to briefing the Gang of Eight when they do not wish to reveal the most sensitive operations to the full oversight committees.

geospatial intelligence (GEOINT). GEOINT is derived from exploitation and analysis of imagery and geospatial information describing and visually depicting physical features and geographically referenced activities on Earth.

groupthink. Groupthink is a concept that refers to faulty group decision-making that prevents consideration of all alternatives in the pursuit of unanimity. Groupthink occurs when small groups are highly cohesive and must reach decisions under severe time pressures. The psychologist Irving Janis developed this notion in studying US decision-making during the Vietnam War. It is sometimes misapplied to analytical failures, where there may have been cognitive errors.

human intelligence (HUMINT). HUMINT consists of collection activities to gain access to people (agents or liaison services), locations, or things (e.g., information systems) to obtain sensitive information that has implications for US security interests. Examples would be information collected clandestinely by agents, obtained from foreign intelligence services of other governments ("liaison"), or more openly by diplomats and military attachés and other US government officials. HUMINT is particularly valuable for analysts when assessing the plans and intentions of governments or nonstate actors.

imagery intelligence (IMINT). Sometimes referred to as PHOTINT (photo intelligence), IMINT is derived from the images collected from a variety of platforms ranging from handheld cameras to space-based and other overhead technical imaging systems controlled by the US government. Imagery analysts study specific intelligence targets through the use of imaging systems and issue reports based principally on those collected images. The National Geospatial-Intelligence Agency processes and analyzes IMINT and geospatial data for use by all-source analysts and other US government agencies.

indications and warning (I&W). I&W is the term for intelligence activities designed to identify on a timely basis foreign developments that could become a threat to US national interests or those of its allies and partners. It can encompass military, political, economic, or cyber activities, including threats from terrorism, nuclear weapons, and other WMDs as well as major political or military developments such as military attacks, political coups, and economic dislocations.

indicator. Any identifiable action or development that focuses on the conditions that might reflect a government or nonstate actor's likely behavior. In a military context, indicators usually reflect capabilities intended for aggressive action. Sociopolitical indicators (e.g., civil disturbances, crime rates, political activities) might precede a government's collapse or state failure. Indicator lists include military, economic, diplomatic, or domestic actions a foreign adversary might be expected to take if it intended to initiate hostilities.

inspector general. IGs are officials empowered to investigate the activities of their respective agencies for evidence of fraud, mismanagement, and illegal or inappropriate activities. The IG typically reports to the director of his or her respective agency, but if the position has been created by legislative statute, the IG must also report significant findings to the appropriate oversight committees. Statutory IGs exist in the Department of State and Department of Defense as well as in the CIA and the Office of the Director of National Intelligence. Their reports often result in management changes, personnel actions (reprimands, dismissals, or criminal proceedings), or sometimes new executive orders or legislative changes.

INT. Abbreviation used to identify specific intelligence disciplines used for collecting raw intelligence. The INTs typically include HUMINT, IMINT, GEOINT, TECHINT, and OSINT.

intelligence community (IC). As of 20018, the IC includes the following sixteen agencies or key elements of them: Air Force Intelligence, Army Intelligence, the Central Intelligence Agency, Coast Guard Intelligence, the Defense Intelligence Agency, the Department of Energy, the Department of Homeland Security, the State Department's Bureau of Intelligence and Research, the Department of the Treasury, the Drug Enforcement Agency, the Federal Bureau of Investigation, Marine Corps Intelligence, the National Geospatial-Intelligence Agency, the National Reconnaissance Office, the National Security Agency, and Navy Intelligence. The director of national intelligence heads the IC.

intelligence cycle. The intelligence cycle is the multistep process of setting intelligence requirements, collecting and processing information, analyzing and producing finished intelligence, and disseminating it to policymakers, who will then provide feedback on what further intelligence they may need or pose questions about the intelligence provided.

intelligence failure. While there is no commonly accepted definition, an intelligence failure occurs when there is a systemic or organizational inability to collect correct and accurate information in a timely fashion or interpret this information properly and analyze it in a timely way in order to alert policymakers to a major new development. Typically an intelligence failure is characterized by collection and analysis problems as well as by insufficient attention to bringing a warning to policymakers so they can respond appropriately.

Intelligence Oversight Board (IOB). The IOB is a small, independent board that investigates intelligence activities to ensure they comply with the US Constitution and other applicable laws as well as executive orders and presidential directives. It reports to the president as part of the President's Intelligence Advisory Board.

Intelligence Reform and Terrorism Prevention Act of 2004 (IRTPA). The IRTPA created the director of national intelligence (DNI) and implemented many of the recommendations of the 9/11 Commission as well as other studies and commissions that focused on intelligence reform. Among the other recommendations that the IRTPA implements were the creation of a National Counterterrorism Center and a National Counterproliferation Center. It also separated the roles of DNI from the CIA director.

interagency policy committee (IPC). IPCs are the lowest level of interagency coordination of policy recommendations and studies that are formed by the National Security Council. IPCs report to the Deputies and Principals Committees and carry out presidential directives that are issued through the NSC system. Policy as well as intelligence agencies are represented at most IPCs, which can cover a wide range of topics.

interagency process. The interagency process involves analysts participating in many interagency meetings, where they present their intelligence assessments for use in policy discussions among the National Security Council, the State Department, and the Defense Department. Working-level interagency meetings are often held prior to more senior-level meetings where decisions will be made. Typically analysts support discussions at the working level and participate in those meetings. For meetings of the Deputies Committee (deputy-secretary level) or Principals Committee (secretary-level), analysts will provide briefing papers or prepare senior intelligence community leaders who will represent the IC at those discussions.

Joint Chiefs of Staff (JCS). The JCS is composed of the military chiefs of the army, navy, air force, and Marine Corps. It is chaired by a four-star general officer (rotating among the services) named by the president and confirmed by the Senate to be the chairman of the JCS.

level of confidence. Analysts must determine how confident they are in reaching analytical judgments based on the quality of the information available and the complexity of the issue. Assigning a "low" level of confidence to a judgment may result from collection gaps, contradictory information, or the presence of deception and denial. "High" confidence may result from having very sensitive HUMINT or extremely precise technical intelligence on a military plan or a weapon system that is corroborated from multiple independent sources.

measurement and signature intelligence (MASINT). MASINT is technically derived intelligence data other than standard imagery and SIGINT. It employs a broad group of disciplines including nuclear, optical, radio frequency, acoustics, seismic, and materials sciences. Examples of MASINT are the detection of low-yield nuclear tests by seismic sensors or by collecting and analyzing the composition of air and water samples.

military analysis. Military analysis encompasses basic as well as current and estimative assessments of a foreign government's or nonstate actor's military capabilities and intentions, including order of battle, training, tactics, doctrine, strategy, and weapon systems. It also examines the entire battle space (i.e., land, sea, air, space, and cyber) as well as transportation and logistics capabilities. Other broad areas are the military production and support industries; underground facilities; military and civilian command, control, and communications (C^3) systems; camouflage; concealment and deception; foreign military intelligence; and counterintelligence.

Military Intelligence Program (MIP). The MIP comprises the combined budgets and programs of the military services' tactical intelligence activities. It was established in 2005 and is separate from the National Intelligence Program, which the Office of the Director of National Intelligence oversees. The MIP is under the control of the secretary of defense and comprises Army Intelligence, Air Force Intelligence, Marine Corps Intelligence, the Office of Naval Intelligence, and Special Operations Command Intelligence. Only the National Security Agency, the Defense Intelligence Agency, the National Reconnaissance Office, and the National Geospatial-Intelligence Agency are considered part of both the NIP and MIP.

mind-set. A mind-set is a type of cognitive filter or lens through which information is evaluated and weighed by the analyst. Beliefs, assumptions, concepts, and information retrieved from memory form a mind-set or mental model that guides perception and processing of new information. Typically a mind-set rests on a series of assumptions about the way the target of the analyst's investigation behaves. Closely related to a mind-set is a "mental model," which connotes a more highly developed set of ideas about a specific subject. Mind-sets and mental models form quickly and become hard to change, particularly when they prove useful in forecasting future trends. Once mind-sets are proven successful, analysts can accept them uncritically despite changes in the environment that would suggest they have become outdated or inaccurate.

mirror-imaging. Mirror-imaging is a cognitive error that occurs when analysts presume that a foreign actor will behave much as they would in the same situation. In this sense, the analysts see their image when they observe the foreign actor. Often analysts have developed a strong expertise on a subject and believe there is a logical way to develop a weapon system, conduct a coup, or reach a decision. They will, then, presume that a foreign actor would go about these tasks as they would. Classic examples include analytical views that assumed risk-averse Soviet behavior in the Cuban Missile Crisis and similar Arab reluctance to start a war with Israel in 1973.

National Counterintelligence and Security Center (NCSC). The NCSC oversees the counterintelligence activities conducted by the CIA, FBI, and Department of Defense and oversees and coordinates the programs and priorities on behalf of the director of national intelligence. It also conducts damage assessments of American counterintelligence cases.

National Counterproliferation Center (NCPC). The NCPC was established in 2005 within the Office of the Director of National Intelligence. It coordinates intelligence support to stem the proliferation of weapons of mass destruction (WMD) and related delivery systems. It also develops long-term strategies for better collection and analysis on future WMD threats.

National Counterterrorism Center (NCTC). The NCTC was established in 2005 as part of the Intelligence Reform and Terrorism Prevention Act of 2004. The NCTC integrates all intelligence—both foreign and domestic—within the US government pertaining to terrorism and counterterrorism. It conducts strategic operational planning and also produces intelligence analysis for key policy agencies. It is part of the Office of the Director of National Intelligence.

National Intelligence Council (NIC). The NIC is responsible for producing National Intelligence Estimates for the US government and for evaluating community-wide collection and production of intelligence by the intelligence community. The NIC is made up of roughly a dozen senior intelligence experts, known as national intelligence officers.

National Intelligence Estimate (NIE). An NIE is usually a strategic assessment of the capabilities, vulnerabilities, and probable courses of action of foreign nations or nonstate actors, produced at the national level as a composite of the views of analysts throughout the US intelligence community (IC). It is prepared under the auspices of the National Intelligence Council, and one or more national intelligence officers will guide the drafting of the estimate. Analysts throughout the IC participate in preparing and approving the text. The NIE is then presented to the heads of the IC and officially released by the director of national intelligence as the IC's most authoritative statement on an intelligence subject.

national intelligence officer (NIO). An NIO is a senior expert on either a region (e.g., Europe, Asia, Africa, Middle East) or a functional area (e.g., weapons of mass destruction, transnational threats, or conventional military affairs) who directs the production of National Intelligence Estimates on those topics. NIOs guide and evaluate the quality of analysis in their substantive areas, represent intelligence community analysts at interagency meetings, and interact regularly with senior policy officials to ensure intelligence production is directed at policy issues of importance.

National Intelligence Priorities Framework (NIPF). The NIPF is an elaborate framework for prioritizing intelligence collection and analysis according to the target country and intelligence topic. The NIPF assigns a numerical priority (1 to 5) according to the importance senior officials attach to the topic, and those priorities are used to allocate and justify intelligence community resources and programs.

National Intelligence Program (NIP). The NIP is the consolidated budget of the sixteen national intelligence agencies, which the director of national intelligence (DNI) is responsible for compiling, reviewing, and presenting to the Office of Management and Budget and Congress. The DNI has some limited authority to revise or prioritize funding and usually works closely with the defense secretary, who has daily budget control of the large military intelligence budgets.

National Security Act of 1947. The National Security Act of 1947 created a unified Department of Defense and the CIA as well as the National Security Council (NSC), which advises the president on national security matters. It specifies the core members of the NSC to be the president, vice president, and secretaries of state and defense and traditionally includes the chairman of the Joint Chiefs of Staff and the director of national intelligence as advisers on military and intelligence matters. This act mandates the NSC as the primary mechanism for advising the president and ensuring that all instruments of national power (diplomatic, military, economic, and informational) be integrated for formulating and implementing national security strategies.

National Security Council (NSC). Established by the 1947 National Security Act, the NSC is chaired by the president and includes the vice president, the secretaries of defense, state, and treasury as well as the national security adviser. The chairman of the Joint Chiefs and the director of national intelligence participate as the president's senior military and intelligence advisers. The NSC directs the work of lower-level committees: the Principals Committee, the Deputies Committee, and interagency policy committees.

national technical means (NTM). NTM is the term applied to intelligence systems used to monitor arms control agreements to ensure that the signatories are abiding by the provisions of those treaties. NTM relies heavily on imagery and electronic intelligence platforms to monitor the activities in countries such as Russia, which have signed a number of nuclear arms control agreements with the United States.

need to know. Senior intelligence managers use the "need to know" principle to determine whether intelligence will be shared with other intelligence professionals or policy officials. By executive order, the knowledge or possession of such information shall be permitted only to persons whose official duties require such access in the interest of promoting national defense.

need to share. Following the 9/11 attacks, the presidential commission examining the intelligence failure concluded that the intelligence community needed to share information more broadly among the various agencies in order to ensure effective coordination of intelligence and to prevent compartmentalization from inhibiting the development of a comprehensive view of future terrorist threats.

Office of Strategic Services (OSS). The OSS was the intelligence organization established during World War II that later became the basis of the CIA. The OSS conducted overseas collection and covert action as well as maintained a research and analysis capability. It was led by William "Wild Bill" Donovan.

open-source intelligence (OSINT). OSINT involves collecting information from unclassified, publicly available sources and analyzing its significance to the US government. Open sources would include newspaper, magazine, radio, television, and computer-based information in many foreign languages; public data found in government reports, press releases, and speeches; and professional and academic journals and conference proceedings. Increasingly, OSINT has focused on exploiting the Internet world of websites and bloggers. The Open Source Enterprise is the intelligence community's primary organization responsible for the collection and analysis of open-source information.

order of battle (OOB). In military analysis, an OOB identifies military units, their command structure, and the strength and disposition of personnel, equipment, and units of an organized military force on the battlefield. It is especially used in warning analysis of major military threats.

policy support. Policy support describes intelligence reporting and analysis that is provided specifically to inform policy decisions and enable decision-makers to conduct or evaluate policy options. It does not imply intelligence advocating any particular policy agenda.

politicization. There is no generally accepted definition of *politicization*, but it commonly refers to the intentional biasing of intelligence analysis to suit a particular set of political goals or agendas. Analysts can be prone to politicization if they allow their personal views to influence their analytical judgments. Likewise, policymakers can politicize intelligence by forcing analysts to tailor their judgments to suit a policy agenda or by misrepresenting analysis as supporting their preferred policies.

presidential finding. A presidential finding is the presidential document authorizing a covert action. It must be signed by the president prior to the operation, and in most cases the finding must be shared with the oversight committees as a "congressional notification."

President's Daily Brief (PDB). The *PDB* is a daily compilation of current intelligence items of high significance provided to the president and key advisers by the CIA, the Defense Intelligence Agency, and the State Department's Bureau of Intelligence and Research. A briefer delivers it to the president, and other briefers provide it to a select group of senior officials designated by the president as recipients. The *PDB* is constantly being refined to suit each president's individual preferences for format, presentation style, and length.

President's Intelligence Advisory Board (PIAB). An outside independent board established by each president, the PIAB can conduct studies of intelligence activities and make recommendations for changes or reforms of the intelligence community.

Principals Committee (PC). The PC is a group of senior cabinet officials advising the president on national security matters. Secretaries of state, defense, treasury, and homeland security along with the director of national intelligence and chairman of the Joint Chiefs of Staff form the core group, to which are often added other cabinet officials when issues within their areas of responsibilities are discussed. The PC is customarily chaired by the national security adviser, and its recommendations are then provided to the president directly or brought to the National Security Council, at which the president and principals meet.

Privacy and Civil Liberties Oversight Board (PCLOB). The 2004 intelligence reforms created the independent PCLOB within the executive branch to advise the president and other officials with respect to privacy and civil liberties when senior officials are developing and implementing laws, regulations, and executive policies related to terrorism.

Red Cell analysis. This structured analytical technique is aimed at countering cultural bias and the mirror-imaging problem by constructing a team of analysts who will consciously try to "think like the enemy" rather than like American intelligence analysts. Red Cell analysts study and then role-play the key decision-makers in a foreign government or perhaps a terrorist cell. They adopt the same decision-making styles, goals, or methods that such adversaries might use in accomplishing their objectives. Red Cell assessments provide US policymakers with an unconventional look at how their opponents might perceive a situation.

rendition. Rendition is the process of transferring a prisoner or detainee from one country to another without a judicial process. Renditions were conducted as part of the US counterterrorism policies after 2001 in order to detain and interrogate individuals at locations outside the United States, including the Guantanamo Bay Naval Base on Cuba.

requirements. Requirements are the general and specific subjects for which additional information is required for effective analysis and eventually decision-making. Analysts most often levy new requirements on intelligence collectors. Some decision-makers will occasionally directly task new intelligence requirements on the intelligence community. Such requirements are part of the intelligence cycle.

signals intelligence (SIGINT). SIGINT is interception and analysis of a target's use of technical signals and communication systems. It encompasses COMINT as well as ELINT and FISINT. The National Security Agency is the principal SIGINT collector in the US government.

signature. Analysts rely on understanding unique "signatures," or patterns, in the way a target operates, equips, or deploys military forces or weapon systems. For example, patterns of military communications can also indicate how military forces are likely to operate in the field; these signatures might indicate levels of readiness or whether operations were underway.

single-source intelligence. Raw information or reporting that is derived from only one collection discipline, such as technical, human, or open source. Single-source reporting is analyzed and then combined with other single-source reports to develop all-source intelligence.

situation report. A situational report (commonly called a "sit-rep") is reporting that is rapidly disseminated as soon as analysts receive it, to give policymakers the most up-to-date information for a quickly developing story. Sit-reps typically focus on what the facts are and any immediate implications of the event. Reporting on coups, deaths of world leaders, military clashes, and sudden breakdowns in public order or negotiations would be the most likely topics of such reports.

sources and methods. Sources and methods are those technical and human means of gathering information clandestinely on intelligence topics. A source can be a satellite imaging system operating high above a foreign country, a diplomat's reporting from an embassy, or a source's clandestine meeting with a case officer to report on a high-level meeting of his government. Analysts must "source" their reports and assessments by demonstrating they have a variety of reporting, preferably from very different kinds of sources and correction disciplines and assess the validity and credibility of the reporting. Such scrutiny reduces the chances of deception or fabrication of reporting if it came from a single source. Protection of "sources and methods" is considered a vital responsibility for intelligence officials.

strategic intelligence. Unlike situational reporting or current analysis, strategic intelligence focuses less on events than on long-term trends. It is usually performed only on subjects of enduring interest to the United States. For example, analysis of foreign ballistic missile developments or of the Chinese military would be of enduring interest to policymakers, regardless of their immediate policy agendas. Such analysis is inherently "estimative," as there is little detailed information on trends beyond a year or more.

structured analytical techniques (SATs). Structured analytical techniques are used to provide more rigor to analytical judgments and to make them more transparent and testable. Various structured analytical techniques—such as devil's advocacy, Team A / Team B exercises, analysis of competing hypotheses, and scenarios analysis—attempt to record the logic employed by analysts in reaching judgments.

By structuring the analysis according to a set of principles (e.g., listing key assumptions, evaluating the quality of information, examining multiple hypotheses, identifying collection gaps, or detecting possible deception and denial), analysts can establish more systematically their levels of confidence in judgments reached. Moreover, they can also track changes in their judgments over time and revisit conclusions that new evidence might appear to challenge.

target analysis. Target analysis is that conducted in direct support of military operations, counterterrorism, or counterproliferation operations and that focuses on understanding, monitoring, and targeting specific individuals, units, or groups for possible apprehension or physical attacks.

Team A / Team B analysis. This structured analytical technique uses separate analytical teams that contrast two or more strongly held views or competing hypotheses about an intelligence topic. Each team will develop its assessments using the available evidence after laying out their key assumptions about the topic. The value comes in arraying the two competing views side by side, which highlights how different premises cause analysts to reach different conclusions.

technical intelligence (TECHINT). TECHINT comprises technical intelligence-collection systems, including IMINT, GEOINT, SIGINT, COMINT, ELINT, FISINT, and MASINT. They are used in combination with HUMINT intelligence to observe and monitor foreign government and nonstate actor actions and behavior. They constitute the largest portion of the US intelligence community's budget and programs.

tradecraft. In analysis, tradecraft comprises the cognitive and methodological tools and techniques used by analysts to gather and organize data, interpret their meaning, and produce judgments, insights, and forecasts for policymakers and other users of finished intelligence products. An example of intelligence tradecraft is the analysis of competing hypotheses.

warning analysis. Warning analysis anticipates potentially threatening or hostile activities and alerts policymakers to the possible implications should the activity occur. "Strategic" warning refers to relatively long-term developments, which provide a lengthy period of time before the event during which a policymaker can develop policies or countermeasures. "Tactical" warning refers to alerting policymakers to near-term events, for which there is little time to prepare.

weapons of mass destruction (WMDs). WMDs are commonly considered to be nuclear, chemical, biological, or radiological weapons that can cause mass casualties.

Worldwide Intelligence Report (WIRe). The *WIRe* has replaced the *National Intelligence Daily (NID)* as the CIA's current publication circulated throughout the US government to senior policy officials. This is now a more Web-based publication that has an electronic dissemination within Washington and overseas. It can be updated frequently throughout the day rather than operate as a once-a-day printed publication like the *NID*.

worst-case analysis. Worst-case analysis occurs when analysts "assume the worst" in reaching judgments about a future event. It can occur when analysts base their analysis on assumptions that an adversary will always select a course of action aimed to create the worst problem for the United States or that the adversary's intentions are uniformly hostile toward the United States. Likewise, analysts are often accused of using such assumptions in an effort to ensure that they never fail to warn a policymaker of a possible surprise. Worst-case analysis, then, becomes a rationale for policymakers to ignore warnings that were actually far more balanced than assumed.

Index

Boxes, figures, notes, and tables are indicated by b, f, n, and t following the page number.

About the Author

Roger Z. George has taught intelligence and national security subjects at Occidental College, Pepperdine University, and Georgetown University's Security Studies Program. He also was professor of national security strategy at the US National War College from 2009 to 2015. During a thirty-year career as a CIA analyst, he also served on policy planning staffs at the Department of State and the Department of Defense and was the national intelligence officer for Europe. He is coeditor with James B. Bruce of *Analyzing Intelligence: National Security Practitioners' Perspectives* (second edition), and coeditor with Harvey Rishikof of *The National Security Enterprise: Navigating the Labyrinth* (second edition). Dr. George earned his PhD from the Fletcher School of Law and Diplomacy, Tufts University, and his BA in political science from Occidental College.

CPSIA information can be obtained
at www.ICGtesting.com
Printed in the USA
LVHW061243170722
723692LV00008B/356

9 781626 167421